North Atlantic Treaty Organization

INTERNATIONAL ORGANIZATIONS SERIES
General Editors:
Robert G. Neville (Executive Editor)
John J. Horton

Robert A. Myers   John Paxton
Ian Wallace   Hans H. Wellisch

John J. Horton is Deputy Librarian of the University of Bradford and currently Chairman of its Academic Board of Studies in Social Sciences. He has maintained a longstanding interest in the discipline of area studies and its associated bibliographical problems, with special reference to European Studies. In particular he has published in the field of Icelandic and of Yugoslav studies, including the two relevant volumes in the World Bibliographical Series.

Robert A. Myers is Associate Professor of Anthropology in the Division of Social Sciences and Director of Study Abroad Programs at Alfred University, Alfred, New York. He has studied post-colonial island nations of the Caribbean and has spent two years in Nigeria on a Fulbright Lectureship. His interests include international public health, historical anthropology and developing societies. In addition to *Amerindians of the Lesser Antilles: a bibliography* (1981), *A Resource Guide to Dominica, 1493-1986* (1987) and numerous articles, he has compiled the World Bibliographical Series volumes on *Dominica* (1987), *Nigeria* (1989) and *Ghana* (1991).

John Paxton was the editor of *The Statesman's Year-Book* from 1969 to 1990. His published works include *The Developing Common Market*, *The Dictionary of the European Communities* (which was commended by the McColvin Medal Committee of the British Library Association), *The Penguin Dictionary of Abbreviations*, *The Penguin Dictionary of Proper Names* (with G. Paton), *Companion to Russian History*, *Companion to the French Revolution*, and *The Statesman's Year-Book Gazetteer*. He was also chief consultant editor of the *New Illustrated Everyman's Encyclopaedia*.

Ian Wallace is Professor of German at the University of Bath. A graduate of Oxford in French and German, he also studied in Tübingen, Heidelberg and Lausanne before taking teaching posts at universities in the USA, Scotland and England. He specializes in contemporary German affairs, especially literature and culture, on which he has published numerous articles and books. In 1979 he founded the journal *GDR Monitor*, which he continues to edit under its new title *German Monitor*.

Hans H. Wellisch is Professor emeritus at the College of Library and Information Services, University of Maryland. He was President of the American Society of Indexers and was a member of the International Federation for Documentation. He is the author of numerous articles and several books on indexing and abstracting, and has published *The Conversion of Scripts* and *Indexing and Abstracting: an International Bibliography*, and *Indexing from A to Z*. He also contributes frequently to *Journal of the American Society for Information Science*, *The Indexer* and other professional journals.

VOLUME 8

North Atlantic Treaty Organization

Phil Williams

Compiler

Transaction Publishers

NEW BRUNSWICK (U.S.A.) AND LONDON (U.K.)

© Copyright 1994 by Clio Press Ltd.

Library of Congress Cataloging-in-Publication Data

Williams, Phil. 1948-
NATO: an annotated bibliography / Phil Williams.
p.cm.—(International organizations series : v. 8)
Includes index.
ISBN 1–56000–154–2
1. North Atlantic Treaty Organization—Bibliography. I. Title. II. Series:
International organizations series (New Brunswick, N.J.) : v. 8.
Z6464.N65W55 1994
[JX1393.N67]
016.365′031′091821—dc20 93–42578
CIP

Library of Congress Catalog Number: 93—42578
ISBN 1–56000–154–2
Printed in the United States of America

Transaction Publishers
Rutgers University
New Brunswick
N.J. 08903

INTERNATIONAL ORGANIZATIONS SERIES

Each volume in the International Organizations Series is either devoted to one specific organization, or to a number of different organizations operating in a particular region, or engaged in a specific field of activity. The scope of the series is wide-ranging and includes intergovernmental organizations, international non-governmental organizations, and national bodies dealing with international issues. The series is aimed mainly at the English-speaker and each volume provides a selective, annotated, critical bibliography of the organization, or organizations, concerned. The bibliographies cover books, articles, pamphlets, directories, databases and theses and, wherever possible, attention is focused on material *about* the organizations rather than on the organizations' own publications. Notwithstanding this, the most important official publications, and guides to those publications, will be included. The views expressed in individual volumes, however, are not necessarily those of the publishers.

VOLUMES IN THE SERIES

1 *European Communities*,
   John Paxton
2 *Arab Regional Organizations*,
   Frank A. Clements
3 *Comecon: The Rise and Fall of an
   International Socialist
   Organization*, Jenny Brine
4 *International Monetary Fund*, Anne
   C. M. Salda

5 *The Commonwealth*, Patricia M.
   Larby and Harry Hannam
6 *The French Secret Services*, Martyn
   Cornick and Peter Morris
7 *Organization of African Unity*,
   Gordon Harris
8 *North Atlantic Treaty
   Organization*, Phil Williams

TITLES IN PREPARATION

Organization of American States,
   David Sheinin
Israeli Secret Services,
   Frank A. Clements

World Bank, Anne C. M. Salda
United Nations System,
   Joseph P. Baratta

Contents

Contents

Preface

The bibliography includes most of the major books written in the English language on NATO. In addition, it includes an extensive listing of journal articles that deal with various aspects of the Atlantic Alliance. Among the journals that have been surveyed are: *Foreign Affairs*; *Foreign Policy*; *International Organization*; *International Affairs*; *World Politics*; *Survival*; *Adelphi Papers*; and the *Journal of Strategic Studies*. There are only a few references from *NATO's Sixteen Nations*, *NATO Review* (formerly *NATO Letter*) and the *Atlantic Community Quarterly*. Part of the reason for this is that they are devoted almost exclusively to NATO issues and for anyone seriously interested in NATO should be perused carefully.

Although they are not annotated, the volume does include a list of doctoral dissertations dealing with NATO issues as well as a short list of congressional documents on NATO to supplement those included in the annotated bibliography. For those interested in particular nations and the Alliance there are sources such as the Annual Statements on Defence in Britain which can be obtained from governments.

No bibliography of this kind can be exhaustive. Nor should it be. There has to be considerable selectivity to cut through the vast outpouring of material on the Atlantic Alliance that has appeared over the years and to present works that are important in their own right, that are representative of a particular point of view or of a particular debate that occurred in the Alliance, or that provide some light on the historical evolution or operations of NATO. At the same time a great effort has been made to ensure that no works of significance are omitted and that all the major debates that have taken place over the last forty years or so are discussed in the citations that are included.

Introduction

NATO has not only been one of the most familiar elements in the international landscape since the late 1940s, but has also proved one of the most enduring military alliances in history. Although there have been periods of turbulence and tension amongst the member-states, the ties that have bound the alliance together have generally been sufficient to outweigh tendencies towards disintegration. Moreover – and in certain respects rather surprising – in spite of the tectonic shifts in Eastern Europe and the Soviet Union between 1989 and 1991, NATO has survived as the premier security institution in Europe. Some critics have argued that it is an outmoded relic of the Cold War and that it has lost not only its enemy but also its traditional role as the major guarantor of European security. In the view of some analysts there are several alternatives better suited for the challenges of the post-Cold War era. These include the Conference on Security and Cooperation in Europe and the Western European Union. Other commentators, however, have argued that the problem is not that NATO lacks a role but that it has failed to meet its responsibility for maintaining peace and security in a European state system that has become far more turbulent in the aftermath of the disintegration of the Warsaw Pact and the demise of the Soviet Union. Although NATO shifted its emphasis from deterrence and defence to crisis management, this has been easier at the level of doctrine than at the level of implementation.

If the crisis in Yugoslavia has not been NATO's finest hour, however, it shares that dubious distinction with the European Community and the Conference on Security and Cooperation in Europe. The institutions that were expected to form part of a complementary European security architecture have engaged in collective buck-passing and have failed to fulfil the aspirations for the creation of an effective collective security and crisis management system in Europe.

If NATO has failed more recently, however, even many of its detractors would acknowledge that it contributed to maintaining peace in the Cold War system in Europe. Before looking at what has been written about NATO, therefore, it seems appropriate to look briefly at its origins, its evolution both in its own terms and within the broader context of Atlantic relations more generally, the evolution of its strategy, the relations with the Soviet Union, and out-of-area issues.

NATO was very much a product of the Cold War between the United States and the Soviet Union. It was an attempt, engineered largely by Britain, to restore a balance of power to a Europe in which there was no indigenous countervailing power to match the Soviet Union. Although the Atlantic Alliance became a key element of the United States strategy of containment – a strategy that would become global in scope – initially Washington was rather reluctant to underwrite the security of Western Europe. It required a systematic campaign by British Foreign Secretary, Ernest Bevin, to persuade the United States that the West Europeans were capable of coordinated action and were actually worth defending. Even after the United States had become committed to the security of Western Europe, however, there were concerns that Washington would end up shouldering a far greater share of the common defence burden than its allies. Closely linked to what became known as the burden-sharing issue was a major question mark about whether the Alliance was really a unilateral guarantee pact in which the United States extended its nuclear umbrella over Western Europe or was intended to be a collective defence organization in which the allies would engage in efforts to meet the Soviet conventional threat at the conventional level.

This ambiguity was reflected in NATO strategy which became particularly contentious as the United States became vulnerable to Soviet missiles. This vulnerability changed the strategic context in which NATO operated and cast question marks over the continued validity of the United States strategy of massive retaliation and the credibility of the American nuclear guarantee to its allies. Many observers argued that it was unrealistic to expect the United States to commit suicide on behalf of its allies. Others contended, however, that the possibility of escalation inherent in any Soviet aggression against Western Europe was sufficient to maintain the credibility of extended deterrence. For its part the United States attempted to minimize the nuclear risk stemming from its commitment to Western Europe. In the 1960s the Kennedy Administration tried to pressure the European allies to increase their conventional forces to a point where NATO could defend successfully against any Soviet invasion and would not find it necessary to resort to nuclear weapons to avoid defeat. This proved extremely divisive in the Alliance during the first half of the 1960s as the Europeans resisted what they saw as a dilution of deterrence. In 1967 NATO reached a compromise agreement in which it adopted the strategy of flexible response, but a rather different version of this strategy from that desired by the United States. Whereas Washington had wanted to remove escalation, the NATO variant of flexible response consisted of both an assured conventional response and the possibility of escalation, either controlled or uncontrolled. Not surprisingly, this compromise did not satisfy the United States and there were subsequent efforts to amend the strategy. The demands for No First Use in the 1980s were simply one more effort to achieve the goal Robert McNamara had set for the United States in the early 1960s – although by then this goal had the support of the European peace movement.

The tension over nuclear weapons in the Alliance resulted in part from the differing geopolitical vulnerabilities between the United States and Western Europe. Various efforts were made to deal with this problem, ranging from the futile efforts at nuclear sharing through the Multilateral Force (MLF) in the early 1960s to the NATO decision of December 1979 to deploy cruise and Pershing missiles in Europe. President Reagan's Strategic Defense Initiative (SDI) can be understood in the same light. As an effort to reduce United States vulnerability, by moving away from the deterrence strategy which was at the heart of the Atlantic Alliance, however, it was inevitable that SDI created another crisis of confidence in the Alliance – as well as proposals to extend strategic defences to Western Europe. Like these earlier efforts to deal with the problems of United States vulnerability, SDI's impact on NATO became the focus of a body of literature which is included in the bibliography.

Closely related to the nuclear issue was the conventional balance. Many of those who wanted to reduce reliance on nuclear weapons argued that such a move was not only highly desirable but also feasible. In their view the conventional military balance in Europe was not nearly as unfavourable for NATO as the orthodox view suggested. Part of the problem was that the military balance itself was not easy to assess. Appraisals of the balance ranged from those who believed that the Soviet Union could not win a conventional war in Europe to those who argued that Soviet forces could reach the Channel very quickly unless NATO resorted to the use of nuclear weapons. Often the source of these divergent assessments could be found in the underlying judgements and assumptions that analysts brought to bear. Indeed, even some of those who agreed the balance was not particularly unfavourable to NATO differed very strongly about the appropriate methodology to reach this conclusion.

Introduction

Another important issue for NATO was the balance of effort and resources to be devoted to security on the Central Front as opposed to the Flanks. Both the Southern and Northern Flanks, however, had a distinct set of problems and efforts by the member-nations to find regional solutions. On the Northern Flank this resulted in the notion of a Nordic balance which was essentially a political arrangement in which Norway and Danish membership in NATO (but accompanied by a Norwegian refusal to allow permanent bases on its territory) was balanced by Swedish neutrality and Finland's deference to Moscow. In the South the problems were rather different and were mainly about containing the potential conflict between Greece and Turkey. Increasingly, however, Southern Europe seemed to be vulnerable not only to the threat from the Soviet Union but also to threats from North Africa and the Middle East.

These external non-traditional threats raised another vexing issue in the Alliance – the extent to which NATO as an alliance could be expected to respond to out-of-area contingencies. Although its formal area of responsibility was limited by the North Atlantic Treaty, the fact that various states had interests outside this area – and expected support or acquiescence from allies when they pursued these interests – created tensions in the Alliance. In the 1950s the pattern was one of European action to retain positions of colonial dominance, with the United States acting as a force for restraint. By the mid-1960s and the United States involvement in Vietnam, however, it was Washington which had become more assertive in the Third World and which demanded European support. What was termed the out-of-area issue became very divisive during the Middle East War of October 1973 and caused even greater rancour in the Alliance in the aftermath of the Soviet invasion of Afghanistan.

Periodic crises in Atlantic relations – whether over strategy, burden-sharing, or out-of-area issues – became the focus of a considerable body of literature. Whereas analyses of NATO in the 1960s were generally dominated by the conflict over strategy and the French decision to withdraw from the integrated military organization, histories of NATO in the mid-1970s focused on the tensions resulting from the Middle East war and the energy crisis. By the late 1970s the question of NATO strategy and force modernization had come to the fore again and was reflected in NATO's decision to modernize its long-range theatre nuclear forces. By the early 1980s the agenda was increasingly crowded as nuclear issues and out-of-area issues became entangled in a crisis of credibility and confidence on both sides of the Atlantic. The level of acrimony between the Reagan Administration and the European allies was perhaps greater than at any previous period in the history of the Alliance.

Part of the reason for this was that in the 1980s security issues had become highly politicized. From being a matter exclusively for governments the Atlantic relationship and NATO strategy became a matter for public and political parties. The domestic politics of NATO countries became central to the future of the Alliance as defence planning took place within a broader public debate about no first use of nuclear weapons and strategies of defensive defence.

Part of the way NATO attempted to alleviate public fears about its strategy was through the pursuit of arms control and confidence-building measures. Although proposals for military disengagement in Europe had been made in the 1950s, it was not until 1973 that formal negotiations between NATO and the Warsaw Pact began with the opening of the talks on Mutual and Balanced Force Reductions. Yet, these were designed initially to contain Congressional pressures for unilateral United States troop withdrawals from Western Europe and were subsequently to bog down in a sterile dispute over data. It was not until the emergence of Gorbachev and the new thinking about foreign and defence policy in the Soviet Union that real progress on arms control was made. With the Reykjavik Summit, however, a new vision was introduced into the arms control negotiations, a vision which resulted in the 1987 INF Agreement.

In the aftermath of this agreement NATO was torn between the traditional emphasis – displayed primarily in London and to a lesser extent in Washington – which suggested the need to modernize its short-range nuclear weapons and the desire – particularly evident in Bonn – to exploit the unprecedented opportunities for the creation of a new peace order in Europe. With the fall of the Berlin Wall and the end of the Cold War political developments overtook arms control. Even so, the agreement on reducing Conventional Forces in Europe at the Paris Summit of 1990 was an effort to bring traditional military structures in line with new political realities.

There has been much debate about the post-Cold War security architecture in Europe and the role of NATO within this architecture. Ultimately, however, the viability of the Alliance will depend upon the extent to which it furthers the interests of its members. During the Cold War there were very different attitudes amongst the member-states, with France opting for greater independence albeit still as an Alliance member, Britain continuing to play the role of loyal ally to the United States, and West Germany walking a thin line between its desire to reassure its allies about its loyalty and its desire to create or maintain a climate of détente in East–West relations in Europe which it hoped would lead eventually to German reunification. Now that Germany has achieved this, it is clear that NATO is far less important to its foreign policy objectives – especially with the disappearance of the Soviet threat.

In speculating about the future of the Alliance, however, it is necessary to consider not only national perspectives but also the way in which NATO has created habits of cooperation among the member-states that are likely to remain useful. The Gulf War revealed that NATO might continue to have a role as an 'Alliance in waiting' for regional contingencies. Consequently, although it can be argued that if NATO did not exist there would be no need to invent it, a balanced appraisal of NATO's prospects must take into account the remarkably smooth way in which the Alliance has adjusted to the loss not only of its major enemy but also of much of its raison d'être. Even if NATO does continue to play a significant role in the management of European security, however, it will have to undergo further change. The most important of these is the internal change – the further devolution of power and responsibility from the United States to Western Europe.

From the inception of the Alliance there was an expectation that once Western Europe was strong economically it would become a second pillar of the Atlantic Alliance, taking on both burdens and responsibilities in ways which would complement rather than challenge the efforts and leadership of the United States. The citations dealing with the European pillar will provide a sound basis from which the reader can assess why this did not occur in the way expected – and consider whether or not the future is likely to be any different.

The mid-1990s is perhaps the most critical period for the Alliance. Unless it is able to respond more effectively to crises such as that in the former Yugoslavia, there will be increasing doubts about its utility and its place as the premier security institution for Europe. The difficulty is that such crises come against a background in which the member-nations themselves are working out new patterns of influence and, in some cases, even new kinds of relationships. A further layer of complexity stems from the fact that these processes are taking place both within Europe and in the Atlantic relationship. Indeed, unless there is both redefinition of the Atlantic link and a reinvigoration of the member-nations' commitment to concerted action in dealing with ambiguous security challenges, there will be a need for an addendum to this bibliography – entitled the demise of NATO.

Acknowledgements

The author would like to thank a number of people who have been helpful in the compilation of this bibliography. These include

Dr. Earl Gibbons, Javad Sedehi, Steve Garber, Steve Hajaar, Mary Beth Cernicek, Peter Duerst, Tracy Naber, and Slobodan Pesic. They were also a source of encouragement in what at times seemed a daunting task. The author would also like to express his appreciation to Enid Johnson, Anita Tilford and Kendall Stanley, all of whom typed various parts of the bibliography. Several colleagues at the University of Pittsburgh Ridgway Center have also been helpful in making suggestions and I am particularly grateful to Paul Hammond, Michael Brenner and Wolfgang Schlör, for their suggestions and a general concern for NATO issues. Thanks too to Lawrence Kaplan for sharing his vast knowledge of NATO and the available literature. Most of all, I want to thank my wife Surratt who has lived with me through every citation and annotation and who has been an unending source of support, love and joy.

Phil Williams
University of Pittsburgh
October 1993

Doctoral Theses on NATO

Origins of the tactical nuclear weapons modernization program: 1969-1979.   Michael David Yaffe, University of Pennsylvania 1991. 764p.

Ambiguous Legacy: The United States, Great Britain and the foundations of NATO strategy, 1948-1957.   Robert Allen Wampler, Harvard University 1991. 135p.

German writers and the intermediate-range nuclear forces debate in the 1980s (nuclear missiles, political literature).   Anne Marie Stokes, The Ohio State University 1991. 232p.

The politics of NATO short-range nuclear modernization, 1983-1990: The follow-on to lance missile decisions.   Jeffrey Arthur Larsen, Princeton University 1991. 539p.

Icelandic security policy: 1979-1986.   Michael Thomas Corgan, Boston University 1991. 345p.

The two faces of consensus: A study of alliance and domestic consensus in NATO's INF policy.   Trine B. Flockhart, University of East Anglia (United Kingdom) 1991. 419p.

The political economy of alliance: Issue linkage in the West German–American relationship.   Karen Erika Donfried, Fletcher School of Law and Diplomacy (Tufts University) 1991. 452p.

'Penetrated System' or 'normal' state? An exploration of INF arms control policy, East–West economic relations, and inter-German policy in the Federal Republic of Germany, 1979-1987.   Cathleen Suzanne Fisher, University of Maryland College Park 1991. 540p.

Soviet reactions to shifts in U.S. and NATO military doctrine in Europe: The defense policy community and innovation. Kimberly Marten Zisk, Stanford University 1991. 344p.

Managing the West Germans: The occupation statute of 1949 from gestation to burial, 1945-1955.   David Aaron Meier, The University of Wisconsin-Madison 1990. 519p.

The United States and the European defense community: 1950-1954.   Joe Knetsch, The Florida State University 1990. 378p.

'Fortress America': The U.S. Senate and the great debate of 1950-1951.   Karen Hunt Exon, University of Kansas 1990. 409p.

Neutralism in the West German peace movement: The question of the evaluative background. (Volumes I and II).   Philipp J. Borinski, Georgetown University 1990. 633p.

Soviet military doctrine and strategy shifts: principal dynamics and implications for conventional warfare. (Volumes I-III).   Howard Ezra Frost, III, The Ohio State University 1990. 1178p.

United States high technology export control policy: An assessment of relative costs and implications for national security.   Doublas Erin McDaniel, The American University 1990. 397p.

The sources of foreign policy: The Carter administration and NATO nuclear forces, 1977-1980.   Vincent A. Auger, Harvard University 1990. 308p.

An analysis of the conventional military balance on the European central front: Some implications for NATO strategy and tactics.   Alex Raymond McKeown, The University of Wisconsin-Madison 1990. 771p.

Military expenditure and economic development, the case of Greece: 1952-1987.   C. Kollias, Council for National Academic Awards (United Kingdom) 1989. 448p.

Dean Acheson: Elder statesman of the Cold War, 1953-1971. (volumes I and II).   Douglas G. Brinkley, Georgetown University 1989. 735p.

Defining Security: The case of southern Europe and the superpowers in the Mediterranean.   Marco Cesa, Boston University 1989. 381p.

How to decide whether to build a ballistic missile defense (NATO, USSR).   David Garland Blair, University of California, Los Angeles 1989. 429p.

Approaching zero: An evaluation of radical reductions in superpower nuclear arsenals.   James Northey Miller, Jr, Harvard University 1989. 322p.

The reliability of East European military forces.   Bradley Roy Gitz, University of Illinois at Urbana-Champaign 1989. 344p.

The evolution of NATO's conventional force posture.   John Stuart Duffield, Princeton University 1989. 565p.

Nordic European security dilemmas: The strategic significance of NATO's northern flank.   Richard David Hooker, Jr, University of Virginia 1989. 385p.

Comiso: The politics of peace in a Sicilian town (Italy).   Laure (Lee) Simich, Columbia University 1988. 450p.

European missile defense.   Randy Keith Willoughby, University of California, Berkeley 1988. 246p.

The penetration of open political systems: A study of the effects of Soviet behavior on public opinion following the NATO dual-track missile decision.   Mark James DeHaven, University of Florida 1988. 275p.

The mutual and balanced force reduction negotiations: The Soviet perspective on verification, 1973-1987.   Nancy Barbara Brendlinger, Kent State University 1988. 280p.

European reserve forces and the conventional defense of Europe. Roy Franklin Phillips, The Rand Graduate Institute 1988. 143p.

Conventional Forces in Europe: A new approach to the balance, stability, and arms control.   Laurinda L. Rohn, The Rand Graduate Institute 1988. 166p.

Western threat perceptions: Implications for NATO nuclear planning.   Eric H. Thoemmes, University of Southern California 1988.

Broker of Power: General Lyman L. Lenmitzer.   Kathleen Frances Anne Kellner, Kent State University 1987. 243p.

The West European public and the Atlantic Alliance (NATO). Andrew Henry Ziegler, Jr, University of Florida 1987. 379p.

Don't rock the boat: Reinforcing Norway in crisis and war.   John Richard Lund, The Rand Graduate Institute 1987. 158p.

Political and military components of Air Force doctrine in the Federal Republic of Germany and their implications for NATO defence policy analysis.   Michael Erie Thompson, The Rand Graduate Institute 1987. 308p.

The second Euromissile crisis (NATO).   James Scaminaci, III, Stanford University 1987. 403p.

Consultation and cooperation in NATO: Nuclear planning, 1975-1987.   Fred Barry Chernoff, Yale University 1987. 364p.

The SDI: Implications for NATO strategy and Western European security. An examination of ballistic missile defense in the context of Western European strategic logic.   Robert Mark Soofer, University of Southern California 1987.

The economics of defense alliances: Burden sharing, free riding and optimality.   Frederick Dix Thompson, University of Virginia 1986. 222p.

Pax Atomica: The nuclear defense controversy in West Germany during the Adenauer era.   Stuart Mark Cioc, University of California, Berkeley 1986. 484p.

A valid heritage: the policy on military tradition in the emergence of the 'Bundeswehr', 1950-1965.   Donald Abenheim, Stanford University 1986. 298p.

The United States, the Soviet Union, and the North Atlantic Treaty, 1948-1949.   Steven Anthony Henstridge, Kent State University 1986. 262p.

Free-riding in NATO: Reality or . . . myth?   Loretta De Luca, Cornell University 1986. 256p.

A study in grand strategy: Eisenhower and NATO.   Douglas Lee Erwin, University of Denver 1986. 338p.

Seapower in the nuclear age: NATO as a maritime alliance.   Joel Jeffrey Sokolsky, Harvard University 1986. 384p.

The struggle for the soul of Faust: The American drive for German rearmament, 1950-1955.   Joseph Bernard Egan, The University of Connecticut 1985. 514p.

Rearming the phoenix: American military assistance to the Federal Republic of Germany, 1950-60.   Andrew James Birtle, The Ohio State University 1985. 488p.

Nuclear weapons decision-making: An application of organization theory to the 'mini-nuke' case.   Jack Leonard Kangas, Stanford University 1985. 303p.

Soviet threat perceptions of NATO's Eurostrategic missiles.   William Vaughan Garner, Georgetown University 1985. 325p.

Fortifications and underground nuclear defense shelters for NATO troops (Policy, Security).   Drew Miller, Harvard University 1985. 859p.

Deterrence as a public good: A journey with the free rider (NATO).   G. Palmer, The University of Michigan 1985. 170p.

Neutralism in the Federal Republic of Germany: Policies and positions of the Social Democratic Party and the Greens.   Diane Hanna Hill Rosolowsky, University of Virginia 1985. 357p.

Allies and adversaries: Policy insights into strategic defense relationships.   Bruce W. Don, The Rand Graduate Institute 1985. 491p.

Alliance Theory: The role of private versus public defense goods.   Carl Harry Groth, Jr, The George Washington University 1984. 198p.

The SPD and NATO: The transformation of Social Democratic alliance policy 1957-1961.   Stephen Joseph Artner, The Johns Hopkins University 1984. 364p.

Approach to alliance: British and American defense strategies, 1945-1948.   Richard A. Best, Jr, Georgetown University 1983. 320p.

Contributions to the economics of military alliances.   James Cameron Murdoch, University of Wyoming 1982. 115p.

Essays on burden sharing and efficiency in alliances.   Michael Allan Schuyler, University of Maryland College Park 1982. 384p.

Scholar versus statesman: The record of Henry Kissinger. The United States and Western Europe.   Jeffry R. Bendel, University of Massachusetts 1982. 304p.

Cold War Rimlands: The United States, NATO, and the politics of colonialism, 1945-1949.   Scott Laurence Bills, Kent State University 1981. 263p.

The United States, Italy and NATO: American policy toward Italy, 1948-1952.   Emory Timothy Smith, Kent State University 1981. 267p.

The politics of weapons standardization in NATO.   Richard Charles Fast, University of California, Santa Barbara 1981. 693p.

NATO and the Mediterranean, 1949-1979: Deterioration on the southern flank.   Benjamin Cameron Sharp, Jr, University of Maryland College Park 1981. 444p.

The US/USSR strategic arms limitation talks: The implications for the security of the Federal Republic of Germany.   Gale Ann Mattox, University of Virginia 1981. 318p.

The collective management of defense: Collaborative weapons acquisition in NATO.   William David Bajusz, The University of Wisconsin-Madison 1981. 329p.

The evolution of Icelandic defense decision making 1944-1981.   John Robin Fairlamb, University of South Carolina 1981. 159p.

French Nuclear Strategy: Continuity and change.   Theresa Anne Lennon. The Catholic University of America 1981. 190p.

Defense Manpower Policy Analysis: NATO ground forces.Ragnhild Sohlberg, The Rand Graduate Institute 1980. 271p.

The Neutron Bomb.   Michael A. Aquino, University of California, Santa Barbara 1980. 298p.

Advanced Technology and NATO defense.   Robert Kennedy, Georgetown University 1978. 226p.

Decision-making process in NATO.   Edward Leon Rowny, The American University 1977. 425p.

Gaullist Foreign Policy: NATO withdrawal and systemic change. Robert Stephen Lockwood, The George Washington University 1976. 443p.

Public goods, the NATO alliance and resource transfers.   Stephen Norris Brown; David Allen Price. University of Denver 1975. 246p.

The influence of threat and alliance setting on national defense expenditures NATO, 1950-1969.   Stephen Michael Shaffer, The University of Michigan 1975. 356p.

The relationship of superpower detente to NATO cohesion. Elizabeth Trocolli Boris, Rutgers The State University of New Jersey-New Brunswick 1975. 216p.

To the NATO review: Constancy and change in Canadian NATO policy, 1949-1969.   Jerome D. Davis, The Johns Hopkins University 1973. 392p.

NATO production and logistics organizations: A study in multi-national political and technical administration.   Gerald Wilbur Cox, The American University 1972. 294p.

NATO nuclear policy-making.   Robert Max Krone, University of California, Los Angeles 1972. 229p.

NATO nuclear-sharing and non-proliferation in Soviet foreign policy, 1960-1967.   Thomas Melvin Magstadt, The Johns Hopkins University 1972. 276p.

NATO without France.   George Roopen Adjemian, Claremont Graduate School 1971. 343p.

NATO and multilateral nuclear force (MLF).   Harry Mason Joiner, University of Kentucky 1971. 347p.

North Atlantic Treaty Organization (NATO) in the perspective of organization theory.   David J. Gould, New York University 1971. 218p.

American public reaction to communist expansion: from Yalta to NATO.   Harold James Sylvester, University of Kansas 1970. 357p.

NATO and national self-interests.   William T. Mohn, Jr, Claremont Graduate School 1970. 287p.

The special committee of NATO defense ministers – a study of political consultation in the Atlantic Alliance.   Harry George Harris, Harvard University 1970.

A theoretical and empirical study of communications relations in the NATO and Warsaw intrabloc and interbloc international systems. Tom Allen Travis, Syracuse University 1970. 376p.

Organizational behavior of smaller nations in a regional defense alliance: A case study of Belgium and Norway in NATO.   Astri Suhrke, University of Denver 1969. 428p.

Political coalitions: NATO and the communist system during the postwar years.   Philip Terrence Hopmann, Stanford University 1969. 301p.

General Alfred M. Gruenther: dedicated spokesman for NATO. Lilyan Mae Alspaugh, Michigan State University 1969. 424p.

NATO in search of cohesion: the quest for means.   Rudolph Gordon, New York University 1968. 346p.

Problems of arms control: United States policy and the defense of NATO.   Stanley Leroy Harrison, The American University 1967. 360p.

The disarray of NATO: a study of the American and French designs for the Atlantic alliance and an appraisal of the resulting crisis they have created for the North Atlantic Treaty adherents.   Edwin B. Strong, Jr, University of Kansas 1967. 499p.

Military bloc formation: The case of NATO, 1949-1962.   Nafhat N. Nasr, Vanderbilt University 1967. 340p.

Norway, the north, and NATO: a study of authoritative elite perceptions as related to foreign policy.   Philip Mark Burgess, The American University 1966. 266p.

The economic allocation of share-costs in joint international ventures: an examination of the NATO and OECD–DAC experience. Stanley Lester Dolins, University of Colorado at Boulder 1965. 331p.

Greek political reaction to NATO and western orientation, 1952-1963.   Theodore Alexander Couloumbis, The American University 1964. 277p.

French attitudes toward NATO.   Wynfred Joshua, University of Pittsburgh 1964. 377p.

Doctoral Theses on NATO

The USSR and NATO: a study in the implementation of Soviet foreign policy.   Frederick J. Yeager, Princeton University 1959. 388p.

Canada and NATO.   Maureen Patricia Cronin, Stanford University 1958. 364p.

US Congressional Documents on NATO

United States Troops in Europe.
Hearings before the combined subcommittee on Foreign Relations
and Armed Services committees on the subject of United States
troops in Europe, United States Senate, 90th Congress, 1st session
on S.Res.49 – to express the sense of the Senate with respect to
troop deployment in Europe, and amendments there to S.Res.83 –
providing study and reevaluation of United States–European
relations, April 26 & May 3, 1967. (U.S. Government Printing
Office, Washington, 1967). 124p.

The Atlantic Alliance: Future Tasks of the Alliance.
Report of the North Atlantic Council submitted by the Subcommittee
on National Security and International Operations (Pursuant to
S.Res.54, 90th Congress) to the Committee on Government
Operations, United States Senate. (U.S. Government Printing
Office, Washington, 1968). 3p.

United States Troops in Europe.
Report of the combined subcommittee of Foreign Relations and
Armed Services committees on the subject of United States troops
in Europe to the Committee on Foreign Relations & Committee
Armed Services, United States Senate, 90th Congress, 2nd
Session. (U.S. Government Printing Office, Washington, 1968).
105p.

The Vandenberg Resolution and the North Atlantic Treaty.
Hearing held in Executive Session before the Committee on Foreign
Relations, United States Senate, 80th Congress. Reaffirming the
policy of the United States to achieve international peace and
security through the United Nations and indicating certain
objectives to be pursued. (U.S. Government Printing Office,
Washington, 1973). 387p.

United States–Europe Relations and the 1973 Middle East War.
Hearings before the Subcommittee on Europe and on the Near East

and South Asia of the Committee on Foreign Affairs, 93rd
Congress, 1st & 2nd Sessions, November 1, 1973 & February 19,
1974. (U.S. Government Printing Office, Washington, 1974). 79p.

Military Assistance Program: 1949.

Joint Hearing held in Executive Session before the Committee on
Foreign Relations and the Committee on Armed Services, United
States Senate, 81st Congress on S. 2388A – a bill to promote the
foreign policy and provide for the defense and general welfare of
the United States by furnishing military assistance to foreign
nations. (U.S. Government Printing Office, Washington, 1974).
736p.

Extension of the European Recovery Program: 1949.

Hearing held in executive session before the Committee on Foreign
Relations, United States Senate, 81st Congress, 1st Session on
S. 833 – to amend the Economic Cooperation Act of 1948. (U.S.
Government Printing Office, Washington, 1974). 380p.

Executive Sessions of the Senate Foreign Relations Committee.

(Historical Series), Volume III, Part 2, 82nd Congress, 1st Session,
1951. (U.S. Government Printing Office, Washington, 1976).
700p.

NATO Posture and Initiatives.

Hearing before the Subcommittee on Manpower and Personnel of the
Committee on Armed Services, United States Senate, 95th Congress, 1st Session. (U.S. Printing Office, Washington, 1977). 78p.

NATO Troop Withdrawals.

Hearing before the Committee on Foreign Relations, United States
Senate, 97th Congress, 2nd Session. (U.S. Government Printing
Office, Washington, 1982). 88p.

The Premises of East–West Commercial Relations.

A workshop sponsored by the Committee on Foreign Relations,
United States Senate and Congressional Research Service, 97th
Congress, 2nd Session, Library of Congress, December 1982.
(U.S. Government Printing Office, Washington, 1983). 196p.

East–West Troop Reductions in Europe: Is Agreement Possible?

Report prepared for the Subcommittee on International Security and
Scientific Affairs to the Committee on Foreign Affairs, U.S. House
of Representatives by the Foreign Affairs and National Defense
Division, Congressional Research Service, Library of Congress.
(U.S. Government Printing Office, Washington, 1983). 42p.

**Implications of Treaty on Final German Settlement for NATO
Strategy and U.S. Military Presence in Europe.**

Hearing before the Committee on Armed Services, United States
Senate, 101st Congress, 2nd Session. (U.S. Government Printing
Office, Washington, 1991). 44p.

Acronyms

ABM	Anti-ballistic missiles
ANF	Atlantic Nuclear Force
ATBM	Anti-theatre ballistic missiles
ATTU	Atlantic to the Urals
AWACS	Airborne Warning and Control Systems
BAOR	British Army on the Rhine
BMD	Ballistic missile defence
C^3I	Command, Control, Communication and Intelligence
CDI	Conventional defence improvement
CDU	Christian Democratic Union
CFE	Conventional forces in Europe
COCOM	Coordinating Committee on Export Controls
CSBM	Confidence- and Security-building measures
CSCE	Conference on Security and Cooperation in Europe
CSIS	Center for Strategic and International Studies
CSU	Christian Socialist Union
EC	European Community
EDC	European Defense Community
ESECS	European Security Study Group
ET	Emerging technologies
FOFA	Follow-on Forces Attack
FOTL	Follow on to Lance
GLCM	Ground-launched cruise missiles
ICBM	Intercontinental ballistic missiles
IEPG	Independent European Programme Group
INF	Intermediate nuclear forces
IISS	International Institute for Strategic Studies
IRBM	Intermediate-range ballistic missiles
LRTNF	Long-range theater nuclear force
LTDP	Long-term Defense Program
MBFR	Mutual and Balanced Force Reductions
MFR	Military force reductions

Acronyms

MLF	Multilateral Force
NACC	North Atlantic Cooperation Council
NFU	No first use
NPG	Nuclear Planning Group
OAS	Organization of American States
PGM	Precision-guided munitions
SAC	Strategic Air Command
SACEUR	Supreme Allied Commander Europe
SALT	Strategic Arms Limitation Treaty
SDI	Strategic Defense Initiative ('Star Wars')
SHAPE	Supreme Headquarters Allied Powers Europe
SPD	Socialist Party of Germany [Deutschland]
START	Strategic Arms Reduction Talks
WEU	Western European Union

Chronology

1947

12 March	Enunciation of Truman Doctrine.
5 June	Announcement of Marshall Plan for economic reconstruction of Western Europe.

1948

22 January	Ernest Bevin proposes establishment of a Western Union.
22 February	Czech coup.
17 March	Signing of Brussels Treaty for collective self-defence.
11 June	United States Senate adopts resolution 239 (The Vandenberg Resolution) recommending association of the United States with regional collective security organizations based on self-help and mutual aid.
6 July	Negotiations entitled 'Exploratory Conversations on Security Problems of Common Interest' begin between the United States, Canada and the Brussels Treaty powers with a view towards a formal alliance.
9 July	The negotiations produce a working document entitled the Washington Paper.
10 December	Negotiations begin on the drafting of the Atlantic Treaty.

1949

4 April	North Atlantic Treaty signed in Washington by Belgium, Britain, Canada, Denmark, France, Iceland, Italy, Luxembourg, The Netherlands, Norway, Portugal, the UK and the USA.

Chronology

6 October	President Truman signs programme for military assistance to United States' allies.

1950

27 January	United States approves plans for integrated defence of the North Atlantic region.
25 June	North Korea invades South Korea.
9 September	Truman announces substantial increases in the strength of United States forces to be stationed in Western Europe.
24 October	Pleven Plan for German rearmament within framework of a European Army.
19 December	General Eisenhower appointed first Supreme Allied Commander Europe (SACEUR).

1951

4 April	Senate passes Senate Resolution 99 voicing its approval of Truman's decision to deploy United States forces to Western Europe.

1952

20–25 February	NATO meeting in Lisbon establishes long-range conventional rearmament goal of 96 divisions.

1954

29 August	French National Assembly rejects European Defense Community.
23 October	Paris Agreements in which the Federal Republic of Germany (FRG) becomes a member of the Western European Union.

1955

5 May	The FRG joins NATO.
14 May	Warsaw Pact established.

1961

13 August	Berlin Wall erected.

1962

4–6 May	NATO Defence Ministers establish Athens Guidelines for the use of nuclear weapons.

1966

10 March	De Gaulle announces decision to leave NATO's integrated military organization.
29 March	Announcement that NATO forces and facilities must be withdrawn from France by 1 April 1967.

26 October	North Atlantic Council decides to move NATO Headquarters to Brussels.
14 December	NATO establishes Nuclear Planning Group.

1967

13–14 December   NATO adopts Harmel Report on Future Tasks of the Alliance which emphasizes deterrence and détente. The Defence Planning Committee adopts the strategy of flexible response.

1973

30 October   Beginning of negotiations in Vienna on Mutual and Balanced Force Reductions.

1974

18–19 June   NATO ministers issue a Declaration on Atlantic Relations.

1975

1 August   Helsinki Final Act in the Conference on Security and Cooperation in Europe.

1976

2 February   Independent European Programme Group established.

1977

17–18 May   Long-term Defence Programme established.

1979

12 December   NATO 'dual-track' decision to deploy 572 cruise and Pershing missiles in Western Europe while also seeking arms control with the Soviet Union.

27 December   Soviet Union invades Afghanistan.

1983

23 March   President Reagan announces his Strategic Defense Initiative.

1984

12 June   Reactivation of Western European Union.

1986

11–12 October   Reagan and Gorbachev meet at Reykjavik and discuss far-reaching arms control proposals.

1987

27 October   Western European Union adopts 'Platform on European Security Interests'.

| 8 December | Intermediate Nuclear Forces agreement signed by the superpowers, eliminating all nuclear missiles in Europe with a range between 500 and 5,000 kilometres. |

1989

2 February	Final meeting of negotiations on Mutual and Balanced Force Reductions which had failed to produce agreement.
9 March	Opening of new negotiations on Conventional Armed Forces in Europe (CFE), covering the Atlantic to the Urals.
29–30 May	NATO fortieth anniversary meeting at which President Bush announces new initiative on conventional arms control.
9–10 November	The crumbling of the Berlin Wall which is widely hailed as marking the end of the Cold War.
3 December	Malta summit between Bush and Gorbachev declares that Cold War has ended.

1990

5–6 July	Summit meeting in London issues 'London Declaration on a Transformed North Atlantic Alliance' which reflects the changing security environment.
3 October	Reunification of East and West Germany in the FRG.
19–21 November	CSCE Summit at which the CFE agreement is signed, reducing NATO and Warsaw Pact forces to a common ceiling. The Charter of Paris for a New Europe is adopted.

1991

25 February	Foreign and Defence Ministers of Warsaw Treaty Organization meet in Budapest to disband the WTO.
7–8 November	NATO's Rome Summit issues Declaration of Peace and Cooperation and adopts new strategy with an emphasis on crisis management.
9–11 December	European Community heads of government hold Maastricht Summit and agree on treaty for European Union.
17 December	Ministerial meeting of North Atlantic Council discusses NATO's role in peacekeeping, strengthening the CSCE, relations with the North

Atlantic Cooperation Council, and relations with the Western European Union.

1993

12 April	NATO begins enforcing no-fly zone over Bosnia.
10 June	Ministerial meeting of North Atlantic Council discusses peacekeeping and the situation in the Balkans.
August	NATO and US threaten strikes against Serbs in Bosnia if siege of Sarajevo is not lifted.
1 October	Yeltsin announces Russian opposition to expansion of NATO in Eastern Europe.

The Origins of NATO

1   **Pattern of Responsibility.**
    Dean Acheson.   Boston, Massachusetts: Houghton Mifflin, 1952. 309p.

This book, edited by McGeorge Bundy, contains excerpts from the major speeches of
United States Secretary of State Dean Acheson, in the period from January 1949 to
August 1951, a key period in the formation of NATO. It includes Acheson's
statements on the Soviet threat, the North Atlantic Treaty, the 'great debate' over
sending troops to Europe and the issue of German rearmament. The book correctly
identifies the Korean War as the key development which led the United States and the
European allies to move from an alliance that was predominantly a security guarantee
to a collective defence organization. It also includes some of Acheson's comments
justifying the decision to send troops to Europe. Both the speeches and the
commentary by Bundy succeed in imparting the flavour of the political debate in a
period when the United States not only departed from the traditional precepts of its
foreign policy and became engaged in an entangling alliance, but also deployed a
substantial number of American forces in Europe. Although it is based on public
sources it has many of the qualities of primary source material and is essential reading
for all serious students of the origins and early years of the Atlantic Alliance.

2   **Present at the Creation: My Years in the State Department.**
    Dean Acheson.   New York: Norton, 1969. 768p.

Although this book covers a far broader canvas than the origins of NATO it does
provide a first-hand account of the creation of the Alliance by one of the main
architects of the postwar security system in Europe. It offers considerable insight into
both the diplomacy and the domestic politics of the late 1940s and early 1950s and
gives a good sense of some of the political opposition that faced the Truman
Administration as it became increasingly committed to the security of Western Europe.
Although one critic subsequently suggested that Acheson had been present, at least in
a leading capacity, on only the sixth day of the creation, he does acknowledge that it
was a particularly busy day. These memoirs not only give a vivid sense of the period
but are also very revealing of the strategic considerations that were the basis for
Acheson's and Truman's policies. They are particularly good on the key personalities

1

involved both in the international negotiations and the negotiations between the Truman Administration and the Senate prior to the North Atlantic Treaty being signed and approved for ratification.

3   **US Role in Negotiations that led to Atlantic Alliance.**
Theodore C. Achilles.   *NATO Review*, Part I vol. 27, no. 4 (August 1979), p. 11-14; Part II vol 27, no. 5 (October 1979), p. 16-18.

Theodore Achilles was the director of the division of West European Affairs in the State Department from 1947 to 1950. As such, he provides an important insider's account of the negotiations leading to the North Atlantic Treaty. With John Hickerson, Director of the State Department's Office of European Affairs, Achilles was the main champion in the State Department of an alliance with Europe. He and Hickerson fought a running battle against George Kennan and Charles Bohlen who thought that an Atlantic Alliance was both unnecessary and undesirable. Although he had been interviewed for numerous previous studies, this is the first public account of the negotiations by Achilles himself. While it does not add a lot that is new or was previously unknown, it does offer a distinct perspective and some inside information. Among the points he makes is that Hickerson insisted that the North Atlantic Treaty be sufficiently clear that it could be understood by an 'Omaha milkman'.

4   **Britain, the Brussels Pact and the Continental Commitment.**
John Baylis.   *International Affairs*, vol. 60, no. 4 (Autumn 1984), p. 615-630.

Looks at the British role in creating the Brussels Pact, which was a prerequisite for the subsequent moves towards an Atlantic Alliance. Also considers this in terms of the perennial British debate over the benefits of a continental versus a maritime strategy. The author looks at wartime planning for a Western European security group and British Foreign Secretary Bevin's interest in a Dunkirk-type Treaty organization for Western security. He also explains the difficulties the United States and the Benelux countries had with a Dunkirk Treaty model and shows how they favoured a Rio-type Treaty or a regional organization of Western Europe under Article 52 of the UN Charter. Bevin's criticism of this type of pact, the changes in the debate after the Czech crisis, and Britain's contribution to the formation of the Atlantic Alliance are also discussed. A useful contribution both to our understanding of the British role and to our knowledge of the origins of the Atlantic Alliance.

5   **The Diplomacy of Pragmatism: Britain and the Formation of NATO 1942-49.**
John Baylis.   Kent, Ohio: Kent State University Press, 1992. 194p.

Looks at the British role in creating the postwar security order in Europe. Based on a careful analysis of the documents now available in Britain, the author charts British planning and policy in relation to security in the postwar world. He focuses on the views of both the Foreign Office and the Chiefs of Staff and the evolving relationships with the Soviet Union, France and the United States. Particular attention is given to the negotiations of 1948 and 1949 over a United States commitment to Western Europe. The author concludes that British policy, carefully orchestrated by Foreign Secretary Ernest Bevin, exhibited pragmatism, patience and vision, and that the formation of the Atlantic Alliance marked a considerable achievement for Britain.

6   **Britain, America and Transition from Economic to Military Assistance, 1948-51.**
Peter G. Boyle.   *Journal of Contemporary History*, vol. 22, no. 4 (July 1987), p. 521-538.
Based on papers from the British Cabinet and the Foreign Office, this illuminating article examines the transition from the United States policy of economic containment exemplified in the Marshall Plan to the more military form of containment embodied in NATO. It looks in particular at British views on this transition and considers the extent to which the British approved and favoured this course as opposed to sharing the reservations of George Kennan. Although Britain was concerned about the effect of increased military spending on economic recovery, these anxieties were put on one side after the outbreak of the Korean War, when Britain came to accept American assumptions about the nature of the threat. Boyle points out, however, that the over-ambitious rearmament programme had severe consequences for the British economy. A valuable article based on serious and detailed historical research.

7   **Strategic Implications of the North Atlantic Pact.**
Bernard Brodie.   *The Yale Review*, vol. 39, no. 2 (December 1949), p. 193-208.
An appraisal of the importance of the Atlantic Alliance by one of the leading strategic analysts of the postwar period. Brodie related the Pact to different American conceptions of how a future war should be fought and in particular to the debate between those who emphasized ground forces and those who advocated greater reliance on air power. He offers what is, in effect, one of the earliest analyses of some of the strategic dilemmas and controversies which were to bedevil NATO throughout the Cold War.

8   **Washington and the Atlantic Pact.**
Marquis W. Childs.   *The Yale Review*, vol. 38, no. 4 (June 1949), p. 577-587.
An interesting contemporary commentary on the formation of the Atlantic Alliance which rightly presents it as a radical departure from past United States policies and commitments. Childs contrasts the expectations of the Europeans that the treaty would be followed automatically by the supply of arms with the reservations and misgivings of many Senators about this. He also discusses the aspirations of the world federalists who saw Atlantic Union as a crucial step towards their long-term goal.

9   **Present at the Creation: The Fortieth Anniversary of the Marshall Plan.**
Edited by Armand Clesse, Archie C. Epps. New York: Harper and Row, 1990. 165p.
The result of a conference organized by the Luxembourg Harvard Association, this volume focuses upon the Marshall Plan, which marked a major milestone on the road towards the creation of NATO. There are fifteen chapters, most of which deal with various aspects of the Plan for European Economic Recovery. Particularly interesting is a chapter by Thomas Schelling which suggests that the Marshall Plan was a rehearsal for the Atlantic Alliance, one by Philip Windsor which has some helpful observations on the nature of the Alliance, and one by Paul Hammond which has an incisive analysis of 'NATO and the infrastructure of reassurance'.

10   **The Compromise that never was: George Kennan, Paul Nitze, and the Issue of Conventional Deterrence in Europe, 1949-1952.**
Jerald A. Combs.   *Diplomatic History*, vol. 15, no. 3 (Summer 1991), p. 361-386.

Although George Kennan was the prime author of the containment strategy, he believed that the Soviet threat was predominantly political rather than military. Consequently, he gave little credence to claims that Soviet military forces were ready to overrun Europe, and believed that American estimates of Soviet military strength were vastly exaggerated. Paul Nitze, Kennan's deputy and then successor at the State Department Policy Planning Staff, had a rather different view of the Soviet threat, however, seeing it as predominantly military in character. In some respects the debate between the two men provided the framework for many of the arguments which took place throughout the Cold War about the nature of the Soviet threat. These differences are discussed by Combs who highlights the continuity in Kennan's approach which led him in the early 1980s to advocate no first use of nuclear weapons. A richly detailed and well-documented analysis.

11   **My Name is Tom Connally.**
Tom Connally.   New York: Crowell, 1954. 376p.

Written by a Senator from Texas, these memoirs are often bombastic, always colourful and sometimes revealing of the politics of the North Atlantic Treaty ratification process. The comments of the flamboyant and irascible Connally have a broad scope and a highly personalized quality. Nevertheless, Connally's position as Chairman of the Senate Committee on Foreign Relations during the period when the Atlantic Alliance was negotiated, signed and ratified means that this is a book which should not be ignored. Although it does not offer much on the negotiations, especially now that the primary documents are available, it does give a flavour of the period, the key personalities involved and some of the subtleties of the relationship between the Truman Administration and the Senate when dealing with the North Atlantic Treaty.

12   **Forging the Alliance: NATO, 1945-1950.**
Don Cook.   New York: Arbor House/William Morrow, 1989. 306p. map. bibliog.

This study provides a straightforward historical account of the events and negotiations that led to the creation of the North Atlantic Treaty Organization and the commitment of US troops to Western Europe. It is largely a diplomatic history and accords a central role to British Foreign Secretary Ernest Bevin in the creation of NATO. According to the author, Bevin's role was twofold. First, by playing on the Anglo-American 'special relationship' Bevin was able to draw the United States and its army back into Europe after the postwar demobilization. Second, by putting together the Dunkirk and Brussels Treaties, Bevin was able to demonstrate to sceptical Americans the ability of Europeans to cooperate. This was crucial in showing the United States that the Europeans were worth defending and that a commitment to the security of Western Europe would also be in the interests of the United States.

13   **Taking the Pledge: Oliver Franks and the Negotiation of the North Atlantic Treaty.**
Alex Danchev.   *Diplomatic History*, vol. 15, no. 2 (Spring 1991),
p. 199-219.

An interesting discussion of the diplomatic manoeuvring that took place among the various governments in formulating the North Atlantic Treaty and endeavouring to ensure that it was approved by the United States Senate. The author focuses primarily on the role and contribution of the British Ambassador, Sir Oliver Franks, in the Ambassador's Committee, and shows how Franks helped to deal with several key issues and played a key role in moderating French demands. The latter part focuses upon Franks' role in the debate over Article 5.

14   **Europe and the United States.**
Vera Micheles Dean.   New York: Knopf, 1950. 349p.

This book provides a survey of European–American relations in the five years after the Second World War. It attempts to place the major changes in the international system in some kind of historical perspective, examines the patterns of recovery in Europe and looks at the United States' role. It places considerable emphasis on the United Nations but acknowledges that expectations for the UN were much lower in Europe than in the United States. Written for the lay person rather than the specialist, this book is of interest mainly as a reflection of some important strands of thinking in the United States in the period leading up to the creation of the Alliance, and does not add much to the scholarly record.

15   **France and the Creation of the North Atlantic Alliance.**
Claude Delmas.   *NATO Review*, vol. 28, no. 4 (August 1980),
p. 21-25.

This article emphasizes the importance of the role of French Foreign Minister Georges Bidault in moving towards Atlantic collaboration in security matters. Delmas traces the crucial shift in French attitudes from an anti-German emphasis to a more Atlanticist outlook, while also emphasizing the domestic opposition from left-wing groups and the Communist Party in France.

16   **The Atlantic Pact Forty Years Later: A Historical Reappraisal.**
Ennio Di Nolfo.   Berlin; New York: Walter de Gruyter, 1991. 268p.

Based on the proceedings of a conference held in Florence on the fortieth anniversary of the signing of the North Atlantic Treaty, this volume contains fourteen chapters by predominantly European scholars. It is divided into three parts, the first of which deals with the negotiations leading to the treaty. The second, and largest, section covers the attitudes of the countries involved and includes a chapter on Scandinavia and one on Belgian and Dutch perspectives. There is also a chapter on Eastern European reactions to the creation of the Western Alliance. The final section has three chapters dealing with Italy and the Pact. A good collection from an unusual perspective.

17 **In Defense of Canada: Growing up Allied.**
James Eayrs.   Toronto, Canada: University of Toronto Press, 1980.
431p.

This is one of several volumes written by Eayrs which deal with the evolution of Canadian foreign and security policy. Its main focus is the Canadian role in the negotiations leading up to the North Atlantic Treaty, but in dealing with this it offers some very illuminating observations on the whole negotiation process and the concerns of the other participants in the negotiations. It makes very good use of the Canadian documents that are available and is a major contribution to our understanding of the origins of NATO.

18 **Breaking the Vicious Circle: Britain, the United States, and the Genesis of the North Atlantic Treaty.**
Martin H. Folly.   *Diplomatic History*, vol. 12, no. 1 (Winter 1988), p. 59-77.

Argues that the British were the main architects of the Atlantic Alliance, that they initiated the negotiations and brought along a very reluctant United States. The author concludes that by tying the United States to the defence of Europe, Britain 'ended the vicious circle of American hesitancy and European lack of confidence which Bevin and his associates had perceived as such a danger in February 1948' (p. 77).

19 **The North Atlantic Treaty in the United States Senate.**
Richard H. Heindel, Thorsten V. Kalijarvi, Francis O. Wilcox.
American Journal of International Law, vol. 43 (1949), p. 633-665.

A detailed and helpful analysis of the North Atlantic Treaty which focuses on the issues discussed by the US Senate prior to ratification. It begins with an explanation of the Vandenberg Resolution and outlines the perceived conflict between the treaty and the United Nations Charter. The article provides a succinct discussion of the obligations undertaken by the United States as a result of Articles 3 and 5, discusses what constitutes an attack on a member-state under Article 5, and how constitutional processes may affect the ability of alliance members to respond to such attacks. The article also examines the selection of certain states for treaty inclusion and the possible admission of new members. Overall this provides the best available discussion of the treaty as a legal document, while revealing the concerns expressed in the United States debate over ratification.

20 **NATO: The Founding of the Atlantic Alliance and the Integration of Europe.**
Edited by Francis H. Heller, John R. Gillingham.   New York:
St Martin's Press, 1992. 470p.

The outgrowth of a conference held at the Harry Truman Library in September 1989, this work contains some very scholarly analyses of the establishment of NATO from a variety of national perspectives. There are contributions dealing with French, Dutch, Italian and United States policies leading up to the creation of NATO as well as a particularly incisive analysis by Peter Foot on 'Britain, European Unity and NATO 1947-50'. The wide variety of contributions covers such issues as German rearmament, the role of the European Defense Community and the nuclearization of NATO. For all serious historians of NATO, this collection is a must. It covers considerable ground in a way which is highly scholarly yet also very accessible. This volume is highly recommended.

21   **The Birth of NATO.**
Sir Nicholas Henderson.   Boulder, Colorado: Westview Press, 1983.
130p.

In the period from 1947 to 1949, Nicholas Henderson was Second Secretary at the British Embassy in Washington. Accordingly he is well placed to provide an inside account of the negotiations that led to the creation of the Atlantic Alliance in 1949. His book provides a step-by-step account of these negotiations, while also offering a series of fascinating vignettes on the main personalities involved. The early chapters look at the genesis of the North Atlantic Treaty, the initial tripartite talks between Britain, Canada and the United States, the opposition to an 'entangling alliance' by Charles Bohlen and George Kennan, two of the key officials in the State Department, and the early sessions of the seven-power negotiations from July to September 1948. Chapter four looks at the period from September to December 1948, while chapter five on the final lap is in many respects the most interesting of all. It shows how the international negotiations and the negotiations between the Truman Administration and Congress became intermeshed in ways which greatly complicated the situation. Throughout the analysis, the contribution to the negotiations made by the representatives of Canada, the United States and Britain is seen as crucial to their ultimate success. The book also has appendices containing the draft text of the Treaty as it stood in December 1948 and the final text as signed on 4 April 1949.

22   **Denmark and the Road to NATO (part I and II).**
Sven Henningsen.   *NATO Review*, Part I vol. 27, no. 6 (December 1989), p. 18-21; Part II vol. 28, no. 1 (February 1980), p. 14-16.

Although Denmark recognized after the Second World War that a policy of neutrality was no longer a viable option, its initial impulse was to look for a Scandinavian security arrangement. This failed in January 1949 – largely because of differences between Norway and Sweden over the relationship between a Nordic pact and the emerging Atlantic Alliance. For Denmark, membership in the Alliance was the only option left given that neutrality was deemed unacceptable and its geopolitical position remained highly vulnerable. Yet Denmark did not have to push hard for membership. The United States was also very anxious for Denmark to be included, partly because of the importance of Greenland: although this was under Danish sovereignty, American bases had been established there and the United States was anxious to retain them.

23   **The Creation of the North Atlantic Alliance, 1948-1952.**
Alan K. Henrikson.   *Naval War College Review*, vol. 32, no. 3 (May-June 1980), p. 4-39.

A richly detailed yet very succinct account of the creation of the Alliance. Makes clear that the Alliance as it had evolved by 1952 was not the kind of Alliance that had been envisaged in 1949. The analysis is particularly good on how the negotiation process affected the final details of the Treaty. Probably the most comprehensive and useful short overview of the origins of the Alliance.

24 **Luxembourg: From Neutrality to the Atlantic Alliance.**
Nicholas Hommel. *NATO Review*, vol. 30, no. 5 (December 1982),
p. 29-33.

This article highlights the fact that for the Duchy of Luxembourg, the calculations which led to membership of the Atlantic Alliance were straightforward. As the Minister of Foreign Affairs, Mr. Bech, stated to the legislative assembly in April 1949, Luxembourg had to replace the illusion of its neutral status and faith in the United Nations with the more tangible guarantees of a system of collective defence. The article outlines the neutrality policy from 1947 onwards and highlights the gradual erosion of Luxembourg's neutral status. As with the other small European countries, considerable importance is placed on the Brussels Treaty as the precursor to the North Atlantic Treaty.

25 **Vandenberg Reconsidered: Senate Resolution 239 and America's Foreign Policy.**
D. J. Hudson. *Diplomatic History*, vol. 1, no. 1 (Winter 1977),
p. 46-63.

A useful appraisal of Vandenberg's role in the evolution of United States policy towards Western Europe leading up to the North Atlantic Treaty. The author provides a particularly good account of the meetings between Under-Secretary of State Lovett and Vandenberg, out of which emerged a draft of the Vandenberg Resolution.

26 **Creating the Entangling Alliance: The Origins of the North Atlantic Treaty Organization.**
Timothy P. Ireland. Westport, Connecticut: Greenwood Press, 1981.
245p.

This stimulating study traces the US commitment to Europe from the end of the Second World War until the assignment of American troops to Western Europe in 1951. Ireland's basic thesis is that the American commitment to Europe in the late 1940s was designed not only to contain the Soviet Union but to re-establish Western Europe and to re-create an indigenous balance of power on the European Continent in ways which would minimize both the cost and the duration of the American commitment. In order to move towards the recreation of an indigenous balance of power in Europe, however, the United States found it necessary to include West Germany in the programmes for recovery and rearmament – a development which created great insecurity amongst other European states, especially France. And in order to alleviate these fears, the United States had to provide reassurances which were made credible only by direct US involvement. This was particularly the case with the decision of September 1950 to send troops to Europe. In essence, the deployment of American troops was the price that the United States paid in order to persuade France to accept German rearmament. Ireland argues his case with great skill and persuasiveness, and even though his thesis is not wholly compelling, the book is a must for all serious students of the origins of the Atlantic Alliance.

27 **A Community of Interests: NATO and the Military Assistance Program, 1948-1951.**
Lawrence S. Kaplan.   Washington, DC: Government Printing Office, 1980. 251p.

A detailed and important study which examines the creation of the United States Mutual Defense Assistance Program. In its early years, this programme was focused primarily on NATO and had considerable impact on the evolution of the Alliance. The author traces the inter-relationships between the programme and the formation of the North Atlantic Alliance as well as the subsequent development of a much stronger military organization. An important and detailed study which is a must for all those interested in the origins and early years of the Alliance.

28 **The United States and NATO: The Formative Years.**
Lawrence S. Kaplan.   Lexington, Kentucky: University Press of Kentucky, 1984. 276p.

This is a very substantial study of the decision of the United States to join Western Europe in a military alliance. The analysis highlights both how anguished this decision was and how easy. It shows how opposition to military alliances from those who supported the United Nations led the Truman Administration to link the UN Charter to the North Atlantic Treaty. The main focus of the book, however, is on the negotiations which led first to the Brussels Pact and from that to the Atlantic Alliance. The analysis traces not only the way in which the Treaty was negotiated but also the move from the Treaty to the Organization, and the impact of the Korean War. Throughout the analysis the author draws on an impressive range of documents from primary sources and provides an invaluable study of the 'formative years' of NATO.

29 **Fingerprints on History: The NATO Memoirs of Theodore C. Achilles.**
Lawrence S. Kaplan, Sidney R. Snyder.   Kent, Ohio: Lemnitzer Center, Kent State University, 1992. 58p. (Occasional Paper 1).

A valuable paper composed of material related to NATO, extracted by the editors from over 900 pages of manuscript written by Theodore Achilles, one of the main architects of the Atlantic Alliance in the State Department. A ten-page introduction by the editors is followed by Achilles' account of the negotiations leading to the treaty and the developments which subsequently put the 'O' in NATO. The memoirs are very colourful and start with the sentence 'Somehow NATO will always be associated in my mind with fishhouse punch' (p. 11).

30 **Memoirs, 1925-1950.**
George F. Kennan.   London: Hutchinson, 1967. 583p.

As the author of containment, George Kennan could be regarded in some senses as the intellectual godfather of NATO. Yet, as he makes clear in a chapter of his memoirs, he was not particularly keen on the idea of a formal alliance with Western Europe, seeing this as an expression of the American penchant for a legalistic and moralistic approach to international politics, and as a move from economic and political containment of the Soviet Union – which followed the lines he had proposed – to military containment which he saw as an unnecessary distortion. Insofar as some action was deemed necessary to supplement the Marshall Plan, Kennan's preference was for a unilateral US guarantee. He was also concerned that the European allies should do more for themselves and should not be overly reliant on the United States. This emphasis on self-help was shared by Senator Vandenberg and was a key theme in the debate over the respective roles of the United States and the West Europeans in the Atlantic Alliance.

31 **The Atlantic Pact and International Security.**
Grayson Kirk. *International Organization*, vol. 3 (1949), p. 239-251.
Kirk looks at the debate over the Atlantic Treaty in the United States and especially its relationship to the United Nations framework for security matters. He also considers the likely impact of the pact on Western Europe, US–Soviet relations and the United Nations.

32 **The Atlantic Alliance: Its Origins and Its Future.**
John J. McCloy. New York: Columbia University Press, 1969. 83p.
This book, based on a series of lectures, by a former official, offers some illuminating and helpful reflections on the origins of the Alliance. McCloy locates the origins of NATO very clearly within the overall struggle between the Soviet Union and the United States for control of Western Europe. He sees the creation of NATO as a natural development of the Cold War and as a measure which clearly complemented the Marshall Plan for European economic recovery. The second lecture looks at the major challenges to the vitality of the Alliance in the 1960s, while the third and final one reiterates the importance of the Alliance and makes some pertinent observations about its future needs.

33 **The Making of the Alliance: A Portuguese Perspective.**
Albano Nogueira. *NATO Review*, vol. 28, no. 5 (October 1980), p. 8-13.
As this article makes clear, Portugal played a non-significant role in the negotiations leading to the North Atlantic Treaty but was invited to participate in the Alliance partly because of the importance of the Azores. The author traces the concerns of Prime Minister Salazar about some of the language of the preamble and the fact that Spain was not invited to join.

34 **Italy's Entry into the Atlantic Alliance: The Role of the Italian Embassy in Washington, 1948-1949 (parts I and II).**
Egidio Ortona. *NATO Review*, vol. 29, no. 4 (August 1981), p. 19-22, 29-33.
The author, who was in the Italian embassy in Washington in the period from April 1948 to April 1949, focuses his remarks upon the obstacles – both domestic and international – which Italy had to overcome before becoming a member of the Atlantic Alliance. The article touches on some of the complications of Italian domestic politics – where the Communist Party was still an important factor – and highlights the importance of the Italian Ambassador in the United States, Ambassador Tarchiani, in influencing the Italian government to participate in the Alliance. Part two develops the themes of the first part and shows how the situation evolved through the first few months of 1949. It also highlights the continued difficulties that bedevilled the issue of Italian participation until very late in the negotiations.

35 **Bargaining Power among Potential Allies: Negotiating the North Atlantic Treaty, 1948-49.**
Nikolaj Petersen.   *Review of International Studies*, vol. 12, no. 3 (July 1986), p. 187-203.
An incisive article which combines theory and history in an effort to explain some of the outcomes of the negotiations leading to the North Atlantic Treaty. An unusual but valuable perspective in which the author looks at the negotiations leading to the formation of the Atlantic Alliance from a bargaining perspective and considers what it reveals about the relative power of the states involved.

36 **Time of Fear and Hope: The Making of the North Atlantic Treaty, 1947-1949.**
Escott Reid.   Toronto: McClelland and Stewart, 1977. 315p.
The author was the number two man, behind Lester Pearson, in the Canadian delegation to the North Atlantic Treaty talks, and has provided one of the fullest and most readable accounts of the negotiations leading to the treaty. Reid participated in the secret Washington meetings between the United States, Britain, and Canada in 1948 and his firsthand account of these and the subsequent meetings is detailed and insightful. The author's personal recollections are supplemented throughout by primary documents drawn largely from US and Canadian government archives. A thorough study, the volume covers the mechanisms for discussion, the conceptual issues at stake, and the specific elements and scope of the final treaty. It gives particular attention to the Canadian agenda in the negotiations and the more obscure elements of the treaty such as the treatment of France's North African territories. The book ends with an assessment of NATO in the 1970s and the author concludes that NATO is not the ideal institution for protecting the free world's values. The value of the book, however, lies not in its prescriptions but in its contribution to the historical record.

37 **The Miraculous Birth of the North Atlantic Alliance.**
Escott Reid.   *NATO Review*, vol. 28, no. 6 (December 1980), p. 12-17.
This article contains reflections by one of the Canadian diplomats who was most centrally involved in the negotiations leading to the creation of the Alliance. Reid looks at United States, French, Belgian and Norwegian perspectives, and highlights the impact of the message from Norway in 1948 that it was under Soviet pressure for some kind of security pact with Moscow. Not surprisingly, but nevertheless very appropriately, Reid also emphasizes the positive role played by Canada in the negotiations.

38 **The Alliance's Anxious Birth.**
Alexander Rendel.   *NATO Review*, vol. 27, no. 3 (June 1979), p. 15-20.
Written by the former diplomatic correspondent of the London *Times*, and based on recently released documents from the British Foreign Office, this article looks at the anxiety created in 1948 by the Czech coup and the Berlin blockade. It also focuses upon the creation of the Western Union, highlighting the crucial role of Britain's Foreign Secretary Ernest Bevin in this task. It argues that the negotiations with Washington which followed the Brussels Treaty began in haste and without a clear plan as to how the European agreement on defence in central Europe should be supported

by the United States. The emphasis on improvisation provides an important element in the analysis and helps to convey the flavour of the late 1940s in Atlantic relations.

39   **Uncertainty Continues as Atlantic Treaty Nears Completion.**
Alexander Rendel.   *NATO Review*, vol. 28, no. 2 (April 1980),
p. 15-19.

In retrospect, there is something of an inexorable quality about the creation of NATO. The period leading up to the Treaty, however, was one of great uncertainty as the debate in the United States Senate cast doubt upon the kind of commitment that would be enshrined in Article 5 of the Treaty. This article discusses the response of British Foreign Secretary Ernest Bevin to these developments.

40   **The Genesis of North Atlantic Defence Cooperation: Norway's Atlantic Policy, 1940-1945.**
Olav Riste.   *NATO Review*, vol. 29, no. 2 (April 1981), p. 19-23.

This article focuses upon the emphasis placed by Trygve Lie, the Foreign Minister of the Norwegian government in exile during the Second World War, on the idea of North Atlantic defence cooperation. This idea was put forward by Lie in December 1940 in a radio broadcast and was subsequently propagated with British officials during the wartime years. Riste also shows how many of the dilemmas which faced Norwegian foreign policy after the war were recognized in the discussions which took place during the war years themselves.

41   **Western Security: The Formative Years: European and Atlantic Defence, 1947-1953.**
Edited by Olav Riste.   New York: Columbia University Press, 1985.
333p.

This book resulted from a symposium held in 1983 which brought together a distinguished group of scholars from Europe and the United States to examine the pre-history and the early history of the Atlantic Alliance. An introduction by Michael Howard, providing an interesting overview of the period, is followed by chapters on British, French and United States approaches to European security in the early Cold War years. The chapter on the United States by John Lewis Gaddis is particularly good and very well documented. The second section includes chapters by Lawrence Kaplan and Olav Riste and deals with the period prior to the Korean War. The third section examines the impact of the Korean War and shows how, building on the steps that had already been taken, the war precipitated not only the creation of an effective Atlantic defence organization but also West German rearmament. Section five deals with the politics of rearmament in Britain and France, while in a final chapter dealing with transition, Thomas Etzold examines the process whereby NATO adopted a nuclear strategy. Several sections have chapters on the Nordic dimension which is often neglected, and the book also contains a useful chronology of the period from 1945 to 1953.

42   **Belgium and the Longest Lasting Alliance.**
Baron Robert Rothschild. *NATO Review*, vol. 30, no. 1
(February 1982), p. 18-22.

Part of a series on the origins of the Atlantic Alliance, this article emphasizes the importance of the Brussels Treaty as a necessary prerequisite for the Atlantic Alliance.

It also emphasizes the role of Paul Henri Spaak, the Belgian Foreign Minister, and it is argued that Spaak was consistently urging the British to adopt a stronger line towards the Soviet Union. The author suggests that Spaak saw the North Atlantic Treaty as something of a personal triumph. Rothschild highlights the solid support in Belgium – unlike France – for both the Brussels Treaty and the Atlantic Alliance.

43   The Fear of Subversion: The United States and the Inclusion of Italy in the North Atlantic Treaty.

E. Timothy Smith.   *Diplomatic History*, vol. 7, no. 2 (Spring 1983), p. 139-155.

Smith argues that one of the main reasons for Italy's inclusion in NATO was the fear of communist subversion. He looks at the opposition to Italian membership, especially from Britain, and how it was overcome, not least through the efforts of Hickerson. This is a good analysis based on careful examination of the documents.

44   Norway and the Atlantic Alliance, 1948-1949.

Grethe Vaerno.   *NATO Review*, vol. 29, no. 3 (June 1981), p. 16-20.

This article traces the Norwegian entry into the Atlantic Alliance and the opposition to this policy from within the ruling Labour Party itself. It also shows how many of the issues in the debate about membership – the 'special relationship' with Sweden, the desire to maintain a low profile toward the Soviet Union, the issue of whether West European or Atlantic ties are most important to Norwegian security – had a resonance in later Norwegian debates about security. Nevertheless Vaerno clearly explains why Norway rejected the Nordic option and chose to join the Alliance.

45   How and Why the Netherlands Joined the Atlantic Alliance (part I and II).

S. I. P. Van Campen.   *NATO Review*, Part I vol. 30, no. 3 (August 1982), p. 8-12; Part II vol. 30, no. 4 (September 1982), p. 20-25.

These two pieces place the Dutch decision to join the Atlantic Alliance in historical perspective and show how this decision departed from the long tradition of neutrality and independence. The author contends that the perceived lack of equilibrium in international relations in Europe in the period from 1945 to 1948 was decisive in the ultimate discarding of Dutch neutrality. Although the Netherlands government initially looked to the United Nations as the primary institution to guarantee its security, the response to the breakdown of four-power cooperation in December 1947 marked a fundamental change in Dutch thinking about security. The Benelux countries placed the emphasis on multilateral regional arrangements rather than bilateralism and as a result were very supportive of the Brussels Treaty. The second article also contains a good account of the domestic debate in the Netherlands about this shift in foreign policy orientation. There was particular concern that nothing in the Treaty should allow the allies to have any say in Dutch policy in Indonesia – a policy that strained relations with Britain and the United States. The analysis also highlights some of the tendencies which came back to the fore in the Dutch debate over European security in the late 1970s and the 1980s.

46   **The Private Papers of Senator Vandenberg.**
Arthur H. Vandenberg, Jr.   Boston, Massachusetts: Houghton Mifflin, 1952. 599p.

Senator Vandenberg was an isolationist Republican who became an internationalist on the day of Pearl Harbor. He was subsequently the key figure in obtaining Republican, and therefore bipartisan, support for the US commitment to Europe in the late 1940s. This volume, which consists of his private notes and comments, offers many insights into the political dimension of United States foreign policy. Vandenberg's writings also help to illuminate key elements in American thinking in the period leading up to the Treaty. The analysis contains some particularly interesting comments on Vandenberg's rivalry with Tom Connally. A good source, this is more substantial than Connally's memoirs.

47   **The Pentagon Negotiations March 1948: The Launching of the North Atlantic Treaty.**
Cees Wiebes, Bert Zeeman.   *International Affairs*, vol. 59, no. 3 (Summer 1983), p. 351-364.

An attempt to supplement the official history of the negotiations leading to the North Atlantic Treaty which suggests that a consensus on the treaty was reached only in 1948. The article explores the history of the Pentagon negotiations, and considers why it took so long to get the treaty signed. The two stages of the Pentagon negotiations are outlined: the first, in which the possible forms of alliance were discussed, and the second in the which the United States wrote the Pentagon Paper. The negotiations over such issues as the mutual assistance pledge, indirect aggression, territorial scope, and the membership of the Alliance are all examined. Considerable attention is given to the role of Ernest Bevin, the British Foreign Secretary, in the moves towards an alliance.

The History of NATO

General overviews

48 **The Alliance: America, Europe, Japan.**
Richard J. Barnet.   New York: Simon and Schuster, 1983. 511p.

Intended as a history of the post-war Western alliance including Japan, this volume focuses primarily on Europe and will appeal to anyone researching the early years of the Atlantic Alliance. Beginning in the early days of the United States' occupation of Germany and Japan, the author traces the vagaries of the relationship between the US and its major allies through to the first years of Reagan's presidency. The narrative focuses on the decision makers who have shaped the evolution of alliance politics throughout its history. These range from Konrad Adenauer to Helmut Schmidt in Germany and Dean Acheson to Henry Kissinger in the United States. The author argues that the alliance moved through three distinct phases: a period of creative innovation during which the United States, in effect, established a new international order; a period of crises within the alliance – particularly the problem of France – and outside (the Cuban and Berlin crises); and a period of growing divergence between the United States and its increasingly independent partners. Well written and thoroughly footnoted, the book is strongest on the early years of the alliance but also provides a good overview of the evolution of Atlantic relations.

49 **The Politics of the Atlantic Alliance.**
Alvin Cottrell, James E. Dougherty.   New York: Praeger, 1964. 264p.

This book, intended as a short guide to the politics of the Atlantic Alliance, offers a useful introduction to NATO. The opening chapter deals with the origins of NATO and its organizational structure, while other chapters deal with 'NATO, Germany and the USSR', with the politics of NATO's military strategy, the politics of economic integration, and the politics of the Alliance. This is a very sensible overview of the Atlantic Alliance and the political factors which influenced its evolution until the early 1960s. For those who want an easy, if obviously dated, introduction to the Alliance, this is a reasonable place to start.

50 **Europe between the Superpowers: The Enduring Balance.**
Anton W. DePorte. New Haven, New Jersey; London: Yale
University Press, 1979. 256p.

This study places in historical perspective the postwar European state system in
Europe based upon the division of the Continent into rival blocs. It highlights some of
the major features of the old balance of power system in Europe, shows how this
system broke down and identifies the main features of the Cold War system in which
Europe was dominated by the two superpowers. It argues that this system was very
stable and explains why challenges to it did not fundamentally undermine its very
stability. It takes on particular interest in light of the way in which the system finally
disintegrated in the 1989 to 1991 period.

51 **The Western Alliance: Its Status and Prospects.**
Edited by Edgar Furniss, Jr. Columbus, Ohio: Ohio State University
Press, 1965. 182p.

This is an interesting collection of essays. Individual chapters include an examination
of the role of the Secretary General of NATO, a good discussion of some of the
defence problems of NATO including the difficulties it would face moving to war, the
issue of political cooperation, French reflections on the Alliance, the German role, and
prospects for the future. A chapter by Frederick Nolting suggests that the Alliance
should adopt a more imaginative role for dealing with challenges outside its immediate
area of responsibility. Perhaps the greatest value of this volume is the eclecticism of the
subjects it covers. Since many of these were perennial problems it offers good insight
into how they were viewed in the mid-1960s.

52 **The Long Peace: Inquiries into the History of the Cold War.**
John Lewis Gaddis. New York: Oxford University Press, 1987. 332p.

A collection of eight conference and symposium papers written and presented by the
pre-eminent historian of the Cold War. Most of the papers focus on the early years and
the events that created the Cold War. The final chapter, 'The Long Peace', is a
thought-provoking investigation into the enduring stability of the postwar international
system. Although this book does not focus on NATO as such, it does offer a very good
analysis of the Cold War system in which NATO played a major role. For those
interested in the broader context of stability which the alliance both operated within
and contributed to, this is a very good study indeed.

53 **35 Years of NATO: A Transatlantic Symposium on the Changing
Political, Economic and Military Setting.**
Edited by J. Godson. New York: Dodd, Mead and Co., 1984. 175p.

A volume which, for the most part, contains eminent contributors rather than eminent
contributions and reproduces with later additions and enlargements a series of essays
published in *The Times* (London) in the first half of 1984. The contributors include
Alexander Haig, Franz Josef Strauss, James Schlesinger, Roy Jenkins, and Abba
Eban, as well as Margaret Thatcher, Ronald Reagan and Helmut Kohl. Conceived to
mark the 35th anniversary of the Alliance, the series was designed to identify
challenges to NATO. This is reflected in the broad approach of the book which has
sections on 'defence, arms control and the transatlantic order', on economic
challenges, on public opinion, and on regional problems outside the Alliance, as well
as on the question of whether Western civilization is an obsolete concept. The essays

give a reasonable flavour of the period but, with a few exceptions have little enduring value. A slightly larger version of this came out as *Challenges to the Western Alliance: An International Symposium on the Changing Political, Economic and Military Setting* (London: Times Books, 1984). 208p.

54 The Fate of the Atlantic Community.
Eliot R. Goodman.   New York: Praeger for the Atlantic Council of the United States, 1975. 583p.

A massive study which provides a very comprehensive analysis of the problems faced by NATO in the 1960s and 1970s. The author traces the idea of Atlantic union and highlights the practical problems this notion encounters. There is a particularly good chapter on the impact of General de Gaulle which considers the role of France as disintegrator. The author also looks at the prospects for and limitations of the notion of Atlantic partnership, issues related to the management of détente, multilateral nuclear sharing, and the economics of the Atlantic Community. The final chapter deals with the role of parliamentary assemblies in NATO. Overall, this is a thorough and useful study which deals in detail with important themes in the history of NATO.

55 The Western Alliance: European–American Relations since 1945.
Alfred Grosser.   London: Macmillan, 1978. 375p.

This study examines patterns of continuity and change and shifts in economic power in US–European relations from 1945 through to the early 1970s. Grosser rejects the negative characterizations of American hegemony, preferring to differentiate between 'humiliating dependence' and 'realistic acceptance' of constraints. Part I looks at Atlantic relations in the period between the end of the Second World War and the creation of the Alliance. Part II deals with harmonies and strains of the 1950s, looking at developments in Europe and European–American differences over issues such as Indo-China, Suez and Algeria. Part III explores the clash between the Kennedy Administration's grand design and General de Gaulle's conceptions of a more independent European role. It also considers the impact of Vietnam on America's relationship with its European allies. Part IV looks at the crisis of the early 1970s and has some incisive comments on the 'Year of Europe'. The author concludes that the leading European nations have suffered a severe identity crisis and that the European community is neither a subordinate configuration in a bloc under American leadership nor a second pillar of the Atlantic structure nor a new superpower between the two giants. In retrospect, this judgement may seem rather harsh. Nevertheless, Grosser provides an excellent overview of the period under review and offers a subtle and sophisticated treatment of the linkages between economic and security issues.

56 Atlantic Community in Crisis: A Redefinition of the Transatlantic Relationship.
Edited by Walter F. Hahn, Robert L. Pfaltzgraff, Jr.   Elmsford, New York: Pergamon Press, 1979. 386p.

The starting point for this edited volume is that the ties of the Atlantic Community which emerged in the late 1940s have been loosened, with the result that the Community is heading towards a crisis. Although it is not clear that the Community was ever as close as is assumed, this remains a useful collection. Diane Pfaltzgraff makes some useful conceptual distinctions relating to community and partnership. There are also sections on technological collaboration, Finlandization, and energy, monetary and trade problems within the Alliance. The volume is broadly conceived and interesting if somewhat alarmist.

57 The Revisionists: Moscow, Bonn, and the European Balance.
Josef Joffe. *The National Interest*, no. 17 (Fall 1989), p. 41-54.
A dated but interesting analysis which identifies the shared interests of the Federal Republic of Germany and the Soviet Union in modifying the postwar European order which was based on the idea of dual containment. Joffe argues that policies based on these interests have to be reconciled with other concerns – Bonn's desire not to lose its Atlantic insurance policy and the cocoon of West European integration, and the Soviet desire to keep the United States as a counterweight to German power and as a means of legitimizing a residual Soviet presence in Eastern Europe. It is interesting to consider how much of Joffe's assessment has survived the changes in Europe since 1989. This offers some good insights into the Cold War security system.

58 The Rationale for NATO: European Collective Security – Past and Future.
Morton A. Kaplan.   Stanford, California: Hoover Institution, 1973. 94p.
The main purpose of this slim volume is to elucidate what the author terms a dissuasion strategy. Before doing this, Kaplan looks briefly at the collapse of the wartime alliance which led to the Atlantic Alliance, the early history of NATO, the Nixon era, and the military balance and geopolitical situation in the early 1970s. The author advocates removing the quick-reaction aircraft and the Pershing missiles in the hope of creating a more pronounced firebreak and removing Soviet incentives to pre-empt. This would also provide a better basis for a dissuasion strategy in which NATO would promise to avoid large-scale damage to Eastern Europe so long as the non-Soviet Warsaw Pact states did not join in aggressive action against Western Europe. An intriguing, if not a persuasive analysis and proposal.

59 American Historians and the Atlantic Alliance.
Edited by Lawrence S. Kaplan.   Kent, Ohio: Kent State University Press, 1991. 192p.
Resulting from a symposium of historians, this volume contains some good chapters dealing with particular episodes in the history of NATO. There are contributions on the formation of the Alliance, NATO and the Korean War, the American commitment to Germany, the French withdrawal from NATO's integrated command, 'Nixingerism, NATO and Detente' the SS-20 challenge, and the INF Treaty and the future of NATO. The author list reads like a who's who of American diplomatic historians and includes Ernest May, Samuel Wells, Gaddis Smith, Walter Lafeber and, not least, the editor himself. Although not a comprehensive coverage, this does highlight some of the most crucial episodes in the evolution of NATO. In all, it is a valuable study.

60 Defending the West: A History of NATO.
William Park.   Brighton, England: Wheatsheaf Books, 1986. 242p.
A useful volume which breaks no new ground but is good on the details of NATO's nuclear force posture. Although the author aspires to update Robert E. Osgood's *NATO: The Entangling Alliance*, in actuality he has written not so much a history of NATO as an analytical history of NATO's nuclear strategy. NATO's rhetoric and

capabilities are identified and probable outcomes in response to Soviet aggression are projected and analysed. The concluding chapter looks at NATO's force posture below the nuclear threshold. The author believes he sees encouraging signs of an evolving Franco-German 'special relationship' that could potentially enhance NATO's conventional deployment.

61 NATO's Future: Toward a New Transatlantic Bargain.

Stanley R. Sloan. Washington, DC: National Defense University Press, 1985. 241p.

This book, written in the mid-1980s, provides one of the best overviews of the evolution of the Atlantic Alliance. Its focus is on the transatlantic relationship, with particular emphasis on the original transatlantic bargain and the ways in which it has changed. It is especially good on the attempts by the Europeans to forge a defence identity and the reasons why this failed. It also contains a good chapter on the evolution of alliance strategy. Sloan analyses the tensions within the alliance over the Soviet threat and threats arising outside the area of NATO's formal responsibilities. He delineates very effectively the different attitudes on how to deal with the Soviet Union and on the appropriate balance between détente and deterrence which caused major problems in NATO in the late 1970s and the first half of the 1980s. A key theme of the book is that a new transatlantic bargain needs to be worked out in which the Europeans not only get together, but forge an equal partnership with the United States. Sloan looks at the pressures for moving in this direction and at some of the obstacles. Although dated in some respects, this book remains essential reading and is one of the best available overviews of the evolution of the Atlantic Alliance.

62 Walter Lippmann on Europe and the Atlantic Community.

Anwar Syed. *Orbis*, vol. 7, no. 2 (Summer 1963), p. 308-335.

Syed examines the views of the famous American columnist, Walter Lippmann, on European and Atlantic security arrangements and shows how these views evolved over time. Lippmann's views on NATO, the Schuman Plan, the European Defense Community, the German problem, De Gaulle and the evolving Atlantic community are all discussed by the author.

63 The Permanent Alliance: The European–American Partnership.

Geoffrey Williams. Leyden, The Netherlands: Sijthoff, 1977. 407p.

Williams looks at the Atlantic relationship in the postwar period and traces its origins, development and decline. He argues that the antithesis between Atlantic unity and European integration was unnecessary. At the same time, the author presents the case for a more equal relationship in the Atlantic Alliance based on a clear division of labour.

64 European Security in the Nuclear Age.

James H. Wyllie. Oxford, England: Basil Blackwell, 1986. 186p.

A good overview of the European security arrangements of the mid-1980s, which explains the background to these arrangements in terms of the ideological conflict between East and West and the nuclear environment within which postwar security policies have been worked out. When he wrote in his preface that the book attempts to explain why these arrangements are the way they are and why it was unlikely that they would change radically in the near future, Wyllie was reflecting the views of most scholars and observers of European security.

NATO in the 1950s

65 **Negotiation from Strength.**
Coral Bell. New York: Knopf, 1963. 248p.

One of the main themes of United States policy throughout the 1950s was the idea of negotiation from strength. This notion is critically and comprehensively dissected in this study. Coral Bell highlights some of the difficulties of negotiating from strength in an alliance of democracies. She also argues that the emphasis on integrating Western Germany into NATO made it very difficult to negotiate effectively with the Soviet Union and its allies.

66 **In the Laps of the Gods: The Origins of NATO Forward Defense.**
James A. Blackwell, Jr. *Parameters*, vol. 15, no. 4 (Winter 1985), p. 64-75.

Blackwell explores the operational origins of the NATO strategy of forward defence in the period from 1949 to 1955. He suggests that forward defence was subject to wide variations in the way it was interpreted, largely as a result of divergent operational concepts and differing national military styles. He also looks at the initial planning for forward defence, the increased sense of urgency from 1949 to 1952 and the stretch-out from 1952 to 1955. A useful discussion of an often neglected aspect of NATO strategy.

67 **Securing Peace in Europe, 1945-62.**
Edited by Beatrice Heuser, Robert O'Neill. New York: St Martin's Press, 1992. 355p.

Sets out to consider the way in which the Western Alliance, in its formative years, laid effective foundations for a new era of European security. Part one of the volume focuses on the formative years of NATO, while the second part considers the problems on NATO's central front, including the Berlin crises, French disenchantment, Britain's alternatives to the European Defense Community, and nuclear weapons and British–German relations. The third part of the volume deals with the Mediterranean and the Far East, while the fourth section deals with problems within the alliance, especially that of coordinating military production and containing Soviet espionage. While the individual contributions are often very good, the overall effect is somewhat disjointed. This is alleviated slightly by a final essay in which Robert O'Neill draws lessons from the historical experience for the future of European security.

68 **NATO – The First Five Years.**
Lord Ismay. Paris: NATO, 1954. 280p.

Written by the first Secretary General of NATO, this book offers a detailed but very traditional account of the origins of the Alliance, and traces the transition from the initial United States security guarantee to the emphasis on balanced collective forces in May 1950, a transition which went much further as a result of the outbreak of the Korean War in June 1950. In effect, Ismay provides an 'official history' both of the origins of NATO and its early evolution. Its main interest stems from the author's unique vantage point on the Alliance.

69 **NATO and its Commentators: The First Five Years.**
Lawrence S. Kaplan. *International Organization*, vol. 8, no. 4
(November 1954), p. 447-467.
An analysis of the kind of literature which was written about NATO in its first five
years. The author looks at writings on political-military affairs, the possible
development of an Atlantic Community and the United States position of leadership.

70 **NATO and American Security.**
Edited by Klaus Knorr. Princeton, New Jersey: Princeton University
Press, 1959. 342p.
A very good snapshot of the strategic and political problems facing NATO in the late
1950s. With the Soviet development of intercontinental ballistic missiles (ICBMs) the
Alliance underwent a major crisis of confidence as many commentators argued that
NATO was relying on an American security guarantee which it would be suicidal for
the United States to implement. This volume contains some interesting analyses of this
crisis and combines some very informative discussions of the evolution of the Alliance,
with calls for NATO to develop a greater capacity for conventional resistance to
conventional attack. A very distinguished contributor list includes Roger Hilsman,
George Rathjens, Denis Healey, Morton Kaplan and Gordon Craig. This not only
provides a very good sense of the some of the debates and arguments of the late 1950s
but is also one of the books which contributed to United States efforts to revise NATO
strategy and move towards greater reliance on conventional defence rather than
nuclear retaliation. This book was reprinted by Greenwood Press in 1984.

71 **NATO and the Defense of the West.**
Prince Hubertus zu Lowenstein, Volkmar von Zuhlsdorff. Westport,
Connecticut: Greenwood Press, 1957 (original reprinted in 1975). 383p.
Looks at the history, organization, and structure of NATO not only in the central
region but also on the flanks. Somewhat ideological in tone and rather conventional,
but it also contains lots of detail about NATO and its evolution in the 1950s.

72 **The German Rearmament Question: American Diplomacy and European
Defense after World War Two.**
Robert McGeehan. Urbana, Illinois: University of Illinois Press, 1971.
280p.
A detailed and valuable account of the negotiations among the Western allies from the
initial decision to rearm Germany to the abandonment of the European Defense
Community (EDC) and the entry of Germany into NATO through the Western
European Union. McGeehan notes that the German rearmament question, by leading
to the EDC project, had very important political results which offset the frustrations
resulting from the delay in West Germany's remilitarization. Although the EDC failed,
the episode provided time for the other European nations to reconcile themselves to
the idea that Germany rearm and become a member of NATO.

73 **The Politics of Western Defense.**
Fred W. Mulley. New York: Praeger, 1962. 282p.
Written by a Labour Member of Parliament who was subsequently to become Britain's
Minister of Defence, this study emphasizes the need to augment NATO's conventional

strength and to enhance military integration. It also explores the problems of joint political control over strategic and tactical nuclear weapons and presses the idea of a European nuclear strike capability within the framework of the Western European Union – a proposal which would have required Britain to give up its efforts to maintain a special relationship with the United States. On this particular issue Mulley was clearly well ahead of his time. In other respects, the book is more orthodox. Nevertheless, it provides a good overview of the kind of political and military problems which confronted NATO in the late 1950s and early 1960s.

74   **Curtis LeMay and the Origins of NATO Atomic Targeting.**
Peter J. Roman.   *Journal of Strategic Studies*, vol. 16, no. 1 (March 1993), p. 46-74.
A detailed and very useful historical analysis which looks at the atomic support for NATO provided by the United States Strategic Air Command (SAC). The author argues that in certain respects the commitment to Europe threatened to undermine LeMay's vision for SAC and his control of targeting operations. The author details the negotiations which occurred about the division of responsibility between Supreme Allied Commander Europe (SACEUR) and Strategic Air Command (SAC) and outlines the agreement that was finally reached. A thorough analysis based on detailed documentary research.

75   **Atlantic Alliance: NATO's Role in the Free World.**
Royal Institute of International Affairs, Chatham House Study Group. Westport, Connecticut: Greenwood Press, 1979 (reprint of 1952 edition). 172p.
Setting NATO clearly within the old British concern over the balance of power in Europe, this is a very informative analysis of NATO's early years. It looks at Soviet objectives and emphasizes Moscow's desire to secure the withdrawal of American forces and bases from Europe. The study group highlights several tensions which were to be endemic problems for NATO. These included the difficulty of combining unity of effort and national independence, the tension between the notions of European integration and Atlantic Community, and the problem of reconciling the desire to harness German power with the fear of German predominance. For an early assessment of the problems and prospects of NATO this is a must.

76   **The Rearming of Germany 1950-1954: A Linchpin in the Political Evolution of Europe.**
B. Mitchell Simpson III.   In: *War Strategy and Maritime Power*, edited by B. Mitchell Simpson III.   New Brunswick, New Jersey: Rutgers University Press, 1977, p. 199-220.
Although based primarily on secondary sources, this is a useful overview of the process whereby Germany was allowed to rearm and enter NATO. It looks at the impulses behind the American decision to press for German rearmament and at the European responses. This is not a major scholarly contribution to the understanding of this process, but it does offer some interesting observations and provides a short and helpful overview for those who just want to understand the main themes rather than come to grips with all the subtleties and nuances of the period.

77   **Toward Atlantic Security.**
     Charles M. Spofford.   *International Affairs*, vol. 27, no. 4
     (October 1951), p. 434-439.

Starting from the premise that the major purpose of NATO is to prevent war, this analysis identifies three stages in the development of collective strength: agreement on principle, planning military forces, and the actual creation of the organization. It also outlines NATO's structure, the consensus model by which it operates, and the role of the permanent international staff. In addition, attention is given to outstanding issues such as the period of conscription of member-nation forces, the level of defence budgets, the creation of integrated forces and the need to keep allied public opinion supportive of the Alliance and its efforts. An interesting snapshot of the prevailing concerns of the period written by a key NATO official.

NATO in the 1960s

78   **The Shape of NATO.**
     Current History, vol. 39, no. 229 (September 1960), 129p.

This publication contains a series of six articles offering an assessment of the state of NATO at the beginning of the 1960s. Contributors include Richard Van Alstyne, Alvin Cottrell and Hans Kohn. There is a useful piece by Allan Nanes on NATO's strategic dilemmas.

79   **Special Issue on the Atlantic Community**.
     International Organization, vol. 17, no. 3 (Summer 1963), p. 521-812.

A useful collection of articles which provides a comprehensive assessment of the Atlantic relationship. Contributors include Stanley Hoffmann, Arnold Wolfers and Lauris Norstad.

80   **Special Issue on NATO and European Security.**
     Orbis, vol. 13, no. 1 (Spring 1969), 372p.

A special issue containing twenty-seven essays on various facets of NATO. The authors include well-known analysts of NATO such as Alastair Buchan, Robert Pfaltzgraff, Pierre Hassner, Eugene Hinterhoff, Morton Kaplan and Timothy Stanley. Among the topics covered are national perspectives on the Alliance, the impact of the Soviet invasion of Czechoslovakia, and NATO's strategy and doctrine. Perhaps the most significant paper was by Denis Healey, the British Minister of Defence, who argued a strong case for maintaining nuclear weapons at the heart of NATO strategy. Healey, of course, subsequently became a supporter of 'no first use'. In his article here, however, he presented a very strong case for continued reliance on nuclear weapons as a way of presenting the Soviet Union with risks it was psychologically unwilling to run rather than attempting the more difficult task of confronting it with force it was physically unable to overcome. Apart from this and a few other particularly good articles, the special issue is useful primarily as a snapshot of the problems on the NATO agenda in the late 1960s.

81 **German Policy toward the East.**
Willy Brandt. *Foreign Affairs*, vol. 46, no. 3 (April 1968), p. 476-486.
This article, written by the then Foreign Minister of the Federal Republic of Germany, examines Bonn's policy towards the East and acknowledges that in spite of the lessening of East–West tensions, the process of reunification would be long and arduous. The main significance of the article lies in the fact that its author was the major architect of the Ostpolitik and it offers a glimpse of his thinking and expectations about détente.

82 **NATO in the 1960s: The Implications of Interdependence.**
Alastair Buchan. New York: Praeger, 1963. rev. ed. 131p.
A study which starts from the assumption that no NATO member is capable of ensuring its own security through a purely national strategy, examines the impact of strategic interdependence between the United States and Western Europe, and concludes that the Alliance members cannot compartmentalize their policies. Buchan examines the threat posed by the Soviet Union as well as issues and problems arising outside Europe. One of his major conclusions is that NATO needs to strengthen its international staff since only a system of joint planning will lead to more concerted policies by the members of the Alliance.

83 **The Reform of NATO.**
Alastair Buchan. *Foreign Affairs*, vol. 40, no. 2 (January 1962), p. 165-182.
Buchan looks at the internal and external pressures on NATO – especially the changes in power between the United States and Western Europe – which suggest that the Alliance needs to be reformed. He focuses on the machinery of political consultation and control in the Alliance, the strategic balance and nuclear control, and concludes that the Alliance needs a stronger centre.

84 **NATO in Quest of Cohesion.**
Edited by Karl H. Cerny, Henry W. Briefs. New York: Praeger, 1965. 476p.
The result of a conference held at Georgetown University in 1964, this edited volume brings together both American and European commentators to discuss the crisis in the Alliance in the early and mid-1960s and what had to be done to restore cohesion. Contributors include Hans Morgenthau, Klaus Knorr, André Beaufre, Robert Kleiman, and other well-known specialists on NATO and international security. Attention is given to the economic, strategic, and political problems confronting the Alliance. Particularly interesting is the record of the discussion which took place at the conference and which included Henry Kissinger and Sir John Slessor. This is combined with a high-quality set of substantive chapters, a preface by General Lauris Norstad, and a chapter by Under Secretary of State George Ball on United States policy towards NATO, all of which make this one of the more enduring and helpful analyses of NATO during the 1960s.

85 **NATO after the Invasion.**
Harlan Cleveland. *Foreign Affairs*, vol. 47, no. 2 (January 1969),
p. 251-265.
Cleveland looks at the Soviet invasion of Czechoslovakia, the NATO reaction – which
was to watch but lie low – and the subsequent changes in NATO force planning. He
also highlights the dilemmas of what to do about détente in response to the Soviet
invasion.

86 **The "Atlantic Community" Reappraised.**
Edited by Robert H. Connery. *Proceedings of the Academy of Political
Science*, vol. 29, no. 2 (1968). 156p.
An interesting snapshot of NATO in the late 1960s in which a series of distinguished
contributors – including William and Annette Baker Fox, Andrew Pierre, Wilfrid
Kohl, Catherine Kelleher – explore various national perspectives on the Atlantic
Alliance. Economic and trade issues are also dealt with.

87 **NATO without France: The Military Implications.**
Kenneth Hunt.   London: International Centre for Strategic Studies,
December 1966. 26p. (Adelphi Paper, No. 32).
Looks at the French decision to leave NATO's integrated military organization and
assesses the implications for NATO. The author examines the impact on the Alliance
of the loss of French land and air space, the removal of NATO's military headquarters
and the loss of bilateral facilities on French territory. This paper is systematic,
thorough and helpful.

88 **The Troubled Partnership: A Re-appraisal of the Atlantic Alliance.**
Henry A. Kissinger.   New York: McGraw-Hill, 1965. 266p.
An excellent analysis of the problems within NATO resulting from the resurgence of
Western Europe and its resentment at continued American domination of the
Alliance, and especially the formulation of NATO strategy in Washington. Although
Kissinger saw NATO's highly contentious strategic debate over nuclear weapons as
debilitating for the Alliance, he also displayed great empathy for the Europeans and
called for a more understanding approach by the United States. The analysis of
French, German, and American preferences and policies in relation to NATO strategy
is particularly incisive. Kissinger's conclusion emphasized the need to move towards a
more genuine Alliance in which Western Europe provided the second pillar. Overall
this provided an illuminating study of the problems in Atlantic relations in the mid-
1960s, although Kissinger's critics would argue that he failed to show a similar level of
understanding of the allies in his subsequent roles as National Security Adviser and
Secretary of State during the Nixon Administration.

89 **NATO: The Entangling Alliance.**
Robert R. Osgood.   Chicago, Illinois: Chicago University Press, 1962.
416p.
Written in the early 1960s, this important book deals with the origins of the Alliance,
the evolution of its strategy and force posture and the different preferences of the
Europeans and the United States. While recognizing the tensions between strategic
logic and the political need for consensus in the Alliance, Osgood's main argument is

that changes in the nuclear balance which make passive deterrence more stable make extended deterrence (the US nuclear guarantee to Europe) less credible. The implication was that Soviet conventional aggression was much more likely in an era of nuclear stalemate than in the period of American predominance. The solution to what was subsequently termed 'the stability–instability paradox' was for NATO to strengthen its conventional forces to be able to deter or contain conventional aggression by the Soviet Union. Osgood's views on this are very similar to those of the Kennedy Administration. Nevertheless, this is a book which goes beyond advocacy and offers some of the most incisive commentary and analysis of the Atlantic Alliance during the first decade or so of its life. For all of those who are interested in the history of NATO, this book is a must.

90 **Implications of the Western Response to the Soviet Intervention in Czechoslovakia**
Andrew J. Pierre. *Atlantic Community Quarterly*, vol. 7, no. 1 (Spring 1969), p. 59-75.

The author examines the impact of the Soviet invasion of Czechoslovakia on Western perceptions of détente and, more significantly, on the strategic assumptions of NATO in relation to force structure and operational planning. He shows how the invasion challenged Gaullist hopes for Europe, set back Bonn's Ostpolitik and placed Soviet forces in a more favourable position for launching offensive operations. He also identifies the long-range implications for Western policy.

91 **NATO in Transition: The Future of the Atlantic Alliance.**
Timothy J. Stanley. New York: Praeger, 1965. 417p.

Stanley's study provides a good snapshot of NATO in the mid-1960s. Starting with an examination of the communist challenge, it offers some interesting comments on the whole issue of European unity on the one hand and Atlantic partnership on the other. In addition, it deals with a variety of issues connected to the alliance's nuclear and conventional strategy. There is a particularly useful chapter which deals with the crisis of confidence over extended deterrence and looks at both British and French nuclear policies. Other chapters deal with the nuclear–conventional links, national political environments and the political economics of defence. Although a good overview, the book suffers from the fact that it was written while the debate over NATO strategy was still in flux and before the final agreement on flexible response. Nevertheless, it remains useful as a perspective on NATO in the mid-1960s.

92 **The Atlantic Community: Progress and Prospects.**
Edited by Francis O. Wilcox, H. Field Haviland. New York: Praeger, 1963. p. 294.

This collection of essays by some of the leading experts on Atlantic relations provides a useful snapshot of some of the main issues on NATO's political agenda in the early 1960s. There is a particularly illuminating essay by Stanley Hoffmann entitled 'Discord in Community' which treats the North Atlantic areas as a partial political system and examines patterns of cooperation and competition in this system. Other contributors include Alfred Grosser who deals with France and Germany, Robert Bowie who examines strategy and the Alliance, and Arnold Wolfers whose chapter, 'Integration in the West: the Conflict of Perspectives', highlights the tensions between the idea of the Atlantic Community and the growing importance of the European Community.

Although dated, some of the ideas and analyses in this volume have an enduring relevance.

NATO in the 1970s

93 **Special Issue on "Year of Europe".**
Orbis, vol. 17, no. 1 (Spring 1973), 292p.
A good collection of articles dealing with the problems and prospects of Atlantic relations in the early 1970s. There are good pieces by Simon Serfaty, Paul Davis and Joseph Coffey. Perhaps most valuable of all, however, is John Yochelson's excellent article on 'MBFR: The Search for an American Approach' which looks at the background of American domestic politics and the pressure for US troop cuts in Europe emanating from the Senate.

94 **Western Europe in Kissinger's Global Strategy.**
Agryris G. Andrianopoulos. London: Macmillan, 1986. 262p.
This study examines Atlantic relations in the early 1970s largely through the perspective of Henry Kissinger, President Nixon's National Security Adviser, who had written extensively on the United States and Western Europe prior to his appointment. The author argues that Kissinger's policy towards Europe can be understood in terms of the ideas and concepts he outlined in his academic writings. He also explores the Nixon Doctrine and the idea of partnership with the Europeans, the linkages between economic and security issues, the controversy over US troops in Europe, and Kissinger's concerns over Ostpolitik and the possibility of a fragmented or differentiated détente between individual NATO members and the Soviet Union. This is a useful historical study.

95 **NATO: A Balance Sheet after Thirty Years.**
S. I. P. Campen. *Orbis*, vol. 23, no. 2 (Summer 1979), p. 261-270.
Campen places considerable emphasis on the need for political solidarity in NATO and contends that there is insufficient attention given to political considerations. The argument that the political role of the alliance is a necessary counterpart to continued defence efforts is persuasive.

96 **New Imperatives for the Old Alliance.**
Robert Ellsworth. *International Security*, vol. 2, no. 4 (Spring 1978), p. 132-148.
Ellsworth sees changes in the world and especially the growth of Soviet military power – both in terms of strategic nuclear forces and the capacity for global power projection – as imposing new imperatives for NATO. Although the Alliance has responded and has planned enhancements to its Command, Control Communications and Intelligence through deployment of airborne warning and control systems (AWACS), modernized its air and naval forces, and increased the flexibility of its nuclear doctrine, the author argues that NATO must go beyond its passive, defensive strategy and be more actively

engaged in formulating the rules of the new international order. He expresses particular concern over access to energy resources.

97 **Defense Politics of the Atlantic Alliance.**
Edited by Edwin H. Fedder.   New York: Praeger, 1980. 187p.
An interesting collection of essays which begins with two general analyses of NATO and US–European relations, one by the editor and the other by Anton DePorte, and follows these with chapters on French, British and German defence policies. There are also chapters on the coordination of détente policy, the state of Atlantic relations, the politics of European defence cooperation, and the economic costs and rewards of US military expenditures. The final chapter looks at the issue of guns and butter and traces patterns in public expenditure in the United States and Western Europe from 1920 to 1975. The whole is a valuable anthology.

98 **The Content of European Detente.**
Gregory Flynn.   *Orbis*, vol. 20, no. 2 (Summer 1976), p. 401-416.
Examines the *modus vivendi* between East and West which developed in the first half of the 1970s and which helped to legitimize the status quo in Europe. At the same time the author acknowledges that the two sides continued to have divergent conceptions of a legitimate European order and the appropriate basis for security in Europe and shows how these divergences were manifested in both the Conference on Security and Cooperation in Europe (CSCE) and the MBFR negotiations. Flynn provides good insights into NATO's approach to détente.

99 **European Security, Nuclear Weapons and Public Confidence.**
Edited by William Gutteridge.   London: Macmillan, 1982. 236p.
This volume stems from a series of meetings held in the late 1970s. The first meeting under the auspices of the Finnish Pugwash Group in 1977, was followed by one organized by the Polish Pugwash Group in 1978 and a third organized by the Finnish group in 1979. Consequently, it brings together contributors from both East and West. The author list includes Poles, Finns, Canadians, Soviets, East and West Germans, Americans, Bulgarians and three British analysts. The title of the book is rather deceptive. Although there is a large section on the military aspects of European security, another section deals with the Baltic and the Arctic while there are also discussions of economic and technical cooperation in Europe. The book does not break much new ground but does have an interesting collection of participants with varying ideological and political perspectives.

100 **Detente: The Other Side.**
Pierre Hassner.   *Survey*, vol. 19, no. 2 (Spring 1973), p. 76-100.
A brilliant and, in many ways, very prescient article which argues that during the Cold War both sides accepted the status quo even though this was hidden by verbal offensives. Détente, in contrast, the author argues, involves a hot peace as each side tries to undermine the other's system through more subtle means. The notion of détente as involving diplomatic rather than military offensives was very insightful.

101 **NATO and Western Security in an Era of Transition.**
Martin J. Hillenbrand. *International Security*, vol. 2, no. 2
(Fall 1977), p. 3-24.

A long-time observer of NATO, Hillenbrand notes that the alliance perpetually appears to be in alternating states of crisis and euphoria. He suggests, however, that the problems facing NATO in the late 1970s are somewhat different from those of the past. After providing a concise historical overview, Hillenbrand argues that the alliance has served its purpose well and continues to be necessary. While détente between the superpowers represents a major change, Hillenbrand argues that there is not really an option for a more independent or self-reliant Western Europe. He also emphasizes the problems of Euro-communism and the economic dimensions of security. Hillenbrand believes that with American leadership and the cooperation of the Europeans, NATO can continue to be the best vehicle for guaranteeing European security in an imperfect world.

102 **New Variations on Old Themes.**
Stanley Hoffmann. *International Security*, vol. 4, no. 1
(Summer 1979), p. 88-107.

Hoffmann argues that the crises facing NATO in the late 1970s are essentially new variations on old themes. The article traces patterns of continuity and change in the Alliance. Among the familiar problems are those stemming from a geopolitical unevenness which gives rise to divergent security concerns on the two sides of the Atlantic; those resulting from an unevenness of political structure and organization which reflects power inequalities among the members; and the sensitivity of NATO to its environment, including the economic context, the 'grey areas', and internal political developments. In terms of the changes, Hoffmann emphasizes the evolving strategic balance between the United States and the Soviet Union, the impact of arms control, especially the Strategic Arms Limitation Treaty (SALT) process, economic developments such as United States unilateralism and the embryonic European monetary system, and the concerns over energy supplies. The final section of the paper explores the issues on NATO's agenda in the late 1970s.

103 **NATO and the Year of Europe.**
Michael Howard. *Survival*, vol. 16, no. 1 (January/February 1974),
p. 21-27. (Reprinted from *Round Table* [October 1973]).

The author looks at the strategic and political reasons for the tensions in Atlantic relations during 1973, the so-called 'Year of Europe'. He argues that the dangers of Finlandization of Western Europe are greatly exaggerated but that they could be rendered wholly unnecessary if Europe relied to a greater extent on its own resources for defence and security.

104 **Europe and the United States: The Future of the Relationship.**
Karl Kaiser. Washington, DC: Columbia Books, 1973. 146p.

Kaiser looks at the issues troubling Atlantic relations in the mid-1970s against a background of major changes in the international system. He explains the European perspectives on these issues and highlights several ways in which Atlantic relations might be restructured across a wide range of issues.

105 **Europe and America: A Critical Phase.**

Karl Kaiser. *Foreign Affairs*, vol. 52, no. 4 (July 1974), p. 725-741.

The author argues that the crisis of the early 1970s in both Atlantic relations and European integration involves more fundamental issues than previous crises in NATO. He identifies three options for the Atlantic relationship – a rejuvenation of partnership, Atlantic partnership without France, and cooperative bilateralism.

106 **America and Western Europe: Problems and Prospects.**

Edited by Karl Kaiser, Hans-Peter Schwarz. Lexington, Massachusetts: Lexington Books, 1978. 447p.

A comprehensive assessment of US–European relations which looks at the impact of public perceptions on both sides of the Atlantic, the prevailing trends in the Atlantic economic system, the evolution of East–West relations in Europe, and at the key issues in security. Not only does it offer some good insights into German perspectives on the evolving relationship, but it also encapsulates many of the strains and tensions in NATO and the wider Atlantic relationship during the mid- and late 1970s.

107 **NATO after Thirty Years.**

Edited by Lawrence S. Kaplan, Robert W. Clawson. Wilmington, Delaware: Scholarly Resources, 1981. 262p.

A good snapshot of NATO at the end of the 1970s, this book is based on a conference sponsored by the Center for NATO Studies at Kent State University which brought together both historians and political scientists to place NATO in historical perspective and explain key relationships within the Alliance. The first three chapters are on NATO in history. These are followed by four chapters on NATO in the world, which deal respectively with: perceptions from the East; NATO and the United Nations; the United States, NATO and the Colonial World; and NATO and the European Community. The final section on NATO in Arms looks at military aspects of NATO and includes chapters on standardization and on arms control. Overall, this is a useful collection, in which the opening chapter by Lawrence Kaplan stands out as a succinct and informative analysis of patterns of continuity and change in NATO.

108 **Western Europe: The Trials of Partnership: Critical Choices for Americans, Vol. 8.**

Edited by David S. Landes. Lexington, Massachusetts: D.C. Heath, 1977. 406p.

This is a very good collection which contributed significantly to the understanding of the tensions in Atlantic relations in the mid-1970s. The editor's introduction is followed by two excellent analyses, one by Raymond Aron, and one by Stanley Hoffmann which discusses Western Europe and the United States as 'uneven allies'. This is followed by chapters on Britain, France, Germany, Italy, Spain and Portugal, and the United States. There are also chapters on trade and industry.

109 **NATO: The Next Thirty Years: The Changing Political, Economic, and Military Setting.**
Edited by Kenneth A. Myers.   Boulder, Colorado: Westview Press, 1980. 469p.

This book, which grew out of a Conference on the future of the Atlantic Alliance held in Brussels in September 1979, contains papers dealing with the Alliance by a variety of commentators including Henry Kissinger, Josef Luns, Uwe Nerlich, Samuel Huntington, Amos Jordan, Michael Howard, Irving Kristol and Alexander Haig. It is divided into four parts: the future of NATO; strategic and military problems; political and economic problems; and organization and leadership. The book provides a valuable encapsulation of the kinds of concerns that were predominant at the end of the 1970s in both the United States and Western Europe. Many of the chapters were also published as articles in the *Washington Quarterly* in 1979 and 1980.

110 **Fading Partnership: America and Europe after 30 Years.**
Simon Serfaty.   New York: Praeger, 1979. 115p.

The author focuses on patterns of discord and collaboration in the Atlantic Alliance in the 1970s and examines them with a wry cynicism. He provides a persuasive critique of the Nixon–Kissinger policies towards Western Europe, an assessment of nuclear fantasies in the Alliance – which includes an analysis of the prospects for a European nuclear deterrent – an examination of Atlantic economic disputes and a discussion of domestic politics with particular focus on French and Italian communist parties. This is a useful study.

111 **The Atlantic Connection: Prospects, Problems and Policies.**
Philip H. Tresize.   Washington, DC: Brookings Institution, 1975. 100p.

Written by a former US Ambassador to the Organization for Economic Cooperation and Development, this volume assesses the state of the Atlantic relationship in the mid-1970s. The author looks at trends in the Soviet Union, the moves towards integration in Western Europe, the common defence effort and burden-sharing, East–West negotiations, and trade and economic issues. His conclusion is that the Atlantic relationship is resilient but that its management is better achieved through pragmatic policies than grand designs.

112 **NATO and Security in the Seventies.**
Edited by Frans A. M. von Geisau.   Leyden, The Netherlands: Sijthoff, 1971. 158p.

An interesting collection of essays which offers a long-range perspective on NATO by Louis Halle, an analysis of NATO's ability to deal with emerging crisis situations, NATO and the Mediterranean, and developments in Eastern Europe. There is a particularly interesting chapter by Nils Orvik outlining what he terms a sub-regional approach to European security. The final chapter – by the editor – looks at the evolution of the alliance and argues, in what was to be an increasingly common theme in the 1980s, that security could be enhanced through greater bilateral contacts and inter-bloc cooperation.

113 **The Year of Europe?**
Z (Pseud.). *Foreign Affairs*, vol. 52, no. 4 (January 1974), p. 237-248.
Looks at the deterioration in relations between Western Europe and the United States in 1973 and suggests that both sides need more goodwill. The author also proposes a yearly summit between European and US leaders.

NATO in the 1980s

114 **Preventing World War III: A Realistic Grand Strategy.**
David M. Abshire. New York: Harper & Row, 1988. 322p.
The author, a former United States ambassador to NATO (1983-87), is the founder and president of Washington's Center for Strategic and International Studies. The title implies a far more dated Cold War work than is actually the case. Writing after the advent of the Gorbachev era, Abshire correctly predicted that the 1990s would be a period of great fluidity. He contends that the danger of world war lies in small conflicts and brushfire incidents which are more likely to get out of hand during a period of instability. He cautions against the dismantling of the NATO alliance and instead argues for a restructuring of alliance commitments and contributions. He favours greater partnership between Europe and America and far less US unilateralism. As for domestic politics in the US, he warns against the intrusiveness of Congress in foreign and security policies and argues for the maintenance of a strong defensive posture.

115 **Europe in NATO: Deterrence, Defense and Arms Control.**
Carol Edler Baumann. New York: Praeger, 1987. 372p.
Based on a conference held under the auspices of the Committee on Atlantic Studies in May 1985, this volume covers several major themes: the challenges facing Western Europe; arms and strategies; arms control; public opinion and the defence consensus; and the prospects for an integrated European defence identity. Its sixteen chapters include contributions from Helga Haftendorn, Wolfram Hanreider, David Garnham, and Werner J. Feld. It provides a useful inventory of the central themes in Atlantic relations in the mid-1980s.

116 **NATO's Mid-life Crisis.**
Richard K. Betts. *Foreign Affairs*, vol. 68, no. 2 (Spring 1988), p. 37-52.
Betts looks at the state of NATO after the INF Treaty and argues that the Alliance is confronting forces and trends that could alter its basic terms of reference. Political initiatives from Moscow raise unprecedented possibilities for negotiated change in the East–West military confrontation. At the same time NATO has to keep itself in shape militarily. After looking at concerns over denuclearization and the political cross-currents in NATO, Betts proposes a three-track strategy: asymmetrically reciprocate in response to Gorbachev's initiatives on arms reductions, continue formal arms control negotiations with the Soviets, and begin reassessing NATO's objectives while avoiding unilateral force reductions. Written prior to the major changes in Europe, this is a very prescient analysis.

117   **The State of the Alliance 1986-1987: North Atlantic Assembly.**
John Cartwright (et al.).   Boulder, Colorado: Westview Press, 1987.
376p.

This volume contains six reports presented to the North Atlantic Assembly by members of parliament from various NATO countries. There are reports on NATO's public legitimacy problem and how it can be dealt with, the economics of alliance security, the military balance, the problems of maintaining consensus, the issue of strategic defence, and nuclear technology and arms control. For those interested in these issues and how they were seen in the mid-1980s this is a good place to start.

118   **The Long-Term Crisis of the Alliance.**
Eliot A. Cohen.   *Foreign Affairs*, vol. 61, no. 2 (Winter 1982-83),
p. 325-343.

Cohen argues that the tensions in the alliance in the early 1980s reflect problems which go much deeper than mutual antipathy between the Europeans and the Reagan Administration. In essence, the problem stems from a mixture of structural factors and long-term trends. He suggests that these problems can be dealt with through a redefinition of NATO in which the United States concentrates on global responsibilities and Europe on regional responsibilities.

119   **The Future of the Atlantic Alliance.**
Christopher Coker.   London: Macmillan for RUSI, 1984. 241p.

An interesting volume in which the author examines NATO defences, the nuclear issue, the failure of European defence cooperation, burden-sharing and out-of-area operations. The second part, entitled 'perceptions of the Atlantic Alliance' is a series of chapters by prominent individuals including General Bernard Rogers, Don Cotter, John Lehman, and Hedley Bull. Topics covered include the flanks, the UK role in NATO and a new strategy for forward defence.

120   **After INF: The Political–Military Landscape of Europe.**
Hugh De Santis.   *Washington Quarterly*, vol. 11, no. 3
(Summer 1988), p. 29-44.

The author argues that the main significance of the INF Agreement is its impact on a range of issues affecting European security and identifies what the author sees as the main problems of alliance management for the United States resulting from the effects of the Treaty. De Santis concludes that it is crucial for the United States to reassure Europe that it will not be abandoned militarily.

121   **NATO in the Fifth Decade.**
Edited by Keith Dunn, Stephen Flanagan.   Washington, DC: National
Defense University Press, 1990. 242p.

Although published in 1990, this book was based on a conference held in Brussels in September 1988. As such, it is inevitably somewhat dated. Nevertheless, within the limits of this, it is a useful collection with papers by Michael Howard, Christopher Donnelly, Helga Haftendorn, John Cross, and Yves Boyer. There are sections on the Soviet factor, European defence cooperation, nuclear options, the conventional arms balance, and other challenges. In a final chapter by the editors, the question of whether NATO's fifth decade will see renewal or mid-life crisis is explored. Overall, this is useful mainly as an analysis of how people were thinking before the revolutions of 1989-91.

122 Securing Europe's Future.
Stephen J. Flanagan, Fen Osler Hampson. London: Croom Helm, 1986. 334p.

This analytical and prescriptive study offers insights into alliance problems and recommendations for dealing with them. Both endemic and new divergences are identified and the authors show how these reflected different national security priorities between the United States and its European allies. The prescriptions include the continued deployment of theatre nuclear weapons; the pursuit of the Strategic Defense Initiative (SDI) in a manner more sensitive to European concerns in exchange for greater European support for research; greater European defence cooperation through the Western European Union and the European Community; and the continued pursuit of détente and meaningful arms reductions.

123 NATO Today: The Alliance in Evolution.
Foreign Relations Committee Staff, US Senate. Washington, DC: GPO, April 1982. 102p. (A Report to the Committee on Foreign Relations, United States Senate).

Written by the Staff of the Foreign Relations Committee in a period of considerable strain and acrimony in Alliance relations, this study reviews the problems facing NATO in the early 1980s. It is careful to emphasize the continued resilience and sense of common purpose in NATO but also acknowledges that the current situation is unique because the Alliance faces multiple strains with a cumulative impact. The report provides a good account of the contentious issues in Atlantic relations ranging from the Siberian gas pipeline through military cooperation and burden-sharing in South West Asia, and economic tensions among trading partners, to the anti-nuclear movement in Europe and the possibility of American troop withdrawals. The conclusion is that NATO is not in crisis but that the issues on its agenda require extremely careful management.

124 Military Power in Europe: Essays in Memory of Jonathan Alford.
Edited by Lawrence Freedman. London: Macmillan, in association with the International Institute for Strategic Studies, 1990. 241p.

This collection of essays, dedicated to the memory of Jonathan Alford, Deputy Director of the International Institute for Strategic Studies, looks at military aspects of European security within the broader political context. The contributors, all friends of Jonathan Alford, include the editor himself, Hugh Beach, James Eberle, Edwina Moreton, Robbin Laird, François Heisbourg, James Thomson, Catherine Kelleher and Donald Daniel. In addition, the volume contains two chapters by Jonathan Alford himself, including one on confidence-building measures, something on which he specialized. Although the chapters were all completed before the 1989 revolutions in Eastern Europe, some of the issues they address, such as national planning in an alliance context and NATO's higher command continue to be of relevance. The volume is particularly valuable on issues at the interface of political and military considerations.

125 **The Atlantic Crisis.**
Lawrence Freedman. *International Affairs*, vol. 58, no. 3
(Summer 1982), p. 395-412.
A succinct and comprehensive review of the problems and tensions in Atlantic relations in the early 1980s, this article discusses disputes over monetary policy, Middle East diplomacy, and relations with the Soviet Union. It considers whether these disputes were more serious than previous ones. Among the specific issues discussed are the decline of Atlanticism, linkages between economic and political–strategic issues, the arguments over burden-sharing, the change in European opinion on conventional versus nuclear forces, divergences in the global perspectives of the United States and Europe, and the use of economic sanctions versus military force in relation to Third World contingencies. The article concludes that NATO needs to move beyond its preoccupation with the Soviet military threat to Central Europe and give greater attention to other challenges.

126 **Fighting Allies: Tensions within the Atlantic Alliance.**
Edited by Walter Goldstein. Washington, DC: Brassey's Defence Publishers, 1986. 235p.
The main question considered in this volume is whether NATO will survive the tensions amongst its members or will collapse in disarray. An opening chapter by the editor sets up the theme very effectively and highlights patterns of convergence and divergence amongst the allies. Key issues such as burden-sharing, nuclear and conventional forces and arms control are discussed in the first section, while the second part of the book consists of country-member studies. The third part looks at trends and prospects and has a chapter on secular change in the alliance by Robert Lieber, one on American public opinion by Werner Feld, and one on the European peace movement by Christopher Coker. The final chapter by Walter Goldstein concludes that the allies will continue to fight but will do so within the alliance framework. A good overview of the issues in Atlantic relations in the mid-1980s.

127 **The Crisis in Western Security.**
Edited by Lawrence S. Hagen. London: Croom Helm, 1982. 247p.
Put together in a period when the dissolution of détente had aroused immense strains in European–American relations, this book has a distinguished cast of contributors. They include Philip Windsor, Lawrence Freedman, Richard Burt, Colin Gray, Pierre Hassner, and Helmut Sonnenfeldt. These authors provide a variety of perspectives on strategy, arms control and the alliance. Yet, although the individual contributions provide considerable insight into the Atlantic crisis of the early 1980s, the book is less than the sum of its parts. There is no coherent sense of direction to the volume because each contributor goes his own way. If the book has little enduring significance, however, it may still be of interest to those investigating the crisis of the early 1980s.

128 **The Western Alliance: Drift or Harmony?**
Stanley Hoffmann. *International Security*, vol. 6, no. 2 (Fall 1981), p. 105-127.
Hoffmann identifies three trends contributing to a sense of crisis in the Atlantic Alliance: collapse of US–Soviet détente, an increasingly unfavourable military balance in Europe, and a heightened belief that the world has become a unified strategic arena. The implications are compounded by disagreements among the allies over Soviet

capabilities and intentions. Such differences are rooted in geography, history, domestic politics, and national character. The author argues that a new rapprochement among the allies is needed to coordinate policy and that new institutions or mechanisms may well be necessary, especially to deal with out-of-area problems. He concludes that intra-Alliance fragmentation is a bigger problem for the Alliance than the Soviet threat and proposes political compromise, strategic integration, and institutional innovations, all of which he argues are needed to preserve the Atlantic Alliance. He concludes by noting that this will require both a turn from American unilateralism and a new European willingness not merely to claim but to play a world role – starting with defence at home.

129 **NATO: The Next Generation.**
Edited by Robert Hunter. Boulder, Colorado: Westview Press, 1984. 272p.

Based on a conference held in January 1984 in Brussels under the auspices of the Center for Strategic and International Studies, this volume assesses the strains in the Alliance in the early and mid-1980s. It contains the text of speeches given at the conference by such figures as Henry Kissinger, Helmut Schmidt, and James Schlesinger as well as papers by analysts such as William Hyland, Robert Komer, James Thomson and Lawrence Freedman. A variety of topics are covered, including Alliance leadership, arms control, out-of-area issues, and the economic dimension. Particularly notable is a very frank exchange of views between Schmidt and Schlesinger, an exchange which gave the proceedings a certain notoriety.

130 **NATO after Forty Years.**
Edited by Lawrence S. Kaplan, Victor S. Papacosma, Mark R. Rubin, Ruth V. Young. Wilmington, Delaware: Scholarly Resources, 1990. 293p.

A very useful survey of the state of NATO on its fortieth anniversary. Growing out of a conference held at the Lemnitzer Center at Kent State University, this volume is divided into four parts. The first section deals with nations and the alliance and has chapters on the United States, the Anglo-American special relationship, Germany, France, the small powers and the Mediterranean states. The second and much shorter section has a chapter on the search for a European pillar and one on the United States, NATO and the Third World. The third section deals with security issues and includes an essay on 'NATO and Detente: Cycles in History' by Anton DePorte. The final section has three essays on NATO, including one by Ronald Steel dealing with what he sees as the European problem and one by Thomas Etzold on NATO's 'unexpected midlife crisis'. A good collection of papers which offer some important insights on the state of NATO just prior to the massive upheavals in Europe.

131 **Can NATO Survive?**
Stanley Kober. *International Affairs*, vol. 59, no. 3 (Summer 1983), p. 339-350.

A rather hawkish American article which is critical of the shift in European attitudes towards the US nuclear presence in Europe. Although it argues that the Reagan Administration should be more flexible on arms control, the European allies are criticized for questioning US motives. Moreover, the author argues that Western Europe is not indispensable to US security, and that if the Europeans want missiles without paying for them, there is nothing in the Atlantic Alliance for the United

States. He also suggests that the Europeans should be prepared to forgo the benefits of détente when the Soviet Union suppresses the freedom of non-NATO members.

132 **NATO in a New Strategic Environment.**
Edward A. Kolodziej. *Arms Control*, vol. 10, no. 1 (May 1989), p. 3-20.

Looks at the external factors pressing for change in NATO as well as those militating in favour of the status quo. The author sees the former as in the ascendancy. He identifies three options – resisting change, limited change and comprehensive change – and concludes that a limited change policy is most appropriate.

133 **U.S.–Western European Relations.**
Richard L. Kugler. *Current History*, vol. 87, no. 532 (November 1988), p. 353-356, 387-389.

Assesses the state of the Atlantic Alliance at the end of the Reagan Administration. Argues that although the first Administration left a legacy of distrust the second term witnessed an important healing process – partly because of the increase in the pace of arms control negotiations.

134 **NATO: Subjective Alliance: The Debate over the Future.**
Robert A. Levine. Santa Monica, California: Rand Corporation, April 1988. 190p. (RAND Paper R-3607-FF/CC/RC).

This is an illuminating study of the debate in Europe and the United States during the 1980s over the future of NATO. Levine categorizes European and American opinions into several schools of thought. The most important European group is the 'couplers' category which, according to Levine, includes governments of all of the European members of the Alliance, as well as major segments of the opposition parties. The couplers want to maintain the American nuclear guarantee to Western Europe and were concerned over the INF treaty which abolished land-based missiles with ranges between 500 and 5,500 kilometres. The second group is the 'removers', that is members of the European peace movement who want US nuclear and conventional forces removed from Europe. This school of thought has support mainly on the left in Europe but evokes sympathy from the American right where there is a group that Levine terms the 'withdrawers'. This group wants a sharply decreased American commitment to Western Europe either because the United States is overstretched or because the European allies are not bearing their fair share of the burden. The most important school in the United States, however, is the 'maintainers' – those who want to keep essential elements in the American security guarantee to Western Europe. Levine not only puts this debate in historical perspective, but uses it to make several observations on the future of the Alliance. His study provides an excellent overview of the strategic and political debates of the 1980s and places them in a coherent intellectual framework.

135 **The United States and Post-INF Europe.**
Michael Lucas. *World Policy Journal*, vol. 5, no. 2 (Spring 1988), p. 183-233.

Writing in the aftermath of the December 1987 INF agreement, the article argues that NATO has reached a crossroads. The author is critical of a United States policy he believes does not take full account of the changed circumstances. Rather than a continuing debate over burden-sharing and modernization, what NATO needs is a new Harmel report and a recognition that NATO is not the only framework for understanding and reacting to the changes in Europe. This in many respects was what West Germany was arguing.

136 Before the Day After: Can NATO defend Europe?
Laurence Martin.   London: Newnes Books, 1985. 159p.

A nice coffee-table book designed for the non-specialist but one which offers a good overview of the military confrontation between NATO and the Warsaw Pact forces in Europe. The author looks at the military problems on the Central Front and the Flanks, the evolution of NATO strategy and various ways in which NATO might enhance its conventional forces. The economic basis for security is also considered in a very accessible way, while the volume has a useful glossary of terms.

137 The Alliance Debate.
Sam Nunn, Henry Kissinger, Pierre Lellouche, Robert Hunter, Barry Blechman, Michael Harrison, Simon Serfaty.   *Washington Quarterly*, vol. 5, no. 3 (Summer 1982), p. 19-81.

A series of articles by a group of distinguished authors on NATO. It looks at various dimensions of the crisis in Atlantic relations in the early 1980s and considers the severity of this crisis. Senator Nunn emphasizes the need for a stronger conventional defence posture; Henry Kissinger discusses nuclear issues and the peace movement; and Lellouche and Hunter both assess the future of NATO. Hunter argues that both Western Europe and the United States have to try to understand each other's perspective. Barry Blechman provides a telling critique of 'no first use' arguments, while both Michael Harrison and Simon Serfaty provide incisive analyses of the trends in US–European relations which need to be managed. This is a useful collection of articles.

138 The Alliance after Afghanistan: A Crisis in US–European Relations.
Robert Osgood.   *Atlantic Community Quarterly*, vol. 18, no. 4 (Winter 1980-81), p. 394-402.

The author looks at what he sees as a latent crisis in NATO stemming partly from the difficulty of responding to détente, growing Soviet power and challenges from outside the NATO area. Osgood also offers a series of prescriptions for coping with the new tensions. These include the restoration of faith in American military power, an agreed concept of the threat, and a coordinated diplomatic strategy.

139 The Atlantic Alliance: Prescriptions for a Difficult Decade.
Bernard W. Rogers.   *Foreign Affairs*, vol. 60, no. 5 (Summer 1982), p. 1145-1156.

Written by the Supreme Allied Commander Europe, this article starts from the premise that NATO members have failed to meet their commitments on defence spending and contends that these commitments need to be reaffirmed. A real increase of four per cent in Allied defence spending would enable the Alliance to field an adequate conventional deterrent.

140 **After Reykjavik: Arms Control and the Allies.**
Jane M. O. Sharp. *International Affairs*, vol. 63, no. 2 (Spring 1987),
p. 239-358.
This article examines the responses of allies to the October 1986 Reykjavik summit,
and highlights the tensions between West European security requirements and the
objectives of superpower arms control. Central to the analysis is the abandonment–entrapment cycle (an eight-stage cycle of anxiety which moves from European
fears that the United States will withdraw extended deterrence to fears that Europe
will be the battleground for a superpower conflict in which European interests are not
directly involved). The difficulty stems partly from the fact that actions taken in
response to one kind of anxiety eventually create another. The article also addresses
the Reykjavik proposals – which consisted of pragmatic arms control limits for the first
five years and radical disarmament measures thereafter – and considers the European
reaction. A very interesting and provocative analysis.

141 **NATO in the 1990s.**
Stanley R. Sloan. Washington, DC: Pergamon-Brassey's, 1989. 347p.
This book is based on the work of the North Atlantic Assembly Special Presidential
Committee on NATO in the 1990s. It contains the committee's report as well as a
number of supporting papers. These supporting papers look at NATO's past history,
the contemporary setting, and new challenges and opportunities. There is a
distinguished list of authors including Catherine Kelleher, David Greenwood,
Lawrence Freedman, Karl Kaiser, and Robert Hunter. Although another book that in
some respects was overtaken by the revolutions in 1989, this book is still worth looking
at for the quality of the contributions to some of the themes it identifies.

142 **Making the Alliance Work: The United States and Western Europe.**
Gregory F. Treverton. London: Macmillan, 1985. 211p.
Written by a thoughtful and knowledgeable analyst of NATO affairs, this book offers a
good overview of NATO's strengths and weaknesses in the mid-1980s. The author
identifies two approaches to the state of the alliance: those who believe that the
Atlantic relationship has always been troubled and that crises come and go without
eroding the underlying framework of cooperation and those who contend that the
problems of the 1980s are less manageable than earlier strains and stresses. His own
position is that there are problems of assessing how serious the difficulties are because
there is no real base-line for comparison. The main substance of the book is an attempt
to correct this deficiency by looking at a series of problems facing NATO – the
arguments over nuclear weapons, the balance between defence and détente, the
problem of collective versus national action outside the NATO area, the impact of
economic strains on security cooperation – in terms of their antecedents and current
manifestations. This allows the author to determine what is a familiar pattern of
acrimony and what is new and different. The final chapter looks at how alliance politics
can be managed. The author suggests that the United States and Western Europe will
remain central to each other's purposes and that this will continue to make the alliance
resilient but that the tasks of managing the alliance will remain formidable.

143 **West European Security after Reykjavik.**
Phil Williams. *Washington Quarterly*, vol. 10, no. 2 (Spring 1987),
p. 37-49.
Looks at European reactions to many of the issues raised at the Reykjavik Summit and
argues that there was discontent with the diplomatic process, disquiet over United
States assumptions, and unhappiness with the substance of the agreements which were
almost reached. It overstates the extent to which Reykjavik undermined long-term
European confidence in the United States.

144 **NATO's Political–Military Challenges.**
David S. Yost. *Current History*, vol. 81, no. 479 (December 1982),
p. 401-404, 435-438.
Argues that NATO has allowed its military problems to worsen partly because of its
inability to make a realistic threat assessment and act upon it. The author asserts that
the Alliance has insufficient vision and unanimity. He makes a well-argued but
overstated case.

Atlantic relations

145 **The Future of the Atlantic Community: Toward European–American
Partnership.**
Kurt Birrenbach. New York: Praeger, 1963. 94p.
Written by a leading member of Chancellor Adenauer's party, this study argues against
any idea of a third force Europe and proposes instead a strengthening and
revitalization of Atlantic ties. It looks not only at the strategic dimensions of Atlantic
relations and the conflicts over strategy that characterized the first half of the 1960s but
also at the economic and cultural dimensions of the Atlantic Community. There is little
here that is new, but it is worth looking at as an example of the kind of ideas proposed
by committed Atlanticists in the early 1960s in their effort to develop and enhance
cooperation between the United States and Western Europe.

146 **Finding America's Place.**
Michael Brenner. *Foreign Policy*, no. 79 (Summer 1990), p. 25-44.
An incisive analysis which looks at the future of the United States' role in Europe in
view of the end of the Cold War and the limits of American power. Brenner argues
that the United States still has essential roles in Europe – as under-writer of a
European settlement, honest broker, and a force for stability – but that new terms of
engagement need to be worked out.

147 **Sources of Strain in Transatlantic Relations.**
Miriam Camps. *International Affairs*, vol. 48, no. 4 (October 1972),
p. 559-578.
This article looks at the sources of strain in the Atlantic relationship in the early 1970s,
as the United States was trying to redefine its international role in view of changes in

superpower relations and the balance of power. The author examines the proposition that bipolarity had given way to a pentagonal world and suggests that Western Europe had become a power centre without power. The US–West European relationship is examined in the 'advanced nations' context and the author highlights the fear of economic warfare and the strains stemming from divergent assessments of the need to include Japan in the coordination of economic policy.

148 **Atlantis Lost: US–European Relations after the Cold War.**
Edited by James Chace, Earl Ravenal. New York: New York University Press for the Council on Foreign Relations, 1976. 273p.

This book was written in a period of turmoil and pessimism about the future of the Atlantic Alliance. This is reflected in the title and in the tone of many of the chapters written by a distinguished list of authors that included Stanley Hoffmann, Zbigniew Brzezinski, Seyom Brown, Edward Morse and Andrew Pierre. The overall thrust is that the Atlantic Alliance was suffering not only from the Middle East and oil crises of 1973-74 but also from more fundamental problems relating to basic structural changes in international politics. The thesis of several of the contributors is that the Atlantic relationship is in disarray but that the Europeans have neither the will nor the capability to provide any alternative. Ronald Steel claims, for example, that Europe lacks the will to move from under American protection. Others saw Europe and the United States emerging as economic competitors even though the European allies were proving unwilling to develop greater self-reliance in security. There was broad agreement that aspirations to transform the Atlantic Alliance into a genuine twin-pillar arrangement in which American power would be both balanced and complemented by that of a stronger and more united Europe had effectively been abandoned. In retrospect much of the analysis seems overly gloomy and pessimistic; yet it does evoke the mood of this period in Atlantic relations.

149 **NATO: The Transatlantic Bargain.**
Harlan Cleveland. New York: Harper & Row, 1990. 204p.

A useful study of the consultative and bargaining processes in NATO. The notion of the transatlantic bargain is a particularly fruitful one and has been frequently used by other commentators on NATO. The author develops this theme while examining the consultation process over a wide range of issues including NATO strategy, détente, burden-sharing, and out-of-area challenges. The author emphasizes the golden rule of consultation – that each NATO member consult with the others as soon, as often and as explicitly as it would wish other governments to consult.

150 **Defense and Detente: US and West German Perspectives on Defense Policy.**
Edited by Joseph I. Coffey, Klaus von Schubert. Boulder, Colorado: Westview Press, 1989. 324p.

An interesting collection of chapters which look at the different ways in which the United States and the Federal Republic of Germany adapted to the Cold War world, at their approaches to deterrence and defence, their perspectives on burden-sharing, and their approaches to détente. As well as the two primary authors the contributors are Dieter Dettke, James Golden, and Gale Mattox. A good analysis of convergence and divergence in what was the central bilateral relationship within NATO.

151 **The United States and the European Pillar: The Strained Alliance.**
William C. Cromwell.   London: Macmillan, 1992. 275p.

A good overview of the US policy towards West European efforts to establish a
European pillar in defence. The author looks at the vagaries of the Atlantic
relationship and highlights the ways in which European preferences and policies
sometimes diverged from those of the United States. He also looks at possible
architectures for post-Cold War Europe and at the United States role in the new
Europe. The author concludes that the period of American predominance in Europe is
over and that progress has been made towards partnership of equals.

152 **Political Problems of Atlantic Partnership: National Perspectives.**
Edited by William Cromwell.   Bruges, Belgium: College of Europe,
1969. 458p.

An excellent commentary on the problems of Atlantic relations in the late 1960s which
focuses upon divergent national perspectives and policies. Cromwell provides a useful
analysis of the United States while Josef Joffe examines German policy, looking at the
cross-pressures from France and the United States. There is also a chapter on Britain.
For anyone interested in looking at the evolution of Atlantic relations in the 1960s this
is a very good source.

153 **Political Community and the North Atlantic Area: International
Organization in the Light of Historical Experience.**
Karl Wolfgang Deutsch (et al.).   Princeton, New Jersey: Princeton
University Press, 1957. 228p.

A major study of patterns of integration in the Atlantic region. The author, one of the
premier political scientists in the world, focuses on transaction flows amongst peoples
of different nations as a measure of integration. The book is also conceptually useful
and develops the notion of a security community which has subsequently been applied
to both the members of the Atlantic Alliance and the European Community. Not
directly on NATO, this is nevertheless an important book about the underlying
patterns of social interaction amongst the members of the Atlantic Alliance.

154 **The Western Misalliance.**
Theodore Draper.   *Washington Quarterly*, vol. 4, no. 1 (Winter 1981),
p. 13-69.

A highly critical analysis of the failure of the European allies to support the United
States in the crisis over American hostages in Iran. Taking this as a starting point,
Draper looks at the other problems in the Alliance, including the dilemmas associated
with NATO strategy in an era of strategic parity, the problems resulting from the
geographical limits of the Alliance, the difficulties associated with changing power
relationships between the United States and the European allies, and the strains
resulting from divergent policies towards the Soviet Union. Draper argues that many
of the problems in Atlantic relations arose from the European effort to combine three
policies: economic competition with the United States, unqualified independence in
global politics, and ultimate dependence on the United States for European defence.
This leads to the conclusion that the Alliance is mortally ill and that there is a large gap
between Alliance commitments and the coincidence of interests necessary to make
these commitments credible. Although Draper sees the Alliance as obsolescent, he
nevertheless suggests in conclusion that there would be major dangers in an isolated

America and an insulated Europe. While some of Draper's arguments are overdrawn, this is a trenchant and important article which both expressed and evoked the profound sense of dissatisfaction with the European allies which existed in the United States during the early 1980s.

155   Managing Alliances.
Lawrence Freedman.   *Foreign Policy*, no. 71 (Summer 1988), p. 65-85.

An interesting set of comments on the problems that confronted NATO throughout the 1980s and some sound advice on dealing with them. Freedman is not blasé, however, and offers the prescient argument that as political relations in Europe become more fluid NATO will increasingly have to justify itself in ways which do not emphasize an immediate sense of threat.

156   The Troubled Alliance: Atlantic Relations in the 1980s.
Edited by Lawrence Freedman.   New York: St Martin's Press, 1983. 170p.

Based on a compilation of papers that were presented at a Conference at the Royal Institute of International Affairs, London in 1983, this book focuses very effectively upon the reasons for tension and conflict within the Atlantic Alliance. It is particularly strong on the linkages between the economic and security dimensions of Atlantic relations. The scene is set with chapters by the late David Watt and by Catherine Kelleher which focus respectively on European images of the United States and American images of Western Europe. This was particularly useful in a period when many Europeans thought the Reagan Administration too bellicose and many Americans thought the Europeans too soft on the Soviet Union. In the second section of the book the focus is on the economic strains within the Alliance. Concerns are expressed over the lack of congruence between the extensive economic interdependence of the allies and the lack of coordination of their respective economic policies. The third part focuses on the adequacy of the existing security arrangements with the predominant view being that the European members of NATO should play a larger role in their own defence and security. A valuable final chapter explores the linkages between economic and security relations.

157   Bonn and Washington: From Deterioration to Crisis.
William E. Griffith.   *Orbis*, vol. 26, no. 1 (Spring 1982), p. 117-133.

Griffith sees the crucial linchpin of the Atlantic relationship as that between Washington and Bonn and argues that major problems are developing in this relationship. As well as divergences over specific problems there is a more fundamental change – knowledge of Germany in the United States is declining, while knowledge of the United States in Germany is also eroding. The author suggests that these trends should be reversed by a process of mutual education which would help rebuild consensus between the governing élites and the majority of the populations in both West Germany and the United States.

158   NATO and the TNF Controversy: Threats to the Alliance.
Morton Halperin.   *Orbis*, vol. 26, no. 1 (Spring 1982), p. 105-116.

Written by a noted academic and former member of the NSC staff under Kissinger, this analysis looks at the dangers to NATO in the controversy over deploying cruise and Pershing missiles to Europe. Halperin argues that the major threats are German nationalism and American isolationism and that it is crucial to deal with the TNF issue in ways which do not exacerbate these tendencies.

159 **The United States and Western Europe: Political, Economic and Strategic Perspectives.**
Edited by Wolfram Hanreider. Cambridge, Massachusetts: Winthrop, 1974. 311p.

This volume offers some extremely incisive analyses of Atlantic relations in the early 1970s by a very distinguished group of analysts which includes Hans Morgenthau, Kenneth Waltz, Stanley Hoffmann, David Calleo, Benjamin Cohen and Paul Hammond. The perspectives are very different and coverage includes the economic dimensions of Atlantic relations as well as the strategic and political dimensions. They are particularly useful as a perspective on the Nixon years which, in spite of the nostalgia that was subsequently expressed in some quarters in Europe, was actually a period of considerable acrimony in Atlantic relations. They highlight the way in which the relationship between the United States and Western Europe had changed and show that although the United States remained the predominant power in the Alliance, by the early 1970s it had to take its allies' views into account to a greater extent than in the past. A particularly useful contribution for giving the flavour of the period is the chapter by John Yochelson on European and American perspectives on the idea of mutual force reduction.

160 **On the Political Integration of the Atlantic Community.**
Livingston Hartley. *Orbis*, vol. 6, no. 4 (Winter 1963), p. 645-655.

Suggests that the era of the nation-state is giving way to the era of political integration, which will lead eventually to world government. Arguing that the North Atlantic leads the world in this trend, the author looks at the ways integration can occur and suggests that the political integration of the West is essential to stop a future world government from being dominated by Communists. Emphasis is placed on the 1962 NATO Convention which recommended the creation of a Permanent High Council, the development of a NATO Parliamentarians' Conference, and the creation of an Atlantic Community High Court of Justice.

161 **A European Perspective on the Reagan Years.**
Michael Howard. *Foreign Affairs*, vol. 66, no. 3 (America and the World 1987-88), p. 478-493.

Argues that 1987 was a nadir for the Atlantic relationship as a result of the Reykjavik Summit, the Iran–Contra scandal and the United States budget deficit. Howard argues that the sheer unprofessionalism of the Reykjavik Summit shocked European governments, while Iran–Contra highlighted once again the divergence between the Reagan Administration and the European allies on policies outside the NATO area. This is a critical but trenchant appraisal.

162 **The Atlantic Alliance: Jackson Sub-committee Hearings and Findings.**
Henry Jackson. New York: Praeger, 1967. 309p.

This volume is the result of hearings held in 1965 and 1966 before the Sub-committee on National Security and International Operations of the Senate Committee on Government Operations. It includes a chapter on Senator Jackson's report which looks at the basic issues in NATO and the Alliance's unfinished business. The contributors, who provided testimony, include Richard Neustadt, Dean Acheson, Christian Herter, Lauris Norstad, Thomas Schelling, John McCloy, Dean Rusk and Robert McNamara. There are also over one hundred pages of documentation. Jackson provides a good assessment of the state of NATO during the period in which there was considerable controversy over flexible response.

163   Europe's American Pacifier.

Josef Joffe.   *Foreign Policy*, no. 54 (Spring 1984), p. 64-83.

Argues that the during the first half of the twentieth century the West European state system failed to preserve the security and independence of its members, to maintain stability and to inhibit the use of force. Joffe argues that the postwar system is, by contrast, ultra-stable. While Joffe attributes this largely to the United States commitment to Western Europe, he contends that this commitment did much more than contain the Soviet Union – it also acted as the crucial foundation for the construction of an international order in Western Europe that removed traditional conflicts and established conditions for cooperation. The commitment removed the search for autonomous defence policies by the states of Western Europe. Joffe also argues that there is no substitute for a continuation of this commitment.

164   Atlantic Crisis: American Diplomacy Confronts a Resurgent Europe.

Robert Kleiman.   New York: William Norton, 1964. 158p.

This slim but informed volume looks at Kennedy's Grand Design for Atlantic partnership and the way in which it was destroyed by General de Gaulle. The author, a highly respected journalist, is critical of both British and American policies but is rather more sympathetic to France. He covers trade as well as security issues.

165   The U.S. and Western Europe: A New Era of Understanding.

Hans Kohn.   *Orbis*, vol. 6, no. 1 (Spring 1962), p. 13-24.

Kohn looks at European and United States approaches and assessments of each other and emphasizes the importance of the trans-Atlantic linkage. He also argues that the problems between the United States and the European allies (i.e. anti-colonialism) are not much different from intra-American or intra-European problems and that trans-Atlantic unity is actually growing.

166   Western Europe and the Reagan Doctrine.

Evan Luard.   *International Affairs*, vol. 63, no. 4 (Autumn 1987), p. 563-574.

Looks at the Reagan doctrine as a major source of controversy in American politics and as a source of disagreement in the Western Alliance. The preference of West European governments for adherence to the principle of non-intervention is outlined, as is European scepticism about the feasibility of Reagan's objectives. Attention is given to US policies towards Nicaragua, Cambodia, Afghanistan, and Angola and the author offers several major criticisms of these policies.

167 **The Atlantic Triangle and the Cold War.**
Edgar McInnis.   Toronto, Canada: University of Toronto Press, 1959.
163p.
Canada is often neglected as a member of the Atlantic Alliance. This study attempts to
correct this deficiency and argues that the triangular linkages and common sense of
identity and outlook among the United States, Canada and Britain provide the
essential basis for Atlantic solidarity and cohesion. There is something slightly artificial
about both this argument and the overall focus of the book. Nevertheless, the author
provides a useful discussion of the three powers and of their different reactions to key
developments and issues.

168 **The United States and West Germany 1945-1973: A Study in Alliance
Politics.**
Roger Morgan.   London: Oxford University Press, 1974. 282p.
Looks at patterns of harmony and discord in the German American relationship and
how these are influenced by domestic politics in the two countries, by the broader
multilateral alliance, and the global international system, especially the policies of the
Soviet Union. Morgan shows how these forces impinged on the relationship as it
evolved through what he identifies as ten distinct phases in the period from 1945 to
1973.

169 **Atlantic Dilemma: Partnership or Community.**
Frank Munk.   New York: Oceana, 1964. 177p.
A useful assessment of the compatibility between European and Atlantic regional
constructions which sets out to investigate alternative courses of action and to locate
the minimum threshold of Atlantic cohesion below which a process of fission and
alienation will occur. Having looked at economic, military and political dimensions of
the Atlantic relationship the author suggests that the first Atlantic community
established in the late 1940s is reaching its limit and the second one awaits its
architects. This slightly idiosyncratic approach nevertheless provides a good sense of
the concepts and aspirations underlying the debate over Atlantic relations in the early
1960s.

170 **The Atlantic Community: A Complex Imbalance.**
Robert L. Pfaltzgraff, Jr.   New York: Van Nostrand Reinhold, 1969.
216p.
Argues that the initial dependence of Western Europe on the United States has been
superseded by new forms of dependence which contribute to 'the crisis of the west'.
The author examines the divergences in strategic perspective between the United
States and its European allies, the technology gap, economic relations, and policies
towards Eastern Europe. The final chapter outlines a new more harmonious Atlantic
relationship and identifies the kind of adjustments both the Europeans and the United
States have to make to bring this about.

171   **The Atlantic Alliance: Perspectives from the Successor Generation.**
Edited by Alan Platt.   Santa Monica, California: Rand Corporation,
December 1983. 195p. (R-3100-nis).
The result of a conference in February 1983 sponsored by Rand, the United States
Information Agency, the NATO Information Service, the State Department and the
Ford Foundation, this paper has an interesting collection of chapters generally from
younger analysts. The paper looks at the historical basis for the Alliance, the strains in
Atlantic relations in the early 1980s and whether or not these constituted a crisis, the
US role in the Alliance, European and American attitudes toward the Soviet Union,
and the management of US–European differences. Contributors include Josef Joffe,
Robert Osgood, Stephen Szabo, and Gregory Treverton while the discussants include
James Thomson, Pierre Lellouche, and Arnold Horelick. An interesting collection
which provides a good sense of the divergent assessments of the condition of NATO.

172   **Western Europe and the United States: The Uncertain Alliance.**
Michael Smith.   Boston, Massachusetts: George Allen & Unwin,
1984. 152p. (Studies in Contemporary Europe, no. 6).
A good analysis of US–European relations and their evolution in the postwar period.
The author identifies patterns of continuity and change and considers the relationship
in terms of the broader environment, the issues at stake and the processes through
which relations are conducted. The volume contains a useful bibliography.

173   **NATO's Last Mission.**
Ronald Steel.   *Foreign Policy*, no. 76 (Fall 1989), p. 83-95.
The author, a long-time critic of NATO, argues that the end of the Cold War will
inevitably undermine NATO unity. He sees three possible ways of dealing with the
alliance's 'crisis of credibility'. The first alternative is the maintenance of the status
quo: US dominance over policy-making coupled with pressures for greater financial
burden-sharing. Second, is the creation of a genuine European pillar in the alliance,
something that would permit the United States role to be downgraded. The third
alternative, and the one Steel favours, is a negotiated settlement of the Cold War
which would leave in place a calm and stable Europe – and allow the United States to
disengage.

174   **An Alliance of Continents.**
Franz Josef Strauss.   *International Affairs*, vol. 41, no. 2 (April 1965),
p. 191-203.
Written by a leading conservative politician in the Federal Republic of Germany, this
article analyses problems in the Atlantic relationship. The author is critical of the
somewhat patriarchal US role in NATO, argues that Europe and the United States no
longer have identical interests and contends that Europe has become overly reliant on
the United States. He also claims that the US desire to maintain the status quo in
Europe is incompatible with European unification. The article discusses the Atlantic
Nuclear Force and the Multilateral Force and the advantages of each to the United
States on the one side and Western Europe on the other. It concludes that NATO
should be a more balanced American–European alliance not an American protectorate. To achieve this there should be a European federation which would create a
European nuclear council and a European nuclear arsenal.

175 **German–American Military Fissures.**
Alex A. Vardamis. *Foreign Policy*, no. 34 (Spring 1979), p. 87-106.
Explores the growth of mistrust between Washington and Bonn during the Carter Administration. Considerable attention is given to nuclear issues as a source of this discord. Although some of the author's predictions proved to be inaccurate, this article nevertheless offers a good introduction to some of the tensions in NATO in the late 1970s.

176 **Issue Linkage among Atlantic Governments.**
William Wallace. *International Affairs*, vol. 52, no. 2 (April 1976),
p. 163-179.
Discusses the interdependence of politico-military and economic issues among NATO members and the change in United States policies on this issue from Kennedy to Nixon. The author suggests that US efforts to create a 'grand design' in foreign policy encounter significant obstacles: the limited attention span and capacity for absorbing information of top leaders, the habits and conventions of the international system and their institutional expression in intergovernmental organizations, and the national administrative structures for managing foreign policy. Differences between the Atlantic and West European systems are highlighted and an attempt is made to identify the conditions under which linkage is legitimate.

177 **A New Transatlantic Bargain.**
Samuel Wells Jr. *Washington Quarterly*, vol. 12, no. 4
(Autumn 1989), p. 53-60.
Argues that after its fortieth anniversary NATO is in exceptionally good health, but that it has to be cautious about Gorbachev's policies, which do not reflect a fundamental shift in Soviet objectives. The author proposes that the Atlantic Alliance continue in its present form but with a modified orientation in which greater emphasis is placed on political and economic considerations. Although written before the fundamental shifts in Europe, it is arguable that this prescription has become more rather than less important.

NATO: Organization, Structure and Procedures

178 **Military Logistic Systems in NATO: The Goal of Integration Part I: Economic Aspects.**
Geoffrey Ashcroft. London: International Institute for Strategic Studies, November 1969. 35p. (Adelphi Paper 62).
Looks at military logistics within NATO, current national activities and the possibilities for the evolution of an integrated system. The author also examines efforts to deal with cost reduction and the possibilities of increasing collaboration for this purpose.

179 **Military Logistic Systems in NATO: The Goal of Integration Part II: Military Aspects.**
Geoffrey Ashcroft. London: International Institute for Strategic Studies, June 1970, 35p. (Adelphi Paper 68).
Looks at the military dimension of logistic problems in NATO and especially the military interest in logistic cooperation or integration. The main focus of the paper is the logistic activities of the NATO military authorities, and the author considers whether these activities are likely to lead to an integrated logistic system. He is very critical of the existing approach and offers some suggestions for achieving better integration.

180 **Integration and Disintegration in NATO: Processes of Alliance Cohesion and Prospects for Atlantic Community.**
Francis A. Beer. Columbus, Ohio: Ohio State University Press, 1969. 330p.
Starting from the assumption that NATO was a corner-stone of the postwar international system but with an uncertain future, Beer tries to assess the degree of cohesion in NATO through a focus on integration, which is defined as a process in which national actors shift their loyalties and activities towards a new centre whose institutions demand or possess jurisdiction over them. This process is assessed in terms of three indicators: institutional autonomy, authority, and legitimacy. This provides the

framework for a study of political consultation, NATO military forces, armaments, NATO infrastructure, and NATO science. At the end of his survey of these areas, the author concludes that compulsory institutional procedures remained weak and that NATO authority remained mostly indirect and of limited effectiveness; there was little authoritative decision-making on matters of major importance to the participants. Finally, Beer looks at the future of NATO in terms of three possible levels of integration – Atlantic Community, Atlantic Partnership and Atlantic Alliance. He is not optimistic that NATO leaders could build new authority or legitimacy for a more integrated alliance. Although this explains the limits of Alliance it does not explain why NATO continued to function in spite of these limits.

181　The Military Committee of the North Atlantic Alliance: A Study of Structure and Strategy.
Douglas L. Bland.　New York: Praeger, 1991. 258p.

Written by a Canadian analyst, this study fills a gap in the literature. Its main focus is the Military Committee, which is the senior military committee in NATO, oversees the actions of the major NATO commanders and is charged with recommending measures considered necessary for the common defence of the NATO area. The book looks at the evolution of NATO strategy and considers the impact on this of the NATO structure. The author suggests that the political and military needs of the alliance are in continual competition and that consequently NATO's strategic choices are ensnared in an 'alliance dilemma'. He also argues that the Military Committee is both an institutional expression of this dilemma and an antidote to it. One of the major recommendations in the book is that the alliance return to a regional military structure supported by a strategy of reinforcement. To achieve this the author recommends that Allied Command Europe, the office of SACEUR, and SHAPE should be eliminated and that the responsibility for the planning, organizing and conducting of European defence should be passed to European regional commanders.

182　Consultation and the Atlantic Alliance.
Manlio Brosio.　Survival, vol. 16, no. 3 (May/June 1974), p. 115-121.

Written by a former Secretary-General of NATO, this article highlights both the need for and the limits of inter-allied consultation. The author examines the instruments or mechanism of consultation, the substance or range of consultation, and most crucial of all, the political will which determines the extent and scope of consultation. A practical approach by a NATO insider.

183　NATO and the SHAPE Technical Center.
Raymond H. Dawson, George E. Nicholson, Jr.　International Organization, vol. 21, no. 3 (Summer 1967), p. 565-591.

Looks at the role of the Technical Center at SHAPE (Supreme Headquarters Allied Powers Europe) and relates it to theories of functionalism. The authors trace the way in which the Center stopped being simply a functional body and became instead an international military organization.

184　The Committee System of NATO.
Bjarne Eriksen.　Oslo: Universitetsforlaget, 1967. 79p.

A useful reference study which looks at the development of the committee system in NATO, the composition of the committees, the role of the international staff and the national delegations, and the Parliamentarians' Conference. As well as dealing with structural issues, the author looks at the process or functioning of the system. He sees the committee system as a very flexible organizational machinery for dealing with complex tasks. Although somewhat dry and rather dated, this volume nevertheless provides a useful discussion of how NATO operates on a day-to-day basis.

185 **No Soft Options: The Politico-Military Realities of NATO.**
Sir Peter Hill Norton. Montreal, Canada: McGill-Queen's University Press, 1978. 172p.

This study, written by a former Chairman of the NATO Military Committee, looks at the history of NATO, the threat, deterrence, the conventional balance, regional perspectives in the Alliance, and some of the tensions in NATO. The author also examines the 'higher direction of NATO' and has a useful, if all too short, chapter on the machinery and procedures for crisis management in the Alliance. Other chapters look at the particular problems facing NATO when the book was written and also at the way ahead. Although this is not a particularly scholarly study it is worth looking at because of the credentials of the author in terms of his experience in NATO.

186 **Fearful Symmetry: The Dilemmas of Consultation and Coordination in the North Atlantic Treaty Organization.**
John W. Holmes. *International Organization*, vol. 22, no. 4 (Winter 1968), p. 821-840.

Looks at some of the problems involved in the consultation process in NATO and shows how the consultation and coordination issues are related to broader issues such as the shape of the Alliance, the distribution of power, and the purposes the Alliance is intended to serve. The analysis is very positive about NATO's move from searching for 'hardware' solutions to the problem of nuclear-sharing to seeing this as a matter for enhanced consultation.

187 **One for All: NATO Strategy and Logistics through the Formative Period (1949-1969).**
James A. Huston. Newark, New Jersey: University of Delaware Press, 1984. 332p.

This volume focuses upon an often neglected aspect of NATO, the cooperation in logistics, which is a crucial complement to both strategy and tactics. It is a well-researched study which looks at the evolution of coordinated logistics efforts through the Mutual Defense Assistance Program. The book covers various aspects of logistics and deals with the NATO infrastructure programme, transportation, and international supply and maintenance. The author identifies both the major achievements and the continued shortcomings in an area that has considerable importance but little glamour. A helpful study which helps to fill a gap in our understanding of NATO.

188 **The NATO International Staff/Secretariat 1952-1957: A Study in International Administration.**
Robert S. Jordan. London: Oxford University Press, 1967. 307p.

This study focuses upon the administrative aspects of NATO as they developed through the mid-1950s. It examines the tradition of international administration, early efforts to administer NATO, and the creation of NATO headquarters. The second section considers the machinery for policy-making in NATO headquarters with particular attention to the operation of the North Atlantic Council and the role of Secretary General. Part Three looks at administrative problems of an international civil service and focuses upon issues such as recruitment, retention and remuneration. Part Four explores the administration of the international staff and secretariat in several areas – press and cultural relations, economics and finance, production and logistics, and infrastructure. Jordan traces the growth in importance of the staff. A great deal of attention is also focused upon the contribution of Lord Ismay, who, it is argued, saw his role first in terms of diplomacy and only second in terms of administration. Jordan concludes that Ismay's great contribution was to create an international climate in which the Council could take political decisions with minimum friction. This book deals with an unusual and often neglected aspect of NATO in an important period when it was consolidating many of its activities.

189   **Generals in International Politics: NATO's Supreme Allied Commander Europe.**
Edited by Robert S. Jordan.   Lexington, Kentucky: University Press of Kentucky, 1987. 229p.

After a foreword by General Bernard Rogers and an introductory chapter by Andrew Goodpaster on the development of the Supreme Headquarters Allied Powers Europe (SHAPE) between 1950 and 1953, this volume has individual chapters dealing with the contribution of each of the SACEURs from 1950 through to 1979. The chapter dealing with Eisenhower, the first SACEUR, focuses on his role in raising European morale, in persuading the American Senate to support the deployment of American troops to Europe, and in organizing SHAPE. His successor, General Matthew Ridgway, played an important consolidating role, but although a brilliant field soldier he was not a diplomat. General Gruenther, the third SACEUR tried to persuade the European allies to deploy larger conventional forces, while his successor General Norstad not only developed the Pause concept but also outlined plans enabling the Europeans to share in the nuclear decision-making – plans that did not endear him to Washington. The main task for General Lemnitzer, SACEUR from 1963 to 1969, was to cope with the French withdrawal from NATO and the ejection of NATO from France; that of his successor, General Goodpaster, was to adjust to détente and to contain Congressional pressures for American troop reduction in Europe. The chapter on Haig as SACEUR is followed by an overall assessment by the editor of the lessons that can be drawn from the NATO experience in multinational military leadership.

190   **NATO Political–Military Consultation: Shaping Alliance Decisions.**
Thomas J. Kennedy Jr.   Washington, DC: National Defense University, 1984. 86p.

A succinct and helpful overview of the patterns and processes of consultation in NATO. The study looks at the general alliance procedures for consultation, and the particular role of the United States in this process. It also focuses upon ways in which the consultative procedures can be improved as well as the kind of consultation that occurs outside the formal NATO procedures. Kennedy concludes that the injection of fresh ideas rather than major organizational changes offers the best prospect for improving the process.

191 **Concerting Policies in the North Atlantic Community.**
R. C. Lawson.   *International Organization*, vol. 12, no. 2
(Spring 1958), p. 163-179.
Looks at the difficulties faced by NATO members in coordinating their policies and the
means that have been devised to overcome these. The role of the Secretary General is
given particular attention as is the NATO method of decision-making without formal
voting.

192 **The Importance of the North Atlantic Assembly.**
A. Glenn Mower, Jr.   *Orbis*, vol. 21, no. 4 (Winter 1978), p. 927-946.
Looks at the role and aspirations of the North Atlantic Assembly and in particular its
desire that its resolutions and recommendations be given greater attention by the
North Atlantic Council. The Assembly's strengths are its freedom of action (it is non-
governmental) and the calibre of its membership (which consists of influential members
of national parliaments). These allow it to play several roles which include a forum for
discussion of intra-NATO concerns such as the effect of national budgets on burden-
sharing and NATO strength. It also has an educational function through the
preparation and dissemination of committee reports, the contributions of specialists
and the provision of technical and political information. The impact of the Assembly
on both national and NATO policies is also highlighted.

193 **Men of Responsibility: A Memoir.**
Dirk U. Stikker.   New York: Harper & Row, 1965. 148p.
Dirk Stikker, a Dutch diplomat, was the Netherlands' Foreign Minister, the Dutch
permanent representative to NATO and eventually NATO's Secretary-General. As
such, he has a valuable perspective on the alliance and its evolution. This book
highlights the role of the Secretary-General but is also good on substantive issues like
the feuds in NATO over strategy and nuclear weapons.

NATO Crisis Management

194 **Surprise Attack.**
   Richard K. Betts.   Washington, DC: Brookings Institution, 1982.
   318p.

Although this analysis of surprise attack by Richard Betts goes well beyond NATO, it does contain several chapters dealing with the problem of surprise on the central front. Having examined sudden attacks both in the Second World War and in the postwar era, and identified the reasons why surprise succeeds, Betts turns his attention to NATO. He identifies some of the ways in which NATO is vulnerable to surprise and highlights many of the dilemmas that the alliance could face in responding to Soviet aggression. The analysis contains one of the best public discussions of warning indicators and of the NATO Alert System. Betts is particularly good at highlighting the dilemmas faced by NATO in responding to warning. These dilemmas are both political and military and involve striking a balance between preparedness as a hedge against the possibility that deterrence might fail, and doing nothing to exacerbate or intensify the crisis. As an analysis of some of the dilemmas that would have been faced by NATO in a Cold War crisis, this study is difficult to surpass.

195 **Surprise Attack: NATO's Political Vulnerability.**
   Richard K. Betts.   *International Security*, vol. 5, no. 4 (Spring 1981),
   p. 117-149.

Argues that NATO's political vulnerability to surprise is not simply a matter of obtaining early warning of a possible Soviet attack. The central issue is the ability to respond to warning. Betts suggests that this should be a priority for the alliance, noting that the focus on intelligence detection and on the military balance, rather than on reaction to warning and the political transition to a decision to mobilize, distorts the defence debate. The article also considers how war might break out in Europe, with particular attention to the notion of compound crises which multiply each other and take events out of control. An important article drawn from Betts' book on the same topic but which stands in its own right.

196 **The Command and Control of Nuclear Forces.**
Paul Bracken.   New Haven, New Jersey; London: Yale University
Press, 1983. 252p.

The author looks at the problems involved with the command and control of nuclear forces at the strategic and theatre levels. He highlights the dangers of a ratchet effect in a crisis as the two superpowers place their forces on higher states of alert, and deals with the particular problems associated with tension in Europe and the alert of theatre nuclear forces. The author explores the advantages and drawbacks of both centralized and decentralized command systems and argues that 'NATO decision makers will not be faced with one choice on nuclear usage but with many. The NATO force structure makes this certain because it is made up of so many parts that interact in a non-simple way' (p. 130). A well-informed and valuable study that focuses on an issue that was not always well understood.

197 **Crisis Management: The New Diplomacy.**
Alastair Buchan.   Boulogne-sur-Seine, France: The Atlantic Institute,
1966. 63p.

Writing at a time when NATO appeared to be in turmoil, Alastair Buchan argued that if an alliance system of crisis management could be agreed upon and translated into institutional terms then the malaise in NATO would be overcome. Accordingly, he set out to explore the notion of crisis management and to consider how it applied to NATO. Buchan was concerned with the rights and duties of allies in relation to crises and with the techniques of collective management that were politically realistic. He surveys different kinds of crises: colonial emergencies, crises within the alliance, Far Eastern crises, American crises, and European crises. On the basis of this he concludes that NATO lacked a system of collective decision-making that would function effectively in a major crisis. Buchan also identifies several ways in which the NATO decision-making system might be improved so that the Alliance would be better able to respond to crises.

198 **Managing Nuclear Operations.**
Edited by Ashton B. Carter, John D. Steinbruner, Charles A.
Zraket.   Washington, DC: Brookings Institution, 1987. 751p.

Although this volume goes well beyond NATO in scope and content, it does have much of relevance to the alliance, its strategy, force posture, and alert system. A chapter by Donald Cotter, for example, deals with peacetime operations involving nuclear weapons and how they are made safe and secure. Also important is a study by Bruce Blair of alert procedures in crisis and in conventional war. This chapter discusses the United States DEFCON alert system as well as the NATO system, highlights some of the dilemmas involved in making decisions about alert status, and identifies the problems of controlling forces on high stages of alert. The other particularly relevant chapter by Catherine Kelleher analyses NATO nuclear operations. Kelleher provides a detailed breakdown of US nuclear weapons deployed in Europe whether available to US forces or to those of America's allies. She also examines the security and storage arrangements for the nuclear stockpile, and the formal structures for release authority at both the military and civilian levels. The chapter finishes with a discussion of the problems related to the command and control of nuclear operations. A valuable study, although one that was relevant to a much higher level of military confrontation than currently exists.

199 **Nuclear Planning in NATO: Pitfalls of First Use.**
Daniel Charles. Cambridge, Massachusetts: Ballinger, 1987. 177p.

This book offers a critique of NATO's strategy of flexible response, largely on the grounds that the weaknesses in command and control would significantly impair the ability of NATO to use nuclear weapons in a limited and deliberate manner. The argument is that the use of nuclear weapons is more likely to be uncontrolled and to spark further escalation. Having set the scene with the discussion of NATO strategy and doctrine, the author identifies some of the dilemmas attendant upon NATO's military posture. There is a particularly good discussion of the advantages and disadvantages of moving to a higher alert status and dispersing nuclear weapons in a period of crisis. The author contends that dispersal would mean a significant loss of control. He also argues that political leaders would be aware of this and would consequently delay decisions about dispersing nuclear warheads. The implication is that reliance on nuclear weapons would actually paralyse the NATO decision-making structure in a period of crisis. The alternative, which the author also points out, is that NATO might find it difficult to refrain from nuclear first use even if it wants to. In conclusion, Charles contends that the ability of NATO to manage and control its nuclear forces in a period of crisis should be improved while at the same time cautioning against over-confidence in the ability to exercise control over these weapons.

200 **Improving International Crisis Communications.**
CSIC Study Group on International Crisis Communications.
Washington, DC: Center for Strategic and International Studies,
March 1991. 50p.

This report of a project directed by Michael Mazarr examines communication links between governments that could be used in periods of tension or crises. It looks at direct superpower communication and Third World crisis communications as well as communications in Europe. The chapter on Europe argues that a multilateral communications network and a multilateral crisis prevention centre could play a role in securing stability in Europe. A useful contribution with relevance to crisis management in Europe after the Cold War.

201 **Peace to Crisis in Europe: Preparedness and Transition.**
John Garnett, JRA Macmillan, Kenneth Hunt, Clive Rose. London:
Royal United Services Institute for Defence Studies, 1986. 37p.
(Whitehall Paper no. 2).

This paper, which consists of essays by the four contributors, starts from the assumption that too little attention has been given to the consultation and crisis management procedures within NATO or to the process of rising tension through crisis to war. The paper attempts to describe this transition in ways which highlight both the strengths and the weaknesses of the NATO procedures. Both John Garnett and Kenneth Hunt highlight the weaknesses and problems, with Garnett arguing that although the alliance has improved pre-crisis consultation, this would not guarantee that the allies would agree on what steps should be taken in a crisis. Kenneth Hunt has a brief but useful outline of the NATO alert and mobilization system for crisis management. The final essay by Clive Rose, a former British permanent representative on the North Atlantic Council, highlights some of tensions and dilemmas inherent in crisis management in the alliance and offers some suggestions for dealing with them more effectively.

202 **Crisis Management in the Alliance.**
Gerd Schmuckle. *Washington Quarterly*, vol. 6, no. 3
(Summer 1983), p. 80-88.
Schmuckle highlights weaknesses in NATO's crisis management system including the clumsy structure of the three top headquarters, the resulting slowness of the command and control system, and the lack of machinery for dealing with out-of-area crises. He argues that the maintenance of effective cooperation within the alliance must be given high priority. In addition, Schmuckle argues, NATO should eliminate its military committee and its military staff – a step which would shorten the decision-making process. Further improvement could be made through the creation of a crisis and defence cabinet composed of deputy prime ministers of Britain, France, Germany and Italy who would participate in the United States President's decision-making process. As well as considering possible objections to this, the article outlines other ways in which NATO's capacity for crisis management could be improved, including making better use of exercises.

203 **Command Performance: The Neglected Dimension of European Security.**
Paul B. Stares. Washington, DC: Brookings Institution, 1991. 240p.
Based on an extensive range of interviews, this important book provides an authoritative, comprehensive and detailed study of NATO's mobilization and alert system, as well as its command, control and communication capabilities. An impressive analysis which fills a major gap in the literature, it looks at the importance of command and control in previous wars, at the way in which NATO had planned to move from peace to war and at the arrangements for command in the event of a war with the Soviet Union. The book has a number of helpful tables, figures and appendices outlining command arrangements. Although the issue discussed is of less importance as a result of the changes of 1989 and 1990, the author has a useful final chapter recommending ways in which NATO can be re-oriented for the challenges of the new Europe.

204 **"I don't need your handkerchiefs": Holland's Experience of Crisis Consultation in NATO.**
Cees Wiebes, Bert Zeeman. *International Affairs*, vol. 66, no. 1
(January 1990), p. 91-114.
Examines conflicts of interest and the process of consultation between the United States and the smaller NATO allies in three international crises – the Cuban Missile Crisis, the Soviet invasion of Czechoslovakia in 1968, and the shooting down of KAL 007 in 1983. The unresolved issues include procedures for crisis management, political consultation, and the role of the smaller NATO members in these processes. The authors are critical of the United States and conclude that Washington often acts unilaterally and then demands European support. In these circumstances, they conclude, the internal cohesion of NATO will not continue indefinitely.

205 **NATO Crisis Management: Dilemmas and Tradeoffs.**
Phil Williams. *Washington Quarterly*, vol. 12, no. 2 (Spring 1989),
p. 29-40.
Looks at the problems, dilemmas and trade-offs associated with NATO's planning for crisis management. The author identifies such dilemmas as the need for responsiveness

versus the need for certainty, the problem of categorizing the type of crisis NATO might find itself faced with, the difficulties of achieving consensus, the preparedness–provocation dilemma, and the competing pressures of political and military considerations. The article also includes several suggestions whereby NATO might improve its capacity for crisis management.

206 **Crisis De-escalation: A Relevant Concern in the New Europe.**
James A. Winnefeld.   Santa Monica, California: July 1990. 29p.
(Rand Note N-3153-CC).

Prepared as part of a project on 'avoiding nuclear war: managing conflict in the nuclear age' supported by the Carnegie Corporation, this paper contains an illuminating analysis of an issue that is often neglected. The author contends that greater attention needs to be given to planning for de-escalation and force disengagement in crises. He highlights several kinds of crises that could take place in post-Cold War Europe and suggests that improvements are needed in planning, in forces and hardware for peacekeeping and crisis communication and in the political frameworks – both inside and outside NATO – for managing conflict in Europe.

The Evolution of NATO Strategy

Extended deterrence

207   America in the 1980s: Reframing our Relations with our Friends and among our Allies.
McGeorge Bundy.   *Survival*, vol. 24, no. 1 (January/February 1982), p. 24-28.
A brief but important contribution to the debate over extended deterrence in which the former National Security Adviser to Presidents Kennedy and Johnson attempts to place the threat posed to NATO by the SS-20 in proper perspective. Bundy argues that in a world of strategic nuclear redundancy political intention is constrained not by the capability of opposing systems but by the inescapable risks of escalation in any use of nuclear weapons that might trigger a response by a nuclear adversary. Bundy also argues that this uncertainty equally applies to a large-scale conventional encounter in Europe. His argument that the certainty of risk and uncertainty is what deters sane leaders is the basis of what subsequently became known as existential deterrence. The implication of this in the NATO context was that Alliance strategy and doctrine mattered far less than the possibility that any war in Europe between East and West, even if it started at the conventional level, could result in large-scale nuclear warfare. And it was this possibility which was most important in maintaining peace.

208   Extended Deterrence: The United States and NATO Europe.
Stephen J. Cimbala.   Lexington, Massachusetts: D. C. Heath, 1987. 229p.
A detailed and useful analysis of the problems of extended deterrence in Europe with suggestions as to how some of the dilemmas can be resolved and some of the risks reduced. The author, a prolific writer on strategic issues, deals with Soviet strategy, operations and objectives, and with the strategic dimensions of any conflict in Europe. The book contains a very useful discussion of some vexing strategic issues such as escalation and coupling and also covers the United States maritime strategy which is an often ignored element in extended deterrence. Although some of the author's

recommendations have been rendered moot by the developments of 1989 and 1990, this remains a useful book for anyone interested in the central strategic dilemmas that traditionally faced NATO.

209 What Interdependence for NATO?
Malcolm W Hoag. *World Politics*, vol. 12, no. 3 (April 1960), p. 369-390.

Argues the case for maintaining strategic interdependence between the United States and Western Europe based on a combination of American strategic nuclear forces to deter Soviet nuclear aggression and sizeable non-nuclear forces to deal with more limited contingencies. The argument is that this would avoid the need to build strategic nuclear forces in Europe and therefore prove less costly. The author acknowledges that there are continued costs to reliance on allies and that European theatre forces would remain vulnerable to nuclear attack.

210 Extended Deterrence and the Prevention of War.
Paul K. Huth. New Haven, New Jersey; London: Yale University Press, 1988. 227p.

A conceptual and empirical analysis of extended deterrence, this study does not focus specifically on the Atlantic relationship. Nevertheless, for those who are interested in the conditions under which extended deterrence is likely to succeed or fail, this book is useful reading. The author goes well beyond many of the issues that are normally discussed in relation to extended deterrence in Europe.

211 NATO: The Next Thirty Years.
Henry A. Kissinger. *Survival*, vol. 21, no. 6 (November/December 1979), p. 264-268.

An important article in which Kissinger cast considerable doubt upon the validity of the United States nuclear guarantee to Western Europe and suggested that the reassurances that he had provided as US Secretary of State had been meaningless. He identified the features of the changing strategic context which had led him to this conclusion and also made some suggestions about what NATO should do in response.

212 Can Europe's Security be 'Decoupled' from America?
Andrew J. Pierre. *Foreign Affairs*, vol. 51, no. 4 (July 1973), p. 761-777.

Examines concerns over the possibility that the United States nuclear guarantee might be removed from Western Europe. The author looks at the issue in relation to the arms control negotiations. He concludes that much depends on domestic attitudes in the United States and that consequently Washington should not link security and divisive economic issues.

213 Counterforce and Alliance: The Ultimate Connection.
Earl C. Ravenal. *International Security*, vol. 6, no. 4 (Spring 1982), p. 26-43.

Arguing that a counterforce strategy stems from the logic of extended deterrence, the author, a long-time critic of the United States commitment to NATO, identifies what he sees as the weaknesses and paradoxes of such an approach. He notes the tension between the idea of coupling – which depends on escalation being virtually automatic – and the United States desire for firebreaks and thresholds – which would help to control escalation. The tension between crisis stability and extended deterrence is also explored, and the author uses this as a rationale for the United States reorienting its policy away from Europe.

214 **Europe without America: The Erosion of NATO.**
Earl Ravenal. *Foreign Affairs*, vol. 63, no. 4 (Summer 1985),
p. 1020-1035.

Argues that the alliance between the American right and the European left directed against NATO is a response to the danger and incredibility of the United States nuclear guarantee to Western Europe. The author considers the logic of extended deterrence and suggests that efforts to patch it up have failed. The author favours a progressive but thorough United States disengagement from the defence of Europe.

215 **The Political Implications of Strategic Parity.**
Walter B. Slocombe. London: International Institute for Strategic
Studies, May 1971. 32p. (Adelphi Paper 77).

A comprehensive and incisive examination of the impact of the Soviet attainment of strategic parity on United States strategy (especially related to limited nuclear options), on Soviet–American confrontations, and on the extension of deterrence to the European allies. The author argues that parity does not really undermine United States credibility since deterrence in Europe 'rests not on technical ability to make a particular kind of response or the validity of any particular strategic doctrine, but on the disastrous effects on the national self-interests of the United States of a successful Soviet attack on Western Europe' (p. 22). Although he also recognizes that parity can change perceptions, this is a balanced and thoughtful analysis which recognizes that deterrence is as much political and psychological as it is military.

216 **Extended Deterrence.**
Walter B. Slocombe. *Washington Quarterly*, vol. 7, no. 4 (Fall 1984),
p. 93-103.

Slocombe describes the problem of extended deterrence in an interesting way. He defines the problem as one concerning the credibility of retaliation when the consequences are suicidal. He also argues that extended deterrence has long been in crisis – and considers the response of the Alliance. One has been to seek alternatives to nuclear response through greater reliance on conventional forces; the other has sought to make nuclear weapons more usable and less suicidal either through changes in nuclear strategy or through nuclear-sharing arrangements or force deployments in Europe. Slocombe outlines a four-point programme for the Alliance, but concludes that extended deterrence will work so long as the independence of Western Europe is seen as essential to the independence of the United States itself. A tightly argued and incisive analysis.

217 **Extended Deterrence: Some Observations.**
Richard Smoke. *Naval War College Review*, vol. 36, no. 5
(September-October 1983), p. 37-49.

Re-examines the problem of extended deterrence which has been central to so many of NATO's strategic problems since the inception of the Atlantic Alliance. The author looks at different strategic variants for extending deterrence and concludes that in the 1980s, although threats by NATO to engage in controlled escalation may lack credibility, the threat of uncontrolled escalation continues to have impact. A useful and persuasive analysis.

Flexible Response

218 **Power and Policy: Doctrine, the Alliance and Arms Control: Part I.**
London: International Institute for Strategic Studies, Spring 1986. 72p.
(Adelphi Paper 205).
The first in a series of three Adelphi Papers based on the 1985 IISS Annual Conference, this paper contains analyses by Supreme Allied Commander Europe, General Bernard Rogers, James A. Thomson, François Heisbourg, Air Vice-Marshal Bernard Jackson and Leon Sloss. The focus is on NATO strategy, the roles of theatre and strategic nuclear forces, and the issues surrounding defence planning and force modernization. The paper by General Rogers argues that although there are inadequacies in Flexible Response, what are needed are the tools to implement the existing strategy rather than shifts to a new strategy.

219 **Power and Policy: Doctrine, the Alliance and Arms Control, Part II.**
London: International Institute for Strategic Studies, 1986. 78p.
(Adelphi Paper 206).
This Adelphi Paper, consisting of articles from the 1985 Annual IISS Conference, focuses upon the interrelationships between the doctrinal choices made by NATO and the policies and strategic choices of the Warsaw Pact states. It also considers the impact of strategic choices on arms control and stability. Contributors include Dennis Gormley, Karsten Voigt, and Dennis Ross. There is also an interesting analysis by Johan Holst which explores NATO's dilemma in relation to strategies of punishment and denial.

220 **Power and Policy: Doctrine, the Alliance and Arms Control: Part III.**
London: International Institute for Strategic Studies, Spring 1986. 76p.
(Adelphi Paper 207).
The third of a series of three Adelphi Papers dealing with strategic choices for the Western Alliance and their impact. This paper, which contains essays by Richard Burt, Phillip Karber, Peter Stratmann, General Farrar-Hockley, and Robert Komer, focuses upon the problems of alliance cohesion and on the need to maintain an appropriate balance of effort and attention between the central front and the flanks and between defence in Europe and out-of-area contingencies. It also contains an excellent summary of the conference themes by the then director of IISS, Robert O'Neill.

221 **NATO Strategy and Nuclear Defense.**
Carl H. Amme Jr. New York: Greenwood Press, 1988. 188p.
Although this is a well-covered subject, the author sets it in an historical context in a way that it is very useful. He looks at both US and Soviet strategy in Europe as well as

the strategic concepts and preferences of the major European allies. A second section of the book deals with the military confrontation in Europe, highlighting imbalances and asymmetries in force postures, arms control in Central Europe, and plans for the use of tactical nuclear weapons in the local battle. The third part focuses on the control of nuclear weapons and offers a critical examination of Flexible Response. The book also contains a useful, if not comprehensive, bibliographical essay.

222 **NATO without France: a Strategic Appraisal.**
Carl H. Amme, Jr. Stanford, California: Hoover Institution, 1967. 195p.
Written in the aftermath of the French withdrawal from the NATO integrated military organization, this study looks at some of the implications of the denial of French territory to NATO. It also looks at the conflict over NATO strategy which helped to precipitate the French withdrawal, highlighting points of both convergence and divergence in the strategies of the United States, the major European members of the Alliance, and the Soviet Union. The volume is also good on imbalances, asymmetries, and instabilities in force posture and provides considerable detail on some of the more tactical aspects related to possible conflict in Europe.

223 **The Great Debate: Theories of Nuclear Strategy.**
Raymond Aron. Garden City, New York: Doubleday, 1965. 265p.
A masterpiece of strategic erudition by the famous French philosopher, sociologist and strategist. Aron looks at the divergent strategic preferences of the United States and Western Europe in the 1960s and comments upon the debate in NATO with a fascinating mixture of insight and empathy on the one side and ruthless strategic logic on the other. An important book which well repays another look by those interested in the evolution of NATO strategy.

224 **NATO Strategy: The Case for a New Strategic Concept.**
John Baylis. *International Affairs*, vol. 64, no. 1 (Winter 1987/1988), p. 43-60.
Argues that NATO's strategy of Flexible Response adopted in 1967 suffers from serious shortcomings. The author also considers several proposals for its replacement, while highlighting the bureaucratic and political restraints on NATO decision-making. Consideration is given to 'no first use' and the notion of an extended firebreak as the major alternatives, and the advantages and shortcomings of both approaches are outlined. John Baylis considers how an extended firebreak would differ from Flexible Response and questions whether a gross disparity really exists between NATO and Warsaw Pact conventional forces. He concludes that NATO needs to recognize the weaknesses of Flexible Response and to take action to overcome these weaknesses.

225 **The Western Alliance and the McNamara Doctrine.**
Leonard Beaton. London: International Institute for Strategic Studies, August 1964. 12p. (Adelphi Paper 11).
An incisive analysis of the evolution of United States nuclear strategy in the Kennedy Administration and the implications of the innovations for the United States security guarantee to Western Europe. Is very good on the subtleties of the doctrinal changes introduced by United States Secretary of Defense Robert McNamara.

226 **Escalation and the Nuclear Option.**
Bernard Brodie. Princeton, New Jersey: Princeton University Press, 1966. 151p.

An important critique of the McNamara strategy and the emphasis that the United States, during the 1960s, placed on conventional defence as the main element of deterrence in Europe. This was something that the European members of NATO disliked but that most American analysts seemed to favour. Brodie was an exception – for reasons he develops in this highly readable and incisive volume. He argues that the most important threshold is not that between conventional and nuclear weapons but that between peace and war. In his view the distinction between non-war and possible destruction was crucial. Building up the capacity to fight a conventional war would weaken rather than strengthen this. The analysis was an important contribution to the strategy debate in NATO in the 1960s and one which helped to strengthen the European position and preference.

227 **The Nature and Practice of Flexible Response: NATO Strategy and Theater Nuclear Forces since 1967.**
Ivo H. Daalder. New York: Columbia University Press, 1991. 411p.

A major study which examines the NATO strategy of Flexible Response in terms of the debate about the credibility of extended deterrence. It focuses not on the origins of Flexible Response so much as the Alliance debate which followed the adoption of the strategy in 1967. The author highlights the different interpretations which were put on Flexible Response by different nations, but shows how, in spite of these, the Alliance was able to maintain a high degree of cohesion. Daalder argues very convincingly that the differences over Flexible Response reflected more fundamental differences both about the seriousness of the threat and about the likelihood and nature of escalation. While he effectively outlines the conceptual issues at the heart of NATO's long debate over Flexible Response, however, he also provides an excellent account of the continuing debates about nuclear force modernization. The study is based on extremely thorough research and provides a very good companion to Jane Stromseth's volume on the origins of Flexible Response (*see* item no. 233). It is a must for any serious student of NATO strategy.

228 **The Evolution of NATO's Strategy of Flexible Response: A Reinterpretation.**
John S. Duffield. *Security Studies*, vol. 1, no. 1 (Autumn 1991), p. 132-156.

A 'revisionist' account of the origins of NATO's strategy of Flexible Response (or MC14/3 as it was commonly known in NATO) which suggests that it was not the major turning point in the evolution of NATO strategy it is often purported to be. The author argues that the Alliance had already moved away from exclusive reliance on massive retaliation with the adoption of MC14/2 – also known as the Pause concept – in 1957. While this is persuasive, his other argument that the Kennedy Administration was willing to work within the parameters of MC14/2 and did not want a formal review is less compelling. Nevertheless, this is an interesting and provocative addition to the literature on the evolution of NATO strategy.

229 **NATO Myths.**
Lawrence Freedman.   *Foreign Policy*, no. 45 (Winter 1981-82),
p. 48-68.
Argues that although NATO depends on the myth that it would go nuclear if necessary, the Soviet Union must still take this myth seriously. Freedman argues that NATO's nuclear strategy nevertheless survives more on its comparative lack of expense than its merits and shows how it has been undermined by American hawks who have been searching for a technological fix on the one side and the disarmers on the other. He concludes that NATO should develop a more compelling conventional strategy – and a doctrine to accompany it.

230 **The Great Strategy Debate: NATO's Evolution in the 1960s.**
Richard Kugler.   Santa Monica, California: Rand Corporation, 1991.
146p. (Rand Note N-3252-FF/RC).
Part of a larger study on the history of NATO's conventional defence forces and strategy, this note focuses on the transatlantic debate of the 1960s over the balance between conventional and nuclear components of NATO strategy. It looks at the Kennedy Administration's initial demands for reform in 1961-62, the period of conflict and consensus formation from 1963 to 1966 and the period of decision-making and policy execution which went through to early 1969. It argues that although NATO cohesion was severely tested the final results were very positive for the Alliance, enhancing deterrence and providing a greater capacity for forward defence. A detailed and rich study, this note includes a helpful discussion of the Multilateral Force episode as well as a good analysis of the changes in NATO's conventional forces and their relationship to the changes in strategy.

231 **NATO's Non-Nuclear Needs.**
Lawrence C. McQuade.   *International Affairs*, vol. 40, no. 1
(January 1964), p. 11-21.
Written during a period of considerable contention in NATO over the appropriate strategy for the Alliance, this article focuses on three problems facing NATO in the first half of the 1960s: reaching consensus on the immediacy of the communist threat, choosing a preferred strategy, and deciding on the allocation of defence resources. After discussing possible military contingencies the author concludes that small, ambiguous crises at the non-nuclear level are most likely. Nevertheless, NATO's shortcomings in combat readiness represent a continued weakness which could be alleviated through increased allocations of resources by the European allies. This was a fairly standard argument for the early 1960s.

232 **NATO's Strategic Doctrine.**
Timothy W. Stanley.   *Survival*, vol. 11, no. 11 (November 1969),
p. 342-349.
This article, reprinted from *Orbis*, looks at the determinants and components of NATO strategy. The author argues that Flexible Response, as adopted by NATO in 1967, has two main components – an 'assured response' (i.e. the certainty of some response that would lead to a substantial and sustained fire fight), and the willingness and ability of NATO to escalate. The escalation may involve extension of the battlefield, but at some point will require that NATO initiate the use of nuclear weapons. The author looks at the capabilities necessary to implement this strategy.

233 **The Origins of Flexible Response: NATO's Debate over Strategy in the 1960s.**
Jane E. Stromseth. London: Macmillan, 1988. 274p.

This volume is the definitive work on the NATO debate during the 1960s over the extent to which it should rely on nuclear weapons as the key element in its deterrent strategy. It looks at the origins of the Kennedy Administration's shift to Flexible Response and greater reliance on conventional forces as well as the responses of France, Britain and the Federal Republic of Germany to United States proposals. The analysis, which is based on an extensive series of interviews both in the United States and Western Europe shows how the United States sent mixed signals to its allies about precisely what it wanted. The volume also highlights the patterns of convergence and divergence in the national responses of the three major European allies. The book argues very convincingly that the strategy formally adopted by NATO in January 1968 was both a military and a political compromise, one of the main merits of which was that it was capable of very flexible interpretation. A final chapter looks at the efforts to improve NATO's conventional forces during the 1980s and shows how the debate over NATO strategy in this period had many echoes of the debate of the 1960s. The study is extremely thorough and the references provide details of further documentation.

Nuclear sharing

234 **The Sharing of Nuclear Responsibility – A Problem in Need of Solution.**
André Beaufre. *International Affairs*, vol. 41, no. 3 (July 1965), p. 411-419.

Written by an eminent French strategic analyst, this article focuses on the nuclear problem within the Atlantic Alliance and the divergences among United States, British, French and German perspectives on the issue. It considers the tensions between European nuclear aspirations and United States efforts to maintain control over NATO nuclear strategy. Emphasis is placed on the position of Germany as a potential battleground with no voice in the decision to use nuclear weapons. The French position is also articulated. Beaufre argues that with nuclear stockpiles on its territory France wants a voice in nuclear planning and decision-making. European antipathy towards the Multilateral Force idea is discussed as is the British proposal for an Atlantic Nuclear Force (ANF) as an alternative. The article calls for a review of NATO strategy and a shift from defence to deterrence, and proposes new guidelines for decision-making and the creation of a crisis management system to coordinate national nuclear forces in time of war.

235 **The Reorganization of NATO.**
Kurt Birrenbach. *Orbis*, vol. 6, no. 2 (Summer 1962), p. 244-257.

Identifies and assesses the arguments of the European allies for co-determination on nuclear issues. It is suggested that this is primarily a political and not a military issue and that the allies should not carry demands for co-determination too far. At the same time the author urges closer cooperation within NATO through military integration, coordination of disarmament policy, and the development of equal burden-sharing.

236 **Tensions within the Alliance.**
Robert R. Bowie. *Foreign Affairs*, vol. 42, no. 1 (October 1963), p. 49-69.
Explains the tensions in Atlantic relations in the early 1960s in terms of differences over how to organize the West. Looks at rival American and French conceptions and concludes that the position of Britain has generally been disruptive. Sees the issue of nuclear sharing as crucial and presents a case for an integrated Atlantic nuclear force.

237 **Strategy and the Atlantic Alliance.**
Robert R. Bowie. *International Organization*, vol. 17, no. 3 (Summer 1963), p. 709-732.
Looks at the changing strategic balance and the implications of this for NATO strategy. Like many other American analysts in this period, Bowie saw larger conventional options as desirable. He also looks at the question of nuclear sharing in NATO, and argues that neither US monopoly nor independent national forces are adequate and prefers an integrated multilateral force. This proposal is fully spelled out in the article. What made this so significant is that Bowie was one of the major architects of the MLF idea within the State Department.

238 **The Multilateral Force: A Study in Alliance Politics.**
Alastair Buchan. *International Affairs*, vol. 40, no. 4 (October 1964), p. 619-637.
Traces the origin of the idea of a multilateral nuclear force, looks at the response of the European allies, and shows how it became entangled in both United States and West European politics. The author concludes that the episode may prove to be no more than a detour on the road to a more effective system of strategic planning in the alliance.

239 **The Control of NATO Nuclear Forces in Europe.**
Marco Carnovale. Boulder, Colorado: Westview Press, 1993. 302p.
Focuses on the problems of control of nuclear weapons in NATO in periods of crisis or war – and to a lesser extent on 'safety and security' in peacetime. The author acknowledges that the issue is predominantly political, and suggests that because of the divergence between United States and European views, nuclear control arrangements in NATO have been deliberately ambiguous. The author considers systems under 'dual key' control of the United States and a European ally, United States forces intended for the European theatre, and the British nuclear force. In each case he analyses the apparatus of control. A detailed study which deals effectively with the technical and political complexities surrounding the issue.

240 **European Deterrence and Atlantic Unity.**
James E. Dougherty. *Orbis*, vol. 6, no. 3 (Fall 1962), p. 371-421.
Looks at the nuclear issue in Atlantic relations in the early 1960s and the nuclear policies of Britain and France. It is suggested that the European desire for nuclear weapons is based partly on the fear that the United States will use nuclear weapons unwisely. Such concerns could be reduced through closer cooperation and intensified consultation. The author notes General de Gaulle's desire that the European Community emerge as a third force between the United States and USSR and claims

that France is more concerned about US influence than Soviet influence. Although a Western European deterrent would be preferable to national deterrent capabilities, even if such a deterrent is created, the United States must stay in Europe to protect non-members of the European Community, coordinate planning and keep Moscow from using divide-and-conquer strategies. An interesting contribution to the debate over nuclear sharing in NATO.

241   **The U.S. Plan for a NATO Nuclear Deterrent.**
Christopher Emmet.   *Orbis*, vol. 7, no. 2 (Summer 1963), p. 265-277.
Looks at arguments for a European and a NATO multilateral deterrent and contends that it would be easier for Washington to share nuclear secrets with a European group in which the United States also has a voice. Moreover, it is suggested that a NATO deterrent would quieten fears of a Franco-German dominated nuclear force. Other disadvantages of a strictly European force are also highlighted, as are the limits of the French *force de frappe*. The relation of conventional forces to the United States nuclear deterrent is also explored and it is argued that the Europeans must increase their manpower contributions to NATO.

242   **LBJ and the Presidential Management of Foreign Relations.**
Paul Y. Hammond.   Austin, Texas: University of Texas Press, 1992. 288p.
A perceptive analysis of Lyndon Johnson's foreign policy which covers the nuclear sharing issue in NATO as one of its three major case-studies. The author examines the MLF issue within the broader framework of both alliance politics and domestic politics in the United States. He also makes some important observations on how influence is exercised in NATO, observations which have relevance well beyond the particularities of the MLF issue.

243   **NATO's Nuclear Crisis.**
William Kintner.   *Orbis*, vol. 6, no. 2 (Summer 1962), p. 217-243.
Argues that NATO's deterrent strategy is not very effective because the Soviets doubt US resolve to use nuclear weapons, especially with regard to political warfare such as the Berlin crisis. Although Kennedy's fear of nuclear escalation led to reliance on conventional weapons in Europe, Soviet conventional troops are armed with nuclear weapons. Consequently, the United States should enhance nuclear deterrence by providing nuclear weapons to the European NATO countries. Kintner argues that NATO must have flexibility in the types of weapons available, must see nuclear defence as morally right, and must have symmetry with the USSR on all weapons. He proposes the creation of a NATO nuclear strike force to give European members greater say in alliance decision-making and suggests that the failure of the United States to share its nuclear assets could divide the alliance.

244   **Nuclear Sharing in NATO and the Multilateral Force.**
Wilfrid L. Kohl.   *Political Science Quarterly*, vol. 80, no. 1 (March 1965), p. 88-109.
A judicious and balanced account of the nuclear sharing problem in NATO which looks at the political and military dimensions of the issue. Kohl concludes that the United States should not press for it if the allies are not receptive.

245 The Case for Nuclear Sharing.
F. O. Miksche. *Orbis*, vol. 5, no. 3 (Fall 1961), p. 292-305.
Argues that nuclear weapons have become a crutch for NATO and that the smaller nations have little influence over nuclear decisions, a situation that has led to growing doubts in non-atomic NATO countries. The author considers a range of solutions. Strengthening conventional forces is seen as expensive and the author suggests that it might be preferable to encourage more countries to acquire nuclear weapons and become responsible for their own defence.

246 NATO's Nuclear Problems: Control or Consultation?
Frederick W. Mulley. *Orbis*, vol. 8, no. 1 (Spring 1964), p. 21-35.
Starting from the failure of the Atlantic Alliance to reshape its policies since the US nuclear monopoly ended, this British politician examines the requirements of NATO strategy and emphasizes the importance of reconciling military and political needs. He suggests that there are no military advantages to MLF and that although it is intended to prevent the rise of a Franco-German military force there is no evidence that Germany is interested in having nuclear weapons.

247 Decentralizing Nuclear Control in NATO.
Timothy W. Stanley. *Orbis*, vol. 7, no. 1 (Spring 1963), p. 41-48.
A knowledgeable analysis of the major nuclear forces of NATO. The author identifies two categories of strategic forces: counterforce capabilities which have been and will continue to be under US control, and purely retaliatory forces which are more open to decentralization, and in relation to which the United States might give up its veto. A distinction is also made between battlefield nuclear weapons and medium-range missiles capable of interdiction. The author believes that a continued US monopoly on control of nuclear weapons is a major problem for Europe and that some decentralization of control in certain categories will end the political deadlock and lead to more efficient management of nuclear weapons in NATO.

248 The Cybernetic Theory of Decision: New Dimensions of Political Analysis.
John D. Steinbruner. Princeton, New Jersey: Princeton University Press, 1974. 366p.
Although this has a theoretical framework regarding the nature of decision-making, the substance of the volume deals with the politics of nuclear sharing between the United States and Western Europe between 1956 and 1964. The author examines the rise and demise of the Multilateral Nuclear Force and contends that the episode can be understood only in terms of traditional limits of rational decision-making.

249 Shaping the Postwar Balance of Power: Multilateralism in NATO.
Steve Weber. *International Organization*, vol. 46, no. 3 (Summer 1992), p. 633-680.
Argues that although the United States has been the dominant power in NATO it has provided security to the allies in ways which reflected multilateral principles. This was manifested in the Eisenhower Administration's plans for nuclear sharing, which the author argues was designed to speed the 'transformation of Europe into an integrated defence community' (p. 634). Under the Kennedy Administration, however, nuclear

strategy took precedence over politics and the scheme was recast in ways which made it unpalatable to the Europeans.

250 **Nuclear Consultation Processes in NATO.**
Thomas C. Wiegele. *Orbis*, vol. 16, no. 2 (Summer 1972), p. 462-487.
Looks at the concept of consultation and examines how it works in NATO, with particular reference to the mechanisms used to formulate nuclear policy. The author looks at the MLF experience and also identifies the agendas of the ten nuclear planning group (NPG) meetings held between 1967 and 1971. Consultation within the NPG is seen as taking place at three levels – ministerial, bilateral and multilateral national staff, and permanent staff. A valuable article which showed how NATO dealt with the problem of nuclear sharing through a consultative mechanism rather than the hardware solution of schemes such as the MLF.

251 **Nuclear Sharing: NATO and the N+1 Country.**
Albert Wohlstetter. *Foreign Affairs*, vol. 39, no. 3 (April 1961), p. 355-387.
An important article which had considerable impact during the 1960s on American military thinking about the European security problem. Wohlstetter looks at the problem of extended deterrence and nuclear sharing and identifies four alternatives: rejection of nuclear weapons and of the American nuclear guarantee; the development of independent national nuclear forces; the idea of a NATO multilateral force in which there is joint control over nuclear weapons and, finally, continued reliance on the American nuclear guarantee. Having argued that the repudiation of nuclear weapons understates the conflict of interest between East and West, that independent national nuclear forces would not only lack credibility but would also cause serious command and control problems; that jointly controlled nuclear forces would weaken rather than strengthen NATO; Wohlstetter claimed that the American nuclear guarantee was the best option for both Western Europe and the United States. Although this was not an assessment that was shared in Europe, especially in France and Britain, it was reflected in Secretary McNamara's speech in Ann Arbor in 1962 in which he attacked independent nuclear deterrent forces as dangerous, expensive, prone to obsolescence and lacking in credibility.

General strategy

252 **Operations FM100-5.**
Washington, DC: Department of the Army, August 1982. 182p.
This document provided the US Army's war-fighting manual and, as such, had considerable relevance for American strategy in NATO. It made clear throughout that the US Army must be capable of operating on a nuclear and chemical battlefield. The document describes US Army operational doctrine and emphasizes manoeuvre and movement rather than attrition; combined arms warfare; and cooperative actions with other services and allies. It provides the basis for the notion of the Airland Battle which was adopted by US forces for the European theatre and subsequently became the basic concept for the prosecution of hostilities in the war in the Gulf in 1991.

253   Cruise Missiles: Technology, Strategy, Politics.

Edited by Richard C. Betts.   Washington, DC: Brookings Institution, 1981. 612p.

As its title suggests, this is a comprehensive analysis of the cruise missile which covers the technologies involved, the kind of missions – including those in the European theatre – for which it might be used and the arms control dimension. The section on the politics of cruise missiles has a very informative chapter on NATO alliance politics by Gregory Treverton, one on the European nuclear powers by Lawrence Freedman, and one on Germany and the non-nuclear NATO countries by Catherine Kelleher. For those interested in the Intermediate Nuclear Forces debate of the early 1980s this book provides valuable background and should be regarded as essential reading.

254   Conflict Termination in Europe: Games against War.

Stephen J. Cimbala.   New York: Praeger, 1990. 268p.

Goes well beyond its title to examine how war might start as well as end in Europe. The author considers problems of pre-emption and the notion of stability and relates these to Soviet strategy and Soviet thinking about war termination. His main theme is that NATO needs to think through the problem prior to the outbreak of war. The author has a particularly good chapter on Soviet and Western concepts of escalation. The book is better than the timing of its publication.

255   European Security and France.

François De Rose.   London: Macmillan, 1984. 143p.

The volume, written by a well-known French strategic analyst of European security issues, has a preface by Henry Kissinger and a series of trenchant observations on both NATO and French strategy. The author argues that conventional defence capabilities need to be enhanced so that NATO strategy is not one of inflexible response. As well as warning of the dangers of Western Europe being decoupled from the United States, De Rose also argues that the Europeans should have greater responsibility for the security of Europe and that the European Community should assume a role in defence matters. An appendix looks at the specific requirements for effective NATO conventional defence.

256   Beyond First-Use.

Jonathan Dean.   *Foreign Policy*, no. 48 (Fall 1982), p. 37-53.

A useful contribution to the debate over No First Use and strengthening conventional forces which helps to explain why reliance on nuclear weapons became such a controversial issue in the early 1980s. The author argues that one of the real issues is whether a strategy of First Use is politically sustainable. Dean argues that arms control and more innovative approaches to conventional defence by NATO could go a long way towards defusing the issue.

257   The Price of Peace: Living with a Nuclear Dilemma.

Lawrence Freedman.   New York: Henry Holt, 1986. 288p.

This book, by the Professor of War Studies at King's College, London, brings together a series of articles, book chapters and papers written by Freedman in the early 1980s as part of the continuing debate over nuclear weapons. It contains several chapters about NATO strategy and force posture, including one which provides an incisive critique of flexible response. Another chapter looks critically at the concept of escalation. In addition, Freedman looks at the causes of the crisis in Atlantic relations in the early 1980s, and the negotiations on nuclear forces in Europe from 1969 to 1983. All the essays manage to be both sensible and lively and remain well worth looking at.

258 **The Airland Battle Doctrine: NATO Strategy and Arms Control in Europe.**
Manfred R. Hamm. *Comparative Strategy*, vol. 7, no. 3 (1988), p. 183-211.

A comprehensive and helpful discussion of the Airland Battle concept which looks at its origins, and its key components. The author also distinguishes it very clearly from the concept of Follow-on Forces Attack (FOFA). He examines the various critiques of Airland Battle and its relationship to arms control in Europe. The author concludes that Airland Battle, along with FOFA, could significantly enhance NATO's capacity to fight outnumbered in Central Europe.

259 **Reassurance and Deterrence: Western Defence in the 1980s.**
Michael Howard. *Foreign Affairs*, vol. 61, no. 2 (Winter 1982-83), p. 309-324.

An article by an eminent British historian which argues that virtually from the outset of the Alliance, the American military presence was wanted in Western Europe not simply as a deterrent to the Soviet Union but as a reassurance for the West European allies. During the 1950s the Europeans were so reassured that they wanted defence on the cheap – and therefore found reliance on American nuclear weapons a comfortable option. The problem, however, was that this option meant that European armed forces became peripheral to a nuclear deterrent, the ultimate control of which lay elsewhere. One result of this was that the European populations began to see the commitment of American power to the security of Western Europe not as a source of reassurance but as a source of danger – a process that was intensified by the emergence of strategic parity. Accordingly, Howard argues the Europeans in the early and mid-1980s required reassurance not against the Soviet threat but against the danger of nuclear war. The final part of the article outlines ways in which deterrence and reassurance can once again be reconciled, placing considerable emphasis on enhanced European capacity for conventional defence.

260 **Problems of National Strategy: A Book of Readings.**
Edited by Henry A. Kissinger. New York: Praeger, 1965. 477p.

A very useful book of readings. Although most of the articles can easily be found elsewhere, the fact that they are generally of a very high quality and make an important contribution to the strategic debate of the 1960s makes this a useful compendium. Only one of the five sections of the volume deals with NATO, but the contributors to that section include Thomas Schelling, Albert Wohlstetter, Robert Bowie (who was one of the prime authors of the Multilateral Force proposal) and Bernard Brodie, as well as Alastair Buchan and Pierre Gallois. Together these authors provide contrasting views on some of the key strategic issues and debates in NATO. The arguments centre around NATO strategy and the appropriate balance between nuclear and conventional capabilities and emphases, and the issue of nuclear sharing in which the multilateral force idea figures prominently. Both the US strategy of flexible response and the MLF proposal find champions and critics in the selections chosen by Kissinger.

261 **New Weapons and NATO: Solutions or Irritations.**
Robert Kromer.   New York: Greenwood Press, 1987. 185p.
This book focuses on the impact of new weapons systems on political cohesion in
NATO. It looks at two case-studies: the development of small-yield tactical atomic
weapons in the 1950s and the introduction of precision-guided munitions (PGMs) in
the late 1960s and the 1970s. The author suggests that the tactical nuclear weapons
issue – in which the United States offered the use but not the control of these weapons,
accentuated American dominance in the Alliance. When set against other changes such
as European recovery this became debilitating as the Alliance in the 1960s became
convulsed in a major debate over strategy. As regards PGMs the results were mixed,
but there was not a significant shift by the European members of the Alliance towards
the adoption of these systems. The author concludes that the reluctance to capitalize
on the military benefits offered by precision weaponry stemmed from a divergence of
views on Alliance strategy fuelled by doubts about American credibility and
accentuated by domestic politics and divergent threat perceptions. Instead of removing
NATO's conventional weaknesses, PGMs simply helped to undermine political trust.
This is an unusual but helpful study which offers a distinct perspective and recognizes
that for NATO political cohesion was always at least as important as military strength.

262 **European Security in the 1990s: Deterrence and Defense after the INF
Treaty.**
Walter Laquer, Leon Sloss.   New York: Plenum Press, 1990. 214p.
Written by two eminent strategic analysts for the Center for National Security Studies,
Los Alamos National Laboratory, this book looks at the major issues facing NATO
prior to the revolution of 1989. It is particularly good on strategic issues and on future
requirements for theatre nuclear forces. It also contains a useful survey of the West
European defence horizon. Many of the arguments and contentions have, of course,
been overtaken by events. Nevertheless, there is an extremely useful appendix which
contains documents on European security from 1948 to 1989. This appendix makes up
almost half of the book and ensures that it is of continuing value.

263 **A Measured Defence for the West.**
Lester B. Pearson.   *Orbis*, vol. 1, no. 4 (Winter 1958), p. 428-434.
Written by the Canadian Foreign Minister who argues that the balance of conventional
weapons in favour of the Soviets is offset by a balance of nuclear weapons in favour of
the United States, so long as surprise attack cannot occur. Argues too that if only one
or two members of NATO make decisions on nuclear weapons usage, then this could
create tensions in the Alliance. Pearson also looks at alternatives to massive retaliation
and argues that the fear of attack would be lessened if European frontiers were
guarded by troops with tactical nuclear weapons. He argues that a weak defence places
onerous burdens on the United States and robs Europe of a stake in its own security.
Consequently, it is necessary to depart from the all-or-nothing approach.

264 **Inadvertent Nuclear War? Escalation and NATO's Northern Flank.**
Barry R. Posen.   *International Security*, vol. 7, no. 2 (Fall 1982),
p. 28-54.
A superb piece of strategic analysis which challenges the view that a major military
clash between NATO and the Warsaw Pact could be limited to conventional hostilities.
Posen starts from the assumption that escalation is not simply a matter of choice or
deliberate decision but is also something which can occur inadvertently and as the

unintended consequence of actions taken as part of a conventional war. The possibility that during conventional hostilities strategic nuclear weapons may be put in jeopardy could lead them to be used before they are lost. Inadvertent escalation is more likely to occur, however, because of offensive tendencies, the narrow distinction between offence and defence, and the 'fog of war'. The Northern Flank of NATO is an especially likely place because of its geography, the nature of the military forces deployed there, and the war-fighting strategy of the United States Navy which includes the forward operation of US attack submarines in the Norwegian and Barents Seas, offensive carrier group operations against the Kola peninsula, and a NATO naval counterattack to defend Norway. Posen argues that more civilian oversight is necessary to reduce the escalation tendency of Western conventional war plans. This is an excellent critique of proposals and strategies intended to raise the nuclear threshold by strengthening NATO's capacity for conventional war-fighting, but which actually might have made the use of nuclear weapons more likely.

265 **Inadvertent Escalation: Conventional War and Nuclear Risks.**
Barry R. Posen. Ithaca, New York: Cornell University Press, 1991.
280p.

A very impressive study which identifies ways in which conventional war between nuclear powers could escalate to include the use of nuclear weapons even though neither side wanted such an outcome. The author develops a model of inadvertent escalation, then looks at the European and maritime dimensions of a war between NATO and the Warsaw Pact and highlights various ways in which escalation could have occurred. The analysis is theoretically sophisticated and the author combines this with detailed knowledge of US and NATO strategy and operations. One of the basic themes is that conventional operations can threaten nuclear forces and thereby lead to pressure for the use of nuclear weapons. In this connection, the author is particularly critical of the United States maritime strategy. Another theme is that the military balance was much less unfavourable to NATO than was usually assumed and that a deliberate NATO decision to escalate was therefore less likely than often suggested. An excellent analysis of the escalatory perils and pitfalls of large-scale conventional war in Europe and at sea.

266 **Notes on the Military Problems of Europe.**
George W. Rathjens, Jr. *World Politics*, vol. 10, no. 2
(January 1958), p. 182-201.

Discusses some of the major problems of European security and NATO strategy in the late 1950s against the background of technological developments. Rathjens considers the objectives of major and minor powers in both general war and limited war, the definition of limitations, the circumstances in which war might be initiated, and the validity of alliances and military postures for the United States. The author argues that the main problem for NATO comes from limited threats.

267 **Defense or Retaliation: A German View.**
Helmut Schmidt. New York: Praeger, 1962. 264p.

A distinguished analysis by a distinguished author who was subsequently to become Minister of Defence and ultimately Chancellor of the Federal Republic of Germany. Schmidt argues that strategic and tactical nuclear weapons deter Soviet use only of strategic and tactical nuclear weapons and cannot be extended to deter conventional attack. The concomitant of this is the argument that NATO's conventional forces

The Evolution of NATO Strategy. General strategy

needed to be strengthened very substantially. As Minister of Defence, however, Schmidt placed rather more emphasis on the nuclear component of NATO strategy. The book contains a good appendix giving details of technical terms, a map with the order of battle of land armies in Central Europe, and a useful bibliography.

268   **The 1977 Alastair Buchan Memorial Lecture.**
       Helmut Schmidt.   *Survival*, vol. 20, no. 1 (January/February 1978),
       p. 2-10.

An important speech by the Chancellor of the Federal Republic of Germany which some see as the genesis of the NATO decision of December 1979 to modernize its long-range theatre nuclear forces. Schmidt argued that SALT codified the strategic balance, in a way which magnified the disparities between East and West in tactical nuclear and conventional weapons. Although it was the theatre nuclear disparities that became increasingly important in 1978 and 1979, Schmidt's remarks were directed primarily at the need to re-establish a conventional balance and/or make progress in conventional arms control.

269   **Terminating Major War in Europe.**
       John F. Scott.   Carlisle, Pennsylvania: Strategic Studies Institute,
       US Army War College, 1989. 87p.

Deals with an often neglected aspect of strategy in Europe – how a war might be brought to an end on terms that are satisfactory to both sides. The author looks at Soviet views on this issue and concludes that NATO needs to put in place both a structure and a strategy for war termination.

270   **European Security in the 1990s.**
       Edited by Dan Smith.   London: Pluto Press, 1989. 176p.

Edited by a leading figure in the British and European peace movements, this volume has eight chapters written by analysts who support alternative approaches to security. Among the themes covered are Soviet new thinking, United States decline, West European defence cooperation, nuclear weapons in Europe after the INF treaty, 'star wars' and the 'threat from the south'. A useful series of reflections on the changing European security agenda.

271   **Deterrence and Defense: Towards a Theory of National Security.**
       Glenn H. Snyder.   Princeton, New Jersey: Princeton University Press,
       1961. 294p.

A brilliant analysis of the relationship of denial and punishment in deterrence strategies. Although cast in much broader terms than NATO, in many respects this volume established the intellectual framework within which much of the debate over NATO strategy subsequently took place. It is essential reading for anyone who wants to understand the strategic debate in NATO during the 1960s.

272   **War in Europe: Nuclear and Conventional Perspectives.**
       Edited by Hylke Tromp.   Aldershot, England: Gower, 1989. 350p.

The book does four things. In the first place it considers how a nuclear war in Europe could start, how it would be fought and what the consequences would be. Second, it looks at the nuclear arms race and arms control in Europe. Third, the book has a series of chapters on alternative strategies for the defence of Europe. The fourth element is a critical assessment of some of the consequences of these alternative strategies and of defensive defence in particular. Containing 23 chapters with a variety of perspectives, this book offers a good overview of the defence debate that evolved in the 1980s. It contains a particularly incisive chapter by John Mearsheimer which offers a stinging critique of the arguments for the No First Use of nuclear weapons.

273 **NATO's Strategic Options: Arms Control and Defense.**
Edited by David S. Yost. New York: Pergamon, 1981. 258p.
A good collection of essays which looks at the nature of the Soviet threat, the prospects for conventional and nuclear arms control, and specific defence options including enhanced radiation weapons, improved command control and communications, and chemical warfare alternatives. Contributors include Peter Vigor, Richard Burt, Uwe Nerlich, and the editor himself.

Nuclear strategy

274 **NATO's Nuclear Modernization Dilemma.**
Hans Binnendijk. *Survival*, vol. 31, no. 2 (March/April 1989),
p. 137-155.
Examines the problems facing NATO as it considered the issue of modernizing its short-range nuclear forces in Europe in the aftermath of the INF Agreement. Military considerations suggested that the Alliance needed a Follow on to Lance (FOTL) but German domestic opinion was strongly against this. Binnendijk analyses the competing pressures. This article was intended as a guide to this debate. It explores the changing strategic setting, NATO's modernization plans, alternative nuclear force postures for NATO, and the arms control dimension. Although the author argued that finding the right balance between modernization and arms control would be difficult, events in Europe unfolded in a way which made the issue moot. Nevertheless, this provides a useful overview of the issues as they were seen in late 1988 and early 1989.

275 **Britain, NATO and Nuclear Weapons: Alternative Defense versus Alliance Reform.**
Ken Booth, John Baylis. London: Macmillan, 1989. 374p.
A book written by two friends and colleagues which encapsulates and elucidates many of the key issues in both the European and British defence debates of the 1980s. Ken Booth presents a case for alternative defence arrangements. He highlights the shortcomings of Britain's existing defence policy and offers arguments for moving towards a non-provocative defence policy and reciprocal or common security. John Baylis, in contrast, argues that what is needed is not radical change – because there are major political and military problems with entirely non-nuclear strategies – but significant reform. He presents the case for an extended firebreak strategy in which nuclear weapons would play a reserve role. The authors juxtapose their differing approaches rather than engaging in a point-by-point discussion. Nevertheless, this captures many of the key issues in the debate and the arguments are presented by both authors in a scholarly, rigorous and judicious manner. A useful and informed

contribution that avoids the emotionalism so characteristic of much of the nuclear debate of the 1980s.

276 **The Nuclear Confrontation in Europe.**
Edited by Jeffrey D. Boutwell, Paul Doty, Gregory F. Treverton.
London: Croom Helm, 1985. 247p.
Looks at the history of NATO's nuclear posture, the deployment of theatre nuclear forces in the 1980s, the role of third-country nuclear forces, nuclear weapons and NATO politics, Soviet force posture, nuclear weapons and the Warsaw Pact, and the future of the nuclear confrontation. As well as the editors, contributors include Lawrence Freedman, Condelezza Rice, Stephen Meyer and Timothy Ireland. A useful collection which brings out the interplay between strategic and political questions in relation to nuclear weapons in Europe.

277 **Tactical Nuclear Strategy and European Defence: Critical Reappraisal.**
Michael J. Brenner. *International Affairs*, vol. 51, no. 1
(January 1975), p. 23-42.
An incisive discussion of possible problems with proposals for reform of the tactical nuclear forces. The author identifies several problems with NATO's tactical nuclear strategy. These include the danger that early nuclear use would reduce diplomatic efforts; problems of command and control; the difficulty of limiting usage to the battlefield; and the possibility that the linkage of intercontinental ballistic missiles (ICBMs) in the US to weapons in Europe would lead to escalation. At the same time he makes clear that there are no easy answers when dealing with the problems of planning, nuclear control, credibility and escalation. This is an informed and judicious analysis.

278 **Strategy, Doctrine, and the Politics of Alliance: Theater Nuclear Force Modernization in NATO.**
Paul Buteux. Boulder, Colorado: Westview Press, 1983. 158p.
An interesting volume which deals with the political uses of strategic doctrine in NATO. It covers the neutron bomb and alliance strategy, the issue of forward-based systems, long-range nuclear forces and the Eurostrategic balance, long-range theatre nuclear force modernization, and the politics of nuclear consultation in NATO. Buteux rehearses the key arguments in a systematic and helpful fashion, but apart from his analysis of consultation does not add a great deal to material that is covered elsewhere. The quality of the printing of this volume leaves a great deal to be desired.

279 **The Politics of Nuclear Consultation in NATO, 1965-1980.**
Paul Buteux. Cambridge, England: Cambridge University Press, 1983. 292p.
This volume focuses on the political process within NATO whereby the members seek to achieve a consensus on nuclear policy. Having established the political and strategic background to the formation of the Nuclear Planning Group (NPG) and highlighted the problem of nuclear sharing, the author provides a very detailed account of the work of the NPG between 1965 and 1980. He looks at the initial McNamara proposal for a consultative group and traces the way this idea was modified and subsequently implemented. The activities of the group in establishing guidelines for the tactical use of nuclear weapons are outlined in some detail, as are the deliberations of the latter

half of the 1970s which culminated in the Long-range Theater Nuclear Force decision of December 1979. The author also offers some observations on the nature of the consultative process and on the implications of theatre nuclear weapons. This is a useful book which deals with an often neglected aspect of NATO.

280   **Massive Retaliation and Graduated Deterrence.**
A. W. Buzzard.   *World Politics*, vol. 8, no. 2 (January 1956), p. 228-237.

This contribution by a British Rear Admiral to the debate over NATO nuclear strategy started from the premise that the major problem was local rather than major aggression and that it would not be deterred by increasingly incredible threats of massive retaliation nor by inadequate conventional forces. The alternative, therefore, was to move to a strategy of 'graduated deterrence' based on the distinction between the tactical and strategic uses of nuclear weapons. Tactical nuclear weapons could be used as an intermediate option to repel local aggression without going to massive nuclear war. Buzzard argued that by not disclosing what level of military action would be employed, all wars would be made less likely.

281   **Cruise, Pershing, and SS-20: The Search for Consensus: Nuclear Weapons in Europe.**
John Cartwright, Julian Critchley.   London: Brassey's Defence Publishers, 1985. 163p. (A North Atlantic Assembly Report).

Written by two British members of Parliament who were the co-rapporteurs of the North Atlantic Assembly's Special Committee on Nuclear Weapons in Europe, this study provides a comprehensive analysis of the origins of NATO's modernization decision of December 1979, the accompanying arms control proposals and the subsequent controversy. The authors also look at how attitudes and policies on the issue evolved in key countries, with individual chapters on the United States, the Soviet Union, the Federal Republic of Germany, Britain, Italy, The Netherlands, Belgium and France. A very helpful and informative study which explains (among other things) how NATO agreed upon the figure of 572 missiles.

282   **NATO Strategies and Nuclear Weapons.**
Stephen J. Cimbala.   London: Pinter, 1989. 276p.

The title on the cover of this book differs from that on the title page – NATO Strategy and Nuclear Escalation. Nevertheless, this is a useful study which explores some of the key dilemmas and problems associated with NATO strategy. Recognizing that the Alliance may well evolve in unpredictable ways, the author identifies and explores the various functions of US and allied forces – deterrence, reassurance, denial, retaliation and control. He argues that the control function is central to everything else, yet least fully understood. Amongst the issues the author deals with are SDI, the Maritime Strategy, Flexible Targeting, and War Termination.

283   **Flexible Targeting, Escalation Control, and War in Europe.**
Stephen J. Cimbala.   *Armed Forces and Society*, vol. 12, no. 3 (Spring 1986), p. 383-400.

Highlights the difficulties of devising a strategy that maximizes both deterrence and escalation control, especially given the divergent geopolitical perspectives of the United States on the one side and the West Europeans on the other. The article also questions the extent to which the Soviet Union is likely to cooperate in escalation control, the difficulties of fighting a controlled war, and the dependency of flexible targeting and escalation control upon the existence of United States strategic defences. The author argues that improving NATO's conventional defence capabilities has ambiguous implications for escalation control. He concludes that deterrence in Europe rests upon the inescapable possibility that any conflict would expand beyond the control of Washington and Moscow and result in mutual assured destruction.

284   **The Neutron Bomb: Political, Technological and Military Issues.**
Samuel T. Cohen.   Cambridge, Massachusetts: Institute for Foreign
Policy Analysis, November 1978. 95p.
Written by a physicist who was one of the people responsible for development of the enhanced radiation warhead or neutron bomb, this book looks at the military and political issues associated with the controversy over development and deployment. It traces the history of the neutron bomb and looks at the debate over it in the Kennedy–Johnson years and the subsequent débâcle in the Carter Administration. The author also looks at the physical principles underlying the neutron bomb and highlights its military advantages, particularly for NATO. He makes a very strong case in favour of deploying the system. His discussion of the controversy of the late 1970s, however, reveals very clearly that these views were not universally shared.

285   **NATO Negotiations on the Intermediate-range Nuclear Forces, 1977-79.**
Don R. Drenth.   University of Pittsburgh, Pittsburgh, Pennsylvania:
1986. 34p. (Pew Case Study in Negotiation).
A straightforward and useful account of the pressures and concerns which led to NATO's decision of December 1979 to deploy 464 ground-launched cruise missiles and 108 Pershing IIs in Europe, while also negotiating with the Soviet Union about arms control. The author highlights European political and strategic concerns both before and after the neutron bomb fiasco, and looks at the deliberations of the High Level Group in NATO, as well as the final decision by the North Atlantic Council. There is little in the study that is new, but it offers a straightforward and effective account of the internal negotiations leading to a major strategic decision by NATO.

286   **Can America Fight a Limited Nuclear War?**
T. N. Dupuy.   *Orbis*, vol. 15, no. 1 (Spring 1961), p. 31-42.
An assessment of some of the fashionable ideas of the late 1950s about conflict in a nuclear environment. The author argues that the United States' focus on ground nuclear capabilities and the erroneous assumption that the European allies would take care of conventional defence has led to excessive dependence of NATO on nuclear weapons. Consideration is given to some of the problems of fighting and surviving in a nuclear environment and the forms that military adaptation might take. It is also suggested that preparing to fight a limited nuclear war would require astronomical budget expenditures, and although the author believes in being ready for feasible contingencies it is unclear whether limited nuclear war is feasible.

287 **Will Tactical Nuclear Weapons ever be Used?**
Philip W. Dyer. *Political Science Quarterly*, vol. 88, no. 2
(June 1973), p. 214-229.
Tactical nuclear weapons have always been an ambiguous weapon system. Their origin and development, their ranges and yields, their deployment in Europe and the doctrines governing their use have all raised serious questions which have never been fully or satisfactorily resolved. Consequently, the author argues, many conditions must be fulfilled before they would be used. He also suggests that it is significant that, during the Korean War when many of these conditions existed, the United States decided not to use its growing arsenal of tactical atomic weapons. He concludes that a weapon whose use cannot be realistically envisaged has little deterrent value.

288 **Project Vista and Nuclear Weapons in Europe.**
David C. Elliot. *International Security*, vol. 11, no. 1 (Summer 1986), p. 163-183.
In 1952, Project VISTA issued a report that advocated reliance on tactical nuclear weapons as a stronger deterrent to Soviet ground forces than strategic bombing. This report, which the Air Force tried to suppress, was one of the first attempts to base Western European security on theatre nuclear weapons. It both foreshadowed and influenced NATO's efforts to rely on tactical nuclear weapons as a compensation for its conventional deficiencies.

289 **The NATO Decision on Theater Nuclear Forces.**
Raymond Garthoff. *Political Science Quarterly*, vol. 98, no. 2
(Summer 1983), p. 197-214.
Garthoff's scholarly and informed review of the process of reaching the NATO decision in 1979 to deploy American Pershing II ballistic missiles and ground-launched cruise missiles (GLCM) in Europe reveals that a complex of internal alliance politics played at least as important a role as the perceived threat from the Soviet Union and its SS-20s. European concerns focused on the credibility of American assurances, and the American decision to support and then to advocate deployment was grounded not in American concerns over deterring the USSR from an attack, but the desire to reassure the Allies. Although in December 1979 this policy seemed to be a great success, the deployment became a divisive issue in alliance politics and in the national politics of several European NATO countries.

290 **NATO Needs a New Missile.**
Andrew Goldman. *Orbis*, vol. 32, no. 4 (Fall 1988), p. 541-550.
Argues that although tactical nuclear weapons have taken on greater importance in Europe, there are inadequacies both in the stockpile and procedures for use. In order to overcome these problems and restore deterrence, NATO must not only modernize its land-based tactical nuclear weapons but should also begin to transfer control of the weapons to the Europeans.

291 **Nuclear War in Suburbia.**
Gary L. Guertner. *Orbis*, vol. 26, no. 1 (Spring 1982), p. 42-69.
Argues that NATO should not only place greater emphasis on conventional defence rather than nuclear weapons but also that in doing this the Alliance could make far

better use of the natural terrain and the many small villages in the forward defence area in Germany. Guertner argues that this not only provides greater concealment for NATO troops but that a conventional defence offers greater prospect of limiting damage than do nuclear options. Improvements in this area would add credibility to NATO's deterrence posture.

292 **NATO and Nuclear Weapons: Reasons and Unreason.**
Stanley Hoffmann.   *Foreign Affairs*, vol. 60, no. 2 (Winter 1981/82), p. 327-346.
Argues that the controversy over nuclear weapons provides NATO with one of its most serious challenges. Looks at the reasons why NATO's modernization decision created such a furore in Europe and offers several recommendations on what could be done to alleviate the problem. This is an incisive analysis.

293 **Nuclear Weapons in Europe.**
William G. Hyland, Lawrence D. Freedman, Paul C. Warnke, Karsten D. Voigt.   New York: Council on Foreign Relations, 1984. 118p.
The first volume in the Council on Foreign Relations Series on European–American relations, this study addresses fundamental issues relating to the role of nuclear weapons in the defence of Western Europe. Each of the authors offers a distinct perspective on the controversy generated by NATO's decisions to deploy cruise and Pershing missiles in Western Europe. For Hyland, who supports the deployment, the nuclear debate is seen as part of a more fundamental question about whether Western Europe would continue to seek security through partnership with the United States. For Voigt, however, nuclear weapons are seen as dangerous, destabilizing and unnecessary, while for Warnke they are seen as lacking in credibility. Freedman, in contrast, argues that nuclear weapons are important for NATO for both symbolic and strategic reasons. At the same time he suggests that NATO should reduce its battlefield nuclear weapons. Taken as a whole, this is a good collection.

294 **The Politics of Euromissiles: Europe's Role in America's World.**
Dianna Johnstone.   London: Verso, 1984. 218p.
An informed study by an American journalist which looks at the NATO decision to deploy cruise and Pershing missiles in Europe and the debate this provoked. Individual chapters deal with the debates in Germany, France and Italy, offering conclusions which are intriguing although far from persuasive. In the chapter on Italy, for example, it is argued that for reasons of its own the Mafia supported the deployment decision. In a concluding section which makes some rather tenuous connections, the author tries to link the deployment in Europe to American designs in the Third World.

295 **The Present as Prologue: Europe and Theater Nuclear Modernization.**
Catherine McArdle Kelleher.   *International Security*, vol. 5, no. 4 (Spring 1981), p. 150-168.
This essay examines the controversy over NATO's decision to use new long-range theatre nuclear force (LRTNF) deployments, places it in historical perspective and identifies novel elements of the problems facing NATO. In the mid-1970s European élites had reflected American enthusiasm for cruise missiles. Nevertheless, the deployment decision was highly controversial. Kelleher looks at the reasons for this and emphasizes three considerations: popular identification of LRTNF with targeting

against the Soviet homeland, scepticism about the benefits of introducing LRTNF into the European balance, and the linkage between deployment and arms control. She also argues that the debate highlights changed features of the European security context, especially the turbulent domestic climate of many European allies and divergent conceptions on the two sides of the Atlantic of the requirements of security. The implications of all this for the future are also considered. The increasingly visible and anomalous position of the Federal Republic of Germany is seen as one of the major problems.

296 **Debate over the Modernization of NATO's Short-Range Nuclear Missiles.**
Catherine M. Kelleher.   New York: Oxford University Press, 1990, p. 603-622. (*SIPRI Yearbook 1990*).

An incisive analysis which focuses on the nuclear weapons debate precipitated by the 1987 INF Treaty and which gradually became an alliance crisis as Britain and the United States demanded modernization of short-range nuclear forces (SNF) and the Federal Republic of Germany placed a higher priority on further arms control. Catherine Kelleher looks at these events and carefully delineates the developments which helped to turn the issue of short-range nuclear force modernization into an alliance crisis. She concludes with an assessment of the military and political implications of the SNF crisis.

297 **Managing NATO's Tactical Nuclear Operations.**
Catherine M. Kelleher.   *Survival*, vol. 30, no. 1 (January-February 1988), p. 59-78.

An informed discussion of NATO's stockpile of tactical nuclear weapons with particular attention to weapon deployment security and storage. There is a valuable discussion of the issue surrounding NATO alerts and the dispersal of the weapons. The political and military procedures for nuclear release are also considered.

298 **The Nuclear Defense of Europe.**
Donald M. Kerr, Steven A. Maaranen.   *Washington Quarterly*, vol. 6, no. 4 (Autumn 1983), p. 93-110.

Written by the director of the Los Alamos National Laboratory and the leader of the strategic analysis group at the Laboratory, this article argues that advances in Soviet capability have jeopardized the efficacy of NATO's strategy of flexible response. The authors suggest that without escalation dominance, flexible response will become untenable. They also argue that the ambiguity over the strategy in the Alliance is a source of division. While recommending that NATO move to a greater emphasis on conventional forces, unlike most proponents of this course the authors acknowledge the difficulties of such a transition and consider how they might be overcome.

299   **Theater Nuclear Weapons and the NATO Strategy of Flexible Response.**
J. Michael Legge.   Santa Monica, California: Rand Corporation,
April 1983. 93p. (Rand paper R2964-FF).

This report examines the evolution of NATO's strategy from 1949 to the adoption of flexible response in 1967. Particular attention is given to the role of theatre nuclear weapons and to the development within NATO's Nuclear Planning Group of the doctrine concerning potential use of these weapons. The rationale behind NATO's decision in 1979 to modernize its long-range theatre nuclear forces is dealt with very fully. The report also examines the debate over flexible response – especially between the Europeans on the one side and the United States on the other – and considers alternative strategies including the argument for a No First Use policy. In addition, the study identifies the key weapon systems in NATO's nuclear stockpile and identifies the roles and missions of each system. It also has three useful appendices which delineate different categories of weapons systems, identifies the composition of the Nuclear Planning Group and outlines the growth of NATO's theatre nuclear stockpile. In sum, this is a very useful study of both NATO's strategy and its nuclear force posture.

300   **The Western Alliance after INF: Redefining US Policy towards Europe and the Soviet Union.**
Michael R. Lucas.   Boulder, Colorado: Lynne Rienner, 1990. 266p.

Looks at the causes and consequences of the shift from the postwar model of security (which was essentially based on confrontation) to an emerging structure of common security. The author focuses on the INF Treaty and the debate surrounding it in relation to these two approaches to security. Written when it was unclear which approach would triumph, the author offers some perceptive insights into the Western debate which preceded the end of the Cold War in Europe. He also highlights the importance of economic détente in establishing the conditions making possible a transition from the Cold War security system to one based much more on cooperation.

301   **The Modernization of NATO's Long-range Theater Nuclear Forces.**
Simon Lunn.   Washington, DC: GPO, 1981. 80p. (Report prepared
for the Subcommittee on Europe and the Middle East of the
Committee on Foreign Affairs, U.S. House of Representatives by the
Foreign Affairs and National Defense Division Congressional Research
Service).

Provides an excellent analysis of the background to the INF decision of December 1979. The author explores the various rationales for the decision and considers the relationship between modernization and arms control.

302   **Nuclear Weapons in NATO's Deterrent Strategy.**
J. J. Martin.   *Orbis*, vol. 22, no. 4 (Winter 1979), p. 875-895.

Argues that NATO strategy must place more emphasis on deterrence of escalation in the event of war as well as the ability to deny military gains to the Soviet Union. The author looks at Soviet strategy, highlighting the Soviet emphasis on pre-emptive nuclear strikes and the capacity of conventional forces to exploit these through a rapid advance. He also looks at the United States debate on NATO doctrine and considers the arguments of nuclear advocates and those who favour more reliance on conventional forces. His own preference is for the triad of forces, and he suggests certain improvements in the forces themselves and the doctrine for using them.

303 **Theater Nuclear Weapons and Europe.**
Laurence Martin. *Survival*, vol. 16, no. 6 (November/December 1974), p. 268-276.
Starts from the premise that the NATO doctrine for the use of tactical nuclear weapons is ill-developed and that the nuclear forces themselves have been carelessly designed and deployed. The author emphasizes the need for greater invulnerability and proposes what he describes as a nuclear covering force, which would be used when the conventional war went badly.

304 **Nuclear Weapons and European Security.**
Edited by Robert Nurick. London: Gower for the IISS, 1984. 142p. (Adelphi Library 13).
A succinct introduction by the editor focusing upon the credibility of extended deterrence sets the scene for five Adelphi Papers – 'The Future of Britain's deterrent force' by Peter Nailor and Jonathan Alford; 'Nuclear weapons in Europe' by Gregory Treverton; 'Deterrence in the 1980s: American strategic forces and extended deterrence' by Anthony Cordesman; 'Nuclear forces and Alliance relations: Updating deterrence in Europe – Inflexible response?' by François De Rose; and 'TNF modernization and countervailing strategy' by Christopher Makins. This is a good collection which explores the problems of nuclear strategy in Europe from several distinct perspectives.

305 **U.S. Nuclear Weapons In Europe: Issues and Alternatives.**
Jeffrey Record. Washington, DC: Brookings Institution, 1974. 70p.
Written at a time when the United States was considering reforms in its tactical nuclear posture in Europe, this succinct study looks at the main elements of this posture, highlights the asymmetries between US and Soviet tactical nuclear postures, and considers four alternatives: a smaller deployment, a smaller and less vulnerable deployment, a war-fighting deployment, and no deployment. After analysing the four options Record recommends the second as the one most likely to meet political and military needs and to enhance security and stability. There are eight informative tables relating to various aspects of NATO's military posture, but no index.

306 **Theater Nuclear Weapons: Begging the Soviet Union to Pre-empt.**
Jeffrey Record. *Survival*, vol. 19, no. 5 (September/October 1977), p. 208-211.
Argues that in a war in Europe NATO might not have the option of first use of nuclear weapons. On the contrary, the author suggests that a major Pact invasion of the central region probably would be initiated by large-scale pre-emptive theatre nuclear strikes. Consequently NATO needed to pay more attention to the survivability of both its theatre nuclear assets and its command and control systems.

307 **Nuclear Strategy in Europe.**
Thomas C. Schelling. *World Politics*, vol. 14, no. 3 (April 1962), p. 421-432.
An important and influential article in which Schelling applied some of his ideas about strategy and risk to the European security situation. He argued that a limited war in Europe would increase the risk of general war, especially if nuclear weapons were

introduced. Moreover, such a step would change the emphasis from the military level to that of political bargaining. This shared danger could be exploited to bring the conflict to an end on favourable terms. This would be more difficult in an environment characterized by strategic stability. In these circumstances the introduction of nuclear weapons would more likely be part of a punitive strategy of limited reprisal. It is arguable that the ideas of manipulating risk contained in this article provided at least part of the intellectual basis for the NATO strategy of flexible response as adopted in 1967.

308 **The Role of Deterrence in NATO Defense Strategy: Implications for Doctrine and Posture.**
David M. Schwartz. *World Politics*, vol. 28, no. 1 (October 1975), p. 118-133.

An argument very much in the Schelling mould, emphasizing that deterrence is most effectively achieved by NATO through a strategy of risk manipulation or what Schwartz refers to as manipulating the nuclear threshold. The prerequisites are that NATO conventional forces are strong but that the exact point of the nuclear threshold is uncertain. Attempting to improve the quality of NATO's nuclear arsenal and thereby make the outcome of nuclear use more predictable would weaken a deterrence posture based on the possibility that, if attacked, NATO might use nuclear weapons with all the uncertainty about the consequences of such a use. Schwartz draws out some of the implications of this for NATO doctrine and force posture, arguing (amongst other things) that NATO's political disunity enhanced deterrence by making its response less predictable.

309 **NATO's Nuclear Dilemmas.**
David N. Schwartz. Washington, DC: Brookings Institution, 1983. 270p.

One of the best analyses of the political and military problems associated with NATO's high level of dependence on nuclear weapons, this book examines five episodes in which the United States attempted to deal with NATO's nuclear dilemmas: the offer of Thor and Jupiter IRBMs to the allies in December 1957; plans developed by SACEUR General Norstad to create a mobile land-based medium-range ballistic missile force for NATO; the multilateral force episode from 1960 to 1965; the debate over flexible response from 1962 to 1967; and the creation of the Nuclear Planning Group in 1966-67. These case-studies are a prelude to an analysis of the December 1979 decision by NATO to modernize its long-range theatre nuclear forces while simultaneously pursuing arms control. Throughout the analysis the author tries to show why the United States pursued each initiative, why the Europeans reacted as they did, and why the initiative succeeded or failed. He is concerned with drawing broad lessons from the 1957-67 period to apply to current issues. The author suggests that many of NATO's problems stem from an addiction to nuclear weapons and that attempts to solve these problems through hardware solutions are less satisfactory than doctrinal or consultative approaches.

310 **The Neutron Bomb for NATO Defense: An Alternative.**
R. G. Shreffler. *Orbis*, vol. 21, no. 4 (Winter 1978), p. 959-973.

Argues that although there would be little benefit to be gained from replacing the warhead on the existing Lance missiles with an enhanced radiation warhead, the debate over the neutron bomb offers NATO an opportunity to reconsider how battlefield nuclear weapons might be used to strengthen deterrence in Europe. The author examines the notion of a fixed defence at the intra-German border based upon these missiles and suggests that deployment would give NATO a strong cheap border defence. What is not fully appreciated is the political difficulty of deploying new nuclear weapons in Europe in this period.

311   **Nuclear Forces in Europe: Enduring Dilemmas, Present Prospects.**
Leon V. Sigal.   Washington, DC: Brookings Institution, 1984. 181p.
Looks at the dilemmas and problems associated with NATO's heavy reliance on nuclear weapons and argues that the paradoxes and inconsistencies of NATO's nuclear doctrine resulted in confusion about the rationale for deploying cruise and Pershing missiles in Europe. The author also examines the politics of the issue and offers a particularly incisive analysis of the Euromissile issue. Writing at a time when the negotiation between the Soviet Union and the West had stalled, the author – in somewhat prescient fashion – looks at the prospects for dealing with the issue through negotiation. This is an informed, informative and judicious analysis.

312   **Tactical Nuclear Weapons: European Perspectives.**
SIPRI.   London: Taylor and Francis, 1978. 371p.
This book, published in the middle of the controversy over the neutron bomb, provides detailed accounts of the kinds, types and numbers of nuclear weapons deployed in Europe as well as discussions of their roles and missions. It also argues that NATO is too dependent on these weapons and that the introduction of new systems such as the enhanced radiation warhead would be a mistake. This book is very informative and a useful counterweight to Cohen's book *The Neutron Bomb* (*see* item no. 284) which argues in favour of deployment of neutron weapons.

313   **European Security, East–West Policy, and the INF Debate.**
Jed Snyder.   *Orbis*, vol. 27, no. 4 (Winter 1984), p. 913-970.
Argues that the INF debate is the most significant development in the long debate over Western deterrence and the Soviet threat. Places it within the familiar problems of extended deterrence and the dilemmas faced by the United States as it tries to reassure the allies that they will not be decoupled, yet simultaneously tries to get them to share more of the burden. The author also shows how the INF debate highlights the increasing divergence of perspective between the United States and the European allies. He also sees it in relation to Soviet efforts to erode the strategic relationship between the United States and Western Europe.

314   **The LRTNF Decision: Evolution of US Theater Nuclear Policy, 1975-9.**
James A. Thomson.   *International Affairs*, vol. 60, no. 4 (Autumn 1984), p. 601-614.
Traces the process between 1975 and 1979 whereby the United States and its NATO allies transformed alliance policy on theatre nuclear forces. The author was in the Office of Secretary of Defence and subsequently a member of the National Security Council staff during this period. Consequently, he had a close-up view of the process. Thomson identifies three phases: American foot-dragging on modernization, a policy shift, and American pressure in the period following the Guadeloupe Summit. He argues that arms control was intended as a complement to, but not a substitute for, deployment – a principle which was eventually undercut by the INF agreement.

315 **Planning for NATO's Nuclear Deterrent in the 1980s and 1990s.**
James A. Thomson.   *Survival*, vol. 25, no. 3 (May/June 1983),
p. 98-109.

Argues that NATO needs a comprehensive review of its nuclear forces, with particular attention to the structure of short- and medium-range forces, the contribution of US sea-based and intercontinental forces, NATO's capacity to direct its forces during hostilities, and the size of the nuclear stockpile in Europe. The author deals with each of these issues and argues that simply because they are likely to be controversial is no reason for NATO to postpone the hard decisions about modernization.

316 **Rethinking NATO Strategy.**
Vincenzo Tornetta.   *Washington Quarterly*, vol. 17, no. 3
(Summer 1984), p. 13-20.

Defends the decision to deploy INF systems on the grounds that it represents an updating of NATO's strategy which is necessary to re-establish credible deterrence in Europe. Emphasizes the need to ensure that there is greater understanding of NATO'S strategy and the role of nuclear weapons within it.

317 **Nuclear Weapons in Europe.**
Gregory F. Treverton.   London: International Institute for Strategic Studies, Summer 1981, 34p. (Adelphi Paper 168).

Places the NATO nuclear modernization decision of December 1979 in historical perspective and looks at the problems against a background of a changed strategic balance. After looking at the Soviet nuclear threat to Western Europe the author highlights the difficulties inherent in any decision to use nuclear weapons. He also explores the current issues surrounding TNF and the prospects for arms control. In conclusion Treverton argues that the underlying ambiguities surrounding the American deterrent will remain and that their management depends ultimately on political will, confidence and skill rather than specific weapons or arms control agreements.

318 **Managing NATO's Nuclear Dilemma.**
Gregory F. Treverton.   *International Security*, vol. 7, no. 4
(Spring 1983), p. 93-115.

Argues that the nuclear dilemma in NATO stems from geography and the fact that NATO's main deterrent against Soviet aggression in Europe, American strategic nuclear forces, are located in the United States. Consequently, Europeans and Americans have fundamentally divergent strategic preferences. This is not a problem that can be solved, but is something which has to be managed. Treverton outlines the limits of the efforts to solve the problem in terms of force posture and emphasizes the need for a satisfactory decision-making process on these matters in the alliance. Treverton also looks at how the problem was dealt with historically, considering the role of the Nuclear Planning Group and particular episodes such as the enhanced radiation weapons imbroglio. The author concludes that the management of nuclear politics is predominantly a political process, influenced as much by the general state of trans-Atlantic relations as by the specifics of military hardware.

319 **The Bomb and European Security.**
Guido Vigeveno. Bloomington, Indiana: Indiana University Press, 1983. 131p.

A sensible overview of the controversial issues which arose in NATO in the late 1970s and early 1980s. After defining the terminology in his opening chapter, the author looks at NATO and Soviet strategy, the military balance, and arms control in Europe. Most interesting are the final three chapters which consider refinements of NATO strategy, the neutron bomb issue and NATO's dual-track approach which sought to combine deployment of long-range theatre nuclear forces with arms control negotiations. A useful overview which deals adequately with the issues.

320 **The Neutron Bomb Controversy: A Study in Alliance Politics.**
Sherri L. Wasserman. New York: Praeger, 1983. 151p.

This book focuses upon the politics of the neutron bomb controversy and explains why this weapons system proved so controversial in NATO. It sets the controversy within the broader context of tactical nuclear weapons in Alliance strategy, looks at the constraints and incentives for the acquisition of neutron weapons, and explores the political debates and pressures in both the United States and West Germany. The author is very critical of President Carter and argues that poor communication with his aides, lack of knowledge about Europe and NATO and the belief that the United States should not be overly assertive in dealing with the allies all contributed to the mis-handling of the issue. A valuable study which illuminates the problems of reconciling divergent political needs between different members of the Alliance.

321 **The History of NATO Theater Nuclear Force Policy: Key Findings From the Sandia Conference.**
David S. Yost. *Journal of Strategic Studies*, vol. 15, no. 2 (June 1992), p. 228-261.

The author outlines the major conclusions to emerge from a conference held in September 1990 at the Sandia National Laboratories in Livermore, California on the history of NATO's theatre nuclear forces. Much of the focus of both the conference – which included testimony from high-ranking officials – and this article concerns the impact of analysis on NATO strategy. Attention is also given, however, to the historical pattern of theatre nuclear force policies, the impact of public opinion, and the influence of the West European members of NATO. The author also highlights issues that were never fully resolved, such as the linkage to US intercontinental forces, control of escalation, and how to be prepared for both conventional and TNF operations. Yost provides a useful analysis.

322 **The Need for Substrategic Weapons.**
Thomas-Durell Young. *Orbis*, vol. 36, no. 2 (Spring 1992), p. 227-238.

Looks at the Bush Initiative of September 1991 which was the most sweeping act of unilateral disarmament in the nuclear era and argues that this causes problems for NATO. The Alliance needs to have substrategic nuclear forces to deal with a disintegrating Soviet Union and the growing threat from the Middle East and North Africa. The political difficulties in the way of modernization of substrategic nuclear weapons, however, leads the author to suggests exploring modernization outside the alliance on a trilateral basis among the United States, France and Britain. In conclusion, the author argues that Europe is not entering a peaceful era and that NATO must retain a nuclear strategy to provide for European security in an unstable world.

Conventional strategy

323 **NATO: Meeting the Coming Challenge (The Project on a Resources Strategy for the United States and its Allies).**
David Abshire.   Washington, DC: Center for Strategic and International Studies, 1988. 91p.

This report was part of a broader study on resources strategy. It focused on short-term measures to improve NATO's conventional defence posture in the aftermath of the INF Agreement. The report looks at the conventional balance in Europe and argues that NATO needs to enhance its crisis management effectiveness. It makes specific recommendations in the areas of equipment modernization, and emphasizes the need for more cooperation in the development and procurement of armaments. The report contains a series of useful appendices with details of collaborative ventures in arms production, including those carried out in accordance with a congressional initiative sponsored by Senator Sam Nunn.

324 **The Alliance and Europe: Part IV – Military Doctrine and Technology.**
Steven L. Canby.   London: The International Institute for Strategic Studies, 1975. 42p. (Adelphi Paper 109).

Starts from the premise that tactical nuclear weapons cannot substitute for conventional forces and that NATO should rely more on conventional strength. The author suggests that revised doctrines can allow NATO to match the Pact in conventional force and contends that a proper employment of forces can favour the defence. To fully exploit technology, it is important to change existing NATO practices. Canby outlines detailed plans for defensive superiority through a checkerboard system of defence by small strong points. A detailed and persuasive account.

325 **NATO: Reassessing the Conventional Wisdoms.**
Steven L. Canby.   *Survival*, vol. 19, no. 4 (July/August 1977), p. 164-168.

Argues that the debate about enhancing NATO forces has led to some misunderstanding and has obscured the real reasons for NATO's inability to stop a Warsaw Pact attack. Canby suggests that NATO suffers from an emphasis on support rather than combat forces and a preoccupation with battlefield firepower for a war of attrition rather than the use of armour for manoeuvre-style warfare beyond the battlefield. Crucially, NATO is lacking in operational reserves.

326 **Dumping Nuclear Counterforce Incentives: Correcting NATO's Inferiority in Conventional Military Strength.**
Steven L. Canby. *Orbis*, vol. 19, no. 1 (Spring 1975), p. 47-71.
Identifies and assesses four approaches to dealing with NATO's conventional inferiority in Europe: reliance on tactical nuclear weapons; aiming for technological superiority; spending more; and relying more on militia. After suggesting that none of these alternatives is adequate, Canby argues that NATO needs to restructure its forces and change its operational practices to provide defence in depth with large operational reserves. Canby also provides detailed guidelines for a new US and NATO posture.

327 **More Troops, Fewer Missiles.**
Steven Canby, Ingemar Dorfer. *Foreign Policy*, no. 53 (Winter 1983-84), p. 3-17.
Argues that the controversy over the deployment of cruise and Pershing missiles in Europe has increased allied awareness of the excessive dependence on nuclear weapons in NATO strategy and therefore made them more willing to strengthen contributions to NATO's conventional defence. The authors contend that the conventional parity that would make new nuclear deployments unnecessary is achievable at relatively low cost. Considerable emphasis is placed on the Dutch creation of two additional armoured brigades and the deployment of another brigade in West Germany as part of an increasing division of labour in which the United States would place more emphasis on tactical air power.

328 **Time for Action.**
Robert Close. Oxford, England: Brassey's, 1983. 233p.
A successor to the author's 'Europe without Defense' this volume emphasizes the global nature of the Soviet threat especially in the Middle East and Southern Africa; the problems of deterrence and defence in Europe; the controversy over nuclear weapons; and the importance of psychological warfare campaigns. The prescriptions are predictable: revitalize the defence of Europe; re-establish nuclear equilibrium; and develop a European intervention force for out-of-area challenges. There is no index.

329 **Alternative Defence: Answer to NATO's Central Front Problems?**
Jonathan Dean. *International Affairs*, vol. 64, no. 1 (Winter 1987/88), p. 61-82.
This article discusses proposals for alternative defence against a background of criticisms of NATO posture since the early 1980s. The author evaluates alternative defence proposals relevant to the defence of West Germany, with particular attention to non-violent defence with total or partial elimination of German/NATO armed forces; re-organization of the forces; and the modification of the traditional system through the addition of a high-technology shield. He concludes that these proposals have contributed significantly to the debate on European defence and helped to provide a vision of more desirable security arrangements in Europe.

330 The Retaliatory Offensive and Operational Realities in NATO.
Keith A. Dunn, William O. Staudenmaier. *Survival*, vol. 27, no. 3 (May/June 1985), p. 108-118.

Provides a critical analysis of Samuel Huntington's proposal that NATO should adopt a retaliatory offensive strategy. The authors evaluate the strategy in terms of suitability, feasibility, flexibility, and acceptability, and conclude that a retaliatory offensive runs into problems on each of these criteria. Although the implications of a retaliatory offensive for crisis stability could have been discussed more fully, the authors nevertheless provide a very incisive and persuasive analysis.

331 NATO's Balancing Act.
John Erickson. *Current History*, vol. 77, no. 451 (November 1979), p. 145-147, 180, 186.

Erickson argues that with the changes in the strategic balance NATO's nuclear strategy is not realistic. He looks at the issue of theatre nuclear forces and at the problems of conventional defence, before concluding that NATO needs to reorganize its defences.

332 Strengthening Conventional Deterrence in Europe: Proposals for the 1980s.
ESECS.   New York: St Martin's Press, 1983. 260p. (Report of the European Security Study).

This study, which proved very influential in the debate of the early and mid-1980s identified a variety of ways in which NATO could improve its conventional capabilities and thereby strengthen deterrence of conventional aggression. The volume contains the report of the ESECS steering group. This is followed by more detailed workshop reports and supporting papers, which deal, amongst other things, with the threat including Soviet operational concepts, the requirements for NATO's conventional defence, and the role that technology could play in enhancing the capacity for defence. Considerable emphasis was placed on the benefits that would be obtained from a capacity to interdict Warsaw Pact follow-on forces and disrupt Soviet C^3I capabilities. In order to achieve this it was argued that NATO should make greater use of new non-nuclear technologies. In a supporting paper by Donald Cotter the key technologies identified were: advanced submunitions; accurate, long-range stand-off missiles; long-range surveillance and target acquisition and tracking; and information processing and distribution techniques. Cotter's analysis helped to provoke an intense debate in the mid-1980s about the value for NATO of what were called emerging technologies or (ET).

333 The NATO Conventional Defense: Back to Reality.
Ori Even-Tov. *Orbis*, vol. 23, no. 1 (Spring 1979), p. 35-50.

A sceptical assessment of hopes that high-technology weapons would enable NATO to compensate for the numerical inferiority of its forces as compared to those of the Warsaw Pact. The author bases much of his argument on an analysis of the performance of precision-guided munitions (PGMs) during the Middle East war of October 1973. He argues that these weapons did not have a decisive impact, nor did they clearly favour the defence over the offence. In addition, he suggests that Soviet doctrine and tactics are well suited to survive PGMs, which are themselves very vulnerable to counter-measures. A useful critique of NATO's tendency to look for technological panaceas for its defence problems.

334 **NATO's Conventional Defenses: Options for the Central Region.**
Stephen J. Flanagan. London: Macmillan, 1988. 161p.

During the 1980s there were many proposals for improving NATO's conventional military posture in Central Europe. This book reviews these proposals, both official and unofficial, and critically assesses them in the light of prevailing military, political, economic and demographic trends. It looks at such issues as opportunities for greater armaments cooperation, the impact of new technologies, changes in concepts and tactics to emphasize deep-strike, and the role of arms control. The conclusions are sober and contend that improving the conventional component of NATO strategy will be a long and complicated process with no shortcuts.

335 **The Defense of Western Europe.**
Edited by Will Gann. London: Croom Helm, 1987. 317p.

The result of a research project at the Hoover Institution, this volume looks at the defence forces of Western Europe, as well as at the United States contribution. In addition to chapters on NATO members, there is a chapter dealing with Austria and Switzerland. The individual chapters provide surveys of the development of national forces since the Second World War; the relations between armed forces and the society within which they exist; military doctrine; organization; the ability of the forces to implement their assigned responsibilities; and their relationship with NATO. Although this has a rather different focus from most analyses of NATO and European security, it is a useful collection of essays for those who want to know more about the organization and disposition of national military forces in Western Europe.

336 **Non-Offensive Defense: An Alternative Strategy for NATO?**
David Gates. New York : St Martin's Press, 1991. 205p.

Provides both a historical perspective on, and a contemporary assessment of, proposals that NATO move toward a strategy based on non-offensive defence. The analysis covers various proposals whereby NATO might move to less provocative postures and the author traces the intellectual roots of these proposals to some of the great political philosophers who discussed issues of war and peace. The concluding chapter suggests that the end of the Cold War has removed the case for defensive defence which the author regards as predominantly dependent on political rationales. The suggestion that NATO retain its strategy of flexible response was, however, rapidly overtaken by events. Overall the book offers a very critical assessment of an idea that had many problems but also encouraged much imaginative thinking about the nature of security relations in Europe.

337 **Conventional Deterrence: Alternatives for European Defense.**
Edited by James R. Golden, Asa A. Clark, Bruce E. Arlinghaus.
Lexington, Massachusetts: Heath, 1984. 245p.

Examines the debate over NATO strategy and considers the possibilities of placing greater emphasis on conventional deterrence within the framework of the existing strategy of flexible response. There are four sections in which the chapters, by a variety of contributors, explore issues related to deterrence, the political context, the military context, and economic context. The discussion is helpful and broad based, and the final chapter by James Golden offers a set of balanced conclusions and sensible policy recommendations. It argues that while conventional deterrence alone is not a viable alternative for NATO, conventional forces are becoming a more important component of the overall deterrence strategy. Moreover, Golden cautions that overstating the impact of new conventional technologies or demanding fundamental shifts in alliance strategy is more likely to destroy rather than sustain support for increased defence spending.

338 **Groping for Technical Panaceas: The European Conventional Balance and Nuclear Stability.**
Fen Osler Hampson. *International Security*, vol. 8, no. 3 (Winter 1983-84), p. 57-82.

Hampson looks at the debate over the need for better conventional deterrence in Europe with particular attention to the recommendations of the Report of the European Security Study Group (ESECS), entitled 'Strengthening Conventional Deterrence in Europe: Proposals for the 1980s'. He compares this with other studies – by the Congressional Budget Office, the Department of Defense, and John Mearsheimer – looking at force structure, mobilization capabilities, geography, and force-to-space ratios. Hampson criticizes the ESECS study for advocating greater reliance on accurate conventional missiles as he believes this would undermine crisis stability and would not therefore raise the nuclear threshold. He argues that in this area in particular, the recommendations of the report are ill-conceived. While recognizing that some remedial measures are necessary Hampson emphasizes the need to consider NATO's strengths and weaknesses vis-à-vis the Pact before making any major changes. Although it is a review essay, this piece contributes to the debate in its own right.

339 **Conventional Deterrence and Conventional Retaliation in Europe.**
Samuel P. Huntington. *International Security*, vol. 8, no. 3 (Winter 1983-84), p. 32-56.

A provocative and important article which argued that NATO's focus on conventional defence in Europe should be replaced by a new emphasis on what Huntington called conventional retaliation. Huntington's starting point is that in spite of the emphasis on strengthening NATO's conventional defence, the United States and its European allies lack the political will to increase capabilities to the point where they can defend adequately. He also argues that even if increased conventional forces did provide a stronger defence of Europe, they would not necessarily enhance deterrence of Soviet aggression. Drawing on Glenn Snyder's distinction between denial and punishment capabilities, Huntington outlines four ways to deter Soviet aggression: defence with conventional or nuclear weapons and retaliation with conventional or nuclear weapons. Nuclear deterrence has the problem of being nuclear but the great advantage of being retaliatory. Consistent with this logic, Huntington devises a proposal for a retaliatory counter-offensive into Eastern Europe in the event of a Soviet invasion of Western Europe. Such a strategy, he argues, would pose great potential costs and risks to the Soviet Union. While Huntington concludes that conventional retaliation is strategically positive, militarily possible, and even politically feasible, he ignores the impact on crisis stability. For all its problems, however, this is a provocative and highly stimulating proposal.

340   **The Alliance and Europe: Part II – Defence with Fewer Men.**
Kenneth Hunt.   London: International Institute for Strategic Studies, 1973. 42p. (Adelphi Paper 98).
Starting from the premise that it would be difficult to maintain the existing force level, Brigadier Kenneth Hunt looks at ways in which the defence of Europe might be implemented with smaller forces. He looks at deficiencies in NATO's force posture, and considers several ways of dealing with the growing constraints, including restructuring, rapid reinforcement in crisis, and greater reliance on reserves.

341   **Precision ATGMs and NATO Defense.**
Robert Kennedy.   *Orbis*, vol. 22, no. 4 (Winter 1979), p. 897-928.
A realistic assessment of the benefits from the deployment of modern anti-tank guided missiles. The author suggests that although these systems can enhance NATO's defensive capability, the impact will be limited by Soviet counter-measures and tactics. They are certainly not likely to bring about a dramatic shift in the balance between offence and defence. This is a useful critique of NATO's tendency to believe that technology provided the answer to many of its military problems.

342   **Conventional Defense and Total Deterrence: Assessing NATO's Strategic Options.**
Robert B. Killebrew.   Wilmington, Delaware: Scholarly Resources, 1986. 159p.
One of the many studies which appeared in the mid-1980s highlighting ways in which NATO could strengthen the conventional components of its force posture and reduce its reliance on nuclear weapons. The author argues that conventional defence of Europe is achievable without spending a great deal more money, although he also makes clear that this is a supplement rather than an alternative to nuclear deterrence. Considerable emphasis is placed on operational factors and there is a particularly helpful discussion of the problems of mobilization.

343   **Ten Suggestions for Rationalizing NATO.**
Robert Komer.   *Survival*, vol. 19, no. 2 (March/April 1977), p. 62-72.
Komer was to become a key figure in the formulation of US policy in NATO during the Carter era. In this succinct article he outlines ways in which NATO could enhance its conventional forces within resource constraints. He argues that NATO members should start thinking in alliance terms, should give high priority to improving C^3 assets, should think more in terms of inter-operability, should give less attention to keeping open the sea lanes and should rationalize NATO's theatre nuclear posture. Komer's influence was subsequently apparent in NATO's Long-term Defense Improvement Program.

344   **U.S. Force Structure in NATO: An Alternative.**
Richard D. Lawrence, Jeffrey Record.   Washington, DC: Brookings Institution, 1974. 136p.
Argues that the US and NATO military posture is inappropriate to meet a Soviet threat that is geared to a short decisive campaign. Having highlighted the deficiencies, the authors also suggest that they can be overcome by such measures as repositioning of US troops, raising the ratio of combat to support troops, upgrading the protection of

pre-positioned equipment and redirecting lines of communication. The book contains a number of tables and four useful appendices.

345 **Surprise Attack and Conventional Defense in Europe.**
John H. Maurer, Gordon H. McCormick. *Orbis*, vol. 27, no. 1
(Spring 1983), p. 107-126.
Argues that the growing Soviet interest in conventional options in Europe has increased the importance of surprise. As a result NATO needs to increase the readiness of forward deployed units and not count on having the time to move forces forward.

346 **NATO's Changing Strategic Agenda: The Conventional Defense of Central Europe.**
Colin McInnes. London: Unwin Hyman, 1990. 201p.
As the author himself notes in his introduction, this book was written at a time of great change. He suggests that at the end of the 1980s NATO was faced with two major problems: how to respond to developments in the Soviet Union and Eastern Europe; and what to do about NATO strategy and criticisms of nuclear reliance. The volume focuses rather more on this second question and after providing a careful analysis of NATO strategy it also looks at one of the most important alternatives, the concept of non-offensive defence. Although critical of some aspects of non-offensive defence, McInnes suggests that along with the idea of common security it may provide an appropriate approach for NATO in the 1990s. While the prescriptions offered by McInnes are sound and sensible, the extent of the political changes he discusses briefly makes much of the discussion of military strategy hypothetical. Although some of the reforms made by NATO since the publication of this book are foreshadowed by the author, the Alliance has moved much more drastically than almost anyone could have contemplated at the end of 1989 when the book was completed.

347 **Maneuver, Mobile Defense, and the NATO Central Front.**
John J. Mearsheimer. *International Security*, vol. 6, no. 3
(Winter 1981-82), p. 104-122.
A critical assessment of proposals for changing NATO's strategy of forward defence based on attrition of attacking forces to a manoeuvre-oriented defence. Proponents of manoeuvre argue that Pact forces could easily pierce NATO's linear defences by concentrating forces at specific points and would then proceed to destroy the Alliance's weak reserves. They also contend that an attrition strategy is foolhardy if the defender is outnumbered. Mearsheimer believes that although the case for a seemingly cost-effective manoeuvre-based defence has some appeal, it has not been outlined in sufficient detail. While such an approach would not improve the prospects for success for an outnumbered defender, mobile defence forces would have a significant offensive capability, and could jeopardize crisis stability. The geography and terrain of West Germany, and the command and control requirements of integrating NATO's six national armies on the Central Front, make a manoeuvre defence a poor choice. Beyond specific military considerations, Mearsheimer contends that the Germans are unlikely to accept a manoeuvre defence which could turn Germany into a battlefield. His conclusion is that it would be preferable for NATO to strengthen its national corps reserves and enhance tactical mobility and flexibility within the framework of forward defence.

The Evolution of NATO Strategy. Conventional strategy

348 **Conventional Deterrence.**
John J. Mearsheimer. Ithaca, New York: Cornell University Press, 1983. 296p.
A major study which looks at the operation of conventional deterrence in the past and shows how its success or failure is related to the strategies available to the protagonists. As well as using a number of case-studies from the twentieth century, the author looks at the prospects for conventional deterrence in Europe.

349 **The Conventional Defense of Europe: New Technologies and New Strategies.**
Andrew J. Pierre. New York: Council on Foreign Relations, 1986. 185p.
This book has chapters by American, French, German and British authors dealing with aspects of the debate of the mid-1980s over enhancing conventional defence in Europe. It provides several diverse points of view on the extent to which the defence of Europe should be non-nuclear, the best means of achieving this, and the cost. It is particularly useful in providing a very good sampling of the defence debate of the mid-1980s on strengthening NATO's conventional forces.

350 **Follow-on Forces Attack (FOFA): Myths and Realities.**
Bernard W. Rogers. *NATO Review Reprints*, no. 6 (December 1984), p. 9.
Written by the then Supreme Allied Commander Europe, this article sets the concept of Follow-on Forces Attack within the overall context of NATO strategy, explains the reasons for the emphasis on attacking the Warsaw Pact's second-echelon forces, and sets out to dispel certain myths about FOFA, including the tendency to confuse it with the Airland Battle concept enunciated by the United States Army. FOFA was developed by Allied Command Europe specifically to deal with the problem of second-echelon forces.

351 **America in NATO: The Conventional Delusion.**
Alan Ned Sabrosky. *Orbis*, vol. 25, no. 2 (Summer 1981), p. 293-306.
A counter to many of the arguments which claim that NATO relied too much on nuclear weapons. The author explores the relationship between the strategic and theatre nuclear balances, the implications of the shifts in the military balance in Europe, and the nature of Soviet objectives. He argues that the Soviet Union sees military power as a way of placing political pressure on the West. The main thrust of the analysis, however, is that NATO should not delude itself about the role of conventional forces in its deterrence strategy and should recognize that the key remains strategic nuclear and theatre nuclear forces.

352 **Rethinking Continental Defense.**
Franz-Joseph Schulze. *Washington Quarterly*, vol. 7, no. 2 (Spring 1984), p. 51-58.
A former Commander in Chief of Allied Forces Central Europe argues that conventional forces have to be strengthened but acknowledges the difficulties of achieving this in view of the shrinking manpower base and constricted defence budgets. The author sees the answer in terms of more effective exploitation of new technologies

which are not manpower intensive and which would extend the battlefield to Soviet second-echelon forces.

353   **Europe's Conventional Defense: Solid Progress but Challenges Remain.**
David Shilling.   *Survival*, vol. 30, no. 2 (March/April 1986), p. 122-133.

Shilling takes issue with American critics who argue that the European allies are not spending enough on defence and traces recent improvements in NATO's force posture. He also argues that the military balance is not nearly as bad as often presented and considers the implications of this for NATO's approach to conventional arms control in Europe.

354   **Conventional Defense in Europe.**
Hew Strachan.   *International Affairs*, vol. 61, no. 1 (Winter 1984/85), p. 27-44.

Starting with an overview of the Campaign for Nuclear Disarmament and the various proposals for alternative defence strategies, this article places the argument for stronger conventional forces in Europe in historical perspective. Arguing that flexible response needs to be replaced, it explores and assesses three ways to enhance conventional credibility: an increase in the number of men; defence in depth; and better capabilities for counter-attack. The principles of territorial defence are outlined, with special attention to the arguments of Kenneth Hunt, Horst Afheldt, Major-General Jochen Loser, and Just Defense. The author's conclusion is that it is time for a NATO strategic review and that doctrine and technology need to be more closely related.

355   **Deep Attack Concepts and the Defense of Central Europe.**
Boyd D. Sutton (et al.).   *Survival*, vol. 26, no. 2 (March/April 1984), p. 50-70.

Looks at two deep-attack concepts – Follow-on Forces Attack and the US Army's concept of Airland Battle. The authors highlight the points of convergence and divergence between them, assess their role in enhancing deterrence in Europe, identify the doctrinal and procedural issues they raise, and consider the likely Soviet response. This is a detailed and knowledgeable article.

356   **The Forward Defense of Europe.**
John C. F. Tillson, IV.   *Military Review*, vol. 61, no. 5 (May 1981), p. 66-76.

Starting with a discussion of the shortcomings of NATO's existing plans for defence of Western Europe, the author suggests that greater emphasis should be placed on prepared defences. He also suggested that greater use be made of reserves in defining these fortified positions, allowing regular forces to provide an operational reserve for counter-attack. The defensive zone could be landscaped in ways which would make a rapid advance very difficult.

No First Use of nuclear weapons

357 Generals for Peace and Disarmament: A Challenge to US/NATO Strategy.
New York: Universe Press, 1984. 151p.

One of the main features of the revolt against NATO's dependence on nuclear weapons in the 1980s was that it was not confined to pacifists and the political forces of the Left. The protest movement was greatly strengthened by the arguments of many former high-ranking military officers from various European countries who were extremely critical of NATO's plans for the use of nuclear weapons in a conventional conflict in Europe. This book provides a good example of this. After denouncing the existing strategy, the group of thirteen generals outlines the need not only for alternative defence concepts but also for the West to be much more serious in negotiations about disarmament.

358 Conventional Deterrence: Predictive Uncertainty and Policy Confidence.
Richard K. Betts. *World Politics*, vol. 37, no. 2 (January 1985), p. 153-179.

Written by an incisive analyst of security issues, this article contends that NATO's strategy of Flexible Response has certain merits which are ignored by those who argue that NATO should adopt a strategy of No First Use of nuclear weapons. Betts highlights the inadequacies of a strategy that relies purely upon conventional deterrence but does acknowledge the merits of an approach that combines enhanced denial capabilities and continued threats of nuclear retaliation in the event that denial fails. He describes this as an incremental shift towards the conventional defence component within the existing framework of Flexible Response. Overall, Betts provides an important and intellectually rigorous contribution to the debate over NATO strategy which occurred in the first half of the 1980s.

359 Compound Deterrence vs. No First Use: What's Wrong is What's Right.
Richard K. Betts. *Orbis*, vol. 28, no. 4 (Winter 1985), p. 697-718.

An incisive contribution to the 1980s debate over NATO strategy which highlights the different dynamics of analytical debate and policy reform – with the former placing more emphasis on optimized solutions while policy is based on compromises between competing preferences. Betts argues very convincingly that transatlantic differences over strategy are the result of objective differences of interest which stem partly from the differing vulnerabilities of the United States and Western Europe. While acknowledging that enhanced capabilities for conventional defence are desirable, he believes it is crucial not to place too much faith in conventional deterrence. Enthusiasm for this, he argues, is based on a natural desire to avoid incoherent doctrine, but overlooks the fact that NATO has several inconsistent goals and that there is an inevitable tension between the best doctrine to enhance deterrence and the best one in the event that deterrence fails. This is a realistic and compelling analysis which cuts through much of the debate over NATO strategy in a very incisive manner.

360   **Nuclear Weapons and the Atlantic Alliance.**
McGeorge Bundy, George F. Kennan, Robert S. McNamara, Gerard
Smith.   *Foreign Affairs*, vol. 60, no. 5 (Summer 1982), p. 753-768.
An article which did much to intensify the debate of the 1980s over the appropriate
strategy for NATO, partly because of the eminence of its four authors, all of whom
were former officials. It starts by noting the disarray over nuclear weapons in NATO
strategy and argues that no use of nuclear weapons could reasonably be expected to
stay limited. The major firebreak against the disaster of general nuclear war is that
between conventional and nuclear conflict. Consequently, it is argued, this firebreak
should be strengthened by NATO adopting a No First Use posture. This should be
accompanied by measures to enhance the capacity for conventional defence in Europe.
The authors argue that NATO could deploy adequate conventional forces for a
successful defence so long as its members have the political will. Although the 'gang of
four' argued that such steps would make NATO strategy less controversial, the
proposal itself aroused considerable controversy, evoking a strong response from
several European analysts.

361   **Policy for Peace.**
Field Marshal Lord Carver.   London: Faber and Faber, 1982. 123p.
Written by a former Chief of the Defence Staff in Britain, this book argues for a shift
away from the NATO strategy of Flexible Response, which the author sees as
excessively dependent on nuclear weapons. Lord Carver argues that nuclear weapons
deter only the use of nuclear weapons and that more emphasis should be placed by
NATO on conventional forces, with greater reliance also placed on reserve forces. The
decision of the British government to modernize its strategic nuclear deterrent through
the acquisition of Trident is castigated as a misallocation of resources that could be
much better spent on conventional forces.

362   **Inflexible Response.**
François de Rose.   *Foreign Affairs*, vol. 61, no. 1 (Fall 1982),
p. 136-150.
Weighs in on the No First Use issue with the argument that NATO needs a general updating of its doctrine of deterrence and defence. The author believes that NATO
should reduce reliance on nuclear weapons but should not make a formal declaration
of No First Use. Also looks at the peculiar position of France in relation to NATO
strategy.

363   **I Exist; Therefore I Deter.**
Lawrence Freedman.   *International Security*, vol. 13, no. 1
(Summer 1988), p. 177-195.
This review of books by Morton Halperin and Robert McNamara discusses their
recommendations for reducing reliance on nuclear weapons and offers a perceptive
discussion of the utility of nuclear weapons. The author looks at arguments in NATO
over First Use and at the history of Flexible Response. He also considers whether the
notion of existential deterrence developed by McGeorge Bundy – and which argues
that deterrence depends simply on the availability of some weapons which could be
used in anger – is sufficient. Most important, for the NATO debate, Freedman
considers the relationship between existential deterrence and extended deterrence and
concludes that if existential deterrence is to be extended to allies, it depends upon a

clear security commitment to the arena of conflict. In other words, in the European context it requires United States forces in Europe. This is a helpful contribution to the understanding of NATO strategy and the issue of extended deterrence.

364 NATO's Nuclear Dilemma.
Colin S. Gray.   *Policy Review*, no. 22 (Fall 1982), p. 97-116.

Gray looks at both the weaknesses and the strengths of NATO's strategy of Flexible Response and offers some trenchant comments on the 'no first use' debate. He suggests that NATO should improve the various elements in Flexible Response while keeping in mind that if the Soviet Union ever does invade Western Europe there is a good chance that it would also be willing to cross the nuclear threshold.

365 Nuclear Fallacy: Dispelling the Myth of Nuclear Strategy.
Morton H. Halperin.   Cambridge, Massachusetts: Ballinger, 1987. 173p.

In this provocative and incisive study Halperin offers a critique of US strategy and force structure which, he argues, are based on the assumption that nuclear devices can be used to fight and win wars. He provides a brief history of American nuclear policy, challenges what he believes is the mythology that nuclear threats have been effective in crises, and offers an alternative model based on the assumption that nuclear explosives can under extreme circumstances be used to demonstrate resolve, but never as weapons to fight wars. He has a chapter which develops his main theme in relation to Europe and the American and NATO force posture there. Halperin argues that changes have to be made in force structure and operational plans rather than simply in declaratory policy, and contends that conventional and nuclear forces have to be completely separated.

366 Stability and its Discontent: Should NATO Go Conventional?
Josef Joffe.   *Washington Quarterly*, vol. 7, no. 4 (Fall 1984), p. 136-147.

An incisive analysis which suggests that in spite of the debate over the dangers of NATO's nuclear strategy, Europe is in fact extremely stable. Joffe provides a powerful critique of the No First Use advocates as well as what he terms the New Conventionalists, and argues that the NATO system of nuclear deterrence has worked too well to be abandoned.

367 Nuclear Weapons and the Preservation of Peace: A German Response.
Karl Kaiser, Georg Leber, Alois Mertes, Franz-Josef Schulze. *Foreign Affairs*, vol. 60, no. 5 (Summer 1982), p. 1157-1180.

The response of a German 'gang of four' to the United States 'gang of four' proposal for no first use of nuclear weapons (*see* item no. 360). They present a variety of arguments against renunciation of first use and argue that NATO should implement its double-track decision of December 1979. An important contribution to the debate.

368   **Strategy and the Atlantic Alliance.**
  Henry A. Kissinger.   *Survival*, vol. 24, no. 5 (September/October 1982), p. 194-200.

Argues that NATO strategic dilemmas stem from its continued reliance on the United States' nuclear guarantee to Western Europe after the United States had lost strategic superiority. This has led to public concern about NATO strategy. Yet Kissinger argues that even in these circumstances, a No First Use strategy would be a mistake. He agrees with the proponents of No First Use, however, that NATO should strengthen its conventional forces. The article also looks at the prospects for nuclear arms control. It is important because of the author rather than because of the arguments.

369   **Nuclear Weapons and Deterrence in Europe.**
  John J. Mearsheimer.   *International Security*, vol. 9, no. 3 (Winter 1984-85), p. 19-46.

This article provides a critique of proposals that NATO adopt a No First Use (NFU) policy on nuclear weapons while acknowledging that strong conventional forces are an essential complement to nuclear deterrence. Although the conventional balance is not nearly as bad as much commentary suggested, conventional forces do not provide the same type of deterrent as nuclear weapons. Furthermore, in spite of all the rhetoric in the early and mid-1980s about enhancing conventional capabilities, Mearsheimer recognizes that it would be difficult to maintain the existing conventional balance let alone improve it. Consequently, nuclear weapons remain essential to NATO strategy and European security.

370   **Alternatives in European Security.**
  Edited by Michael Randle, Paul Rogers.   Aldershot, England: Dartmouth, 1990. 175p.

Stemming from an international conference held at the University of Bradford in 1986 and organized by the Alternative Defense Commission, the chapters in this volume focus on change in the prevalent approach to European security. While some of the authors focus on reforming NATO strategy to place more emphasis on defensive defence, others propose dissolving the blocs. In spite of the claims of the editors, this volume was made less rather than more relevant in the period between its genesis and its publication. Nevertheless, it provides a good sampling of the ideas articulated in the 1980s by European critics of NATO and its deterrence strategy.

371   **Making Europe Unconquerable: The Potential of Civilian-based Deterrence and Defense.**
  Gene Sharp.   Cambridge, Massachusetts: Ballinger, 1985. 190p.

Emphasizing the instability resulting from NATO's existing strategy, the author outlines an alternative approach which would train populations for massive non-cooperation and defiance that would deny the Soviet Union its objective in a war and therefore contribute significantly to deterrence in Europe. This is a very radical approach.

372 **Alliance Security: NATO and the No-first-use Question.**
John D. Steinbruner, Leon V. Sigal. Washington, DC: Brookings Institution, 1983. 222p.

An interesting and incisive series of essays dealing with the balance between nuclear and conventional forces in NATO strategy and posture. There is a good historical overview of the nuclear issue by David Schwartz, chapters on both nuclear deterrence and conventional deterrence in Europe by William Kaufmann, a Pentagon official during the Kennedy Administration and author of a book on the McNamara Strategy, and chapters on the advantages of and prospects for No First Use by Leon Sigal. European perspectives are represented in a chapter on strategy by Jonathan Alford, an analysis by three German scholars of the No First Use debate in West Germany, and a chapter by Johan Holst on how NATO could move towards No First Use in practice. A useful chapter by John Steinbruner identifies areas of consensus and divergence in the debate over the role of nuclear weapons in NATO strategy. A serious contribution to the debate over No First Use, this is an informative and informed book.

373 **No First Use of Nuclear Weapons.**
Richard H. Ullman. *Foreign Affairs*, vol. 50, no. 4 (July 1972), p. 669-683.

An early statement that the United States should consider moving to a policy of No First Use of nuclear weapons. In fact, the author suggests that if a No First Use policy accompanied a reduction in American forces in Europe, this would break the linkage between lower force levels and a lower nuclear threshold. He also suggests that No First Use would remove ambiguity from NATO strategy and therefore make it more likely that NATO would respond decisively in a crisis.

Emerging technology and NATO strategy

374 **New Technology and Western Security Policy: Part I.**
London: International Institute for Strategic Studies, Summer 1985. 59p. (Adelphi Paper 197).

This is the first of three Adelphi Papers on the broad topic of security and technology which includes papers from the 1984 IISS Annual Conference. The series of three papers deals with a variety of themes relating to the relationship between technology and strategy. This one includes two incisive essays, by Ingemar Dorfer and John Roper, on 'Technological Development and Force Structure within the Western Alliance: Prospects for Rationalization and Division of Labour'. Dorfer's analysis discusses the nature of emerging technologies, while Roper offers a series of balanced observations on both the potential and the limitations of these technologies for NATO.

375 New Technology and Western Security Policy: Part II.
London: International Institute for Strategic Studies, Summer 1985.
56p. (Adelphi Paper 198).

The second in a series of three Adelphi Papers on the broad theme of technology, this publication contains several papers which assess the impact on the military balance between NATO and the Warsaw Pact of new conventional weapons technology. The highlight is the juxtaposition of two papers coming to very different conclusions on this issue. Steven Canby provides a powerful critique of policies which emphasize new technologies to target Soviet follow-on forces; Donald Cotter, in contrast, argues that the new technologies can be harnessed very effectively and will help reduce NATO's dependence on early use of nuclear weapons. This is a good place to get a sense of the debate between the advocates and critics of emerging technologies.

376 New Technology and Western Security Policy: Part III.
London: International Institute for Strategic Studies, Summer 1985.
57p. (Adelphi Paper 199).

The third in a series of three Adelphi Papers based on the 1984 IISS Annual Conference, this paper begins with an essay by David Abshire which looks at the impact of new technologies on intra-Alliance relations. It also contains two essays on defence research and development and Western industrial policy, one by Sir Ronald Mason, former Chief Scientific Adviser to the British Ministry of Defence, and one by Henri Martre. There are also essays by Fred Hoffman and Lawrence Freedman offering contrasting views on the Atlantic Alliance and strategic defence.

377 NATO's Conventional Defense Improvement Effort: An Ongoing Imperative.
David Abshire. *Washington Quarterly*, vol. 10, no. 2 (Spring 1987), p. 49-60.

Argues that Reykjavik underlined the need for NATO to enhance its conventional forces but places the renewed focus on this issue within the context of existing efforts. These included NATO's 1984 decision to improve reinforcement and sustainability and, more importantly, the Conventional Defense Improvement (CDI) effort. The CDI began in 1985 and was implemented in accordance with NATO's Conceptual Military Framework which defined the critical war-fighting mission components of NATO strategy. Critical deficiencies were identified and systematic efforts made to remedy them. These are discussed and assessed in the remainder of the article.

378 New Conventional Weapons and Western Defense.
Edited by Ian Bellany, Tim Huxley. London: Cass, 1987. 198p.

Based on papers presented at a conference held at Lancaster University in 1985 this book looks at what it describes as the inward and the outward faces of defence policy, especially that of the United Kingdom, in the NATO context. The inward dimension is concerned with the impact of new technologies on defence budgets. Consequently, there are chapters dealing with technical innovation, research and development, and the respective advantages of indigenous production versus off-the-shelf purchases for weapons procurement. The other part of the book is concerned with the impact of technologies, with particular attention to maritime operations, military aviation and the concept of the land–air battle in Europe. Questions about the impact of emerging technologies on the nuclear threshold are also discussed. Whereas the conventional wisdom was that new technologies would allow NATO to raise the nuclear threshold (i.e. become less dependent on the first use of nuclear weapons) this is challenged with the argument that some new technologies, particularly those relating to the development and deployment of ballistic missiles with conventional warheads, could actually blur the threshold between conventional and nuclear war in Europe, thereby increasing the chances of inadvertent escalation. The final chapter by Tim Huxley provides a useful summary of the debate over emerging technologies and suggests that the European allies were concerned about the costs, about the prospect of perpetuating American technological dominance, and about the impact on arms control and strategy.

379 NATO and the New Technologies.
David Hobbs.   Lanham, Maryland: University Press of America, 1989. 142p.

A useful analysis of new weapons technologies and how they might be better exploited by NATO in order to maintain its technological edge over the Warsaw Pact. The author argues that NATO needs both to achieve better value for money in its procurement practices and vigorously adopt new technologies. The analysis by the Director of the North Atlantic Assembly's Scientific and Technical Committee covers electronics technology, battlefield technology, aerospace technology and naval technology. The final chapter explores issues related to NATO's adoption and use of these technologies. The book has no index.

380 Beyond Nuclear Defense: New Aims, New Arms.
Edited by Johan Jorgen Holst, Uwe Nerlich.   New York: Crane, Russak & Co., 1977. 314p.

This was one of the first serious studies to argue that NATO should adopt new technologies of surveillance, target acquisition, discrimination and precision to refine its strategy and force planning. Individual chapters by analysts from West Germany, Britain, the United States, and France deal with particular aspects of the issue. The contributors include Pierre Hassner, Laurence Martin, Albert Wohlstetter, Graham Allison, James Digby, David Greenwood and Richard Burt. The first section looks at the political setting. This is followed by two chapters dealing with the doctrinal framework for limited military responses, while the third section looks at the promises of technology. Section four examines some of the constraints on changing the alliance posture and the final section identifies some of the ways that NATO can develop a greater capacity for more selective military responses. This was quite an important and influential book and was the forerunner to many of the debates of the 1980s over improving NATO's conventional forces.

381 Diminishing the Nuclear Threat: NATO's Defense and New Technology.
The British Atlantic Committee.   London: The British Atlantic Committee, 1984. 63p.

A study by a group of former high-ranking civil servants and military officers, which argues that technology can act as a force multiplier and not only reduce NATO's over-dependence on nuclear weapons but allow the Alliance to replace the strategy of Flexible Response with a strategy which places more emphasis on conventional defence. New technologies for surveillance, target acquisition and command and control are discussed briefly and it is argued that these should be integrated into the NATO force structure for both European and out-of-area contingencies.

382 **Strengthening Conventional Deterrence in Europe: A Program for the 1980s, ESECS II.**
The European Security Report of the Special Panel. Boulder, Colorado: Westview Press, 1985. 150p.

Prepared by General Andrew Goodpaster, former Supreme Allied Commander Europe, Dr. William Perry, General Franz-Joseph Schulze and Air Chief Marshal Sir Alasdair Steedman, this volume provides a follow-up to the initial ESECS report which identified ways in which NATO could strengthen its conventional capabilities through the use of advanced technologies. After examining Soviet strategy and operational concept this volume reiterates some of the arguments contained in the initial report while elaborating on certain points and responding to some of the criticisms and questions that were raised about the utility and wisdom of utilizing emerging technologies in the ways ESECS had argued.

383 **New Technologies, Defense Policy, and Arms Control.**
Kosta Tsipis. New York: Harper and Row, 1989. 138p.

Written by an eminent scientist and security analyst, this slim volume offers a useful guide to emerging technologies, considers their possible applications and their implications not only for strategic systems and the conventional battlefield in Europe but also for arms control. The author provides an incisive critique of the concept of Follow-on Forces Attack and suggests that technology makes alternative such as defensive defence much more feasible.

384 **Emerging Technologies and European Security.**
Phil Williams, William Wallace. *Survival*, vol. 26, no. 2 (March/April 1984), p. 70-78.

A somewhat sceptical analysis of emerging technologies which questions the likely costs and the likelihood of political acceptance. The authors argue that they are unlikely to serve European, as opposed to American industrial interests. They also argue that they are likely to blur rather than raise the nuclear threshold and that they will not necessarily provide safe options.

NATO and strategic defence

385 **SDI: The Challenge to West Germany.**
Christoph Bluth. *International Affairs*, vol. 62, no. 2 (Spring 1986), p. 247-264.

One of three articles looking at West European responses to SDI, this analysis traces the evolution of the German position. It highlights the initial response – which was negative – and examines the reasons for this. The changes towards a more cooperative – although still qualified – policy of support are also examined. The author looks at West German interest in ballistic missile defence in Europe and considers the effect of SDI on European security collaboration.

386 **Strategic Defenses in NATO Strategy.**
Richard I. Brody.   London: International Institute for Strategic
Studies, Autumn 1987. 45p. (Adelphi Paper 225).

Brody discusses the role of strategic defence in the broad context of deterring an attack on NATO – and more specifically, a theatre attack in Europe. He highlights the potential impact of strategic defence on the security environment. In addition he looks at contrasting views on Mutual Assured Destruction and shows how these influence the divergent approaches to strategic defences. The analysis also focuses on the strategic objectives to be served by defences at both the strategic and the theatre levels. At the NATO level these include extended air defence which, the author contends, is becoming critical to NATO's conventional defence capability. The impact of defence on the capability for a selective nuclear exchange is also considered. This is an informed and helpful analysis which is based on careful logic and is argued with considerable subtlety.

387 **The Impact of Strategic Defenses on European–American Relations in the 1990s.**
Stuart Croft.   London: International Institute for Strategic Studies, Spring 1989. 66p. (Adelphi Paper 238).

This study examines strategic defences as an issue which impinges significantly on US–European relations. It looks at the impact on alliance politics of the United States debate on the ABM issue during the late 1960s and the debate on SDI during the mid-1980s. Attention is given to European reactions to SDI and to how Britain, France and Germany saw the United States commitment to strategic defence as impinging on their interests. The analysis also explores the preferences of different schools of thought in the United States debate and considers how these might impinge on European security interests. The author argues that the SDI issue will continue to have relevance for the Atlantic relationship.

388 **NATO Strategy and Ballistic Missile Defense.**
Ivo H. Daalder.   London: International Institute for Strategic Studies, Winter 1988. 88p. (Adelphi Paper 233).

A theoretically informed and interesting analysis which looks at the importance of images of escalation as well as perceptions of the threat for strategic preferences within the overall concept of Flexible Response. A variety of strategies for extended deterrence are outlined and assessed and the author examines the impact on extended deterrence of different options in relation to the level of ballistic missile defences (BMD). Particular attention is given to the issue of whether these are deployed unilaterally by NATO or by both sides. The author recommends that although NATO should be prepared to respond to a Warsaw Pact deployment of BMD, it should not precipitate such a decision by moving towards significant defence deployments itself.

389 **The SDI Challenge to Europe.**
Ivo H. Daalder.   Cambridge, Massachusetts: Ballinger, 1987. 185p.

A perceptive and detailed analysis of European reactions to President Reagan's Strategic Defense Initiative. The author looks at the political, strategic and technological challenges to Europe posed by SDI and also considers the impact on NATO cohesion of US unilateralism and insensitivity to its allied interests.

390 **The SDI and European Security Interests.**
Louis Deschamps.   London: Croom Helm, 1987. 61p. (The Atlantic
Papers 62).
A good overview of the Euro-American debate on SDI which traces European
reactions to SDI, highlights the divisions amongst the Europeans and claims that the
United States initiative reflected the marginalization of Western Europe. The author
concludes with the suggestion that this might provide the impetus for the Europeans to
provide a more coherent and concerted response to security issues.

391 **France and the Strategic Defense Initiative: Speeding up or Putting on
the Brakes.**
John Fenske.   *International Affairs*, vol. 62, no. 2 (Spring 1986),
p. 231-246.
The second of three articles in this issue of *International Affairs* looking at European
reactions to SDI. Fenske argues that France sees SDI as a technological and strategic
challenge not only to France but to Western Europe as a whole. He looks at both the
official response and the political debate and pays particular attention to the
differences within France over the programme – with the Right being much more
supportive.

392 **ATBMs and Western Security.**
Edited by Donald L. Haffner, John Roper.   Cambridge,
Massachusetts: Ballinger, 1988. 325p.
During the mid-1980s, as a result of President Reagan's Strategic Defense Initiative,
the question of whether the European allies needed anti-theatre ballistic missiles
(ATBMs) became a serious item on the security agenda. This study, carried out under
the auspices of the American Academy of Arts and Sciences and the Royal Institute of
International Affairs in London provides a comprehensive overview of the issue. It
contains thirteen chapters which deal with the technology and the politics of the
ATBM issue. Alternatives to ATBMs are considered and the politics of the ATBM are
examined in both the United States and Europe. The implications for arms control are
also discussed. Although the issues seem to fade into insignificance with the changes in
the European security context in 1989 and 1990, the war in the Gulf and the
performance of the Patriot anti-missile missile may create renewed interest in this
book.

393 **A European Antitactical Ballistic Missile System, Deterrence and the
Conventional Defense of NATO.**
Manfred R. Hamm, Kim R. Holmes.   *Washington Quarterly*, vol. 10,
no. 2 (Spring 1987), p. 61-78.
Seeks to develop an over-arching strategic rationale for European tactical ballistic
missile defence system that reconciles the strategic goals of SDI with the conventional
defence imperatives of NATO strategy. The authors argue that a NATO ATBM
system would reduce Western vulnerabilities, counter disturbing trends in Soviet
strategy, and deny the Soviet Union a conventional war-winning posture below the
nuclear threshold. The analysis sets out the technical requirements and options and
also offers counters to European critics of an ATBM system.

394 **The Transatlantic Politics of Strategic Defense.**
Manfred R. Hamm, Bruce W. Weinrod. *Orbis*, vol. 29, no. 14
(Winter 1986), p. 709-734.
Examines the European response to President Reagan's Strategic Defense Initiative and looks at US efforts to co-opt the allies into the programme through industrial cooperation, and to reassure them about the impact of SDI on nuclear deterrence and arms control. The authors suggest that although there are some risks associated with European participation in SDI, these are worth taking, not least because missile defence in Europe would enhance deterrence and improve NATO's capacity for conventional defence. They acknowledge, however, that integrating BMD into NATO strategy is a delicate operation requiring close consultation.

395 **Strategic Defense and the German–American Security Connection.**
Wolfram F. Hanreider. *Journal of International Affairs*, vol. 41, no. 2
(Summer 1988), p. 247-268.
Locates the divergences between the United States and German over SDI in a broader perspective. As the author points out, arms control has always been of paramount political significance for Germany as has deterrence which has been viewed as a prewar military posture. Defence, in contrast, is a wartime posture and signifies the ultimate calamity. The West German response to the idea of strategic defence was also influenced by the ideological and political stance of the Reagan Administration. The effects of SDI on the German–American security connection can be seen in three areas corresponding to three time-frames: the short-term effect on arms control; the medium-term effect on the principle of strategic deterrence; and the long-range effect on the principle of political containment. A useful contribution to our understanding of why SDI proved so divisive.

396 **Swords and Shields: NATO, the USSR, and New Choices for Long Range Offense and Defense.**
Fred S. Hoffman, Albert Wohlstetter, David S. Yost. Lexington, Massachusetts: D. C. Heath, 1987. 371p.
The theme of the book is summed up in the sub-title. It examines the new technologies of offence and defence and how they might further the objectives of NATO and the Warsaw Pact. Considerable attention is given both to SDI and to proposals for a ballistic missile defence of Western Europe. The book is divided into four parts. The first deals with the context; the second with new Soviet military doctrines and emerging Soviet offensive and defensive capabilities; the third with Western choices; and the fourth with the implications for security and stability. The fifteen chapters include contributions by Albert Wohlstetter, Dennis Gormley, William Odom, Uwe Nerlich, and James A. Thomson. This volume offers many insights into the interaction between technology and strategy.

397 **SDI: A View from Europe.**
Robert C. Hughes. Washington, DC: National Defense University Press, 1990. 254p.
Written by a United States Air Force colonel who spent the mid-1980s as part of the US delegation to NATO, this book looks at European responses to the proposed Strategic Defense Initiative enunciated by President Reagan in March 1983. The author traces the European reactions at both the public and the private levels. He

identifies several reasons why the West Europeans were unable to provide a single concerted response and looks at the national reactions of the leading allied countries. In addition, Hughes assesses the implications of SDI for NATO strategy. The study is both easily accessible to the reader and very good on the reasons why the Europeans were never very comfortable with SDI.

398 **Thinking about the Strategic Defense Initiative: an Alliance Perspective.**
Arnold Kanter. *International Affairs*, vol. 61, no. 3 (Summer 1985), p. 449-464.
The author highlights the variations in European responses to SDI, then considers the impact of the programme on the credibility of the United States security guarantee, on the countervailing strategy, NATO plans for deliberate escalation, NATO conventional defences, third-country nuclear forces, Soviet strategic defence forces, and arms control. He concludes his perceptive and helpful analysis with some suggestions for alliance management.

399 **The Role of ATBM in NATO Strategy.**
David Rubenson, James Bonomo. *Survival*, vol. 29, no. 6 (November-December 1987), p. 511-527.
Written by two analysts at Rand this article examines the potential role of ATBMs within NATO's existing strategy and separate from SDI. It sees ATBMs as a potential counter to Soviet conventionally armed theatre ballistic missiles as well as low-yield nuclear armed systems. The authors look at the NATO targets for Soviet missiles and suggest that many of these can be protected through passive defences. They conclude that ATBM might have merit as a long-term option for airbase protection. A sensible analysis of an issue which was all too often bound up with discussion of SDI.

400 **Missile Defenses and West European Security: NATO Strategy, Arms Control and Deterrence.**
Robert M. Soofer. New York: Greenwood Press, 1988. 174p.
A study which outlines and assesses the reactions of the major West European nations to President Reagan's Strategic Defense Initiative of March 1983 and to subsequent suggestions that an anti-tactical missile system should be deployed in Europe. It attempts to place these reactions in perspective, not only by examining the earlier European reaction to the American debate over anti-ballistic missiles in the period from 1965 to 1972, but also by looking at French, British and German perspectives and preferences on nuclear deterrence and arms control. The author is very critical of the notion of escalation uncertainty which was central to the NATO strategy of Flexible Response and also argues that although political factors may intercede to dampen support for anti-tactical missiles in Europe there is a strong strategic rationale for their deployment. This book is valuable mainly as an exercise in a particular kind of American strategic logic which is insensitive to the strategic preferences and needs of the European allies, and which tells the Europeans that they do not really know what is good for them.

401 **Ballistic Missile Defense for Europe.**
David E. Sorenson. *Comparative Strategy*, vol. 5, no. 2 (1985),
p. 159-178.
With the debate over SDI beginning to focus on the theatre dimension, Sorenson explores the case for deployment of theatre ballistic missile defences. He highlights the problems and the potential of theatre defences and concludes that although it might be controversial it would provide one way of dealing with the Soviet SS-20 threat.

402 **Britain's Response to the Strategic Defense Initiative.**
Trevor Taylor. *International Affairs*, vol. 62, no. 2 (Spring 1986),
p. 217-230.
One of three articles in this issue of *International Affairs* looking at the reaction of the European allies to President Reagan's Strategic Defense Initiative. The author shows how Britain has been hesitant, has given qualified political support, and has sought technological benefits.

403 **Ballistic Missile Defense and the Atlantic Alliance.**
David S. Yost. *International Security*, vol. 7, no. 2 (Fall 1982),
p. 143-174.
Writing with great prescience months before President Reagan's Strategic Defense Initiative, Yost notes that ballistic missile defence (BMD) policy options are being reviewed in the United States and that this could have important consequences for European security. Looking back at the earlier European reactions to the ABM debate in the United States Yost examines European views on BMD, particularly those of Britain, the Federal Republic of Germany, and France. US BMD alternatives, such as limited or extensive homeland defence and anti-tactical missiles, are also discussed. Yost favours this new agenda item, arguing that it is time to reassess the lack of Western damage-limiting capabilities. While doubts exist about the technical maturity and economic costs of BMD, the author suggests it is still worth pursuing as a potential damage-limiting strategy.

404 **Western Europe and the U.S. Strategic Defense Initiative.**
David S. Yost. *Journal of International Affairs*, vol. 41, no. 2
(Summer 1988), p. 269-323.
Examines West European perspectives on SDI and shows how the Reagan vision of US–Soviet defence–dominance has been seen to entail a perplexing endorsement of ongoing Soviet strategic defence programmes as stabilizing. While many West Europeans would be pleased to see a reduction in the strategic vulnerability of the United States, the advantages for the West in a lessening of Soviet vulnerability to Western retaliation are not obvious. Although this sentiment has figured in the West European debate over SDI, Yost emphasizes the capacity for the Soviet Union to develop its own strategic defence irrespective of what the United States does.

405 **European Anxieties about Ballistic Missile Defense.**
David S. Yost. *Washington Quarterly*, vol. 7, no. 4 (Fall 1984),
p. 112-129.
The author argues that although European anxieties about the Reagan Administration's Strategic Defense Initiative are understandable, they are not fully justified.

Surveying the European reactions he identifies the irritations over lack of consultation, the concerns over the future of French and British strategic nuclear forces, and the worries about the impact on arms control and détente. His main thesis is that the real problem is the Soviet ballistic missile defence programme and that the Reagan Administration has failed to emphasize that it is responding to this rather than simply taking the lead on strategic defences.

NATO and maritime strategy

406 **Naval Power and National Security: The Case for the Maritime Strategy.**
Linton F. Brooks. *International Security*, vol. 11, no. 2 (Fall 1986),
p. 58-88.

This article seeks to demonstrate the centrality of a maritime component to US military strategy and the commitment to NATO. Brooks argues that a forward naval strategy can strengthen deterrence, contribute strongly to European security and NATO cohesion, and also check Soviet global influence. After elucidating Soviet naval strategy, Brooks identifies three main goals of the maritime strategy: to deny the Soviet Union its kind of war, to destroy the Soviet Navy, and to influence the course and outcome of a land battle in Europe. The author also challenges three major criticisms of the maritime strategy: its irrelevance to conflict in Europe, its high-risk nature, and its opportunity costs. Although the case is not wholly convincing, Brooks does a very good job of presenting the arguments in favour of the Maritime Strategy.

407 **Maritime Strategy, Geopolitics and the Defense of the West.**
Colin S. Gray. New York: Ranmapo Press, 1986. p. 85.

A trenchant and provocative analysis which not only argues that the United States is first and foremost a maritime power but also offers a critique of NATO strategy which claims that the Europeans draw far too rigid a distinction between pre-war deterrence and subsequent military strategy in the event that deterrence fails. Gray argues that efforts to identify, negotiate, and implement strategically rational defence plans for the Western Alliance are usually undermined by political considerations. He subsequently recommends that NATO conventional forces be improved and that the lead in this come from the European allies, thereby allowing the United States to place more emphasis on its maritime forces.

408 **The Maritime Strategy and the Atlantic Alliance.**
Robert S. Jordan. *Journal of the Royal United Services Institute for Defence Studies*, vol. 132, no. 3 (September 1987), p. 45-54.

Looks at the historical evolution of maritime strategy in NATO from the early years of the Alliance. The author also considers NATO's interests in the Mediterranean before examining the United States forward Maritime Strategy and the ways in which it diverges from European preferences and concerns.

409 Alliance Strategy and Navies: The Evolution and Scope of NATO's Maritime Dimension.
Robert S. Jordan. New York: St Martin's Press, 1990. 182p.

Discusses the origins and evolution of NATO's maritime dimension, the difficulties of defining and demarcating the various NATO maritime commands, and the evolution of the strategies that were designed to deter or defeat the Soviet maritime threat during the Cold War. The author provides considerable information on organizational arrangements and on the divergent problems faced in the Atlantic and Northern waters on the one side and the Mediterranean on the other. Attention is also given to NATO's maritime nuclear capacity. Although the volume does not explore some of the critical appraisals of the US Navy's Maritime Strategy it is a valuable study on a subject that is all too often neglected. There are useful appendices containing details of NATO's maritime commanders.

410 Maritime Strategy or Coalition Defense.
Robert W. Komer. Cambridge, Massachusetts: Abt Books, 1984. p. 116.

This analysis, written by a former Under-Secretary for Policy in the United States Department of Defense, starts from a concern that the United States in the early 1980s was drifting towards an unbalanced national strategy in which maritime forces were being emphasized at the expense of ground forces, especially those on the European continent which were deployed as part of a coalition strategy. Komer argues that allies are crucial and that the United States has had a tendency to under-estimate the contributions the Europeans have made to the common defence. As well as a defence of NATO this volume was an attack on the Reagan Administration's 'global unilateralism' which Komer argues was damaging to America's relations with its allies.

411 A Strategic Misstep: The Maritime Strategy and Deterrence in Europe.
John J. Mearsheimer. *International Security*, vol. 11, no. 2 (Fall 1986), p. 3-57.

A vitriolic critique of the Reagan Administration's desire for a 600-ship navy and of the Maritime Strategy which accompanied and justified this target. Mearsheimer's criticisms are comprehensive. He complains that the Maritime Strategy has been defined differently at different times and is still somewhat elusive. More substantively, he argues that not only does the strategy do nothing to help deterrence in Europe but, by diverting resources from ground and air forces, is actually detrimental to deterrence. He also claims that the emphasis on horizontal escalation, offensive sea control, and counterforce coercion would prove destabilizing in a crisis. In his view the Maritime Strategy has few redeeming qualities to offset its undesirable features.

412 Naval Strategy and National Security.
Edited by Steven E. Mille, Stephen Van Evera. Princeton, New Jersey: Princeton University Press, 1989. 389p.

This book brings together a collection of articles initially published in *International Security*, one of the leading journals in the field of security studies. It is important in the NATO context, both because of NATO's reliance on the sea lines of communication and because the Maritime Strategy enunciated by the United States in the first half of the 1980s envisaged a major contribution by the United States Navy to a war in Europe. One of the highlights of the volume is a piece by John Mearsheimer entitled 'A Strategic Misstep: The Maritime Strategy and Deterrence in Europe' which offers a blistering critique and contends that the Maritime Strategy endangers crisis stability but contributes little to deterrence in Europe. The other is a superb analysis by Barry Posen of the way inadvertent escalation could occur in Europe. Although the focus of Posen's piece is on the Northern Flank, many of his arguments have much broader relevance. This is a very useful compilation.

The United States and NATO

413 **The U.S. Military Presence in Europe and French Security Policy.**
Yves Boyer. *Washington Quarterly*, vol. 11, no. 2 (Spring 1988),
p. 197-207.
Considers the argument that there are trends in the United States – especially greater
reliance on technology and the budgetary crisis – which could lead to a significant
military withdrawal from Western Europe, but argues that, geopolitically as well as
militarily, the United States could withdraw from Europe only at the cost of its own
security and influence. The final section of this useful article considers the implications
of this for French defence policy. Although written before the end of the Cold War
some of the analysis continues to be relevant.

414 **The Politics of Negotiation: American Dealings with Allies, Adversaries
and Friends.**
Linda P. Brady.   Chapel Hill, North Carolina: University of North
Carolina Press, 1991. 269p.
A useful book which focuses on the impact of politics on the success or failure of
negotiations involving the United States and its European allies during the 1970s and
1980s. The author provides a framework for analysing negotiation which identifies the
multiple influences on government behaviour. Part two of the book looks at the
negotiations resulting from NATO's Long-term Defense Program agreed upon in 1978.
In this context, the two case-studies are negotiation on Host Nation Support and the
negotiations leading to the 1979 decision to deploy new theatre nuclear forces in
Europe. Part three looks at negotiations with adversaries, focusing upon the MBFR
and the INF negotiations. Part four of the volume focuses upon mixed relationships
and includes a chapter on the out-of-area issue. The succinct conclusions offers some
policy implications drawn from the case-studies. A systematic and valuable study which
offers a novel and important perspective.

415   **The Atlantic Fantasy: The US, NATO and Europe.**
       David Calleo.   Baltimore, Maryland: Johns Hopkins University Press,
       1970. 182p.

A strong critique of NATO, which argues that it has been the means of organizing an American protectorate in Europe, and that it has reflected European dependence rather than Atlantic interdependence, and American hegemony rather than integration. The author explores the Gaullist challenge to American dominance in NATO, the domestic constraints on the United States, and the financial strains in the Atlantic relationship. He suggests that the real replacement for American troops in Europe is a European nuclear force and recommends that the United States gives the allies technical assistance in the creation of such a force.

416   **Beyond American Hegemony: The Future of the Western Alliance.**
       David P. Calleo.   New York: Basic Books, 1987. 288p.

In a study that builds upon earlier analyses which developed many of the same themes, David Calleo argues that the Atlantic Alliance is little more than an American protectorate for Europe and, as such, is becoming increasingly unreliable and irrelevant. NATO, he believes, was appropriate in a period of American hegemony but is less appropriate to the more pluralistic world that has developed since the Alliance was created. Having concluded that NATO in its present form cannot remain viable, Calleo considers possible alternatives and emphasizes the need for a devolution of power and responsibilities from the United States to Western Europe. This is an articulate and persuasive presentation of the American devolutionist argument which emphasizes the need to redress the relative share of the security burden between Western Europe and the United States. To this, Calleo adds a theory of hegemonic decline. He presents a pluralist interpretation of a world in which continued American hegemony is neither possible nor desirable. Calleo does not favour the dissolution of NATO but argues that it is no longer viable in its present form. At the heart of his recommendations is the need to reverse two trends: American military over-extension and European military under-development. His conclusion is that Western security need not be jeopardized by American hegemonic decline if NATO's European members rise to the challenge.

417   **U.S. Policy and the New Europe.**
       Frank C. Church.   *Foreign Affairs*, vol. 45, no. 1 (October 1966),
       p. 49-57.

A perspective from the United States Senate in a period of growing sentiment for United States troop cuts in Europe. Amongst other things Church argues that the Supreme Allied Commander Europe (SACEUR) should be a European rather than an American organization. This idea has surfaced periodically since, but has not been acted upon partly because an American SACEUR has been the custodian of the United States nuclear guarantee to Western Europe.

418   **Europe and the "Structure of Peace".**
       William C. Cromwell.   *Orbis*, vol. 22, no. 1 (Spring 1978), p. 11-36.

An excellent and informative article which looks at the Nixon–Kissinger foreign policy towards Europe. It discusses the conceptual underpinnings of United States policy, Senate demands for US troop reductions in Europe which led the administration to pressurize the Europeans to share more of the burden through increased defence spending, and the deterioration of EC–US relations during Nixon's term in office. The

Year of Europe is given particular attention and the author discusses both the issue of the linkage between security and economic issues and the impact of the 1973 Middle East war and its aftermath. The United States military alert, the European Community's declaration on a European identity and the Washington Energy Conference are all discussed in an incisive manner. The author points out that although the United States had supported European unity when Europe was politically divided and accepted Washington's leadership, it was dismayed when Europe was for the first time unified on an issue and adopted a different position from that preferred by the United States.

419 **US Foreign Policy and European Security.**
Arthur Cyr. New York: St Martin's Press, 1987. 156p.

Looks at the problems facing NATO in the latter half of the 1980s and places them in a broad historical perspective. Although the thrust of the volume is historical, the author derives from his survey a series of sensible lessons which he outlines in the final chapter. A slim volume, but one which offers some good insights on the nature of Atlantic relations and makes some persuasive prescriptions. The author concludes that the interests of NATO members have sometimes been very different, but that NATO's limited goals have ensured continuity of Alliance institutions and understandings. A corollary of this position is that there are lots of competing or incongruent interests which the allies had best leave alone in their common planning efforts.

420 **The Debate on the American Presence and Role in Europe.**
Olivier Debouzy. Paris: The European Strategy Group, January 1991. 127p.

A good overview of the United States military presence in Western Europe which explores the initial US desire to qualify the commitment to Western Europe and the European desire to obtain an irrevocable commitment. Debouzy also surveys the history of NATO, locating the issue of the American military presence within a broader set of issues and problems, and offers some incisive conclusions relating to NATO's ability to live with ambiguity. The concluding section is aptly entitled NATO in the Twilight Zone.

421 **Commitment in American Foreign Policy.**
Terry Deibel. Washington, DC: National Defense University, April 1980. 70p.

This is interesting primarily as a study of commitment rather than as an analysis of European security. Nevertheless, some of the ideas and arguments about the dimensions of commitment could prove very useful in understanding both the United States' commitment to Western Europe in the past and the reappraisal of this commitment resulting from the end of the Cold War. The author examines legal (or formal), physical, behavioural and psychological aspects of commitment. All in all, a helpful study.

422 **United States Military Forces and Installations in Europe.**
Simon Duke. New York: Oxford University Press for SIPRI, 1989. 435p.

A very informative study which provides considerable detail about American military installations and military personnel in Europe. It contains a short but useful introductory chapter which briefly outlines the role of US forces and bases in Europe and comments on the domestic debate in the United States about these forces. The main body of the study, however, is concerned with identifying the historical background and the legal basis for American military installations in individual European countries. The chapters on the Federal Republic of Germany (FRG), Spain, and the United Kingdom are particularly important and informative. In addition, the book has valuable chapters on command, control, communications and intelligence, and on logistics. The final chapter looks at the future of US military basing in Europe and assesses the prospects for change. Although this chapter is dated, the book as a whole remains a valuable resource: for anyone looking for facts and figures relating to the American military presence in Western Europe through the Cold War there will be little need to go further. The analysis is not quite as good as the detail, but this is a well-researched volume which provides much essential information. It contains interesting maps and tables and some extremely helpful annexes with extensive details of forces, weapons systems and organizational arrangements.

423   **In Defense of NATO: The Alliance's Enduring Value.**
Keith A. Dunn.   Boulder, Colorado: Westview Press, 1990. 114p.
This study highlights the continuing relevance of NATO to US global security interests and the importance of Western Europe to the United States. It is a direct response to some of the criticisms levelled at the United States commitment to Western Europe during the 1980s or what the author describes as 'NATO bashing'. Dunn looks sceptically at the most prevalent criticisms, assesses American interests on a region-by-region basis, emphasizes the strategic importance of Western Europe to the United States, looks at the contribution of Western Europe to its own defence, and provides a critique of proposals for substantial cuts in American force levels in Europe. There is also a chapter on policy initiatives for NATO in the future. This is a sensible and succinct study, and many of Dunn's arguments for the maintenance of the American military presence in Western Europe remain relevant, although somewhat less compelling in the aftermath of the revolutionary changes of 1989 to 1991 and the disappearance of the Soviet Union as the primary threat to European security.

424   **NATO's Enduring Value.**
Keith A. Dunn.   *Foreign Policy*, no. 71 (Summer 1988), p. 156-175.
Challenges critics of NATO who contend that Europe is not as important to the United States as it was, that Europe has not been good at burden-sharing, that scaling back the United States commitment would lead to Europeanization and that withdrawing troops would save money. The author claims instead that because of economic considerations, its geostrategic location and cultural factors, Europe should remain a priority area of United States foreign policy. He also notes that the Europeans are doing far more in terms of burden-sharing than they are often given credit for and looks at the potential costs to the United States of withdrawal. Many of the arguments are developed in Dunn's book.

425   **Strategic Implications of the Continental–Maritime Debate.**
Keith Dunn, William Staudenmaier.   Washington, DC: Center for Strategic and International Studies, 1984. 136p. (The Washington Papers, no. 107).
A useful contribution to the debate which took place in the early and mid-1980s about whether the emphasis of the United States defence effort should be on maritime forces

or on alliance defence in Europe. This succinct study offers incisive and critical comments on the competing approaches and contains an illuminating discussion of some of the proposals for strengthening NATO's capacity for sustained conventional resistance. It also argues that Western Europe should remain the top regional priority for the United States.

426 **The American Stake in Europe: Retrospect and Prospect.**
Edward Mead Earle. *International Affairs*, vol. 27, no. 4
(October 1951), p. 423-433.

This article discusses American foreign policy towards Europe after the Second World War. It contrasts the isolationism after the First World War and the Senate's refusal to ratify the Treaty of Versailles with the strong support of the Senate for NATO and the United Nations after 1945. Possible reasons for this change are discussed and the milestones of American foreign policy under Truman are identified. Argues that the European Recovery Program is in America's self-interest and not just a humanitarian effort and concludes with a summary of the political, moral and psychological motives underlying US foreign policy.

427 **U.S. Forces in Europe: How Many: Doing What?**
Alain C. Enthoven. *Foreign Affairs*, vol. 53, no. 3 (April 1975),
p. 513-532.

Presents a strong rationale for the maintenance of United States forces in Europe and challenges some prevalent claims about burden-sharing and the balance of payments costs of US troops in Europe. Enthoven also explores various ways of enhancing NATO's conventional and tactical nuclear posture.

428 **NATO and Congress.**
Annette Baker Fox. *Political Science Quarterly*, vol. 80, no. 3
(September 1965), p. 395-414.

One of the complications for the European allies in dealing with the United States has always been the role of Congress. This article examines the Congressional role on four policy issues related to American membership in NATO: military assistance, the deployment of American troops in Europe; burden-sharing; and provision for the nuclear defence of the alliance. Although different Congressional powers were relevant in each case, the author's examination of the first fifteen years of NATO produced little evidence that Congress had either significantly hindered or conspicuously promoted the use of NATO for achieving US and allied objectives.

429 **NATO and the Range of American Choice.**
William T. R. Fox, Annette B. Fox. New York: Columbia University
Press, 1967. 352p.

This is a distinctive and helpful analysis which looks at (among other things) the way in which NATO developed as an organization. It also provides an excellent account not only of the roles that NATO plays as an instrument of United States foreign policy – which include providing a channel for communication and diplomatic pressure, and extending the American resource base – but also the roles that the United States plays in NATO – to make good the deficiencies of the alliance as a whole, to act as pilot in strategic planning, to guide general policy, to energize the allies, to fill principal military commands, to manage NATO nuclear deterrence, and to demonstrate by example what others might do in terms of conventional defence. While these roles have been modified – or in some cases challenged – since this book was written, the analysis provides a good starting point for thinking about the changing nature of the Atlantic relationship. The other particularly valuable feature of this book is that it examines the impact on NATO of United States decision-making processes both in the executive branch and Congress, and looks at the impact of the United States on the decision-making process within NATO itself.

430   Why West Europe needs 300,000 GIs.
Leslie Gelb, Morton H. Halperin.   *Atlantic Community Quarterly*,
vol. 9, no. 1 (Spring 1971), p. 56-60.

A succinct analysis of why the early 1970s was a bad time to reduce troops in Europe. The authors take issue with the arguments put forward by Senator Mike Mansfield and his supporters for unilateral cuts in American troop levels in Europe.

431   The United States and West Germany: Cracks in the Security Foundation.
George A. Glass.   *Orbis*, vol. 23, no. 3 (Fall 1979), p. 535-548.

Looks at the controversy over the neutron bomb and the modernization of long-range theatre nuclear forces and shows how these raised once again questions about the United States' commitment to Europe and the role of Germany in NATO. United States' willingness to deploy these weapons in Europe ran into the reluctance of a Bonn government concerned about domestic pressures. To make nuclear modernization acceptable, Bonn set conditions for the deployments, something which caused considerable strain in the relationship with Washington.

432   NATO: An Uneasy Alliance.
Norman A. Graebner.   *Current History*, vol. 58, no. 345 (May 1970),
p. 298-303, 308.

An interesting article which argues that the United States' commitment to Western Europe guarantees stability but nothing more.

433   NATO: Time to Call it a Day?
Colin S. Gray.   *The National Interest*, no. 10 (Winter 1987-88),
p. 13-26.

A critical analysis by a prominent conservative strategic analyst who argues that NATO suffers from a failure to reform its force structure. This has created a disparity between plans and expectations on the one side and prospective crises or wartime reality on the other. Gray argues that the Alliance has to adapt to survive. Although containment of Soviet power remained an appropriate guiding concept, it was in danger of being overtaken by political, economic, and military change. The major alternatives considered are devolution and Fortress America, both of which have become more attractive as a result of the subsequent demise of the Soviet Union.

434 **Can the Atlantic Alliance Last out the Century?**
François Heisbourg. *International Affairs*, vol. 63, no. 3
(Summer 1987), p. 425-438.

Assessing the future prospects for NATO as it approaches forty, this article, written by the Director of the International Institute for Strategic Studies, focuses on American domestic pressures stemming from the Gramm–Rudman Amendment. The author suggests that this is likely to have an impact on United States force structure. Possible European reactions to such changes are discussed. Guidelines are also proposed for alliance responses on arms control initiatives.

435 **Will the United States Remain a European Power?**
Robert Hunter. *Survival*, vol. 30, no. 3 (May/June 1988), p. 210-231.

In an interesting and carefully developed analysis, Hunter argues that although NATO has always suffered from crises, several developments in the latter half of the 1980s led the allies to ask more fundamental questions than ever before about the United States' commitment to Europe. The central thesis is that by 1988 it was no longer clear that the Europeans trusted their security arrangements with the United States, or that the United States was willing to continue playing a role as a European power. Hunter explores the issues surrounding the US nuclear guarantee, and although he argues that the whole debate about extended deterrence has an air of unreality, he acknowledges the symbolism of US nuclear weapons deployed in Europe. He also considers other reasons why there are question marks over a continuing US role in Europe, including both the sense that the job has been done and also the corrosive effects of economic competition between Europe and the United States. Finally, Hunter offers some prescriptions for avoiding further estrangement between Western Europe and the United States but acknowledges that, even if these are followed, questions about the continued role of the United States in Europe security are likely to become increasingly insistent.

436 **Restructuring Alliance Commitments.**
Edited by Robert Hunter. Washington, DC: Center for Strategic and International Studies, 1988. 56p. (Significant Issues Series).

Written just before the transition between the Reagan and Bush Administrations, this study explores the value of traditional alliances to the United States in a period when the Soviet threat (even before the revolution of 1989) seemed to have diminished very markedly. Three of the four sections of this short volume concern the United States' role within NATO and the Transatlantic alliance. The remaining section focuses solely on US–Japan relations. The study includes an analysis of strategic problems in NATO by Robert Komer and a chapter by Harald Malmgren looking at economic and political changes in the Transatlantic alliance. The theme underlying each contribution is the need to curb US unilateralism and recognize the new strength of Western Europe. Only by doing this, the authors argue, can a genuine European pillar be developed and a more equitable sharing of burdens be accomplished. Overall this is a useful snapshot of the state of Atlantic relations in the late 1980s but little more. It contains some sensible recommendations, although these were largely overtaken by events in Europe in 1989 and 1990.

437 **The Limited Partnership: Europe, the United States, and the Burdens of Alliance.**
Josef Joffe. Cambridge, Massachusetts: Ballinger, 1987. 225p.
Joseph Joffe is a committed Atlanticist and this book has all the virtues and shortcomings of such a perspective. Joffe places considerable emphasis on the importance of the United States as a unifying and pacifying force in a Europe that historically has been unable to conduct its own affairs without resort to destructive wars. He stresses too the importance of the United States as a counter-weight to the Soviet Union. Yet he is also aware of many of the difficulties the Alliance faces on both sides of the Atlantic. Accordingly, this study examines the tensions between détente and Alliance cohesion, the structural problems relating to nuclear weapons, the impact of popular opinion against nuclear weapons, and the issues related to conventional deterrence. The final chapter examines the potential costs to the United States of disengagement from Europe. An incisive and important analysis, which represented an important strand in German thinking throughout the Cold War.

438 **NATO and the United States: The Enduring Alliance.**
Lawrence S. Kaplan. Boston, Massachusetts: Twayne, 1988. 237p.
An excellent overview which traces the history of NATO from its origins through to the mid-1980s. Lawrence Kaplan looks at the origins of the revolution in United States foreign policy which took place in 1949; the Brussels Treaty connection and the Treaty of Washington; the impact of the Korean War; the move to a 'New Look' strategy; the French challenge to the Alliance from 1958 to 1966; détente and the Nixon Doctrine; the Dual Track decision of 1979; and the subsequent arms control negotiations. His final chapter looks at NATO in retrospect and prospect and notes that although NATO suffers from certain weaknesses and frictions among its members, it retains its overall importance as a guarantor of security of the United States and Western Europe.

439 **NATO and the Nixon Doctrine Ten Years Later.**
Lawrence S. Kaplan. *Orbis*, vol. 24, no. 1 (Spring 1980), p. 149-164.
Places the Nixon Doctrine in proper perspective and looks at the changes which took place between the enunciation of the doctrine – also known as the Guam doctrine – in 1969 and the end of the 1970s. The author argues that Europe has a higher priority in US policy than anticipated in the doctrine, but also suggests that Soviet involvement in Asia and Africa requires that the Alliance members coordinate their positions on issues beyond Europe. A valuable look at the gap between doctrines and their implementation.

440 **Eagle in A New World: American Grand Strategy in the Post-Cold War Era.**
Edited by Kenneth A. Oye, Robert Lieber, Donald Rothchild. New York: Harper Collins, 1992. 451p.
The latest in a series which includes *Eagle Entangled* (1979), *Eagle Defiant* (1983), and *Eagle Resurgent* (1989), this volume provides a set of incisive analyses of the central issues facing American foreign policy in the aftermath of the Cold War. Particularly relevant are the introduction by Kenneth Oye, which argues that the widening disjunctions between military and economic strength was one of the key factors leading to the end of the Cold War; the essay by Charles Glaser and George W. Downs, 'Defense Policy: US Role in Europe and Nuclear Strategy' which argues that there are

still security needs in Europe demanding American involvement; and the chapter by Robert Lieber on 'The United States and Western Europe in the Post-Cold War World' which concludes that 'although both the United States and the countries of Western Europe have fundamental interests in common that point toward the maintenance of their long-standing relationship, the intrinsic difficulties posed by the post-Cold War era are enormous. These problems stem not only from the international environment but also from the resources and the domestic foundations – in America as well as in Europe – on which foreign policy and grand strategy ultimately rest' (p. 333).

441 How NATO Weakens the West.
Melvyn B. Krauss.   New York: Simon and Schuster, 1986. 271p.
A very strong critique of NATO, of the Atlanticist impulse in United States policy and of the US commitment of forces to Western Europe. Starting from a neo-conservative perspective, the author argues that the European allies are guilty of free-riding, that the United States' commitment distorts the US defence budget, that the allies have failed to support the United States adequately in the Third World, and that they have substituted a policy of détente for deterrence and defence. He concludes that the United States should abandon NATO through a phased withdrawal of troops which would allow the allies to take on greater responsibility themselves. This is one of the fullest statements of the neo-conservative position on NATO.

442 The Unipolar Moment.
Charles Krauthammer.   *Foreign Affairs: America and the World 1990/91*, vol. 70, no. 1 (1991), p. 23-33.
An influential article in which the author challenges three conventional assumptions about the shape of the post-Cold War era: that a bipolar world will be replaced by multipolarity; that there will be an increased consensus for an American internationalist foreign policy; and that the absence of an overt Soviet threat automatically improves global security. He contends that bipolarity has been replaced by unipolarity, with the United States as the pre-eminent world power. It is not clear, however, that the American public will continue to support this position. Nevertheless, the author argues, United States leadership in imposing a degree of international order is essential in a world which is increasingly disorderly. The problem, as he notes, is that 'averting chaos is a rather subtle call to greatness' (p. 33).

443 Continental Divide: Time to Disengage in Europe.
Christopher Layne.   *The National Interest*, no. 13 (Fall 1988), p. 13-27.
A familiar refrain from a critic of NATO and the US commitment to Western Europe. The author argues that the United States should take the initiative in seeking mutual superpower disengagement in Europe. The rationale is that this will deprive the Soviet Union of its diplomatic advantage in Western Europe, while signalling to the Europeans that US policy will change. Layne also emphasizes that this would pass the responsibility to Western Europe as to whether Europe should be defended with nuclear weapons. Layne argues that a failure to acknowledge the decay of NATO's foundations will lead to Alliance disintegration in an acrimonious atmosphere.

444 Atlanticism without NATO.
Christopher Layne.   *Foreign Policy*, no. 67 (Summer 1987), p. 22-45.
Layne, a long-time critic of NATO, argues that attempts to reform or restructure the Atlantic Alliance in an effort to preserve the postwar order in Europe are misguided

and that the United States should adopt bolder measures designed to bring about a real transformation in its relationship with Western Europe. He sees NATO as perpetuating a US protectorate over Western Europe and removing Western Europe's incentive to become more self-sufficient. He criticizes schemes for reform and argues instead that the United States should become the champion of 'Euronationalism' and European unification. This could be started by the United States initiating a process of devolution and Europeanization in the Alliance. Although arguing for radical change, Layne contends that in the long term this would make for a more harmonious relationship between the United States and Western Europe.

445　**The Declining Hegemon: The United States and European Defense, 1960-1990.**
Joseph Lepgold.　New York: Praeger, 1990. 225p.
An excellent analysis which looks at the US role in European security matters and relates this to the notion of the United States as the declining hegemon in world politics. The analysis deals with theoretical considerations and offers considerable insight into the issue of hegemonic stability and adaptation. There is also a good discussion of the issues related to the US role in European defence from the 1960s through to the 1980s. The author examines the problems of extended deterrence, burden-sharing and the domestic debate about the commitment to Western Europe. The final chapter explores the future of the US role in Europe in view of changing conditions both in the United States and the international system. In short, this is an important book which should be looked at by all those interested in NATO, Atlantic relations, and United States security policy.

446　**Keeping US Troops in Europe: The Real Reason Why.**
Robert A. Levine.　Santa Monica, California: Rand Corporation, September 1990. 16p. (Rand Note N-3085-AF).
Outlines a rationale for maintaining US forces in Europe which is not linked to the Soviet threat. The main argument is that the United States has interests in Europe – including stability, prosperity and political influence – all of which are enhanced by the maintenance of a military presence on the Continent.

447　**U.S. Ground Forces and the Defense of Central Europe.**
William P. Mako.　Washington, DC: Brookings Institution, 1983. 137p.
The author examines the structure and strength of US ground forces from 1940 until the early 1980s, highlights the demands on ground forces in Central Europe in the 1980s and asks should the United States' contribution to NATO change. This is a highly detailed study which deals with such matters as force to space ratios, operational reserves and the like. The author concludes that a convincing case for significant changes in deployments and force structure has not been made but that there is a good case for a change of direction from rapid to more deliberate reinforcement.

448　**U.S. Troops in Europe: Issues, Costs, and Choices.**
John Newhouse, Melvin Croan, Edward Fried, Timothy Stanley.
Washington, DC: Brookings Institution, 1971. 177p.
A major contribution to the United States debate of the latter half of the 1960s and the first half of the 1970s over the level of the American military presence in Western

Europe. The opening chapter by Newhouse examines the pressures for troop reduction led by Senator Mike Mansfield. This sets the scene for subsequent analyses of Soviet policy, the military balance, the burden-sharing issues, and the financial cost to the United States of its NATO commitment. The conclusion, which has echoes in the post-Cold War debate about the US force level in Europe is that the presence does not fit a precisely calculable military requirement but has to meet a variety of political and strategic considerations related to the kind of world order the United States seeks to encourage; the kind of lasting relationship it seeks with Western Europe; and the degree of stability it wants in Europe. After reading this book, those who look at the current debate over US troops in Europe will feel a strong sense of *déjà vu*.

449 **Nunn 1990: A New Military Strategy.**
Sam Nunn. Washington, DC: The Center for Strategic and International Studies, 1990. 84p. (Significant Issue Series).
Consisting of a series of statements made in March and April 1990 by the Chairman of the Senate Armed Services Committee, this volume highlights the response of a key figure in Washington to the revolution of 1989 in Eastern Europe. Nunn examines the changed threat environment and considers some of its consequences. He also outlines a new military strategy, arguing that American forces in Europe should be reduced to between 75,000 and 100,000 within the next five years. He suggests that there should be greater specialization in NATO and that US ground forces should be primarily 'reception' forces for reinforcement in a crisis.

450 **The American Commitment to European Security.**
Colin L. Powell. *Survival*, vol. 34, no. 2 (Summer 1992), p. 3-11.
This is the text of the Alastair Buchan lecture given at the International Institute for Strategic Studies in April 1992 by President Bush's Chairman of the Joint Chiefs of Staff. Powell reiterates the importance of Western Europe to the United States and makes very clear the desire to retain a substantial American military presence in Western Europe. He also argues that there must be greater sharing of burdens by the European allies. The overall emphasis, however, is on the factors of continuity rather than of change in United States policy.

451 **SAIS Review.**
Laurence Radway. *US Forces in Europe: The Case for Cautious Contraction*, vol. 5, no. 1 (Winter-Spring 1985), p. 227-242.
Although recognizing that there is no groundswell for American disengagement from Western Europe, the author recommends that the United States should begin the process of reducing its military forces gradually and carefully. He anticipates the criticisms of his proposal by committed Atlanticists and contends that these are not particularly compelling. At the same time the author advocates that changes be made gradually and in ways which allow for a constant monitoring of the situation to detect destabilizing consequences. This is primarily useful as a moderate rather than an extreme critique of the Atlantic security framework.

452 **American Military in Europe: Controversy over NATO Burden Sharing.**
Christopher S. Raj. New Delhi: ABC Publishing House, 1983. 380p.
Based on some impressive research, this book provides an excellent overview of the American military presence in Europe, and the political and economic issues

associated with it. The study traces variations in the size of the American troop contingents in Europe and is particularly good on the debates within the Kennedy Administration in the early 1960s. It offers one of the fullest and most comprehensive analyses of this issue and, although hard to get, should be read by anyone interested in the evolution of the United States' commitment to Western Europe.

453 Should America Pay for Europe's Security?
Jeffrey Record. *Washington Quarterly*, vol. 5, no. 1 (Winter 1982), p. 19-24.

After noting that the United States devotes over half its defence budget to its NATO commitment, the author contends that what really preserves European security is the collective strength of United States and allied forces. He is critical of the failure of the European allies to bear a fair share of the burden and considers ways in which they could be prodded into doing more. Some of Record's ideas on this were subsequently embodied in the Nunn Amendment of 1984 which failed to pass but which linked the maintenance of US troop levels in Europe to greater European defence efforts.

454 Alliances in American Foreign Policy: Issues in the Quest for Collective Defense.
Edited by Alan Ned Sabrosky. Boulder, Colorado: Westview Press, 1988. 150p.

This is an interesting collection of essays. The editor looks at the role of alliances in American foreign policy; Earl Ravenal argues that extended deterrence is a very risky policy for the United States; and James O'Leary explores economic relationships among the allies, seeing them as a source of both cohesion and tension. There are also essays on Congress and NATO, and one on public opinion, which really looks much more at the sources of continued cohesion in NATO before identifying what the author, Gregory Foster, describes as a new public opinion strategy.

455 Europe after an American Withdrawal: Economic and Military Issues.
Edited by Jane M. O. Sharp. Oxford, England: Oxford University Press for SIPRI, 1990. 501p.

This comprehensive volume, which is a companion to the study on the American military presence in Western Europe by Simon Duke (*see* item no. 422), examines the possible consequences for Western Europe of a withdrawal of United States forces from the Continent. The assumption was not that such a withdrawal was imminent but that it was necessary to consider the possible implications should it take place. The contributors assessed the economic and military consequences of two hypothetical withdrawal options – one in which all US forces and facilities were withdrawn from Europe and demobilized even though the United States remained a member of the Alliance, and one in which a skeleton presence remained. After assessments of how much of the United States defence budget is actually devoted to the commitment to Western Europe, attention is given to the economics of US bases and facilities in Western Europe. A helpful overview of this by David Greenwood is followed by more specific chapters which examine the economic impact of US forces and bases in the FRG, the Benelux countries, Portugal, Greece, Spain, Turkey, Italy, the United Kingdom, and the Northern Flank states. The third section of the book assesses the military implications of a US military withdrawal. Particularly noteworthy is the chapter which deals with the contribution of US C^3I to the defence of Europe. The final section looks at some of the problems the Europeans would have in providing for their security after an American withdrawal. Although overtaken in some respects by the events of 1989 and 1990, this book is a valuable starting point for anyone interested in the consequences of a much smaller American military role in Western Europe.

456   **The End of Alliance: America and the Future of Europe.**
Ronald Steel.   New York: Viking, 1964. 148p.

The author argues very strongly that by the early 1960s NATO had become a sacred cow of United States foreign policy. Among his charges is that the Alliance had developed a vested interest in the perpetuation of the adversarial relationship with the Soviet Union. Part of Steel's argument is that the increasing vulnerability of the United States had rendered the US nuclear guarantee incredible and made the Alliance itself of dubious value. He also claimed that the Alliance must either develop into a political federation or disintegrate. Although many of the prognoses proved wrong, this is interesting as an early statement of a recurrent, if subordinate, theme in United States scholarly analysis of the Alliance.

457   **The United States Commitment to Western Europe: Strategic Ambiguity and Political Disintegration?**
Phil Williams.   *International Affairs*, vol. 59, no. 2 (Spring 1983), p. 195-210.

An analysis which looks at the political and strategic dimensions of the United States commitment to Western Europe. The author argues that strategic ambiguity is inevitable, but that so long as the political links are strong this need not undermine deterrence in Europe or the cohesion of NATO.

458   **The Senate and U.S. Troops in Europe.**
Phil Williams.   London: Macmillan, 1985. 315p.

This study examines the politics of the American commitment to Europe. It looks at the initial steps whereby the United States became committed to Europe, the subsequent decision to deploy troops, and the debate over this deployment in the American senate. It also traces the later efforts of Senator Mike Mansfield and others to bring about reductions in the size of the American contingent in Europe. It looks in detail at the Mansfield resolutions from 1966 to 1970 and the Mansfield amendments from 1970 to 1975. Attention is given to the way successive administrations responded to Congressional pressures. The Nixon Administration, in particular, engaged in extensive lobbying efforts to defeat the Mansfield Amendments of 1971 and 1973. These efforts are discussed very fully in an analysis which shows how the debates of the 1960s and 1970s over troop withdrawals had echoes of the great debate of 1951 about sending troops to Europe.

459   **U.S. Troops in Europe.**
Phil Williams.   London: Routledge & Kegan Paul for the Royal Institute of International Affairs, 1984. 87p. (Chatham House Papers, no. 25).

An overview of the American military presence in Western Europe which looks at the historical background to this deployment, the rationale and costs of the presence, and the pressures for its reduction. In addition, the study highlights the difficulties in the way of efforts to strengthen NATO's conventional defence forces in the 1980s as well as the possible consequences of United States troop cuts.

460 **Alliance Policy in the Cold War.**
Edited by Arnold Wolfers.   Baltimore, Maryland: Johns Hopkins
University Press, 1959. 314p.

A volume of essays dealing with different aspects of American policy towards its allies during the first decade of the Cold War. The volume contains a number of incisive essays – the editor deals with 'Stresses and Strains' of cooperation with others, and also explores the distinction between collective defence and collective security; Paul Nitze, one of the principal authors of military containment, looks at 'Coalition Policy and the Concept of World Order'; and Hans Morgenthau examines 'Alliances in Theory and Practice'. There is also a very good chapter by Roger Hilsman which explores NATO strategy. Many of the issues that are raised are fundamental to the long-term American debate about foreign policy and national security and are particularly relevant now that the United States is searching for its bearings in the post-Cold War world.

461 **The American Military Presence in Europe: Current Debate in the United States.**
John Yochelson.   *Orbis*, vol. 15, no. 3 (Fall 1971), p. 784-807.

Looks at the American military presence in Western Europe as a focus of debate in the United States. The author explains why Senator Mike Mansfield introduced legislation to cut troops in Europe and also highlights the arguments used by the Administration to counter the Congressional pressure. A well-informed and informative analysis.

The European Nations and the Alliance

France and NATO

462 France Troubled Ally: De Gaulle's Heritage and Prospects.
Edgar S. Furniss. New York: Harper and Brothers, 1960. 512p.
Explains the continuity in French foreign policy from the Fourth to the Fifth Republics and examines the aspirations of de Gaulle to restore French grandeur. There are good chapters on France and NATO and on France and the United States, but these are placed within a much broader context.

463 De Gaulle's France and NATO: An Interpretation.
Edgar S. Furniss. *International Organization*, vol. 15, no. 3 (Summer 1961), p. 349-365.
Furniss explains the origins of de Gaulle's dissatisfaction with the French position in NATO and what was seen as subordination to the Anglo-American alliance. For those interested in the origins and rationale of the policy which led to the 1966 French decision to withdraw from NATO's integrated military organization this is a very good place to start.

464 France, the European Crisis and the Alliance.
James O. Goldsborough. *Foreign Affairs*, vol. 52, no. 3 (April 1974), p. 538-555.
Looks at tensions between the United States and Western Europe during 1973, the Year of Europe, and in particular at the role played by French Foreign Minister, Monsieur Jobert. Also argues that the events of the year highlighted for the Europeans the need for greater unity and that psychologically this was crucial.

465 **The Reluctant Ally: France and Atlantic Security.**
Michael M. Harrison. Baltimore, Maryland: Johns Hopkins
University Press, 1981. 304p.

A comprehensive and stimulating analysis of the French relationship with NATO.
Harrison looks at French policy in the Fourth Republic; at Gaullist perspectives; the
challenge to Atlantic hegemony; the joint policy of military independence and de-
alignment from 1958 to 1968; and France as a partial ally for NATO from 1968 to 1980.
A systematic and detailed account.

466 **Mitterrand's France in the Atlantic System: A Foreign Policy of
Accommodation.**
Michael M. Harrison. *Political Science Quarterly*, vol. 99, no. 2
(Summer 1984), p. 219-246.

Shows how the foreign and defence policy framework established during the first
decade of the Gaullist Fifth Republic serves as both guideline and constraint for
political groups and governments in France. French security policy is insulated from
debilitating experimentation because of a national élite consensus in favour of the
Gaullist framework. This prevents radical shifts in policy and allows those closest to
the core of the Gaullist paradigm to prevail in intra-governmental disputes. The
implication is that there are limits to French willingness to move closer to NATO.

467 **De Gaulle, Europe and the Atlantic Alliance.**
Stanley Hoffmann. *International Organization*, vol. 18, no. 1
(Winter 1964), p. 1-28.

An incisive analysis of de Gaulle's foreign policy and how it attempts to use both
Germany and the idea of a European Europe to compensate for French weakness – a
tactic that Hoffmann describes as using others as an elevator (p. 20). For all those
interested in the evolution of Gaullist policy towards the United States and NATO,
this is a must.

468 **Consensus of Silence: The French Socialist Party and Defense Policy
under Mitterrand.**
Jolyon Howorth. *International Affairs*, vol. 60, no. 4 (Autumn 1984),
p. 579-600.

Suggests that the old Gaullist consensus on foreign policy and defence has quietly
evaporated and that French strategic thinking is increasingly concerned with
conventional defence in Europe. The author highlights the French desire to restructure
the Alliance and create a European pillar. A detailed and persuasive analysis.

469 **France, NATO and European Security.**
Jean Klein. *International Security*, vol. 1, no. 3 (Winter 1977),
p. 21-41.

Considers the French relationship with NATO after the retirement of General de
Gaulle. The author, a noted French strategic analyst, argues that this became an issue
of major importance both in domestic politics and in the relationship with the United
States. Klein discusses de Gaulle's view of NATO and shows how he moved from
seeing it as a necessity during the early years of the Cold War, to the conclusion that it
was a burdensome 'bureaucratic machine' imposed on the Europeans by the United

States. Klein traces French engagement and disputes with NATO through the Pompidou and d'Estaing administrations, paying particular attention to efforts to develop better coordination with SHAPE and to the issue of arms standardization within NATO. The subtle changes in the French strategic concept and the issue of broadened sanctuarization are also considered. This article highlights issues in French security policy which were subsequently to become even more salient and provides some excellent insights into French relations with NATO.

470 **French Nuclear Diplomacy.**
Wilfrid L. Kohl. Princeton, New Jersey: Princeton University Press, 1971. 412p.

French nuclear policy and alliance policy were inextricably linked. Although the main focus of this volume is on the development of French nuclear policy, the author examines how nuclear issues impinged on General de Gaulle's policy towards Britain, the United States and NATO. Kohl provides a good analysis of the nuclear-sharing issue and the MLF episode.

471 **French International Policy under de Gaulle and Pompidou: The Politics of Grandeur.**
Edward A. Kolodziej. Ithaca, New York: Cornell University Press, 1974. 618p.

This volume assesses French foreign policy under the Fifth Republic from de Gaulle's return to power in 1968 to 1974. Although one part of the book deals with French policy in the Third World, the main bulk of it is taken up with analysis of French policy in the Western bloc, and French policy in Europe. Kolodziej traces de Gaulle's policies within NATO and examines the French proposal for a three-power global directorate, as well as French strategic preferences. He also looks carefully at the rationale for the French decision to leave NATO's integrated military organization and at the subsequent emphasis placed by France on the maintenance of the Alliance and the American connection. This is a valuable study of French policy towards both NATO and Europe and brings out the nuances and subtleties in this policy. The Gaullist vision for Europe is also explored. The continuity between de Gaulle and Pompidou and the Gaullist legacy in foreign policy and national security policy are also given careful consideration.

472 **France, the Soviet Union, and the Nuclear Weapons Issue.**
Robbin F. Laird. Boulder, Colorado: Westview Press, 1985. 142p.

This book deals with the conflict between the Soviet Union and France over the role of nuclear weapons in European defence in the context of the broader debate over NATO's 1979 decision to deploy cruise and Pershing missiles in Europe. It argues that the Soviets attempted to denuclearize Europe, to create tensions in the Atlantic relationship, and to forestall trends towards the emergence of a stronger and more independent Western Europe. France, in contrast, tried to bolster the legitimacy of nuclear weapons, to strengthen the Atlantic nuclear connection and to enhance West European security cooperation. The book provides much detail on both Soviet and French nuclear forces. It is based primarily on translations of Russian- and French-language sources.

473   **The French Strategic Dilemma.**
Robbin F. Laird.   *Orbis*, vol. 28, no. 2 (Summer 1984), p. 307-328.
The author highlights the French strategic dilemma which stems from the traditional French emphasis on nuclear weapons to protect French territory and the external pressures which highlight the need to include West Germany in an extended security concept. This is a valuable article.

474   **French Security Policy: From Independence to Interdependence.**
Robbin F. Laird.   Boulder, Colorado: Westview Press, 1986. 186p.
This collection of essays examines the evolution of French security policy, with particular emphasis on the tension between independence and interdependence. The book provides a historical background and an assessment of future possibilities for France. There is an analysis by François Heisbourg of French security policy under Mitterrand from 1981 to 1985 which emphasizes the impact of fiscal constraints. The editor himself has several chapters, including one on French nuclear capabilities and one on the dilemmas attendant upon French doctrine for the use of these capabilities. There are chapters dealing with the impact of French nuclear weapons on Franco-German relations and on European solidarity. A chapter by Yves Boyer looks at high technology and the security relationship between the United States and Western Europe. The book contains several very useful tables and a succinct conclusion by the editor.

475   **Foreign Policy and Interdependence in Gaullist France.**
Edward L. Morse.   Princeton, New Jersey: Princeton University Press, 1973. 336p.
Goes much broader than French policy towards NATO but is very good on both French aspirations for independence and the limits to which this can be achieved given the increased interdependencies of the international system. Morse highlights the importance of welfare goals in setting limits to the French nuclear weapons programme and the French desire for independence in foreign and defence policies.

476   **De Gaulle and the Anglo-Saxons.**
John Newhouse.   London: André Deutsch, 1970. 374p.
A well-written, straightforward and informative account of relations between France, the United States and Britain in the period from just before General de Gaulle became President of France until his departure from office. It looks at de Gaulle's philosophy on foreign policy; his proposals for a trilateral directorate for the global defence of the West; the clash between the Kennedy Administration's conceptions of Europe and the Gaullist vision; the Skybolt episode and de Gaulle's veto of the British application to join the European Community; and de Gaulle's subsequent decision to withdraw from NATO's integrated military organization and to seek openings towards the Soviet Union and Eastern Europe.

477   **France: Preparations for European Leadership.**
Robert S. Rudney.   *The National Interest*, no. 9 (Fall 1987), p. 33-48.
Shows how the strategic ambiguities underlying traditional French security policy have been reassessed as France has adapted to emerging realities in Europe. The author examines the 1984-88 French defence programming law and argues that this reveals a greater French willingness to make military commitments to their European allies.

Attention is also given to French initiatives within the Western European Union and in the bilateral defence relationship with West Germany. Although there is an emerging domestic consensus in favour of increased European defence cooperation the difficulty has been in moving from the declaratory to operational levels. Nevertheless, the author believes France is in a unique position to propose a reform of the transatlantic security system.

478 **Mitterrand's New Atlanticism: Evolving French Attitudes towards NATO.**
Robert S. Rudney. *Orbis*, vol. 28, no. 1 (Spring 1984), p. 83-101.
Argues that the Socialist government of Mitterrand has not only given a high priority to modernizing its strategic nuclear forces but has also decided to reinforce its links with NATO particularly at the conventional level. Mitterrand's support for the INF deployment is examined and the author concludes that French efforts to promote a collective West European consciousness on matters of defence should be encouraged.

479 **Between the Rhine and the Elbe: France and the Conventional Defense of Europe.**
Diego A. Ruiz Palmer. *Comparative Strategy*, vol. 6, no. 4 (1987), p. 471-512.
Examines the potential role of France in the conventional defence of Europe against a background of increased NATO emphasis on conventional options and increased Franco-German defence cooperation. Attention is given to the Rapid Action Force, to French concepts of operations and to future French options.

480 **The Covert French Connection.**
Richard H. Ullman. *Foreign Policy*, no. 75 (Summer 1989), p. 3-33.
An important article which revealed that although France had left NATO's integrated military organization in 1966 and had consistently emphasized the virtues of independence it had received considerable assistance from the United States for its strategic nuclear programme. Part of the United States motivation for this assistance – which began during the Nixon Administration – was Washington's desire to enable France to save money on its nuclear capabilities and to allocate the resources to conventional forces. Cooperation was kept secret because of domestic considerations in both the United States and France.

481 **France's Deterrent Posture and Security in Europe: Part I: Capabilities and Doctrine.**
David S. Yost. London: IISS, Winter 1984/85. 72p. (Adelphi Paper 194).
Looks at French deterrence doctrine and French relations with the Atlantic Alliance since de Gaulle's decision to withdraw from the integrated military command. The author explores the issue of possible French participation in a conflict in Europe in the event of a Soviet attack on Germany. He also highlights the major components of France's deterrent posture.

482 **France's Deterrent Posture and Security in Europe: Part II: Strategic and Arms Control Implications.**
David S. Yost. London: IISS, Winter 1984/85. 75p. (Adelphi Paper 195).

Looks at the implications of the French strategic posture for NATO as well as for France itself. Yost explores the feasibility of the French notion of sanctuarization and considers the implications of failure as well as success. He argues that France's special status creates operational uncertainties but also has certain advantages for NATO. This and the first paper (*see* item no. 481) provide an excellent analysis of the dilemmas and ambiguities surrounding both French nuclear policy and the French relationship with NATO.

483 **France, the Cold War and the Western Alliance, 1944-49.**
John W. Young. Leicester, England: Leicester University Press, 1990. 309p.

Explores French motivations for joining NATO and shows how French concerns and objectives differed from those of other countries. There was, of course, some convergence, especially in the French desire for US financial assistance and its concern over the Soviet threat. What made French policy distinctive, however, was the concern over German resurgence, the loss of Great Power status, and the domestic pressures stemming from the existence of a large communist party in France. This is a useful and informative study.

Britain and NATO

484 **The Debatable Alliance.**
Coral Bell. London: Oxford University Press, 1964. 130p.

Looks at the special relationship between Britain and the United States and shows how this had a major impact on Britain's relations with its West European allies. Considerable attention is also given to the nuclear issue. A useful study which offers insight into Britain's policy towards NATO.

485 **British Defense Policy in the 1990s.**
Christopher Coker. London: Brassey's Defense Publishers, 1987. 186p.

Deals with the dilemmas and choices facing British defence policy-makers and planners in the late 1980s against a background in which the consensus on defence had disintegrated. The author looks at the changing international environment, at economic pressures on the defence budget and at party preferences, especially the Labour Party's commitment to a non-nuclear defence. This has much to say on British attitudes and policies towards NATO and the United States.

486 **US Defense Bases in the United Kingdom: A Matter for Joint Decision?**
Simon Duke. London: Macmillan, 1987. 261p.

Focuses on an important bilateral relationship within the overall multilateral framework of NATO. The author traces the development of United States bases in Europe and considers the principles upon which they are founded in terms of consultation and decision-making. This became a major political issue in the 1980s because of the use of US bases in Britain to launch attacks against Libya. Here, however, the focus is analytical.

487 **Britain's Contribution to NATO.**
Lawrence Freedman. *International Affairs*, vol. 54, no. 1
(January 1978), p. 30-47.

Discusses the level of Britain's expenditures for the commitment to NATO, and the impact of economic pressures. After outlining the decline of resources allocated to defence and the efforts to prevent a rise in military costs, the author concludes that the only place left to cut is Britain's two NATO roles – the Central Front or the East Atlantic and the Channel. Although the British Army on the Rhine (BAOR) takes up an increasing part of the annual defence budget, this could be offset by multilateral cost-sharing through Deutschmark payments to Britain and German purchases of British military equipment. The potential costs to Anglo-German relations of BAOR cutbacks are assessed, and it is suggested that NATO would become more of an American–German alliance if BAOR was removed.

488 **BAOR and NATO.**
J. C. Garnett. *International Affairs*, vol. 46, no. 4 (October 1970),
p. 670-681.

One of the few articles which focuses on the role of British forces on the Central Front in the overall context of European policies and NATO strategy. It begins with an overview of the British role in European security, arguing that Britain has been sharing in the collective defence of Western Europe, limiting the power of West Germany and playing a substantial role in ground defence. John Garnett also provides a good overview of the evolution of defence arrangements on the Central Front and discusses the shift from the Medium Term Plan for falling back to the Rhine to the Forward Strategy of defence closer to the Iron Curtain. He also reviews the changing role of BAOR within NATO strategy. The article ends by highlighting the uncertainty about whether BAOR's main role is to act as a small mobile force for frontier disputes and deterrence or to prepare to fight a major European war. This ambiguity, of course, reflected a more profound uncertainty about NATO's strategy.

489 **British Security Policy and the Atlantic Alliance: Prospectus for the 1990s.**
Edited by Martin Holmes, Gerald Frost. Washington, DC:
Pergamon-Brassey's with Institute for Foreign Policy Analysis, 1987.
140p.

This volume examines the domestic political context within which British policy towards NATO has been formulated; the Conservative Party and defence; economic constraints and defence choices; British collaboration in collaborative defence procurement; and British attitudes towards the United States. It provides some useful commentary.

490 **Britain's Security Policy and Arms Control in the 1990s.**
Dan Keohane. *Arms Control: Contemporary Security Policy*, vol. 12,
no. 1 (May 1991), p. 72-81.

A succinct and informative analysis of British policy towards NATO and European security in the 1990s which starts from that assumption that the real 'special relationship' will be that between the United States and Germany and that Britain will no longer be able to act as a bridge between the United States and Western Europe. After looking at the attitudes of both parties the author warns that remaining aloof from European integration will reduce Britain's influence not only on the Continent but also in Washington.

491 **Trident: The Only Option?**
Colin McInnes. London: Brassey's, 1986. 235p.

This book provides an excellent analysis of British decision-making concerning the choice of a successor to the Polaris strategic nuclear force. It looks at the ways the decision to opt for Trident was made, at the costs and benefits of this programme and at other options, including cruise missiles and the possibility of Anglo-French nuclear collaboration. Although the focus is on Britain, there is much that is of relevance to NATO and to the understanding of Britain's relations with both the United States on the one hand and France and the other European allies on the other.

492 **Britain's Strategic Role in NATO.**
George Richey. London: Macmillan, 1986. 174p.

Written by a former serving officer, this volume argues that Britain is bearing an unfair share of the burden of the common defence in Europe. Consequently, the author recommends that Britain revert to a maritime emphasis – which he claims would also be in NATO's interest. He also argues for a return of National Service and the enlargement of the territorial army. There are detailed, if not always persuasive, analyses of the threat, the problems of conventional defence, and nuclear deterrence.

493 **Britain, Europe and the Alliance.**
Michael Stewart. *Foreign Affairs*, vol. 48, no. 4 (July 1970),
p. 648-659.

Written by the British Foreign Secretary, this article welcomes the Nixon Administration's emphasis on Atlantic partnership – involving both burden-sharing and sharing in decision-making – while arguing that the Europeans can best improve their contribution to common security by closer defence cooperation. Most interesting for its very supportive attitude towards West European integration.

Germany and NATO

494 European Security and the German Problem.
Christoph Bertram. *International Security*, vol. 4, no. 3
(Winter 1979-80), p. 105-116.

The author, a former director of the International Institute for Strategic Studies,
assesses Willy Brandt's Ostpolitik and looks at the changing relationships in the
Atlantic Alliance. He argues that Germany could not be reunified without the collapse
of the Soviet empire. Bertram suggests that the Federal Republic of Germany is
becoming a more independent and less malleable alliance partner. He also notes that it
is more affected by East–West relations than any other European country. At the same
time, it remains reliant on the American nuclear umbrella. Consequently, nuclear
issues such as medium-range missiles and the neutron bomb cause tensions for
Germany and create disharmony in the alliance. For Germany, the other key question
for the coming years concerns the exercise of political and economic leadership responsibilities, especially vis-à-vis the US and the European Community. Bertram argues
that former Atlanticists now see the European Community as a positive alternative to
national self-reliance and are becoming Europeanists. In conclusion, he suggests that
the German question will be manageable as long as the Federal Republic can find a
place in a common Western and European framework. Some of these same arguments
are still relevant to the discussion of the future of Germany now that it is unified.

495 The Silent Partner: West Germany and Arms Control.
Edited by Barry M. Blechman, Cathleen S. Fisher. Cambridge,
Massachusetts: Ballinger with Institute for Defense Analysis, 1988.
266p.

Although Germany has refrained from acquiring nuclear weapons, its policies,
preferences and attitudes on nuclear weapons have played a major part in arms control
in Western Europe. In this volume, five experts on West Germany examine the sources
of German policy on arms control. The positions and preferences of the CDU/CSU,
the SPD, the Free Democratic Party, and the Social Democrats are explored and
illuminated. In addition, there is a chapter on public attitudes on arms control and a
chapter on arms control decision-making. A useful appendix contains biographies of
key actors in FRG decision-making on arms control. Overall, a valuable study which
illuminates a key aspect of West German policy in the decade before unification.

496 Germany's Westpolitik.
Willy Brandt. *Foreign Affairs*, vol. 50, no. 3 (April 1972), p. 416-426.

This article by the Chancellor of the Federal Republic of Germany is, in essence, an
effort to reassure the United States and the European allies that Bonn's Ostpolitik did
not mean an abandonment of West Germany's traditional policy in NATO and
Western Europe.

497 The Germans.
Gordon A. Craig. New York: G. P. Putnam's and Sons, 1982. 350p.

A collection of essays, accessible to the general reader, written and assembled by the
pre-eminent historian of modern Germany. Several chapters, relate to security issues
and the future European political order. Craig looks at the German commitment to
democracy, the rejection of nationalism, the creation of the new German army and the

total reformulation of the German military ethic. The author emphasizes the efforts of the Bundeswehr to create a citizen-soldier cognizant of democratic responsibilities.

498 **Germany Rejoins the Powers.**
Karl W. Deutsch, Lewis J. Edinger.   Stanford, California: Stanford University Press, 1959. 320p.
A study of the process whereby German re-established its legitimacy as an international actor. This was symbolized and consolidated by its entry into NATO and other international organizations.

499 **West German Rearmament.**
Lewis J. Edinger.   Maxwell Air Force Base, Alabama: Documentary Research Division, Air University, October 1955. 154p.
Offers a useful perspective on the problems surrounding German rearmament in the 1950s. The author traces the origins of German rearmament, looks at the new German military establishment, and considers both the political and military implications. Although written for the Air University, this study is well worth a look by scholars interested in German rearmament and how it was discussed in the United States.

500 **Security and Detente: Conflicting Priorities in German Foreign Policy.**
Helga Haftendorn.   New York: Praeger, 1985. 324p.
A valuable and subtle study of the inherent tensions in the foreign policy of the Federal Republic stemming from its need for security in the NATO framework on the one side and the imperatives of the Ostpolitik on the other. The author, a leading German scholar at the Free University of Berlin, provides a detailed and comprehensive analysis of the FRG's foreign policy from its early integration into the Western security system through to the early 1980s. The study also covers the development of the Ostpolitik and NATO's dual-track decision of December 1979. It argues that the tension between security and détente was particularly evident in the disagreement of the early 1980s over the construction of the Yamal gas pipeline, a disagreement which reflected a growing disjunction between détente policy on the one hand and defence policy on the other, and in the relative importance West Germany and the United States attached to each. The study provides an excellent framework for understanding subsequent controversies such as that over the modernization of short-range missiles.

501 **Germany and the Politics of Nuclear Weapons.**
Catherine McArdle Kelleher.   New York: Columbia University Press, 1975. 372p.
Provides a comprehensive analysis of German policies regarding the deployment, control and potential use of nuclear weapons in the period from 1954 to 1966. The study is chronologically organized and is based upon interviews with members of the German policy-making élite under Chancellors Adenauer and Erhard. Kelleher looks at nuclear-sharing schemes in NATO and concludes that Germany followed a cautious policy which combined total abstinence from anything which smacked of direct control over nuclear weapons with efforts to obtain greater influence over United States policy on the nuclear issue. Although the book was published in a period when nuclear issues had little salience, the author concluded that such issues could easily emerge once more – as they did with the NATO dual-track decision of 1979. This is a detailed and

scholarly study which is (among other things) a case-study of a German non-proliferation policy. For those thinking about German policy towards nuclear weapons in the post-Cold War era this valuable analysis is a good place from which to start.

502 **The Federal Republic of Germany and NATO: 40 Years After.**
Edited by Emil J. Kirchner, James Sperling. New York: St Martin's Press, 1992. 270p.

Initially intended as a stocktaking of West Germany's role in NATO over a forty-year period, this volume, as the authors note, was transformed by events into a retrospective of what NATO meant for West Germany and its partners between 1949 and 1989, and what NATO may mean in the future for a united Germany, a Europe no longer divided, and the United States. Amongst the themes that are dealt with very effectively are domestic pressures and German security policy, and the impact on German security of the policies of such states as France, the Soviet Union and the United States. There are also some pertinent observations by the editors on the various options that could form the basis for a new European security order. In addition to its value as a historical study, therefore, this volume is useful as a preliminary analysis of the consequences of the end of the Cold War and of German unification.

503 **The Two German States and European Security.**
Stephen F. Larrabee. New York: St Martin's Press in association with the Institute for East–West Security Studies, 1989. 330p.

Although the Revolution of 1989 and the reunification of Germany have rendered this volume's title an anachronism, many of its chapters remain relevant. The focus throughout is on the inter-German relationship, dialogue, and prospective reassociation. The multinational list of contributors provide French, Polish, and American, as well as both East and West German perspectives on the 'German problem'. Of particular note are the essay on the Polish view of European security and the companion piece on French views. Also of interest are analyses of the economic relations between the two states provided in separate essays by the Free University of Berlin's Gert Leptin and Juergen Nitz of the Institute of International Politics and Economics in the former German Democratic Republic (GDR). Both contain tables on inter-German trade current through 1986. The volume's overall focus on German–German dialogue and rapprochement in some ways presages their unification just months after publication.

504 **Germany at the Crossroads: Foreign and Domestic Policy Issues.**
Edited by Gale A. Mattox, A. Bradley Shingleton. Boulder, Colorado: Westview Press, 1992. 217p.

Although this volume deals with economic, political and technological issues, the first section focuses on security and examines issues related to the future of German defence policy and the future of NATO. In the first essay, Dana Allin and Daniel Mudd argue that NATO should continue in order to promote stability and well-being in the Atlantic region. They are sceptical, however, about efforts to reorientate NATO, arguing that suddenly to reorientate the system to some new (and possibly contrived) goal would court failure. The chapter also argues for specialization and for the further development of multinational forces. A second chapter deals with Franco-German arms cooperation, while a third looks at United States–German cooperation after the Cold War.

505 **Germany and NATO.**
John A. Reed Jr. Washington, DC: National Defense University, 1987. 265p.
A comprehensive account of Germany's evolving relationship with NATO written by a former Political-Military Attaché at the United States Embassy in Bonn. It looks at how Bonn tried to achieve security through membership in NATO and some of the problems to which this has periodically given rise. There are chapters dealing with the troubled path to German membership, the German contribution to NATO, the debates over strategy and the impact of domestic considerations. There are also several useful appendices, one of which provides the text of the Brussels Treaty of 1954. This very useful introduction to the subject offers some pertinent and sensible observations.

506 **Germany and the Atlantic Alliance: The Interaction of Strategy and Politics.**
James L. Richardson. Cambridge, Massachusetts: Harvard University Press, 1966. 403p.
This is an excellent study, not only of the position of Germany within the Atlantic Alliance, but also of crucial episodes and issues. The volume has a particularly good section on the Berlin Crisis of 1958 to 1961, on the issues this posed for NATO and the tension it created between West Germany on the one side and Britain and the United States on the other. It also contains an incisive discussion of NATO strategy. The main focus, however, is on the place of Germany within the Alliance: the first section of the book looks at West German policy in NATO, and the final section looks at German–Allied relations on the issues of reunification and détente. A scholarly and incisive study which repays looking at from the post-Cold War perspective.

507 **German Security Policy.**
Wolfgang F. Schlör. London: Brassey's for IISS, June 1993. 83p. (Adelphi Paper 277).
This paper examines the course of German security policy after the Cold War. It covers the sources and institutions of German security policy, the security objectives after the Cold War, and the policies that Germany conducts in pursuit of these objectives. The paper argues that there are formidable obstacles that prevent Germany from taking up a larger role in international security affairs. While this fact should mitigate fears that a united Germany might revert to old-style power politics, it also inhibits Germany as a facilitator of emerging international security institutions. During the Cold War, Germany pursued a policy of multilateralism, largely through NATO, which slowly turned from a necessity to an end in itself. This led it to neglect developing national security interests beyond the defence of the homeland. Today, this neglect contributes to Germany's problems in finding a new security identity. Germany also faces problems in mustering the resources and the domestic support for a larger role in international security. The author skilfully explores these problems in this excellent analysis.

508 **Germany in the Era of Negotiations.**
Helmut Schmidt. *Foreign Affairs*, vol. 49, no. 1 (October 1970), p. 40-50.
This article, by the then German Minister of Defence, outlines German thinking about security after the end of the postwar era – as the late 1960s and early 1970s were often

described. It places great emphasis on NATO as the key institution in providing security, argues against United States troop withdrawals and explains the key elements in the Federal Republic's Ostpolitik. Schmidt argues that Ostpolitik is not an attempt to break away from the Alliance but an attempt to engage the political strength of the Alliance to overcome the sterile confrontation in Europe.

509 **Germany Debates Defense: The NATO Alliance at the Crossroads.**
Rudolf Steinke, Michael Vale. Armonk, New York: M. E. Sharpe, 1983. 208p.

Provides a sense of the German debate over security and nuclear weapons in the early 1980s, with particular emphasis on ideas for alternative defence enunciated by the Social Democratic and Liberal parties and the German peace movement. There are three sections, one assessing whether the Soviet threat is real; a second which looks at the German Question and European Security; and the third of which suggests alternative approaches to security in Europe. Such alternatives include Egon Bahr's exposition of the SPD's security platform, the development of an independent European defence community, and various peace movement proposals. Of special interest are the alternative 'defensive defence' models detailed in the chapters by Thomas Trempnau and Theodor Ebert. Overall, this provides a good sense of one end of the spectrum in Germany.

510 **Germany and the Western Alliance: Lessons for the 1980 Crises.**
Philip Windsor. London: International Institute for Strategic Studies, 1981. 30p. (Adelphi Paper 170).

Windsor deals with some of the difficulties of West Germany's role in the Western alliance which came to the fore in 1980 following the Soviet invasion of Afghanistan. He examines the context of the 1980 crises to see why they had such an impact. Prior to 1980, alliance problems focused on the credibility of the United States as guarantor of European security; after the Soviet invasion of Afghanistan, they focused on the credibility of the Europeans as allies of the United States. Some Americans questioned whether the allies were worth defending, given their lack of support for the United States reaction – which came on top of disagreements on force modernization, arms control, and relations with the Soviet bloc. Windsor concludes that the only power capable of resolving these issues was the Federal Republic of Germany which, in spite of its weaknesses, was particularly suited to mediating between the various pressures related to security, arms control, and political and economic relations in Europe.

Security on NATO's Flanks

The Northern Flank

511 **The Nordic Balance: An Overview.**
Nils Andren.   *Washington Quarterly*, vol. 2, no. 3 (Summer 1979),
p. 49-62.

Looks at the notion of the Nordic Balance – which is a political not a military concept –
and the strains to which it increasingly may be subjected. The notion of the balance
rests upon the fact that Denmark and Norway are members of NATO but have neither
nuclear weapons nor allied troops on their territories, that Sweden is non-aligned, and
that Finland works within the framework established by its Treaty of Friendship and
Cooperation with the Soviet Union. Although the analysis is a description of the
existing reality, the author also notes that the Nordic Balance has become a normative
concept as the states in the region try to avoid actions which might disturb the political
equilibrium that has been established.

512 **Northern Waters: Security and Resource Issues.**
Edited by Clive Archer, David Scrivener.   London: Croom Helm for
the Royal Institute of International Affairs, 1986. 240p.

This volume focuses upon the maritime areas within the latitude of 80 degrees North
and 60 degrees North and from longitude 90 degrees West to 40 degrees East, an area
which stretches from the Kola Peninsula to the Eastern shores of Canada and which
the editors argue is strategically important as an avenue of commercial and military
transit. There are chapters dealing with various aspects of the region, including legal
issues and resource problems. The bulk of the book, however, is focused on strategic
and security aspects. Steven Miller, for example, has a very good chapter on United
States strategic interests in the region, while Elizabeth Young looks at the control of
conflict in the area. For those interested in NATO's Northern Flank this volume is a
must, especially as it goes well beyond a simple rehash of the military balance in the
region.

513 **Iceland, Greenland, and North Atlantic Security.**
Robert T. Arnason. *Washington Quarterly*, vol. 4, no. 2
(Spring 1981), p. 68-81.

Highlights the importance of Iceland and Greenland to NATO's strategic and tactical planning. The location of the islands in terms both of sea lanes and air routes is emphasized, as is the crucial role of the base at Keflavik. The author also examines the political, socio-cultural and economic contexts and considers their implications for the future involvement of the islands in NATO military planning. An informative article which deals very effectively with an area that is often neglected.

514 **Nordic Security and the Great Powers.**
John C. Ausland. Boulder, Colorado: Westview Press, 1986. 202p.

Written by a retired US Foreign Service Officer, this volume provides a comprehensive examination of the security problems on NATO's Northern Flank in the mid-1980s. The introductory section looks at the Soviet build-up in the North and at NATO's slow reaction. Part one of the volume focuses upon peacetime competition in the region, and includes such issues as the intelligence game, the electronic war, espionage, the contest for the Nordic mind, public opinion, problems of arms control, efforts to stop the flow of sensitive technology to the Soviet Union, and the purpose and impact of military exercises. Part Two looks at the strategies for war-fighting and considers not only NATO and the Warsaw Pact but also the roles of Finland and Sweden. Particular attention is given to the strategic importance of Iceland in a conflict in Northern Europe. This book has no index.

515 **Iceland's Position in NATO.**
Bjorn Bjarnason. *Atlantic Community Quarterly*, vol. 15, no. 4
(Winter 1977-78), p. 393-403.

A useful overview, written by the Deputy General Secretary in the office of the Icelandic Prime Minister, this article explores the reasons for Iceland's involvement in NATO. It looks at the defence agreement of 1951 between Iceland and the United States, the base at Keflavik, and the political controversy over these in Iceland.

516 **Nordic Security.**
Erling Bjol. London: International Institute for Strategic Studies, 1983. 50p. (Adelphi Paper 181).

A comprehensive analysis of security issues on NATO's Northern Flank. The author surveys individual Nordic states then focuses upon their common security problems. He explores the growing influence of left-wing parties and their radicalization on security issues, and also considers the importance of the Norwegian Sea in both NATO and US strategy. The author argues that the main question for NATO is whether the Nordic balance will continue to function in a way which maintains stability on the Northern Flank.

517 **Canadian Security and Defence: the Legacy and the Challenges.**
R. B. Byers. London: International Institute for Strategic Studies, Winter 1986. 88p. (Adelphi Paper 214).

Looks at the issue of how military commitments and capabilities could be balanced by Canada and presents what the author describes as a 'sustainable' approach to Canadian defence. Byers concludes that the Canadian government has failed to grasp the requirements of 'second-order' defence, i.e. actions that can be taken in combination with other members of the NATO alliance to improve the credibility of collective defence.

518 **Northern Europe: Security Issues for the 1990s.**
Edited by Paul M. Cole, Douglas M. Hart. Boulder, Colorado: Westview Press, 1986. 160p.

A series of essays which looks at the changing context for security on NATO's Northern Flank in the mid-1980s. The volume focuses on growing Soviet naval power and increasing superpower competition in the region. Particularly notable is a chapter which highlights the major contribution made to the defence of the north by the Federal Republic of Germany. Consideration is also given to energy security and vulnerabilities in Northern Europe as well as to the implications of deep-strike technology for the region. The final chapter offers a very good synthesis of new threats in the region and how they might be met.

519 **The Defense of NATO's Northern Front and US Military Policy.**
Sherwood S. Cordier. Lanham, Maryland: University Press of America, 1989. 80p.

Written in the aftermath of the INF Treaty, this study argues that conventional forces have become more important and that NATO should regard the Northern Flank as central to the Western position in Europe. The study examines the geopolitics of Northern Europe, and the dilemmas facing the United States and Norway in considering possible reinforcement of Norway. Among the prescriptions are that greater resources be devoted to air and sea lift.

520 **NATO's Northern Allies: The National Security Policies of Belgium, Denmark, the Netherlands, and Norway.**
Edited by Gregory Flynn. London: Croom Helm, 1985. 294p.

This book focuses on public opinion about NATO and security issues in the countries identified in the sub-title. It considers the interaction between domestic considerations and security policy priorities and assesses the implications of this for alliance policy and cohesion. There are very useful informative chapters on individual nations, including one on Denmark by Martin Heisler and one on the Netherlands by Jan Siccama, and a useful concluding chapter by Johan Holst which looks at the problems faced by small states in an alliance dominated by great powers. The editor's introduction contains some pertinent observations. Flynn notes that the four nations will seek more influence in the alliance while avoiding more responsibility and burden-sharing. An interesting and detailed set of studies which illuminates both the domestic peace movements in the 1980s and the limits of small-power influence in alliances.

521 **Norway and the Bear: Soviet Coercive Diplomacy and Norwegian Security Policy.**
Robert F. German. *International Security*, vol. 7, no. 2 (Fall 1982), p. 55-82.

German examines the 'Finlandization' phenomenon of Soviet pressure on Norway, arguing that the Norwegian decision not to have NATO foreign troops or nuclear weapons on its soil has been exploited by Moscow. The author traces the historical background to the Norwegian 'base policy' and provides an account of Oslo's involvement with the U2 and RB47 incidents of May 1960 and June 1960 respectively, as well as the 1961 Finnish Note Crisis. Although Moscow achieved some success in its efforts to keep Norway as malleable a neighbour as possible, German concludes that the Norwegians were not excessively intimidated and have continued to make important contributions to NATO in antisubmarine warfare, electronic warfare, airfield defences, and repositioning of allied equipment.

522 **Nuclear-free Zones: Norwegian Interest, Soviet Encouragement.**
Robert F. German.   *Orbis*, vol. 26, no. 2 (Summer 1982), p. 451-476.
Explores the notion of a nuclear-free zone in Northern Europe and suggests that if this was accepted it would be the first step towards the neutralization of the Nordic area – an outcome that would benefit the Soviet Union but harm the West.

523 **Clash in the North: Polar Summitry and NATO's Northern Flank.**
Edited by Walter Goldstein.   Washington, DC: Pergamon-Brassey's, 1988. 208p.
Although this volume has a familiar set of themes dealing with various aspects of security on NATO's Northern Flank, it also has a particularly good group of contributors. These include Robert Osgood, Christoph Bertram, James Eberle, Finn Sollie and Steve Smith.

524 **NATO's Defense of the North.**
Edited by Eric Grove.   London: Brassey's (UK), 1989. 104p.
A slim but useful volume which looks at the Northern Flank as NATO's first line of defence and considers the threat posed by Soviet forces especially those on the Kola Peninsula, how NATO might defend the Northern allies against this threat, the vital importance of reinforcements, and the interactions with the maritime and air situations. Contributors include British, Dutch and German defence analysts.

525 **North Atlantic Security: The Forgotten Flank?**
Kenneth A. Myers.   Beverly Hills, California: Sage, 1979. 72p.
(The Washington Papers, No. 62).
The basic theme of this short study is that the military trends in the North Atlantic area during the 1970s were moving in favour of the Soviet Union and that this is particularly the case on NATO's Northern Flank. The author emphasizes the strategic importance of NATO's Northern Flank including the US base at Keflavik, examines the plans for reinforcement on this flank in the event of a crisis, and then contends that greater attention needs to be given to the region. He looks at Norwegian relations with the Soviet Union and concludes that the NATO allies must ensure that the Northern states do not lose their self-confidence in dealing with Moscow.

526 **Canada: The Not So Faithful Ally.**
Joel Sokolsky, Joseph T. Jockel.   *Washington Quarterly*, vol. 7, no. 4 (Fall 1984), p. 159-169.
A very critical analysis of the Canadian contribution to Atlantic security. The authors emphasize the benefits to Canada of participation in NATO and argue that Canada is shirking its share of the burdens. They also contend that Canada has tried to continue

playing too many military roles and that the allies should push it towards greater rationalization and specialization. Sokolsky and Jockel argue that one of the major roles for Canada is reinforcement of Norway and that it should be encouraged to devote more resources to this task.

527 **Britain and NATO's Northern Flank.**
Edited by Geoffrey Till. New York: St Martin's Press, 1988. 187p.
Based on a conference which brought together a group of distinguished British and Scandinavian security analysts, this volume offers a good analysis of the security problems on NATO's Northern Flank and the implications for Britain. As well as the formal papers, there are also summaries of the conference discussions. The various sections of the book cover the political and economic context; security in Northern Europe; Britain and the North; the sea campaign that would be fought in the event of hostilities; and the land campaign. In the final section, Admiral Sir James Eberle considers future policy options, and Lawrence Freedman provides some pertinent concluding observations.

528 **Nordic Security at the Turn of the Twenty-First Century.**
Edited by Ciro Elliott Zoppo. New York: Greenwood Press, 1992. 247p.
An eclectic collection of essays which looks at the security problems of NATO's northern members as well as Finland and Sweden. The essays look at both the Scandinavian context for Nordic security and the role of the superpowers. Particularly useful is a chapter by Richard Bitzinger on the politics of defence in Denmark, Norway and Iceland. Although the volume is supposed to be looking ahead it is firmly embedded in the Cold War framework.

The Southern Flank

529 **Southern European Security in the 1990s.**
Edited by Robert Aliboni. London: Pinter, 1992, 147p.
The result of a research project carried out under the auspices of the Italian Institute for International Affairs, this volume is a useful contribution to the emerging debate on the threat from the south to NATO and one which explores the various national perspectives of NATO's Southern Flank members. There are chapters on France, Greece, Italy, Portugal, Spain and Turkey, as well as on the notion of a sub-regional identity and a southern position on European Political Cooperation.

530 **Turkey's New National Security Concept: What it Means for NATO.**
Michael Boll. *Orbis*, vol. 23, no. 3 (Fall 1979), p. 609-632.
The author identifies a shift in Turkey's security policy as a result of the 1974 Cyprus crisis, the subsequent United States arms embargo, and conciliatory overtures from the Soviet Union. Although Turkey in the mid-1970s attempted to achieve greater self-reliance, the author highlights several other options including the re-establishment of

the linkages with NATO and the United States. A useful snapshot of the cross-pressures on Turkey in the mid- and late 1970s.

531 **Delicately Poised Allies: Greece and Turkey – Problems, Policy Choices and Mediterranean Security.**
James Brown. London: Brassey's (UK), 1991. 184p.
A comprehensive study of the political and national security policies of Greece and Turkey and how their actions and interactions have influenced NATO's strategies on its southeast flank. The author argues that NATO strategy in the region is complicated by the juxtaposition of three operational theatres as well as by the tensions between Greece and Turkey. He provides a succinct and balanced analysis of the issues dividing the two nations, the domestic pressures they face, their relations with the United States, the military forces in the region, and the problems posed by Moscow and its allies. The conclusion is that long-term stability will depend as much on diplomatic tact as on military prowess.

532 **NATO's Southern Allies: Internal and External Challenges.**
Edited by John Chipman. London; New York: Routledge, 1988. 399p.
An analysis of the nations on NATO's Southern Flank and the internal and external threats to their national security. The book assesses the place of the southern region in the strategic perceptions of the Soviet Union and NATO, and highlights the difficulties of arranging a proper coalition defence against both the Soviet threat and threats from other sources. Attention is also given to the domestic determinants of the foreign policies of NATO's Southern Flank members and the tensions between national and alliance assessments and priorities. Some very useful chapters on the individual nations are tied together very effectively in introductory and concluding chapters by the editor.

533 **Instability and Change on NATO's Southern Flank.**
CSIA European Security Working Group. *International Security*, vol. 3, no. 3 (Winter 1978-79), p. 150-177.
Looks at the deteriorating relationship in the 1970s between Greece and Turkey on the one side and the United States and NATO on the other. The Greek withdrawal from the NATO command structure, Turkish moves towards a similar loosening of ties with NATO, the continued enmity between the two countries, and the doubts about the viability of their democratic institutions are all discussed. The authors argue that to restore stability on the Southern Flank, greater efforts should be made to address new security concerns, such as post-Tito Yugoslavia. It is also suggested that one of the key tasks for the United States and NATO is to manage political change in an environment in which both Greece and Turkey will continue to pursue independent foreign policies.

534 **Turkey, NATO and Europe: A Deteriorating Relationship.**
Nuri Eren. Paris: Atlantic Institute, December 1977. 54p.
(The Atlantic Papers, No. 34).
Written by a Turkish official, this paper explains why Turkey feels so alienated from NATO, the United States and the European Community in the aftermath of the Cyprus crisis. It looks at the way in which Turkey has subsequently promoted rapprochement with the Soviet Union, and its Balkan and Arab neighbours. It also pleads for greater understanding by its allies.

535 **Spain's Entry into NATO.**
Edited by Federico G. Gil, Joseph S. Tulchin.   Boulder, Colorado:
Lynne Rienner, 1988. 179p.

An interesting collection which examines the inter-relationships between domestic politics in Spain and Spain's entry into NATO. It looks at the role of the Spanish media and the nature of public opinion on the Alliance and the link with the United States. There is a mix of Spanish and American contributors and the latter group includes Gregory Treverton and Glenn Snyder who looks at Spanish policy in terms of semi-alignment and the free-rider issue.

536 **Two NATO Allies at the Threshold of War – Cyprus: A Firsthand Account of Crisis Management, 1965-1968.**
Parker T. Hart.   Durham, North Carolina: Duke University Press, 1990. 222p.

Written by the American Ambassador in Turkey from 1965 to 1968, this study focuses on the events of November and December 1967 in which Cyrus Vance, President Johnson's special emissary, engaged in very successful shuttle diplomacy which helped to avoid war between Greece and Turkey. This is a detailed study which draws heavily on documents and contains several useful appendices.

537 **NATO's New Front Line: The Growing Importance of the Southern Tier.**
William T. Johnsen.   Carlisle, Pennsylvania: SSI US Army War College, August 1992. 115p.

This study identifies and assesses the risks facing the nations in NATO's southern tier, looks at the applicability of NATO's new strategic concept to the region and evaluates the ability of the alliance to execute its operational concepts in the region in the event of violence. The author argues that the southern tier is NATO's new front line. He also emphasizes the importance to European security of NATO's ability to handle the emerging challenges.

538 **NATO and the Mediterranean.**
Edited by Lawrence S. Kaplan, Robert W. Clawson, Raimondo Luraghi.   Wilmington, Delaware: Scholarly Resources, 1985. 263p.

A very good collection, dealing with the major security issues in Southern Europe and the Mediterranean. The book is divided into four sections. The first looks at East–West competition in the Mediterranean and contains a very useful historical perspective by Kaplan and Clawson. The second section deals with air, land and naval forces on NATO's Southern Flank. The third part of the book explores the Iberian connection and looks at Portugal's relationship with Britain and NATO as well as the arguments surrounding Spain's entry into NATO. There is also a section on France, Italy and North Africa. The fifth section of the volume focuses on the Balkans. The book also contains an appendix with comments by the Italian chiefs of staff. This is a very well-done collection which offers an unusual and important focus, and which, in moving to a more regional approach to European security, was ahead of its time.

539 **Turkey and NATO: Past, Present, and Future.**
Bruce R. Kuniholm. *Orbis*, vol. 27, no. 2 (Summer 1983), p. 421-445.
Looks at the links and the tensions between Turkey and the West. The author argues
that the linkages are solid and that difficulties such as allied concerns over human
rights violations should ease as the military regime eases its grip on power. He also
suggests that Turkish membership in NATO benefits both Turkey and NATO.

540 **Italian NATO Policy: The Next Five Years.**
Ian Lesser. Santa Monica, California: Rand Corporation,
November 1989. 36p.
Assesses the likely evolution of Italian attitudes and policies towards NATO through
to the mid-1990s. The author identifies tension between the Italian role in NATO's
central region and its rediscovery of traditional interests in the Mediterranean as well
as between the European and Atlantic dimensions of its security policy. He concludes
that Italy will remain a loyal member of NATO but that the details of its security
policy will be more difficult to predict.

541 **Defending the Fringe: NATO, the Mediterranean and the Persian Gulf.**
Jed C. Snyder. Boulder, Colorado: Westview Press, 1987. 149p.
This volume starts from the premise that the southern region of NATO presents the
Alliance with a range of unique challenges. These are dealt with very effectively in a
volume which looks at the importance of the Mediterranean, the conflict between
Greece and Turkey, and the Spanish entry into NATO. The second part of the volume
looks at the regional security problems and superpower rivalry in the Persian Gulf. A
useful survey, although framed very much within the context of the Cold War.

542 **Spain: Domestic Politics and Security Policy.**
Gregory F. Treverton. London: International Institute for Strategic
Studies, Spring 1986. 45p. (Adelphi Paper 204).
Looks at Spanish security policy and the importance of domestic politics for the choices
Spain makes. In relation to membership in NATO, Treverton argues that it is not
essential for the organization but would underline the vitality and diversity of the
alliance and draw Spain more firmly into the body of Western democracies. The author
also looks at relations between Spain and the United States.

543 **The Turkish Straits and NATO.**
Ference A. Vali. Stanford, California: Hoover Institution Press, 1972.
348p.
The first part of this book looks at the geopolitical significance of the Bosporus and
Dardanelles; the rule of the Ottoman Empire; the Montreux Conference and
Convention; and Soviet designs on the Straits. In essence it provides the background
for the second part which deals with NATO and United States interests in ensuring
that Moscow does not obtain control over the Straits. As valuable as the analysis itself
are the 33 appendices which include a variety of statements and diplomatic notes
regarding the Straits. A study which combines the legal and the geopolitical aspects of
the subject.

544   **Greek Security: Issues and Politics.**
Thanos Veremis.   London: International Institute for Strategic
Studies, 1982. 42p. (Adelphi Paper 179).
This paper deals with Greece's attempt to redefine its security priorities and NATO's
response to this process. Veremis feels that problems arose because American and
NATO officials failed to appreciate the threat to Greek interests from Turkey, or to
understand that Greek threat perceptions are not simply the result of domestic politics.
Because of the importance of Greece to the Western Alliance (i.e. Sixth Fleet support,
communications with Turkey, intelligence, and storage), Greek security pursuits merit
greater attention, especially as Greece will attempt to assert its independence. The
author rightly places emphasis on the Greek preoccupation with the threat from
Turkey and highlights the difficulties this is likely to cause to both NATO and the
United States.

The Soviet Union and NATO

545 Soviet Risk-taking and Crisis Behavior: From Confrontation to Co-existence?

Hannes Adomeit.   London: International Institute for Strategic Studies, Autumn 1973. 40p. (Adelphi Paper 101).

An incisive analysis which categorizes Soviet risk-taking in terms of risks of crisis, risks of war, and risks of mutual annihilation; examines Soviet risk-taking behaviour during the Cold War; and considers the determinants of Soviet crisis behaviour. The author assesses the impact of ideology, of Soviet military power, and of domestic factors. He concludes that the Soviet Union will not exploit strategic parity to gain the upper hand in military confrontations, but will try to avoid confrontations and achieve its objectives without the risks of war. Although Adomeit does not address NATO directly, his analysis has significant implications for NATO, one of which is that deterrence in Europe was much easier than military planners in NATO often seemed to believe.

546 Soviet Readiness for War: Assessing One of the Major Sources of East–West Instability.

Les Aspin.   Report of the Defense Policy Panel of the Committee on Armed Services, House of Representatives One Hundredth Congress, Second Session (Washington: Government Printing Office, 5 December 1988). 17p.

This report assessed two major types of threat from the Soviet Union – that of a standing start attack and an attack after full mobilization. It concluded that the standing start attack was the riskiest for the Soviet Union and that the Warsaw Pact advantage was likely to be greatest after full mobilization. Consequently, it argued for a broader planning focus by NATO to include both kinds of attack and the problems of responding to warning. The Committee also argued that more emphasis should be placed on 'actionable' warning, i.e. warning that the European publics will find convincing enough to allow their governments to take necessary mobilizations steps.

This could be done through improved intelligence dissemination and arms control measures.

547 NATO and Soviet Security Reform.
Stephen R. Covington. *Washington Quarterly*, vol. 14, no. 1 (Winter 1991), p. 39-50.
Examines the Soviet military's view of the defence doctrine enunciated by Gorbachev, the rationales behind its war prevention emphasis and the implications of conventional and nuclear force reductions. The author is cautious and suggests that the Soviet military is making a virtue out of necessity and that it recognizes the effectiveness of NATO's deterrent capabilities.

548 The Soviet Union and Northern Waters.
Edited by Clive Archer. London: Routledge, 1988. 261p.
This analysis of the Soviet presence in northern waters focuses upon the northern part of the North Atlantic, the Norwegian and Barents Seas and includes the islands of Arctic Canada, Greenland, Iceland, the Faroes, Shetlands, and Svalbard and extends to the Kola Peninsula. It is far more sophisticated and comprehensive than many of the studies of the Soviet threat in the North and looks at the legal aspects, resource questions and the strategic implications of the Soviet presence in the region. There are also four chapters on the responses of the major Western states to this Soviet presence, responses that have emphasized increased military presence and attempts at reassurance. A comprehensive and balanced study of a region that is too often treated simply in military terms.

549 The North Atlantic Alliance and the Soviet Union in the 1980s.
Julian Critchley. London: Macmillan, 1982. 210p.
Critchley tries to trace the probable course in the 1980s of the continuing trial of strength between the Soviet Union and the West. A very traditional analysis which emphasizes the continuing nature of the Soviet threat.

550 The Soviet Operational Manoeuvre Group: A New Challenge for NATO.
C. N. Donnelly. *International Defense Review*, vol. 15, no. 9 (1982), p. 1177-1186.
An important analysis which looked at the changes in Soviet organizational structure and doctrine and the threat they posed for NATO. The author focuses on the operational manoeuvre group and its likely role in the event of hostilities. He also highlights the new challenges this presents for NATO force planners.

551 Soviet Threat Perceptions of NATO's Eurostrategic Missiles.
William V. Garner. Paris: Atlantic Institute, November 1983. 113p. (The Atlantic Papers, No. 52-53).
A very unusual perspective which considers how the Soviet Union assessed the threat from NATO's deployment of cruise and Pershing missiles. The author makes extensive use of Soviet public statements and press comments and tries to evaluate what was real concern and what was propaganda. This very informed and informative work is amplified by tables.

552   **The Soviet SS-20 Decision.**
Raymond L. Garthoff.   *Survival*, vol. 25, no. 3 (May/June 1983),
p. 110-119.

Argues very persuasively that the Soviet deployment of the SS-20 was the result of a modernization decision rather than an effort to obtain a military advantage and political leverage over Western Europe. The decision reflected Soviet military assessments of regional security needs and was not an effort to achieve regional superiority. Because the Soviet leadership saw the SS-20 as a necessary modernization, Moscow found it difficult to understand the NATO decision to deploy cruise and Pershing missiles. An informed and judicious analysis.

553   **Double Zero and Soviet Military Strategy: Implications for Western Security.**
Dennis M. Gormley.   London: Jane's, 1988. 229p.

Looks at the impact of the INF Treaty on Soviet military planning and then considers how the Soviet Union is taking steps to compensate for the constraints. Dennis Gormley also argues that the second zero – short-range intermediate nuclear forces – was not in NATO's interest. He suggests that NATO and the United States should be more careful about integrating arms control and military planning. He also argues that NATO needs to find ways to deal with conventionally armed ballistic missiles. Carefully argued, this book gives a good flavour of some of the concerns raised by the INF Treaty.

554   **Soviet Views on Escalation.**
Dennis M. Gormley, Douglas M. Hart.   *Washington Quarterly*, vol. 7,
no. 4 (Fall 1984), p. 71-84.

Looks at Soviet strategy and its relation to the debate in NATO about using precise, discriminate conventional ballistic missiles in the event of a conflict in Europe. The authors offer a critical assessment of arguments that such an option might be escalatory. They survey Soviet views on escalation from 1960s onwards and examine Soviet escalation incentives and disincentives within the framework of the evolving NATO military strategy. The conclusion is that greater reliance by NATO on advanced conventional weapons would exert a dampening effect on escalation, especially when compared with the instabilities in the existing strategy.

555   **The Soviet Union and the Politics of Nuclear Weapons in Europe 1969-87.**
Jonathan Haslam.   Ithaca, New York: Cornell University Press, 1990.
227p.

A very thorough study which examines and assesses the various interpretations for the Soviet deployment of the SS-20. Having identified the major contours of the debate, the author explores the background to this issue, looking at both the SALT process and the Chinese problem for the Soviet Union. He has chapters on the SS-20 decisions during 1974-77, the Western reaction, the arms control negotiations, and the Soviet reversals which led to the INF Agreement. All told, this is a useful analysis.

556 **Soviet Theater Nuclear Forces: Implications for NATO Defense.**
Robert Kennedy. *Orbis*, vol. 25, no. 2 (1981), p. 331-350.

Kennedy looks at the improvements in Soviet theatre nuclear capabilities during the 1970s and suggests that the shift in the European nuclear balance has serious implications for NATO. The appropriate NATO response, according to the author, is to change the emphasis from short-range battlefield nuclear systems to long-range theatre nuclear systems capable of striking the Soviet Union itself. Certain reforms in training, doctrine, force structure and force dispositions are also proposed to enhance deterrence and NATO's capacity to respond to Soviet combined arms operations in the event that deterrence fails.

557 **The Soviet Union and European Security.**
L. C. Kumar. New York: Advent Books, 1987. 329p.

A study by an Indian scholar which looks at Soviet policy towards Europe and in particular the efforts by the Soviet Union to pursue policies of conciliation towards the West and to initiate a pan-European security conference. The author looks at the moves towards the Conference on Security and Cooperation in Europe, the Conference itself and its aftermath. It is overly sympathetic and uncritical in its assessment of Soviet policies and its argument that the Helsinki Conference of 1975 and its Final Act symbolized the triumph of Soviet objectives is patently wrong, given the way the West used the Helsinki process to pressurize the Soviet Union on human rights.

558 **The USSR and the Western Alliance.**
Edited by R. F. Laird, S. L. Clark. Boston, Massachusetts: Unwin Hyman, 1990. 269p.

With contributions by Hannes Adomeit, Charles Gati, Erik Hoffmann, Phillip Petersen and Notra Trulock III, this is a useful collection of essays. It deals with the increased flexibility imparted to Soviet foreign policy by Gorbachev and highlights the kinds of challenges this flexibility poses for NATO and its members. The basic theme is that the Soviet Union under Gorbachev continued to pursue an anti-coalition strategy designed to weaken NATO politically. There are good chapters on Soviet perspectives on France, Britain and Germany as well as on Soviet public diplomacy. Although the book was overtaken by the traumatic events of 1989 and the disintegration of the Soviet empire, it nevertheless provides a useful survey of the kind of foreign policy being pursued by Moscow prior to the major political changes in Eastern Europe and, subsequently, the Soviet Union itself.

559 **The Soviet Offense in Europe: The Schlieffen Plan Revisited.**
Richard Ned Lebow. *International Security* vol. 9, no. 4 (Spring 1985), p. 44-78.

An incisive analysis which compares Soviet plans for a conventional offensive to the infamous Schlieffen Plan of 1914 finally adopted by the Germans in 1940. The author suggests that such an offensive would be incompatible with overall Soviet interests in taking Western Europe intact. He also argues that the shaky allegiance of Warsaw Pact members, as well as problems of resupply, and Command control and communications would hamper the Soviets. Nor could Moscow count on NATO accepting defeat and not resorting to nuclear weapons. A good assessment which highlights some of the constraints on potential Soviet aggression in Western Europe.

560 **Soviet Policy Perspectives on Western Europe.**
Neil Malcolm. London: Routledge for the Royal Institute on
International Affairs, 1989. 117p. (Chatham House Papers).

This study, based largely on an examination of writings by Soviet scholars, examines
Gorbachev's policy towards Western Europe. It argues that this arises from Soviet new
thinking on international relations, which emphasizes bridge building and interdependence. Neil Malcolm also argues that Gorbachev based his policy on acceptance of the
strength and durability of the links between the United States and Western Europe
and, in effect, provides an interpretation which differs from those who saw
Gorbachev's approach as an anti-coalition strategy.

561 **Soviet Strategy toward Western Europe.**
Edited by E. Moreton, G. Segal. London: Allen and Unwin, 1984.
296p.

This is a useful collection of essays on Soviet foreign policy towards Western Europe.
The introduction by the editors highlights the dilemmas and predicaments faced by the
Soviet Union in devising a strategy towards Western Europe. This theme is then
developed in three sections. The first section deals with domestic influences on Soviet
policy and has an essay by Karen Dawisha on the impact of ideology on Soviet
perceptions and one by Hannes Adomeit which examines Soviet decision-making
processes. The second sections focuses on the external influences on Soviet foreign
policy. Among the contributions, there is one by Lawrence Freedman which highlights
the impact of superpower relations on Soviet policy towards Western Europe. In
addition, there is a chapter by Edwina Moreton on the German factor and one by
Gerald Segal on the China factor. The third section of the book has chapters on Soviet
military, economic and arms control strategies. The substantive chapters elaborate on
the central theme of a Soviet Union facing major dilemmas in how to deal with
Western Europe. The value of the book lies in large part in the skill with which the
pressures and dilemmas are delineated.

562 **Soviet Power and Western Negotiating Policies, Vol. 1: The Soviet Asset:
Military Power in the Competition over Europe.**
Edited by Uwe Nerlich. Cambridge, Massachusetts: Ballinger, 1983.
365p.

A valuable, if somewhat hawkish, collection of essays which argues that the Soviet
Union is winning the military competition in Europe both at the conventional and at
the theatre nuclear level. The focus is on the Soviet conception of military power, how
it might be used to achieve political objectives, and how NATO might respond. The
contributors include Phillip Karber, Robert Legvold and Fritz Ermarth.

563 **Soviet Power and Western Negotiating Policies, Vol. 2: The Western
Panacea: Constraining Soviet Power through Negotiation.**
Edited by Uwe Nerlich. Cambridge, Massachusetts: Ballinger, 1983.
434p.

An impressive collection of essays which looks at the utility and limitations of arms
control as a means used by the West to constrain Soviet power. After a section
reappraising arms control, a second section deals with what is termed 'misconceived
negotiation and the dynamics of failure'. Part three considers a framework for
redirecting negotiating policy, while part four looks at NATO's strategic requirements

and the roles for negotiated constraints. The final section considers arms control as a vehicle for political change. Contributors include Lawrence Freedman, Phillip Karber, Lothar Ruehl, Pierre Hassner and Philip Windsor.

564 **NATO and the New Soviet Threat, Report of Senator Sam Nunn and Senator Dewey F. Bartlett to the Committee on Armed Service, United States Senate.**
Sam Nunn, Dewey Bartlett. Washington, DC: GPO, 1977. 20p.
A report which had considerable impact on the NATO strategic debate in the late 1970s. The central thesis was that the Soviet Union and its East European allies were moving towards a decisive conventional military advantage over NATO. Soviet emphasis on firepower and readiness and the transformation of tactical aviation into an offensive force gave the Warsaw Pact the capability to initiate a conflict from virtually a standing start. The Report examined the implications of this decreased warning time for NATO and identified ways in which the Alliance should respond.

565 **The Changing Western Analysis of the Soviet Threat.**
Edited by Carl-Christoph Schweitzer. New York: St Martin's Press, 1990. 318p.
A very interesting collection of essays which explores changing threat perceptions in both Western Europe and the United States from the 1950s to the 1980s. The study focuses upon threat perceptions by NATO itself, by the United States, Britain, France, the Federal Republic of Germany, and The Netherlands. The value of the book is enhanced both by the historical perspective and by the fact that the authors of the individual chapters operated within a broad framework of questions they wanted to answer. In addition, attempts were made by the authors to obtain access to unpublished sources. This is a useful book which offers a good basis for comparison. The conclusions are somewhat short and disappointing, but for those who are interested in how the Soviet Union was perceived during the Cold War this is a very good place to start.

566 **Soviet Atomic Blackmail and the North Atlantic Alliance.**
Hans Speier. *World Politics*, vol. 9, no. 3 (April 1957), p. 307-328.
Speier focuses on how the Soviet Union attempted to use nuclear blackmail to deepen the cleavages in NATO. He looks in particular at Soviet nuclear threats during the Suez crisis and argues that they were very vague and were designed partly to increase the impact of lesser threats such as Soviet intervention in Egypt. Speier also assesses the impact of these threats on NATO.

567 **Military Power and Political Influence: The Soviet Union and Western Europe.**
R. John Vincent. London: IISS, Autumn 1975. 29p. (Adelphi Paper 119).
An erudite examination of the political impact of Soviet military power. The author looks both at the circumstances in which the presence of Soviet military power might have a decisive impact, and at the more general influence of Soviet power on the domestic and foreign policies of West European states. In the former case, Moscow tries to use its military power for specific purposes; in the latter, the Europeans are deferential simply because the power is there. John Vincent looks at the notion of

Finlandization and concludes that although it cannot be dismissed, it is only one of a wide range of possibilities.

568 **Soviet Power and Europe 1945-1970.**
Thomas W. Wolfe. Baltimore, Maryland: Johns Hopkins Press, 1970. 534p.

This book, by an analyst at the Rand Corporation, focuses upon the strategic and political threat which NATO was designed to meet. It looks at the development of Soviet policies towards Western Europe under Stalin, and under Khrushchev and his successors. Specific chapters deal with Soviet thinking on theatre nuclear warfare, the Soviet diplomatic offensive of the late 1960s and the impact of the invasion of Czechoslovakia on Soviet European policy. Throughout the volume the author deals with Soviet views of NATO and with developments in the Atlantic Alliance itself. He brings out particularly well the impact of the Czech invasion in restoring NATO cohesion.

569 **Soviet Ballistic Missile Defense and the Western Alliance.**
David Yost. Cambridge, Massachusetts: Harvard University Press, 1988. 405p.

A well-researched volume which examines the implications of Soviet ballistic missile defence for the Atlantic Alliance. The author is careful in his analysis and, for the most part, judicious in his conclusions. He focuses on the strategic problems that could stem from Soviet development of a significant ballistic missile defence capability and also looks at the political problems resulting from divergent assessments of these capabilities in Western Europe and the United States.

570 **Soviet Ballistic Missile Defense and NATO.**
David S. Yost. *Orbis*, vol. 29, no. 2 (Summer 1985), p. 281-292.

Yost assesses the implications of the Soviet ballistic missile defence programme for NATO and argues that it could undermine the strategy of flexible response; improve Soviet prospects for conventional victory in a war; reduce the credibility of the French and British independent nuclear deterrent forces; and give the Soviet Union more opportunity to control escalation. He suggests that NATO should respond both by enhancing its capabilities to penetrate Soviet defences and by a defence programme of its own.

NATO and the Military Balance in Europe

571 **The European Conventional Balance: A Reinterpretation of the Debate.**
Stephen D. Biddle.   *Survival*, vol. 30, no. 2 (March-April 1988),
p. 99-121.
Starts from the premise that estimates of the conventional balance range from
optimism to gloom and that the proponents of each perspective talk past one another.
Accordingly, the author examines the debate, identifies some of the underlying
differences that explain the diversity of views, and offers some policy recommendations. He argues that the extreme variance in assessments of the balance stems from
the application of unstable equilibrium models to a relatively narrow range of
disagreement between analysts as to the balance of combat inputs. The author suggests
an alternative approach, but concludes that there is a problem because we do not fully
understand stability or its requirements.

572 **European Security: NATO, SALT and Equilibrium.**
Kurt Birrenbach.   *Orbis*, vol. 22, no. 2 (Summer 1978), p. 297-308.
A somewhat alarmist assessment which contends that NATO is in a critical situation
and needs to increase dramatically its conventional capabilities. Birrenbach focuses
largely upon areas of Soviet military superiority and concludes that most attention
should be paid to the 'grey area' lying between intercontinental and conventional
weapons. Although pessimistic it does represent what was a strong strand of opinion in
West Germany in the late 1970s – and one which contributed to NATO's December
1979 decision to modernize its strategic forces.

573 **Assessing the Conventional Balance in Europe, 1945-1975.**
Richard Bitzinger.   Santa Monica, California: Rand Corporation,
May 1989. 40p. (Rand Note N-2859-FF/RC).
This study examines the state of the conventional balance as it was perceived at various
junctures in a thirty-year period, and describes the types of analyses on which the
prevailing assessments were based. It traces a shift from the pessimistic assessments
which predominated between 1945 and 1961 to the more optimistic and sophisticated

assessments of 1961 to 1969 which largely came out of the studies initiated by US Secretary of Defense Robert McNamara. The author also argues that there was a third phase (1969-75) which saw increasing sophistication in the assessments but which also detected a major Soviet quantitative build-up. Because NATO was believed to have a qualitative edge, this was a period in which optimistic and pessimistic analyses vied for acceptance. Although this assesses the assessors it is also very helpful in explaining how the conventional balance was seen at different times. It places a great deal of the debate over the military balance in an overall perspective.

574 **Urban Sprawl and NATO Defense.**
Paul Bracken. *Survival*, vol. 18, no. 6 (November-December 1976), p. 254-260.
Argues that the urban conurbations which have grown up in West Germany could aid a Warsaw Pact advance, especially one based on city-hugging tactics. The author argues that NATO should recognize this danger, acknowledge the trend of urbanization and adjust its strategy and force posture to exploit this trend. NATO could make greater use of urban areas as fortified defensive positions – a strategy which would also require large mobile reserves – but needs to design weapons for hostilities in urban areas. This article deals with a dimension of the military balance that was usually ignored, and makes a good case for its relevance and importance.

575 **The NATO Defense Problem.**
Paul Bracken. *Orbis*, vol. 27, no. 1 (Spring 1983), p. 83-105.
Provides a useful overview of NATO's defence problem while also pointing out that Soviet incentives for embarking upon large-scale military aggression in Europe are minimal. The author also looks at the difficulties of nuclear war planning. His main theme, however, is that the key to European security is a NATO capacity to deter Soviet reinforcement of its forces deployed forward in Eastern Europe.

576 **Alternative Conventional Defense Postures in the European Theater, Vol. 1: The Military Balance and Domestic Constraints.**
Hans Gunter Brauch, Robert Kennedy. New York: Taylor and Francis, 1990. 203p.
This is an interesting collection of essays, predominantly by German and American analysts, but also containing a Soviet perspective. The volume explores the changing political and strategic dimensions of East–West relations, the conventional military balance in Europe from American and West German perspectives, and the constraints likely to be imposed on defence planning in the 1990s. Although there are some good analyses on such subjects as the intricacies of military force assessment and the manpower and budgetary problems likely to confront the United States and its European allies, especially Germany, throughout the 1990s, this was one of the books that was rapidly overtaken by the radical changes in the European political and strategic landscape between 1989 and 1991.

577 **The Future of Europe and NATO's Outdated Solutions.**
Steven L. Canby. *International Security*, vol. 1, no. 4 (Spring 1977), p. 160-162.
Canby argues that with its population and economic base, NATO should be able to afford a better defence against the Soviet Union. This requires a lessening of the

differences between the Western Europeans and the United States over deterrence in Europe and a willingness to make better use of existing resources. In this context, Canby proposes that reserve forces be doubled or even tripled. He claims that this could be done at relatively modest cost, that it would ease the political debates over burden-sharing among the allies, and that it would neutralize Soviet forces without bringing the ritual of mutual force reduction negotiations to a successful conclusion.

578   Is there a Tank Gap? Comparing NATO and Warsaw Pact Tank Fleets.
Malcolm Chalmers, Lutz Unterseher.   *International Security*, vol. 13, no. 1 (Summer 1988), p. 5-49.

As the title implies, the authors believe that the conventional wisdom about Soviet tank superiority is misguided. While the Pact does have a significant quantitative edge, NATO has more important qualitative advantages in terms of observation, firepower, mobility, and armour protection. The authors also point out that many of the Soviet tanks are not even assigned to Europe, let alone Central Europe. Moreover, they contend that other factors such as mobilization effectiveness, technical innovation, industrial production rates, and the average age of tanks actually deployed, narrow the 'tank gap' to rough parity. They conclude that the Soviets' real numerical advantage of between 1.24:1 and 1.64:1 is very modest in view of NATO's qualitative advantages. Although they conclude that the Warsaw Pact does not have a significant advantage in conventional war-fighting capability in Central Europe, they acknowledge that a stable security environment requires greater disincentives against offensive actions.

579   Europe without Defense? 48 Hours that could Change the Face of the World.
General Robert Close.   New York: Pergamon Press, 1979. 278p.

A highly controversial book which caused considerable consternation in NATO circles. The author argued that the Soviet Union, basing its strategy on offence, surprise, speed and shock effect, had the capability to take possession of West Germany within 48 hours. He also contended that the rapidity of the strike and the attainment of deep penetration would make it impossible for NATO to use its tactical nuclear weapons. The increasing Soviet capabilities are contrasted with what is presented as the Balkanization of that Atlantic Alliance, a juxtaposition of outdated national defences rather than a well-integrated and effective force structure. The study also offers various remedial measures for NATO. Although dismissed by many critics, this book helped to focus the debate of the early 1980s on measures to improve NATO's capacity for conventional resistance.

580   Toward Better Net Assessment: Rethinking the European Conventional Balance.
Eliot Cohen.   *International Security*, vol. 13, no. 1 (Summer 1988), p. 50-89.

This article analyses the thinking of two optimists about the military balance – Barry Posen and John Mearsheimer – who contend that the Warsaw Pact's quantitative edge would not translate easily into a quick victory in Central Europe. Cohen highlights what he sees as flaws in the optimists' arguments, including inaccurate assumptions about Soviet military doctrine, inaccurate quantitative figures, and inappropriate modelling. Cohen's own assessment emphasizes the importance of how the war begins, concepts of operations and the impact of force structure asymmetries – all things which qualify optimism.

NATO and the Military Balance in Europe

581   The New Maginot Line.

Jon Connell.   London: Secker and Warburg, 1986. 308p.

Written by the Washington correspondent for the *Sunday Times*, this book highlights what the author sees as the three fallacies of Western defence: pinning too much faith in advanced conventional technologies, placing too much reliance on nuclear weapons, and trying to create space-based defences. The argument is, in essence, that there is no technological solution to the threat posed by the Soviet Union. This was a welcome effort to inject greater realism into the debate over security at a time when NATO, in particular, was emphasizing the importance of emerging technologies in strengthening its conventional forces.

582   The Role of Uncertainty in Assessing the NATO/Warsaw Pact Central Region Balance.

Paul K. Davis.   Santa Monica, California: Rand Corporation, 1988. 39p. (Rand Note N-2839-RC).

Argues that it is essential to recognize that the outcome of a war in Europe would depend upon sets of factors, many of which are often ignored. Consequently, assessments should consider a range of scenarios based on assumptions about such things as the political–military context, warning times, mobilization times, alliance operational strategies, force effectiveness, quality of leaders and troops, and rates of advance and attrition. Davis also suggests that the assessment should be based on a gaming approach because the confrontation of opposing strategies and tactics is so fundamental. He uses this multi-scenario approach to suggest that disaster-ridden scenarios are at least as likely as good scenarios for NATO. He also uses a fault tree depicting various paths to disaster for NATO. This is a useful study which has a degree of sophistication that goes well beyond most analyses of the balance between NATO and the Warsaw Pact.

583   Precision Guided Weapons.

James Digby.   London: International Institute for Strategic Studies, 1975. 24p. (Adelphi Paper 118).

A comprehensive discussion of precision-guided munitions (PGM) stimulated by their use in Vietnam and in the Middle East War of October 1973. Having outlined the principles and technologies underlying PGMs, the author assesses their likely impact on force posture and the conduct of hostilities. He concludes that PGMs assist the defender, and that their acquisition is likely to enhance stability. He also suggests that they will not only increase the intensity of non-nuclear warfare, but may threaten the viability of large, expensive systems, such as advanced tactical fighters and aircraft carriers. An interesting study of weapons systems which increasingly became a key component in NATO's force posture.

584   Not Over by Christmas: NATO's Central Front in World War III.

Elmar Dinter, Paddy Griffith.   New York: Hippocrene Books, 1983. 178p.

An analysis which looks at some of the military issues facing NATO in terms of understanding war as an 'Operational Art'. It examines the balance of power in Central Europe, the tactical conditions of modern war, the evolution of operational doctrine, and defensive operations and the future battlefield. The authors make proposals for NATO's doctrine and organization and relate them to the various possible phases of a European battle. They also argue that NATO should strengthen its conventional forces. An unusual perspective although made less relevant by political events.

585 **What Forces for NATO? And From Whom?**
Alain Enthoven, Wayne Smith. *Foreign Affairs*, vol. 48, no. 1 (October 1969), p. 80-96.
Written by two of Robert McNamara's systems analysts this article argues that the only justification for maintaining an American military presence in Western Europe is that it provides significant capabilities for fighting limited war. The arguments are familiar – without strong conventional forces NATO would have only a choice between holocaust and humiliation. Nevertheless, the authors contend that the balance is not nearly as bad as the standard view suggests – and argue that by correcting its deficiencies NATO would be able to maintain a conventional balance without major increases in overall manpower and budgets. It is also suggested that there has to be greater equity in sharing burdens and that the European allies need to do much more. A good summary of the official United States position through much of the 1960s.

586 **How Much is Enough? Shaping the Defense Program 1961-1969.**
Alain C. Enthoven, K. Wayne Smith. New York: Harper & Row, 1971. 364p.
This volume, which goes well beyond NATO in its scope, was written by two of Robert McNamara's systems analysts at the Pentagon. As well as justifying the need for independent analysis and examining the sizing of nuclear forces, the book looks at NATO's strategy and force posture. Its main importance is that it was one of the first studies to take issue with the idea of massive Soviet conventional superiority. The authors argued that the conventional wisdom of 175 Soviet divisions facing 25 NATO divisions was inconsistent with aggregate economic data. They felt that the Soviet Union would not be able to support such a massive force. They also challenged the idea that Soviet and NATO divisions were the equivalent of each other, claiming that NATO divisions were much larger and more combat-ready. The importance of this study was partly analytical – it prepared the way for later, more comprehensive analytical assessments of the conventional balance in Europe – and partly political, in that it was designed to support Secretary of Defense McNamara's claims that NATO was not outnumbered and with more effort on the part of the Europeans could match the Soviet's conventional forces. In other words, it was not only a major contribution to the debate over the conventional balance but also part of the continuing transatlantic debate over appropriate NATO strategy.

587 **Dynamic Analysis and the Conventional Balance in Europe.**
Joshua M. Epstein. *International Security*, vol. 12, no. 4 (Spring 1988), p.154-165.
An article which sparked a major debate over the appropriate methodology for assessing the conventional balance in Europe. Joshua Epstein argues that to evaluate the conventional force balance in a theatre setting, an explicit mathematical model is often the most appropriate method. After examining some of the most common models for military analysis in Central Europe, he notes that many analysts who are pessimistic about the NATO–Warsaw Pact balance rely much too heavily on 'bean-counting' and ignore qualitative considerations. His criticisms, however, are not aimed solely at the pessimists and he also argues that more optimistic analysts invoke static

'rules of thumb' such as the well-worn '3:1 attacker to defender rule' which are vague and unsubstantiated. He concedes, however, that even the more sophisticated Lanchester Models, which link attrition rates to force levels, are not accurate predictors. Epstein concludes that no serious analysis has demonstrated unequivocally that the Warsaw Pact actually enjoys the massive military superiority over NATO that the conventional wisdom asserts.

588 **On Conventional Deterrence in Europe: Questions of Soviet Confidence.**
Joshua Epstein.   *Orbis*, vol. 26, no. 1 (Spring 1982), p. 71-86.
Argues very persuasively that Western analysts have overlooked the weaknesses in Soviet offensive doctrine and capabilities which mean that the Soviet Union would not be able to embark with great confidence upon a military offensive in Europe.

589 **The 3:1 Rule, the Adaptive Dynamics Model and the Future of Security Studies.**
Joshua Epstein.   *International Security*, vol. 13, no. 4 (Spring 1989), p. 90-127.
This is Joshua Epstein's response to John Mearsheimer's response (*see* item no. 596) to Joshua Epstein's critique of assessments of the conventional balance in Europe which emphasize the 3:1 rule of thumb (*see* item no. 587). An incisive and highly methodological analysis, it argues that one of the key issues is whether or not security studies is to move in the direction of greater scientific rigour. This is part of a debate that specialists will probably find fascinating and the non-specialist will find perplexing given that the participants agreed on the conclusions. Both Epstein and Mearsheimer were ultimately optimistic about the military balance between NATO and the Warsaw Pact.

590 **The Tenuous Balance: Conventional Forces in Central Europe.**
James M. Garrett.   Boulder, Colorado: Westview Press, 1989. 273p.
An analysis of the conventional military balance in Europe which does not set out to be definitive, but which attempts to provide a holistic assessment of the conventional military situation in Central Europe and to suggest ways in which NATO could enhance its capabilities for defence. The author examines not only the forces of NATO and the Warsaw Pact, but also their strategy, operations and tactics. He deals with mobility and firepower issues as well as logistics, tactical airpower, command and control, and terrain. His solution for what he regards as NATO's shortcomings is an area defence backed by substantial operational reserves, enough counter-battery firepower to prevent Soviet artillery from neutralizing dispersed NATO anti-tank defences, and sufficient tactical air power to gain superiority in critical areas. Based as it was on the situation prior to 1989 this volume was quickly superseded by events, but may still have some interest for those concerned with operational details and tactics.

591 **Redressing the Conventional Balance: NATO's Reserve Military Manpower.**
Andrew Hamilton.   *International Security*, vol. 10, no. 1 (Summer 1985), p. 111-136.
Hamilton argues that the NATO–Warsaw Pact conventional balance is thin but repairable, principally by equipping and reorganizing already-trained European military units. He calculates that to ensure a strong NATO defence against a Soviet

attack would require 20 additional 'division equivalents' beyond the roughly 52 divisions currently planned. To acquire these forces at relatively low cost, greater emphasis should be placed on reserve manpower. Other cost-effective measures include using slightly older equipment that would still match that of the Pact, using fewer tanks per infantry squad, substituting light infantry for heavy armoured divisions, and preparing defensive positions.

592 Not by Numbers Alone: Assessing the Military Balance.

Andrew Kelly. Bradford, England: School of Peace Studies, University of Bradford, 1984. 80p. (Peace Studies Papers, No. 11).

This study provides a critique of traditional assessments of the East–West military balance at the arms control level, at the level of theatre nuclear forces and at the level of conventional forces. The author argues that traditional assessments focus on 'bean counts' of troops and weapons and exclude geographical, political and economic factors. The result is that threat assessments are often exaggerated. The author argues that this is true of the conventional balance in Europe and that a close study of Soviet forces and equipment reveals a force that not only has distinct limitations but is also dogged by bureaucracy and inefficiency. This is an interesting analysis.

593 Treating NATO's Self-inflicted Wound.

R. W. Komer. *Foreign Policy*, no. 13 (Winter 1973-74), p. 34-48.

Argues that although conventional defence and deterrence have become more important because of the emergence of strategic parity, NATO faces considerable resource constraints. The author argues that the solution is to be found in force restructuring based on hard choices which would make better use of active personnel. Komer makes three proposals: smaller leaner divisional slices; greater reliance on cheap European territorial forces and on cadre units; and greater emphasis on anti-armour capabilities.

594 Numbers, Strategy, and the European Balance.

John J. Mearsheimer. *International Security*, vol. 12, no. 4 (Spring 1988), p. 174-185.

Mearsheimer is relatively optimistic that NATO forces can successfully repel a Warsaw Pact incursion into Central Europe. In analysing the European conventional balance, he looks at six main factors: the relative strength of NATO and the Warsaw Pact in terms of firepower, mobility, and survivability; the nature of the physical terrain; force-to-space ratios; reinforcement capabilities; reserve capabilities; and the initiative and flexibility of Pact commanders. While NATO conventional forces would probably be strong enough to prevent the Soviets from overrunning Germany, reductions in these forces, even if bilateral, would seriously undermine Western European security because of the force-to-space ratio. He cautions that quantitative parity is not necessarily synonymous with stability or security.

595 Why the Soviets can't Win Quickly in Central Europe.

John J. Mearsheimer. *International Security*, vol. 7, no. 1 (Summer 1982), p. 3-39.

The conventional wisdom about the military balance in Europe was that the Soviet Union had decisive advantages and could win a non-nuclear war fairly rapidly. This view was challenged by several analysts who approached the balance in ways which went beyond simple 'bean counting'. Mearsheimer's was one of the most trenchant of these challenges. He questioned the orthodoxy that the Soviet Union and its allies had a decisive advantage which would enable them to launch a successful Blitzkrieg against NATO and exploit this through deep penetration. Even in the most threatening axis of attack, the Fulda Gap, force-to-space ratios would significantly constrain a Soviet advance. Mearsheimer warns, however, that NATO must continue to improve its force structure, develop good intelligence to provide warning time of Pact mobilization, and plan for ways to mobilize quickly without unnecessarily provoking the Soviets.

596 Assessing the Conventional Balance: The 3:1 Rule and its Critics.
John Mearsheimer. *International Security*, vol. 13, no. 4
(Spring 1989), p. 54-89.

Responding to criticisms by Joshua Epstein (*see* item no. 587), John Mearsheimer defends the validity of the rule that an offence needs a 3:1 advantage over the defence to be successful. He also criticizes Epstein's approach based on dynamic models. The irony is that Mearsheimer and Epstein agree that the conventional balance in Europe is not nearly as bad for NATO as the orthodox view argues. The two analysts disagree about the validity of different ways of getting to this conclusion. An esoteric controversy over methodology, the debate can be seen as either fascinating or as a futile exercise in strategic scholasticism. Whatever the case, this is a trenchant analysis which produced an equally trenchant response.

597 NATO under Attack: Why the Western Alliance can Fight Outnumbered and Win in Central Europe without Nuclear Weapons.
F. W. Von Mellenthin, R. H. S. Stolfi, E. Subik. Durham, North
Carolina: Duke University Press, 1984. 161p.

Written by two German military officers and a Professor of European history, this volume offers what the authors consider a more realistic and relatively optimistic assessment of the military balance in Europe. The argument is based upon several historical case-studies designed to reveal the basis for successful military operations in Europe. In addition, the analysis highlights several major weaknesses of Warsaw Pact forces which, the authors contend, help make the balance less unfavourable to NATO than most conventional wisdom suggests. Contending that superior command style is a very important advantage for NATO, it is argued that the Alliance should not allow itself to be drawn into a war based on attrition, but instead should try to ensure that in the event of hostilities it could regain the initiative by mobile counter-attacks and by setting a tempo of operations which the more rigid Soviet approach would find difficult to deal with.

598 Is NATO Decisively Outnumbered?
Barry R. Posen. *International Security*, vol. 12, no. 4 (Spring 1988),
p. 186-202.

Posen offers a reassessment of the common view that Warsaw Pact forces could quickly and easily prevail over NATO in a conventional land battle in Central Europe. He re-examines the quantity, quality, and mix of each side's weapons; combat readiness and reserve capabilities; and command and logistics abilities. The conclusion is that NATO and Pact forces are 'fully competitive' and that Pact superiority in firepower is generally over-estimated. Posen is unimpressed by Soviet mobilization capabilities and command, control and communication assets. He also contends that NATO's defensive task is easier to achieve than the Pact's offensive strategy. All in all, a powerful challenge to the more pessimistic analyses of the conventional balance in Europe.

599 **Measuring the European Conventional Balance: Coping with Complexity in Threat Assessment.**

Barry R. Posen. *International Security*, vol. 9, no. 3 (Winter 1984-85), p. 47-88.

An important effort to analyse the military balance in Europe in terms of operational complexities rather than 'bean counting'. Posen starts from the need to assess the tactical battlefield situation in Central Europe against the backdrop of Western and Warsaw Pact military doctrines and force characteristics. Posen develops an 'Attrition-Forward Edge of the Battle Area Expansion Model' which takes into account relative military capabilities over time, the impact of tactical air power, force-to-space ratios, exchange rates, and advance rates. His conclusion is that NATO should recognize the progress that it has made in countering Pact capabilities and should spend resources wisely on improvements that are achievable. If NATO's doctrine is fundamentally sound in its assumptions about the nature of a future war, then its forces will serve it well in defending Europe. But the underlying assumptions about mobilization capability, for example, and other elements of military doctrine need to be considered carefully.

600 **Addressing Europe's Conventional Instabilities.**

James A. Schear, Joseph S. Nye. *Washington Quarterly*, vol. 11, no. 3 (Summer 1988), p. 45-58.

One of two articles in this issue of *Washington Quarterly* exploring European security after the INF agreement, this piece looks at instabilities in the conventional balance in Europe in the aftermath of the INF Treaty and identifies four areas in which NATO should strengthen its capabilities: improving combat effectiveness against first-echelon Soviet forces, using emerging technologies to attack second-echelon forces, taking measures to enhance survivability of aircraft against pre-emption, and enhancing readiness. In addition to this force planning agenda the authors also look at how the instabilities can be addressed through arms control – an analysis which was useful but overtaken by progress in the negotiations on conventional forces in Europe (CFE).

601 **NATO–Warsaw Pact Force Mobilization.**

Edited by Jeffrey Simon. Washington, DC: GPO for National Defense University Press, 1988. 563p.

Focuses upon an important and often neglected issue and provides both a general discussion of the problems of mobilization and reinforcement and looks at capabilities of both the front-line states and the states on the flanks. The initial section examines US and Soviet capabilities and options and there is also a section on communication and transportation issues. This is a very detailed set of papers which includes many charts, tables and maps and which helps to fill a major gap.

602   **Security and Stability in Conventional Forces: Differing Perceptions of the Balance.**
Leonard Sullivan, Jr.   Washington, DC: Atlantic Council of the United States, May 1988. 72p.

Written by a former official in the Department of Defense, this study not only provides an extremely helpful analysis of the military balance in Europe but also explains why perceptions of this balance often differ very markedly. The paper focuses upon such issues as quantity versus quality, the importance of force posture and such factors as force-to-space ratios, and the differences between side-by-side and face-to-face comparisons. It also looks at the implications of the uncertainty in assessment for the possibility of force reductions, concluding that a stable equilibrium could be achieved at widely varying levels of force composition and posture.

Burden-sharing in NATO

603 **Burden-sharing in NATO: The Economics of Alliance.**
C. Gordon Bare. *Orbis*, vol. 20, no. 2 (Summer 1976), p. 417-436.
Starts from the premise that a reasonable distribution of costs and benefits of
membership is central to the maintenance of an alliance. A narrow concept of burden-
sharing focuses on the budgetary costs of alliance missions and the balance-of-
payments costs of force deployments overseas. Having established the general
framework for burden-sharing, the author explores specific initiatives taken to alleviate
United States concerns such as the offset agreements between the United States and
Germany and Britain and Germany in the late 1960s. He also shows how this issue
became bound up with larger questions concerning the Atlantic relationship and the
US military presence in Western Europe. From 1970 to 1974 the issue became
entangled with Congressional pressure for unilateral troop withdrawals. After 1974,
however, the issue was defused, partly as a result of changed economic circumstances.
A useful analysis which helps to place the burden-sharing debate of the early 1970s in
its appropriate political and strategic context.

604 **The Political Economy of Alliances: Benefits, Costs and Institutions in
NATO.**
Francis A. Beer. Beverly Hills, California: Sage, 1972. 37p.
Beer examines the Olson and Zeckhauser economic theory of alliances and suggests
that it does not adequately explain the patterns of burden-sharing in NATO. He argues
that complex patterns prevailed in which the process of institutionalization was very
important. A contribution to the theoretical debate about alliance burden-sharing.

605 **Who will Staff NATO?**
Susan Clark. *Orbis*, vol. 32, no. 4 (Fall 1988), p. 521-539.
Looks at the population base from which the members of NATO will draw the
conscripts for military service. The author highlights the fact that seven of the fourteen
countries examined will face a decline of more than twenty per cent of males aged 18

to 22, and suggests ways in which the consequences of this might be alleviated. She also looks at the situation facing the Warsaw Pact.

606 Shifting into Neutral? Burden Sharing in the Western Alliance in the 1990s.
Christopher Coker.   London: Brassey's UK, 1990. 160p.

Although this book was put together just before the revolution of 1989, it raises some issues which remain relevant. One of its basic themes is that the United States is in decline and that the Europeans will have to share the costs as well as the benefits of global security to a greater extent in the future than in the past. There is a particularly good chapter on sharing the costs of global security, written by Michael Brenner. The book suffers from the lack of a real conclusion and from the date it was put together. Nevertheless, for those interested in the continued argument over burden-sharing in NATO this is a useful study.

607 Drifting Apart: The Superpowers and their European Allies.
Edited by Christopher Coker.   London: Brassey's Defense Publishers, 1989. 182p.

The main argument presented here is that the financial burden resulting from ever greater armaments expenditures has led to a paradoxical situation. Contrary to their intentions, the nations of East and West Europe have not purchased more security, but rather less. Escalating armaments expenditures do not enhance either side's security vis-à-vis the other and in fact weaken each side's abilities to respond to other threats and problems that often emanate from areas beyond Europe. These other threats – environmental damage, hunger, overpopulation, instability – grow steadily worse but European governments, burdened with defence spending, lack the resources to work towards solutions. In the book's conclusion, Harry Maier argues that this predicament led Gorbachev to opt for a policy of purchasing greater overall security through decreased armaments expenditure. Maier suggests that the 'more for less' strategy is now being adopted by many others. Despite the subsequent demise of the Warsaw Pact and the Soviet Union, this alternative conception of how to build and finance security remains relevant.

608 World Military Expenditures: European NATO.
Saadet Deger.   New York: Oxford University Press, 1989, p. 141-149.
(*SIPRI Yearbook 1989*).

Summarizes the increasing pressure for cuts in defence spending both in NATO member-states and in Eastern European countries. The author concentrates on the issue of burden-sharing, giving a concise analysis of the various positions, with particular reference to the FRG and Britain. The interplay between burden-sharing and burden-shedding is also given attention.

609 World Military Expenditures: European NATO.
Saadet Deger.   New York: Oxford University Press, 1991, p. 126-137.
(*SIPRI Yearbook 1991*).

Provides a brief but useful overview of patterns of military expenditure by NATO members since 1977 when the Alliance formally adopted the goal of a three per cent per annum real increase in defence spending – a goal which was rarely met but not formally abandoned until 1990. The impact of the political changes in Europe on defence budgets is also discussed. A succinct and informative piece which includes six pages of tables on military expenditure and other relevant economic data.

610 **Constraints on Strategy: The Economics of Western Security.**
Edited by David B. H. Denoon. Washington, DC: Pergamon-Brassey's, 1986. 254p.

A useful, if inevitably rather dated, volume which assesses the likely economic performance of the United States and its major allies, looks at the relationship between economic performance and defence spending and considers how economic factors are likely to shape defence options in the United States; Britain, France and West Germany; and Portugal, Spain, Greece and Turkey (as well as Japan and South Korea). This volume contains a wealth of information and offers both descriptions and economic analyses of patterns of defence expenditure and burden-sharing. A very good conclusion by the editor effectively integrates the major findings of the various chapters.

611 **The Politics of Defense Allocations in Western Europe.**
Yehezkel Dror. *Public Budgeting and Finance*, vol. 3, no. 1 (Spring 1983), p. 3-22.

An unusual and interesting perspective by an analyst whose main area of expertise is public administration. Dror argues that defence allocation in Western Europe is a case of budgeting under conditions of diminishing capacity to govern, combined with more severe constraints on public expenditure. In spite of their unique characteristics, defence allocations share many common features with other budgetary sectors. Adds an often neglected dimension to the narrow arguments over burden-sharing and budgetary allocations to defence.

612 **International Regimes and Alliance Behavior: Explaining NATO Conventional Force Levels.**
John S. Duffield. *International Organization*, vol. 46, no. 4 (Autumn 1992), p. 819-856.

An intriguing analysis which sets out to explain the stability of NATO conventional force levels throughout the Cold War. It suggests that force levels cannot be understood either in terms of public goods analysis or balance-of-power theory. Rather, the stability of these levels is best understood in terms of norms and rules established in the Alliance in a regime. The author uses this to explain why there were not greater variations in force levels.

613 **Defense Burden-sharing in the Atlantic Community 1945-1954.**
Peter Foot. Aberdeen, Scotland: Centre for Defence Studies, University of Aberdeen, 1981. 60p. (Aberdeen Studies in Defence Economics, No. 20).

Foot deals with the emergence of the controversy over burden-sharing in NATO's formative years. This fills an important gap as most studies of the NATO burden-sharing issue focus on the 1960s onwards. Foot demonstrates very clearly that the issue was on the agenda – albeit in a low-key way – from the inception of the alliance. This is a valuable study of a neglected issue by an accomplished British historian of NATO.

614 **Problems of Equity in Alliance Arrangements.**
Peter Foot. Aberdeen, Scotland: Centre for Defence Studies,
Aberdeen University, Summer 1982. 43p. (Aberdeen Studies in
Defence Economics, No. 23).

An interesting study which looks at the problem of defining equity or fairness in burden-sharing in NATO and suggests ways in which the issue can be redefined so that the Atlantic Alliance could remove a source of irritation and resentment. Foot suggests that it would be better to focus on equality of effort rather than equality of sacrifice and on defence outputs rather than inputs. He also argues that the allies have already achieved a surprising degree of equity. A constructive and helpful contribution to the debate over burden-sharing.

615 **The Three Per Cent Solution and the Future of NATO.**
Foreign Policy Research Institute. Philadelphia, Pennsylvania:
Foreign Policy Research Institute, 1981. 118p.

Examines the background to, and the consequences of, the NATO agreement of May 1977 to increase members' defence budgets by three per cent per annum in real terms over a five-year period. Known as the 'three per cent solution' this was partly a response to continued increases in Soviet military capabilities. It also reflected an attempt by the Carter Administration to reaffirm the US commitment to Western Europe. In the event, however, as the authors of this report show, the three per cent commitment became a source of aggravation in the Alliance as most of the European nations failed to meet the target. The episode highlighted the problem of allocating resources to defence in an era of détente, the welfare state, and low growth.

616 **NATO Burden-sharing: Risks and Opportunities.**
James R. Golden. New York: Praeger, 1983. 103p.

Shows how the burden-sharing issue in the early 1980s was driven by divergent outlooks between the United States and Western Europe. Whereas the United States believed that détente had failed and that increased military spending was essential, the Europeans believed that détente had not only produced benefits but that it was crucial to maintain a dialogue with Moscow. As well as exploring the underlying causes of the controversy, Golden identifies the areas where a redistribution of effort might be both feasible and desirable.

617 **NATO's Three Per Cent Solution.**
David Greenwood. *Survival*, vol. 23, no. 6 (November-December 1981), p. 252-260.

An incisive analysis of the burden-sharing issue as it developed in the late 1970s. Greenwood looks at the background in which the United States was arguing that it was bearing too much of the burden and the Europeans were claiming otherwise. The effort to provide a way around this and make a concerted effort to devote more resources to defence resulted in the 1977 agreement by the NATO members to increase defence spending in real terms (after allowing for inflation) by three per cent per annum. Rather than alleviating the controversy, however, this became an additional source of tension. Although an approach to burden-sharing using a single indicator of this kind had the great virtue of simplicity, as Greenwood shows, it also became a source of highly divisive dispute which was more trouble than it was worth.

Greenwood concludes that NATO should get rid of a yardstick which it uses simply to beat itself.

618   Towards Role Specialization in NATO.
David Greenwood.   *NATO's Sixteen Nations*, vol. 31, no. 3 (July 1986), p. 44-49.

Argues that the effort to strengthen NATO's conventional capabilities without devoting more resources to defence is best achieved through greater role specialization among the member-nations. The author looks at the prospects for incremental improvements and at the possibility of more comprehensive changes. He concludes that the NATO planning process is a major obstacle to significant change and suggests ways in which it might be improved.

619   Defense Policy in the North Atlantic Alliance: The Case of the Netherlands.
Jan Willem Honig.   Westport, Connecticut: Praeger, 1993. 263p.

Looks at the impact of the Atlantic Alliance on Dutch defence policy from 1949 through to the end of the Cold War. The author follows the transition in Dutch policy through the period when it tried to be an exemplary ally in burden-sharing and other ways through the 'kidsland' or pilot country approach in which the Labour Government tried to lead NATO in détente in the 1970s and the reversion in the late 1970s to the initial conception. He concludes that the key to understanding the defence policy of the Netherlands is the role of the services in creating and maintaining relatively large forces and that being a good ally was something the military was able to use to justify relatively large forces for a country its size. The conclusion of what is a highly detailed and thorough analysis is that neither loyalty nor free-riding concepts really applied to Dutch defence policy.

620   Burden-sharing in NATO.
Gavin Kennedy.   New York: Holmes & Meier, 1979. 117p.

An analysis of burden-sharing which treats defence as a public or collective good and relates this theory to NATO. The author highlights the free-riding in NATO and suggests that rather than focusing exclusively on benefits more attention should be given to the ability to pay. There is much good information here about the contributions of NATO members, and the author also makes some interesting proposals.

621   Burden-sharing in NATO: Aspects of US Policy.
Klaus Knorr.   *Orbis*, vol. 29, no. 3 (Fall 1985), p. 517-536.

A refreshing analysis of the burden-sharing controversy which argues that most discussions of the problem are conceptually flawed and partial in their approach. Knorr argues that burdens cannot be seen separate from the benefits that are obtained from the alliance. He also contends that economic comparisons must be related to non-economic benefits and disadvantages. A variety of problems limit the comparability of even strictly economic data such as budget figures. Consequently, it is not possible to demonstrate incontrovertibly that the United States has carried an unfair share of the burden associated with membership of NATO.

622 **NATO at Thirty: Looking Ahead.**
Robert Komer. *International Security*, vol. 4, no. 1 (Summer 1979),
p. 108-116.

A short article, which identifies four periods of Alliance history and then focuses on NATO's new Long-term Defense Program (LTDP) and the commitment to a three per cent per annum real increase in defence budgets engineered by the Carter Administration at the London Summit in May 1977. Komer highlights the major elements in the LTDP which include enhanced readiness, improved air defence and an improvement in command, control and communication capabilities. He also emphasizes the need for enhanced collaboration in armaments and for theatre nuclear modernization. The rationale for all this is the coincidence of the end of US nuclear domination and the increase in Soviet conventional strength. Komer also emphasizes the United States' role in what he sees as a major revitalization of the Atlantic Alliance.

623 **Burden-sharing: Has the Term Outlived its Usefulness?**
Jack Le Cuyer. *Atlantic Community Quarterly*, vol. 24, no. 1
(Spring 1986), p. 63-65.

A short but useful article which argues that in spite of the asymmetries in economic and political power of its members, NATO has not only outlasted other alliances but has matured to a point where its members are both more able and more willing to share more equitably the risks and opportunities of countering Soviet global military power. There are still obstacles to this, however. Consequently, a first step, the author argues, would be to discard the idea of burden-sharing in terms of budget statistics and to broaden the discussion to cover the full range of policy instruments that the NATO nations must use to guarantee national and collective interests.

624 **The View from London.**
Michael Legge. *The National Interest*, no. 12 (Summer 1988),
p. 34-42.

Written by a British official, this article is paired with one by Richard Perle. The theme is burden-sharing. While Perle argues that the US share of defence expenditures is disproportionately large, Legge defends European achievements, even while acknowledging that the pressure to reduce US trade and budget deficits gives new salience to the issue. Although the United States devotes more resources and a higher proportion of gross domestic product (GDP) to defence, Washington must take into account other factors such as different perceptions and goals as well as the increases in European spending over the last decade.

625 **NATO after Afghanistan.**
Simon Lunn. Washington, DC: Government Printing Office, 1980.
64p.

This report was prepared for the Subcommittee on Europe and the Middle East of the Committee on Foreign Affairs, US House of Representatives, by a British analyst working in the Foreign Affairs and National Defense Division, Congressional Research, Library of Congress. It is an excellent study which looks at the strains on NATO resulting from the Soviet intervention in Afghanistan and the Iran hostage crisis. The author shows how these rises have become linked to the burden-sharing issue. He examines the European contribution to NATO and the response of the

European allies to the Afghan crisis – which includes indirect assistance through the adoption of additional responsibilities in Europe. A valuable contribution to the burden-sharing debate.

626 **Burden-sharing in NATO.**
Simon Lunn. London: Routledge and Kegan Paul for the Royal Institute of International Affairs, 1983. 88p.

This is an excellent analysis of the burden-sharing debate in NATO which starts from the presumption that determining fair shares is a virtually impossible task. At the same time, the author shows how the issue took on a new dimension in the early 1980s as a result of the Soviet military build-up, the invasion of Afghanistan, and the response of the Carter and Reagan Administrations in the United States. Lunn argues that the debate over burden-sharing became a surrogate for more fundamental issues such as US doubts about the loyalty of the Europeans and European doubts about the wisdom of United States policy towards Moscow. Although this gave the issue even more potential for mischief than in the past, Lunn makes some suggestions for alleviating the tensions in the Alliance.

627 **Burden Sharing in NATO: A New Debate with an Old Label.**
Michael Moodie. *Washington Quarterly*, vol. 12, no. 4 (Autumn 1989), p. 61-71.

Examines the reasons why the burden-sharing debate in NATO became more intense during 1988. These include US economic problems, a more conciliatory Soviet Union, a coalescing Europe, and changing attitudes towards NATO. As a result the debate is no longer about fairness, it is about two fundamental issues – the nature of the future global security role of the United States and the nature of the burden in a rapidly shifting security environment in Europe. Moodie argues very persuasively that since burden-sharing is a surrogate for these more fundamental issues, the terms of the debate themselves must be changed.

628 **NATO Burden Sharing and the Forces of Change: Further Observations.**
James C. Murdoch, Todd Sandler. *International Studies Quarterly*, vol. 35, no. 1 (March 1991), p. 109-114.

Challenges the work on burden-sharing by Oneal and Elrod (*see* item no. 633) partly on methodological grounds. The essay is followed by a short rejoinder from Oneal.

629 **Defense Manpower Policies and Problems Among Member Countries of NATO. Presentation by Members of the Subcommittee on Manpower and Personnel of the North Atlantic Assembly to the Military Personnel and Compensation Subcommittee of the Committee on Armed Services, House of Representatives, Ninety-Seventh Congress, First Session, 5 May 1981.**
North Atlantic Assembly (NAA). Washington, DC: US Government Printing Office, 1982. 35p.

The presentation focuses on the problems of recruitment, retention and reserves in the major NATO countries, and discusses differences between the problems of countries with volunteer forces and those with conscript forces. It also gives a useful summary of the problems facing individual countries.

630 **Enhancing Alliance Collective Security: Shared Roles, Risks and Responsibilities in the Alliance; A Report by NATO's Defence Planning Committee.**
North Atlantic Treaty Organization. Defence Planning Committee. Brussels: NATO, 1988. 79p.

This document reflected an important attempt by NATO, in the late 1980s, to defuse burden-sharing as a highly divisive issue in Atlantic relations. Whereas in the past, the emphasis had been solely on burden-sharing, this study broadened the focus and discussed the sharing of roles, risks and responsibilities in an equitable manner. It not only recognized that this embraced a wide range of contributions by member countries that went beyond financial and human resources to include land and facilities, but also acknowledged that not all contributions were quantifiable or comparable. As well as emphasizing the indispensable contribution of the United States, the Report noted that the European members of the integrated military structure not only provided the bulk of the ready forces available in Europe but also contributed through host-nation support. The Federal Republic of Germany was singled out as bearing a particularly high social cost as a result of the density of military activity on its territory. The report also identified specific areas of improvement for individual countries as well as areas where the collective defence effort needed to be enhanced, including assistance to the three NATO members with less developed defence industries.

631 **An Economic Theory of Alliances.**
Mancur Olson, Jr., Richard Zeckhauser. Santa Monica, California: Rand Corporation, 1966. 38p. (Memorandum RM-4297-ISA; Q180.A1R36, No. 4297).

An important article which suggested that in an alliance like NATO where security is a public good the larger powers bear a disproportionate share of the burden and the smaller powers fail to provide their fair shares. This established the economic framework within which much of the burden-sharing debate subsequently occurred and set the scene for criticisms of free-riding in the Atlantic Alliance.

632 **The Theory of Collective Action and Burden Sharing in NATO.**
John R. Oneal. *International Organization*, vol. 44, no. 3 (Summer 1990), p. 379-402.

Examines the continued relevance of Mancur Olson's theory of collective action as an explanation for variations in burden-sharing. The author suggests that the association between economic size of and defence burden borne by a particular nation – something which was evident earlier in NATO's life – has declined. After examining the reasons for this, the author concludes that the Olson theory still has relevance to the alliance.

633 **NATO Burden Sharing and the Forces of Change.**
John R. Oneal, Mark A. Elrod. *International Studies Quarterly*, vol. 33, no. 4 (December 1989), p. 435-456.

Approaches burden-sharing in NATO from the perspective of the theory of collective action and public goods. It reviews the history of the debate over burden-sharing in

NATO, discusses the theory of collective action and highlights its limits in accounting for national defence expenditures. The article also looks at the impact of the declining economic preponderance of the United States and assesses the future of the Atlantic relationship. In essence, it challenges collective goods interpretations of alliance and offers an alternative model based on hegemonic stability theory.

634 **Corralling the Free Rider: Deterrence and the Western Alliance.**
Glenn Palmer. *International Studies Quarterly*, vol. 34, no. 2 (June 1990), p. 147-164.

This article explores alliance behaviour from a public goods perspective which suggests that larger allies spend proportionately more on defence than do smaller allies. If the larger states spend more on defence, however, it does not follow that the smaller will spend less. In fact, the conclusion of the article is that because of intra-alliance bargaining, when the larger states devote more money to defence the smaller ones are likely to do the same. Although this does not challenge the basic free-rider argument, it does imply that there are limits to free-riding.

635 **Can NATO Assess Dues Fairly?**
Stanley K. Ridgley. *Orbis*, vol. 34, no. 3 (Summer 1990), p. 343-458.

Ridgley considers whether NATO will endure in view of the changes in Europe, and argues that NATO is still a general defence pact and is not directed exclusively against Warsaw Pact forces. The European desire to keep NATO as a check on unified Germany is also highlighted. Attention is given to the burden-sharing issue and European and American claims and counter-claims are contrasted. The author believes that a new method of assessment is needed and that this should be based – as the Europeans argue – not on economic input but on military output. He concludes that the Germans have had a large burden in intangible costs and that all countries must agree on a new and fair system.

636 **Rethinking the Debate on Burden-sharing.**
James B. Steinberg. *Survival*, vol. 29, no. 1 (January-February 1987), p. 56-78.

Another critique of simplistic approaches to burden-sharing, this article argues that too much of the controversy has focused on quantitative measures of national contributions to collective defence. Assessments of the appropriateness of national efforts, however, must address the benefits of NATO membership for the various nations. Moreover, theoretical models of alliance behaviour oversimplify the attempts to determine whether some nations obtain a 'free ride' at the expense of others. The author also notes that the political and social costs of membership should not be ignored and concludes that judgements about the fairness of national contributions must include the broader political context and take into account the central goal of maintaining alliance cohesion in the face of diversity.

637 **Political and Economic Issues within the Alliance: The Future of Burdensharing and the Southern Region.**
James Steinberg, Charles Cooper. Monterey, California: Rand Corporation, August 1990. 25p.

Argues very effectively that disputes over burden-sharing are often a way of masking more fundamental disagreements about both goals and means in NATO – especially arguments about strategic preferences. The authors also look at the economic and financial aspects of the burden-sharing debate. The final part of the paper deals with the specific consequences for Greece and Turkey of trends such as the decline of terrorist threats, the CFE negotiations, and the European Community's growing involvement in Eastern Europe. Although the various parts of the paper are not as fully integrated as they could have been, the authors make a useful start in efforts to assess the impact of the changing political context in Europe and its impact on the burden-sharing debate.

638 **A New Approach to Burden-sharing.**
Leonard Sullivan, Jr. *Foreign Policy*, no. 60 (Fall 1985), p. 91-110.
An innovative and persuasive analysis which argues that the basis of burden-sharing amongst the OECD nations must be redefined to reflect broader political, economic and ideological goals and not simply an emphasis on military security. The author suggests that among the appropriate indicators for burden-sharing are such things as aid to the Third World and disapproval of radical regimes. He also advocates a stronger and more self-reliant regional alliance led by the G-7 nations. In terms of NATO it is suggested that greater reliance be placed on European reserve forces and less on active United States forces which are very expensive.

639 **The Dollar Drain and American Forces in Germany: Managing the Political Economics of Alliance.**
Gregory F. Treverton. Athens, Ohio: Ohio University Press, 1978. 226p.
A detailed and theoretically informed study of the negotiations between Washington and Bonn over the 'mechanisms' for offsetting the balance-of-payments costs to the United States of maintaining a military presence in Europe. The author shows how this became linked to the number of American soldiers deployed in Germany. The main focus is on the crisis of 1966 which led to a summit between Johnson and Erhard in Washington and contributed to the subsequent downfall of the Erhard government. The author highlights the complex linkages between domestic politics and alliance issues and offers some lessons for alliance management.

640 **WEU and the Gulf Crisis.**
Willem van Eekelen. *Survival*, vol. 22, no. 6 (November-December 1990), p. 519-532.
Written by the Secretary-General of the Western European Union, this article looks at the WEU role in coordinating European efforts in the Gulf Crisis. Van Eekelen argues that this marked an important contribution to burden-sharing in out-of-area contingencies and that the European actions have been very positive.

641 **The Nunn Amendment, Burdensharing and US Troops in Europe.**
Phil Williams. *Survival*, vol. 27, no. 1 (January-February 1985), p. 2-10.
Explains the background to, and the content of the Nunn Amendment, which was introduced into the Senate in June 1984 and, had it been passed, would have mandated United States troop reductions in Europe unless the allies met certain specific requirements such as increased ammunition stocks, three per cent increases in their defence budgets, or greater contributions to NATO infrastructure. The Europeans saw

the amendment as the beginnings of another Congressional effort to reduce forces in Europe. In fact, it was an attempt to prod the allies into strengthening conventional forces and thereby reducing reliance on nuclear weapons. The amendment was really about NATO strategy rather than about burden-sharing as such.

642   **Burden-sharing in NATO: Myth and Reality.**
       Jonathan Paul Yates.   *Atlantic Community Quarterly*, vol. 24, no. 1
       (Spring 1986), p. 67-79.

Attempts to place the burden-sharing controversy in the context of broader national roles and responsibilities as well as national interests. The author argues that a careful comparison of the defence expenditures of NATO members reveals that the disparity of effort stems not from European negligence but from the additional costs of strategic nuclear forces and personnel in the United States – as well as the broader strategic responsibilities the United States accepts as a global power. Moreover, the United States is in NATO to serve its own security interests. If it were to withdraw from the alliance or NATO were to dissolve then, the author argues, it would have to increase its nuclear arsenal to compensate for the loss of allied conventional forces, French and British nuclear forces and forward bases in Europe. Although such considerations no longer have the same impact, this was a useful corrective to much of the criticism of the European allies in the United States.

The European Pillar of NATO

643 **NATO and the European Union Movement.**
Mary Margaret Ball. Westport, Connecticut: Greenwood Press, 1974
(reprint of 1959 ed.). 486p.

Looks at the regional organizations of Western Europe and their relationship to each
other and to NATO. The author also traces the evolution of NATO, with particular
emphasis on its organizational structure and military and non-military functions. He
also examines the various fora in which European cooperation takes place, including
the Western European Union. The final chapter is entitled 'European or Atlantic
Community – or Both?'. This work is rich in detail.

644 **NATO and Europe.**
André Beaufre. London: Faber and Faber, 1967. 141p.

This study, by a well-known French general and strategic analyst, offers an overview of
the evolution of NATO and an assessment of the Alliance's future. As a Frenchman
writing in the mid-1960s, Beaufre was acutely aware of many of the problems facing
the Atlantic Alliance, and was particularly sensitive to the issue of what was called
nuclear sharing. His solution to this was a proposal for inter-allied coordination of
national deterrent strategies in peacetime. Beaufre also argued that Europe should
move towards greater unification in defence, while acknowledging that the national
character of territorial defence would be maintained. He proposed a European defence
system which would coordinate the various national defence systems in peacetime and
implement strategy in the event of conflict. While this European system should
complement that of the United States, it should not be subordinate to the Atlantic
system. Although Beaufre argued for the reorganization of NATO and the
establishment of a European political and military pillar of the Alliance, his ultimate
goal seems to have been much in the Gaullist mould – a European Europe distinct
from the United States.

645 **Strategic Interdependence and the Politics of Inertia: Paradoxes of European Defense Cooperation.**
Michael Brenner. *World Politics*, vol. 23, no. 4 (July 1971), p. 635-664.

Looks at the prospects for a European nuclear force centring on Anglo-French nuclear cooperation. The author looks at the bases of the independent national policies of Britain and France, considers how these purposes would be served by a joint force, and assesses the prospects for cooperation in terms of financial requirements, technology policy formation, short-term payoffs and political will. The conclusions are negative.

646 **Europe's Futures, Europe's Choices: Models of Western Europe in the 1970s.**
Alastair Buchan. London: Chatto and Windus for the Institute for Strategic Studies, 1969. 167p.

Although obviously very dated in terms of its details, this book has relevance for the debate over the future of Europe that is taking place in the early and mid-1990s. After identifying the factors bearing on the future of Europe, Buchan identifies six alternatives: Evolutionary Europe, which is diplomatically weak but has looser ties with the United States; Atlanticized Europe which exhibits greater dependence on the United States; a Europe des États in which common political structures are less important but individual European states are confident of their power and position; Fragmented Europe in which the European idea has receded completely; Partnership Europe in which a federal Europe has very close links with the United States – i.e. a twin-pillar alliance; and independent Federal Europe which is essentially a third force rather than a second pillar. The characteristics of each kind of Europe are spelled out in some detail, and the author suggests that it might be possible to combine key elements of each one. The European idea has gone much further than seemed likely when Buchan wrote this book, but there is much here that remains of interest and value to students of NATO, the Atlantic relationship, and European security cooperation.

647 **European Self-reliance and the Reform of NATO.**
Hedley Bull. *Foreign Affairs*, vol. 61, no. 4 (Spring 1983), p. 874-892.

An incisive article which argues that there is a third course for Western Europe between continued Atlanticism and the neutralism advocated by many members of the peace movement during the early and mid-1980s. Bull identifies this alternative as Europeanism. The underlying principle is that Western Europe should not only take a greater share of the burden of its own defence but also more of the responsibility for decisions on security. The author argues that such a course is necessary because of the increasing divergence of European and American interests. He also explores what it would involve (strengthening conventional forces and the creation of a European Planning Committee) and how to deal with the problems it might precipitate. He acknowledges that Europeanism, as he terms it, requires the full participation of West Germany and that care should be taken to assess Soviet reactions.

648 The Defense of Western Europe.
Bernard Burrows, Geoffrey Edwards.   London: Butterworth
Scientific, 1982. 155p.

A slim but incisive exploration of the security situation facing Western Europe. It focuses not only on military threats in Europe but also on challenges from outside the NATO area, and especially the threats to energy sources. The main theme of the book is the need for closer European defence cooperation, and particular attention is given to European armaments collaboration and to the idea of a European defence identity. At the same time the book avoids posing this as a choice between greater European independence and a continuation of the Atlantic Alliance, arguing that a more united Western Europe would also provide a more reliable partner for the United States. For those interested in the principle and practice of European defence cooperation this is an extremely good primer.

649 The Security of Western Europe: Towards a Common Defense Policy.
Bernard Burrows, Christopher Irwin.   London: Charles Knight, 1972.
189p.

This book sets out to examine the strategic and political context of West European security in the 1970s. It is also concerned with identifying the choices available for a more united and self-reliant Europe. Having provided a historical background, and an overview of the political and strategic context, it looks at the various forms that European cooperation could take. There is a useful chapter on methods of cooperation and consultation which looks at possible changes in command structures and who fills the various command positions. This is followed by a discussion of joint procurement and production of defence equipment. Another chapter contends that the Europeans could move towards a more equal partnership with the United States in the wider context of NATO and suggests ways in which this could be achieved. It argues that a new 'defence Europe' should be created to complement economic Europe, and considers the various organizations through which this could be done. The Western European Union and the Euro-Group are seen as having too many disadvantages to provide the basis for a European pillar and the authors propose instead a European defence agency that is closely linked to the European Economic Community. Although many of the details have subsequently changed, much of this discussion provides a dress rehearsal for the current debate over Europeanization of NATO.

650 The Western European Union (WEU) and NATO: Strengthening the Second Pillar of the Alliance.
Alfred Cahen.   Washington, DC: The Atlantic Council of the United
States, 1990. 44p.

A brief organizational history and description of the WEU written by a former Secretary-General of the organization. This slim volume emphasizes the WEU's role in promoting Atlantic solidarity and argues that it provides a suitable basis for NATO's European pillar. The appendix contains an interesting presentation of the parallels between the October 1987 WEU's Platform on European Security Interests and the March 1988 Atlantic Summit Communiqué it is said to have inspired.

651 **The Western European Union and NATO: Building a European Defence Identity within the Context of Atlantic Solidarity.**
Alfred Cahen. London: Brassey's, 1989. 114p.
Written by a former Secretary-General of the Western European Union (WEU), this volume proceeds from the assumption that the construction of a European pillar of the Atlantic alliance is both desirable and necessary. Short and succinct, the book includes a history of the WEU, and a description of its institutional basis followed by a treatment of the organization's problems, its prospects for enlargement, and its achievements and future potential. A useful documentary resource, its five appendices include the texts of the Brussels Treaty, the Rome Declaration, and the October 1987 Platform on European Security, as well as other relevant items.

652 **NATO's Middle Course.**
David Calleo. *Foreign Policy*, no. 69 (Winter 1987-88), p. 135-147.
Written with an eye to NATO's fortieth anniversary, this article considers proposals for NATO reform in three categories: burden-sharing, devolution, and disengagement. Calleo argues that in view of the deterioration of American global predominance and the changes in the Alliance the most appropriate alternative is devolution, but to be effective this must have a nuclear component. This requires a shift in United States thinking about nuclear weapons in the Alliance and a recognition that the European allies must have greater nuclear responsibilities.

653 **Why NATO–Europe needs a Nuclear Trigger.**
Marco Carnovale. *Orbis*, vol. 35, no. 2 (Spring 1991), p. 223-234.
Starting from the premise that the Europeans must still be concerned with a nuclear Soviet Union, this article outlines the case for the creation of a European nuclear force and identifies several conditions which must be met: German involvement; compatibility with NATO, which must continue to have a US conventional and nuclear presence; acceptability in Europe which should be possible because of the Europeanization of nuclear forces; and Soviet acquiescence. The primary mission of this force would be to increase the credibility of NATO's nuclear deterrent in Europe. Submarines would provide the most appropriate systems and the command and control network should be tied to the US–NATO system. A Supreme Allied Commander for European Nuclear Forces should have day-to-day authority. An interesting proposal for changing the basis of responsibility for European security.

654 **European Defense Cooperation: America, Britain and NATO.**
Edited by Michael Clarke, Rod Hague. Manchester, England: Manchester University Press, 1990. 177p.
The result of a conference sponsored by the Fulbright Commission, this book has two main themes: the Anglo-American special relationship and the Europeanization of NATO. There is some tension, however, between these two themes even though the editors treat Anglo-American relations as a subset of the transatlantic relationship. Contributors include Alfred Cahen, Simon Lunn, Robbin Laird, Gale Mattox, Trevor Taylor, Phil Williams and the editors themselves. This is a useful collection.

655   **The Atlantic Idea and its European Rivals.**
Harold Van B. Cleveland.   New York: McGraw-Hill, 1966. 186p.
An appropriately titled volume which looks at the pressures for continued Atlanticism
and the idea of a more independent Europe. The author examines both the economic
and the military aspects of Atlantic relations. He acknowledges that there is some
conflict between greater European unity and a close Atlantic relationship but argues
that Western Europe and the United States still have overriding common interests.

656   **The Eurogroup and NATO.**
William C. Cromwell.   Philadelphia, Pennsylvania: Foreign Policy
Research Institute, 1974. 55p. (Research Monograph Series, Foreign
Policy Research Institute, No. 18).
A very good discussion not only of why the Eurogroup was established in NATO in the
late 1960s but also of its activities in the early 1970s. As the author notes: the
Eurogroup was an informal association of the European members of NATO which
aimed to increase the effectiveness and cohesiveness of the European defence
contribution. It was a political response to the Congressional pressure for a reduction
in the size of the American military presence in Europe. Cromwell makes very clear
that the Eurogroup could not provide the basis for a European defence identity to
parallel the European Community, a judgement borne out by subsequent developments.

657   **Europe Together, America Apart.**
Pieter Dankert.   *Foreign Policy*, no. 53 (Winter 1983-84), p. 18-33.
Written by the President of the European Parliament, this article argues that Western
Europe cannot continue to make an artificial separation between economic and
defence issues. It also argues that because of the rigidity of the Reagan Administration
there is growing divergence between the United States and Western Europe over the
nature of the Soviet challenge. The author proposes a series of pragmatic steps
whereby the European allies can coordinate their positions on security issues.

658   **European Integration and Security.**
Jacques Delors.   *Survival*, vol. 33, no. 2 (March-April 1991),
p. 99-110.
The text of the 1991 Alastair Buchan Memorial Lecture in which the President of the
European Commission argues that Western Europe needs a common defence policy as
part of the move towards European union. Delors looks at the relationship between
European defence cooperation and Atlantic relations and argues that although the
United States has been uncomfortable with moves in this direction there are
advantages for Washington as well as the Europeans in the development of a common
European defence policy.

659   **France, Germany and the Western Alliance: A Study of Elite Attitudes
on European Integration and World Politics.**
Karl W. Deutsch, Lewis Edinger, Roy C. Macridis, Richard L.
Merritt.   New York: Charles Scribner's Sons, 1967. 324p.
A study based on extensive interviews with French and German élites which set out to
discover if national policies were being superseded by supra-national loyalties, the

implications of nationalistic or supra-national currents in European politics for arms control and disarmament, and the trends in West German and French domestic politics which impinge on foreign policy. Points of convergence and divergence on such issues as NATO, Europe, and nuclear weapons, were identified in France. Cleavages and conflicts in West German politics were also identified. The authors presented a rich survey of élite attitudes on foreign policy and security issues. The volume also contains a comparison of the views of the élites in the two countries. On the basis of this comparison and additional data including an assessment of the flow of transactions (statistics of international trade, mail, travel, and the exchange of students) in the Europe of the Six (as it then was), it is argued by Karl Deutsch that the process of European structural integration had been halted. It would be very interesting if a similar study were to be done today of élite attitudes in France and Germany.

660 **A New European Defense Community.**
François Duchene. *Foreign Affairs*, vol. 50, no. 1 (October 1971), p. 69-82.
Has a rather broader scope than the title suggests and looks at the prospects for greater East–West cooperation and at the United States role in Europe, before turning to the prospects for enhanced West European cooperation on defence. The author sees the enlarged European Community as the vehicle for what he describes as a European Defence Organization. He argues that European policies could be better coordinated on such issues as arms control and that there should be joint programmes in arms production. The issue of a Joint European Command, however, he acknowledges to be more problematic. An interesting discussion which highlights themes that are around once again over twenty years later.

661 **European Security Cooperation and British Interests.**
James Eberle, John Roper, William Wallace, Phil Williams.
International Affairs, vol. 60, no. 4 (Autumn 1984), p. 545-560.
Written by four analysts at the Royal Institute for International Affairs, this article emphasized the need to strengthen the European pillar of NATO and for Britain to contribute to rather than obstruct this process.

662 **The Future of European Security and Defense Policy.**
Werner J. Feld. Boulder, Colorado: Lynne Rienner, 1993. 178p.
Starting from the premise that although NATO has some residual tasks it faces an uncertain future, the author looks at growing demands for a new security framework in Europe, and at the efforts of the Europeans themselves to achieve political union. He not only assesses the implications of the Single European Market for security but also looks at the usefulness of the CSCE, the relationship between the European Community and the Western European Union, the lessons learned from Franco-German defence cooperation, and the prospects for the future. Although the analysis reflects many of the uncertainties that currently exist, it is a good preliminary exploration of likely changes in the European security system.

663 **The European Defense Community: A History.**
F. W. E. Fursdon. New York: St Martin's Press, 1980. 360p.
The definitive history of Europe's first formal attempt to forge an integrated defence community. Beginning with a long introductory section on the origins of René Pleven's

proposal for a European Defence Community with a single army, the book presents a readable and well-documented analysis of the four-year debate. It contains a thorough analysis of the various treaty articles and provisions. The author traces the gradual deterioration of the internal EDC consensus, as the threat of Soviet military action against Western Europe seemed to diminish somewhat. He also looks in some depth at the actions of the French Assembly and the government of Mendès-France in the weeks immediately before the Assembly killed the draft treaty in a procedural vote. Although this does not offer a full assessment of the EDC legacy for future European defence cooperation, this is a very good place to start when considering the idea of a European pillar or defence identity.

664   **Prospects for West European Security Co-operation.**
Ian Gambles.   London: International Institute for Strategic Studies, Autumn 1989. 83p. (Adelphi Paper 244).

Gambles examines West European collective defence efforts and explains both the limits of these efforts and why American leadership in the Atlantic alliance has persisted. He suggests that efforts to modify the balance of power in security matters and make it commensurate with economic and political balances have failed. During the 1980s, although a multitude of unconnected elements of West European security cooperation evolved, a lack of synergy inhibited the development of a coherent European defence entity. Even so, the author suggests, these various elements have created a cooperation 'reservoir' with possible future application. The author acknowledges that the prospects for West European security cooperation are dependent upon changes in Atlantic relations, European political integration, and changing East–West relations. The most likely scenario for the future, however, is a continuation of security cooperation between North America and Western Europe either within a relatively unchanged alliance or through a new integrated system based partly on West European role specialization. A less likely scenario involves a collapse of US leadership leading to either a 're-nationalization' of security policies or to an increase in collaboration under the direction of the European Community. The author suggests that the actual course of events will be determined much more by broad political movements, than by the weak internal dynamics of West European security cooperation. Interesting and incisive, while also very judicious in its conclusions.

665   **European Security Integration in the 1990s.**
Ian Gambles.   Paris: Institute for Security Studies, Western European Union, November 1991. 43p. (Chaillot Papers, No. 3).

Analyses the concept of European security integration, recognizing that traditionally integration has been an issue for the European Community while security has been a matter for NATO. After a brief history of the idea of European security cooperation the author turns to the issue of European security integration, looking at its goals, and the problems of membership and participation. Gambles argues that a rational configuration of European security would be guided by several principles – transparency, openness, internal stability, flexibility, non-redundancy, and compatibility with European construction. His subsequent discussion focuses on the modalities of European security integration, examining the present state and future prospects of integration in the European Community, the Western European Union and NATO. Throughout the study, emphasis is placed on the persistence of sovereignty as an obstacle to integration. Overall this is a valuable and cogent analysis which provides a very good introduction to the major issues involved in security integration in Europe.

666   **The Politics of European Defense Cooperation: Germany, France, Britain, and America.**
David Garnham.   Cambridge, Massachusetts: Ballinger, 1988. 204p.

The author contends that the future prospects for European defence cooperation will be determined by the four nations mentioned in the title. Although published shortly before the momentous changes of 1989, Garnham's central argument, that European security is evolving as the result of two dynamics – European integration and American disengagement – remains relevant. The author systematically considers Europe's changing relationship with the United States; bilateral relationships between the three major NATO European powers; divergence and convergence in national military strategies, force structures, and foreign policies; alternative multilateral institutions for defence cooperation outside NATO; and European public opinion. In the final analysis, he concludes, it is American behaviour which is the prime determinant of European action. A well-informed and useful study.

667   **Extending Deterrence with German Nuclear Weapons.**
David Garnham.   *International Security*, vol. 10, no. 1 (Summer 1985), p. 96-110.

Starting with the proposition that flexible response is not a credible deterrent to Soviet aggression in Europe, Garnham looks at three alternatives: US efforts to obtain nuclear superiority, withdrawal from Europe, and stronger conventional defence. Because none of these is entirely feasible Garnham proposes a fourth alternative – what he calls 'selective proliferation'. In his view, German acquisition of nuclear weapons would provide more effective deterrence and be part of an effort to share burdens and create greater European self-reliance on security issues. The author offers a prospectus of what a West German nuclear force would look like, while also emphasizing the merits of closer German–French nuclear cooperation. A controversial but intriguing article.

668   **Untangling an Alliance.**
S. F. Giffin.   *Orbis*, vol. 7, no. 3 (Fall 1963), p. 465-477.

Reconsiders the roles of the United States and Europe in Atlantic Alliance and argues that neither superpower can share with allies ultimate authority over nuclear weapons. Consequently, these allies must either accept the lead of the United States or of the Soviet Union in the ultimate security sense or, if they opt for independence, recognize that this means a loss of protection. The author argues that the dissolution of the alliance would lead to several smaller security pacts. Attention is also given to the possibility that Europe will be politically integrated and could have its own nuclear deterrent force. US concerns that three superpowers would imperil global stability are highlighted.

669   **NATO and European Integration.**
Lincoln Gordon.   *World Politics*, vol. 10, no. 2 (January 1958), p. 219-231.

An interesting article which reveals American ambivalence about European integration. Although Gordon argues that the creation of the European Community should help NATO by strengthening the economic base of the European members, he also notes that it is important to avoid excessive protectionism and tension between Europe and the United States. Emphasis was also placed on the need for closer transatlantic cohesion in the economic and political as well as military spheres.

670   **Alliance within the Alliance: Franco-German Military Cooperation and the European Pillar of Defense.**
David G. Haglund.   Boulder, Colorado: Westview Press, 1992. 213p.
This book explores the old notion of a European pillar within the Atlantic Alliance. It also puts in perspective the emphasis which developed in the early 1990s on Franco-German defence cooperation. Although the idea of a European defence identity has a long pedigree, it has been inhibited by several factors. Indeed, the United States remains ambivalent about it. Nevertheless, as the author makes clear, it could provide the basis for a reconfiguration of NATO that would help ensure the relevance of the alliance through the remainder of the 1990s.

671   **NATO and the European Economic Community.**
Walter Hallstein.   *Orbis*, vol. 6, no. 4 (Winter 1963), p. 564-574.
Explores the nature of the European Community and argues that considerable progress has been made towards economic and political integration. Also suggests that the United States has always supported European integration and that this is not inconsistent with Atlantic solidarity. In fact, the United States would not be as reluctant to have a European nuclear force as to have individual national forces. Hallstein also considers the issue of future British membership in the Community and its impact.

672   **European Defence: The Role for WEU.**
Eric Hintermann.   *European Affairs*, vol. 2, no. 3 (Autumn 1988), p. 31-38.
A well-constructed argument for the creation of a European defence entity built upon the foundations of the existing Western European Union, written by a former Assistant Secretary-General of the organization. Although written in 1988, the article remains relevant to the current debate over the creation of a new European defence community. Hintermann presents ten proposals for the creation of an efficient European defence organization and concludes that WEU comes closest to bringing them to fruition.

673   **American Foreign Policy and European Integration.**
H. Holborn.   *World Politics*, vol. 6, no. 1 (October 1953), p. 1-30.
This article identifies the difficulties in the way of moves towards European union. Emphasis is placed on the depth and vitality of national traditions in Europe, the implication of which is that the interaction process has to be incremental and long-term. Given the problems of European integration after Maastricht this article would repay another look.

674   **Europeanizing NATO.**
Kim R. Holmes.   *Washington Quarterly*, vol. 7, no. 2 (Spring 1984), p. 59-68.
Argues that a divisible détente and an unprecedented divergence of European and US perceptions of the Soviet threat have promoted a revival of interest in a European

defence identity. The author discusses previous efforts at Europeanization, looks at the prospects for an independent European nuclear force – which he does not see as particularly high – and argues that there is a discernible trend towards greater coordination of European defence efforts. He sees greater Europeanization as a positive possibility and contends that it would represent a growing maturity in the Atlantic Alliance rather than its demise.

675 **The European Pillar.**
Geoffrey Howe. *Foreign Affairs*, vol. 63, no. 2 (Winter 1984-85), p. 330-343.

Argues that the twin-pillar metaphor for the Atlantic Alliance is highly appropriate and that European needs America and America needs Europe. After looking at the burden-sharing issue, the British Foreign Secretary highlights ways in which the Europeans can strengthen the European pillar of the alliance both on economic and security issues. A good snapshot of British thinking on these issues in the mid-1980s.

676 **Nuclear Aspects of West European Defence Integration.**
Christopher Irwin. *International Affairs*, vol. 47, no. 4 (October 1971), p. 679-691.

Focusing on the debate about unification of British and French nuclear forces and the lack of a common nuclear doctrine in NATO Irwin argues that a US–Soviet No First Use rule would leave Europe defenceless against a conventional attack but that the use of nuclear weapons would cause devastation to Europe. He also highlights the problems caused by the absence of France from the nuclear planning process. Irwin assesses proposals for the unification of British and French nuclear forces which some argued would give Western Europe greater strategic autonomy. He also considers proposals for coordinating the deployment of French and British nuclear submarines to double the number on patrol. The problem he sees is that Britain and France could not maintain the pace of technological advancement set by the two superpowers. Consequently, a European nuclear force could never replace the US nuclear umbrella. Moreover, he argues, a truly European nuclear force would not be feasible without a European state to operate it.

677 **United States Foreign Policy in a Changing World.**
Edited by Alan Jones. New York: McKay, 1973, p. 149-175.

This volume contains an excellent chapter by Robert Lieber entitled 'Britain joins Europe'. Going well beyond the title, Lieber's analysis offers an incisive and extremely helpful discussion of European–American relations in a period of transition. Lieber focuses on the degree of unification in Western Europe and on European affinity with the United States and uses these two axes to create a matrix identifying nine possibilities. Among the possibilities he identifies are twin-pillar Alliance or Atlantic partnership, a third-power Europe, a Finlandized Europe and a dependent and Atlanticized Europe. Having identified the possibilities, Lieber then ranks them in a hierarchy ranging from most likely to least likely. As a short and incisive analysis of possible variations in European–American relations, this chapter is hard to beat.

678 **Integration and Security in Western Europe: Inside the European Pillar.**
Edited by Mathias Jopp, Reinhardt Rummel, Peter Schmidt.
Boulder, Colorado: Westview Press, 1991. 316p.

The editors of this study start by noting that the notion of a European security pillar at the beginning of the 1990s, although not new, was very different from what it had been in the past. They suggest that in the 1970s and 1980s the Europeans were simply attempting to protect their specific interests within the Atlantic framework. Today, in contrast, enhanced West European security and defence cooperation would modify the structure of NATO and contribute to the creation of a European pillar which could deal with pan-European and global security issues. The first two chapters explore the trends which support integration and those which obstruct it as well as the institutional frameworks for security cooperation. This sets the scene for discussion of views from the central region and the flanks and for a series of twelve chapters which deal with individual national views on West European security policy. Part four of the volume has chapters on European Political Cooperation, the European Parliament, NATO and the Western European Union. In the conclusion, the editors acknowledge that no unanimous sentiment for closer security cooperation among West European countries can be discerned and that there are no converging views on a single organization. Since this was written there has been a degree of convergence on the Western European Union, but differences remain as to whether this will be a second pillar in NATO or ultimately the security arm of the European Community. Although the issue is still in flux, however, this survey helps the observer to understand how and why the various nations take the positions they do. There is, unfortunately, no index.

679 **British–German Defense Co-operation: Partners within the Alliance.**
Karl Kaiser, John Roper. London: Jane's, 1988. 308p.

Produced under the auspices of the Royal Institute of International Affairs and its counterpart in Bonn, this volume brings together British and German analysts to examine the defence relationship between Britain and the Federal Republic and to highlight patterns of convergence and divergence in their approach to security problems. There is a useful overview of the relationship from 1950 to 1980 by Christoph Bluth. This is followed by chapters which deal with particular issues, such as British nuclear weapons deployed in Germany, the military balance, cooperation on the Northern Flank, and collaboration in arms production. In some cases there are, in effect, pairs of chapters with one by a British author and one by a German contributor dealing with similar themes. Contributors include Jonathan Alford, Christoph Bertram, Keith Hartley, Lawrence Freedman, Peter Stratmann and other well-known analysts of NATO and European security issues.

680 **A Plan to Reshape NATO.**
Henry Kissinger. *Time*, 5 March 1984, p. 20-24.

A strongly stated challenge to the European members of NATO to play a more active role in supporting the Alliance. Kissinger argues that if they fail to do this the United States should withdraw up to half of its ground forces deployed in Europe. Among the measures he believes are necessary to re-invigorate the Alliance are a more solid effort to establish consensus around its political goals, the assumption of greater responsibility for conventional defence by the Europeans; and the appointment of a European to serve as NATO's SACEUR.

681 **France, Germany, and the Future of the Atlantic Alliance.**
Robbin Laird. *Proceedings of the Academy of Political Science*,
vol. 38, no. 1 (1991), p. 50-59.

French–German interaction regarding security in the 1980s centred on reinforcing NATO while enhancing the European role therein. The transformation of East–West relations reinforced the perceived need for European cooperation in the security field and the Europeanization of the Atlantic alliance. The revolutions of 1989 unleashed tensions between nationalism and multilateralism which are at the core of the building of the new Europe and the restructuring of the Atlantic alliance.

682 **The Europeanization of the Alliance.**
Robbin Laird. Boulder, Colorado: Westview Press, 1991. 143p.

Starting from the premise that even before the revolution of 1989 there was a strong movement towards Europeanizing the Atlantic Alliance, the author provides an excellent analysis of the moves in this direction. He argues that the greatest contribution of the Western Alliance is that it established a habit of cooperation which is relevant to the post-Cold War security challenges. At the same time, it has to be recognized that the Western Alliance is a 'mix of institutions – NATO, bilateral, multilateral, non-NATO, and national defense efforts defined with collective purposes in mind' (p. 3). Keeping this in mind, Laird focuses upon the process of Europeanization since the mid-1980s, looking at the revitalization of the Western European Union, the growth of bilateral ties, the Franco-German dynamic, and the future of European nuclear deterrence. He also argues that the main task for the future is not deterrence and defence but crisis management and conflict prevention.

683 **Strangers and Friends: The Franco-German Security Relationship.**
Edited by Robbin Laird. London: Pinter, 1989. 150p.

This book provides a comprehensive overview of the Franco-German security relationship as it evolved in the 1980s. After a helpful introduction by the editor, there are chapters on French and West German policies, on cooperation in conventional force planning, and procurement cooperation. The final chapter looks at the accomplishments of bilateral security cooperation. There is also a useful set of appendices including a chronology of Franco-German defence cooperation, excerpts from the 1963 treaty between France and Germany on cooperation and the 1986 Franco-German agreement on defence cooperation. This is a concise and valuable study of one of the key elements in the Europeanization of Atlantic defence.

684 **France Defeats EDC.**
Edited by David Lerner, Raymond Aron. New York: Praeger, 1957.
225p. 4 maps.

Contributors to this volume are drawn from the ranks of both the European Defense Community's advocates and opponents as well as foreign observers. However, the study, undertaken by the Institut d'Études Européennes in the immediate aftermath of the French Assembly's rejection of EDC, endeavours to present an objective analysis of France's long and decisive national debate. A detailed chronology of EDC's troubled life is included. Divided into four sections, the volume begins with a historical sketch of the debate. Part Two examines the issues at stake within France, in the wider European political arena, and between France and Germany. The role of the French press and the shifting emotions of the French public are explored in Part Three. Both chapters of this section include substantial data gleaned from contemporary public opinion polls. Part Four focuses on the manoeuvring within the Assembly. David Lerner concludes that budgetary concerns and an abiding distrust of Germany were at the heart of EDC's failure. Some tables are included.

685 NATO and the Future of Europe.
Ben T. Moore.   New York: Harper and Brothers, 1958. 263p.

Growing out of work done on the Council of Foreign Relations, this study suggests that while the United States has encouraged European economic union, it has not done the same in terms of a European defence union seeing this as less important than the Atlantic Alliance. To justify this argument, the author traces the idea of European union and has a useful chapter on the whole issue of the European defence community. He also surveys European institutions in both security and economic fields. His most radical proposal is for a European nuclear defence union. Seeing this as preferable to the development of national nuclear forces. All in all, Moore provides one of the strongest American endorsements of European union, arguing that American interests would be advanced by a European defence union controlling the entire range in modern military power including nuclear weapons. He sees this as essential to a more equal Atlantic relationship and argues that a relationship of equality is likely to be more enduring than one of European dependence on the United States.

686 The Defense Policies of Nations: A Comparative Study.
Edited by Douglas J. Murray, Paul R. Viotti.   Baltimore, Maryland: Johns Hopkins University Press, 1989. 702p.

Although this study does not focus on NATO as such, it does have six chapters on Europe and the North Atlantic as well as a chapter on the United States. Particularly useful are the chapter on Britain by David Greenwood, that on France by Alan Sabrosky and that on the Federal Republic of Germany by Catherine Kelleher. For those interested in patterns of convergence and divergence in the defence policies of the major West European states this is very helpful.

687 Europe without America?: The Crisis in Atlantic Relations.
John Palmer.   Oxford, England: Oxford University Press, 1987. 217p.

Written by the European editor of Britain's *Guardian* newspaper, this book was prompted in large part by the disastrous performance of the Reagan Administration in the area of alliance relations. The author argues that trade disputes, economic rivalries, arguments over the burdens of defence, and the declining hegemony of the United States all foreshadow a dramatic shake-up in transatlantic relations. Although Palmer stops short of predicting the imminent demise of the NATO alliance, he explores four perspectives for the future: what he terms Atlantic reformism involving the creation of a European Pillar in the Atlantic Alliance; European reformists who want to hedge against the disintegration of the Atlantic Alliance by strengthening the European Community but do not want to make a formal choice between an independent Europe and links with the United States; European neo-Gaullism which presumes a more independent Western Europe; and a socialist United States of Europe. The potential and difficulties of each of these possibilities are explored in the concluding chapter.

688   **Nuclear Diplomacy: Britain, France and America.**
Andrew J. Pierre.   *Foreign Affairs*, vol. 49, no. 2 (January 1971),
p. 283-301.
Looks at the future of European strategic nuclear forces and considers the prospects for Anglo-French nuclear collaboration. The author sees the main goal as a European nuclear role within the Atlantic Alliance and suggests that the United States should take steps to facilitate this.

689   **Defending Europe in the 1990s: The New Divide of High Technology.**
Joseph C. Rallo.   London: Frances Pinter, 1986. 135p.
The title is somewhat misleading. Although high technology is identified as the main instrument of policy, the author believes the goals of that policy can be accomplished only through greater European integration. It is a recitation of the merits of integration and the failures of fragmented national technology programmes that make up the body of the book. Rather than NATO, Rallo sees the European Community (EC) as the most logical institutional choice for the unification of European high-technology efforts. The 'symbiosis' between the EC and the Western European Union is also regarded as an asset. The author's conclusions are tentative since the prospects for a collective European security policy remain uncertain. Tables are included.

690   **Modernizing Transatlantic Relations: West European Security Cooperation and the Reaction in the United States.**
Reinhardt Rummel.   *Washington Quarterly*, vol. 12, no. 4
(Autumn 1989), p. 83-92.
Rummel argues that key elements of the Western security arrangement need to be updated. He looks at the incentives for and impediments to West European security cooperation and suggests that enhanced cooperation is likely, partly because West Germany has become much more interested in this possibility. Consideration is also given to how the United States is likely to react to further steps in this direction. The author identifies several strands of American opinion – the isolationists and unilateralists, the multipolarists, the traditionalists, and the devolutionists – before going on to argue that a more efficient type of cooperative leadership in the alliance is needed.

691   **The Atlantic Community and Europe.**
Robert Schuman.   *Orbis*, vol. 1, no. 4 (Winter 1958), p. 408-410.
Written by one of the architects of the movement towards European integration, the analysis argues that the North Atlantic Pact provides a framework for military cooperation in Europe but that the Council of Europe provides for economic, political, and cultural cooperation. The author argues that there is no conflict between the Atlantic idea and European integration and that there is a need for a broader Atlantic dialogue to create an Atlantic community that goes beyond military cooperation.

692   **Benelux Security Cooperation: A New European Defense Community.**
George J. Stein.   Boulder, Colorado: Westview Press, 1990. 166p.
Belgium, Netherlands, and Luxembourg, three of NATO's smallest and weakest member-states, are the focus of this study. The author begins with a detailed exposition of each nation's security polices, force posture, and contributions to NATO

collective defence and proceeds to a prescriptive programme for reform and rationalization. Arguing that the three nations are among the most integrationist-minded of European states and have a long tradition of cooperation within their Benelux community, Stein proposes they extend their cooperative efforts to the military sphere. Although each of the three belongs to NATO, the European Community, and the Western European Union, the author believes the WEU would offer the best framework within which to accomplish this restructuring. Stein's prescription is for the integration of the national armed forces of the three and the reconfiguration of those forces along mission-specific lines. The author believes these measures would both rationalize Benelux defence investment and contribute to NATO's overall defensive capability.

693 **European Defense Cooperation.**
Trevor Taylor.   London: Routledge and Kegan Paul, 1984. 97p.
(Chatham House Papers, No. 24).

This is a helpful survey of European defence cooperation. It looks at NATO's problems in the early 1980s and contends that some of these problems could be alleviated by closer cooperation amongst the European members of NATO. At the same time, Taylor is realistic about some of the obstacles. After the historical survey of previous attempts at cooperation, he looks at the possibilities in four areas: nuclear weapons and strategy; arms control; conventional forces; and out-of-area activities. Emphasis on the Western European Union as the most appropriate institutional basis for further European defence cooperation seems to be largely borne out by subsequent events.

694 **The Reactivation of WEU: Statements and Communiqués, 1984-1987.**
The Western European Union.   London: Secretariat-General of the Western European Union, 1988. 79p.

A compilation of official documents pertaining to the reactivation of the WEU and the evolution of European security policy. The text is in both English and French. Presented in two parts, Part One contains the official texts of 27 October 1987, Rome Declaration; The Platform on European Security Interests of the same date; 23 April 1985, Bonn Communiqué; 30 April 1986, Venice Communiqué; and 28 April 1987, Luxembourg Communiqué. Part Two contains a thematic presentation of European security policy as drawn from the aforementioned official documents.

695 **Crisis in European Defense: The Next Ten Years.**
Geoffrey Lee Williams, Alan Lee Williams.   New York: St Martin's Press, 1974. 334p.

A book which provides some historical perspective on, and an overview of, the problems facing NATO in the 1970s. Written by two brothers, it looks at the pressure from the Soviet Union against Western Europe and the particular problems caused by nuclear weapons and the changing nuclear balance. It also examines British, French, German and United States perspectives on security problems and identifies what the authors believed would be the main patterns of conflict and instability over the next ten years. The authors conclude with what they describe as a search for European equilibrium. A moderately useful volume, but not one which breaks any new ground.

696   The European Defense Initiative; Europe's Bid for Equality.
Geoffrey Lee Williams, Alan Lee Williams.   London: Macmillan,
1986. 242p. bibliog.

The authors favour a twin-pillar structure for NATO though they caution against a premature and ill-conceived 'Europeanism'. The European initiative they advocate retains the United States as the centerpiece of the alliance's deterrent posture. France, Germany, and Britain are exhorted to step up their own contributions to bring them more in line with what the authors regard as those nations' real military capabilities. They also advocate Britain's adoption of the Trident sea-based nuclear programme because, in their estimation, it is the best alternative available. In general, however, the authors support an upgrading of NATO's conventional capabilities. Ultimately, they favour the Europeanization of NATO as a means of recapturing the support of West European publics that they deem all too vulnerable to pressures for neutralism and unilateral disarmament.

697   France, Germany, and the New Europe: 1945-1963.
F. Roy Willis.   Stanford, California: Stanford University Press, 1965.
397p. bibliog.

Franco-German union is widely considered to be the foundation upon which the European Community and European integration are built. This volume chronicles the transformation of Franco-German relations and the creation of this cornerstone relationship. It is very well documented and provides the definitive work on the rapprochement between France and the German Federal Republic. Although concerned with all aspects of the relationship between these two nations, the book is dominated by the military dimension. The historic enmity between the two is traced through the Second World War and the French role in the occupation of Germany, after which it is gradually transformed, first, into one of cooperation by the Schuman and Pleven plans and finally into friendship by the Elysée Treaty. The author devotes substantial space to the failed European Defence Community initiative and his book is a valuable source for information on the French occupation zone in western Germany.

NATO and Out-of-Area Challenges

698 NATO's Out-of-Area Problem.

Marc Bentinck.   London: International Institute for Strategic Studies,
Autumn 1986. 84p. (Adelphi Paper 221).

This detailed and well-documented study examines how the members of NATO
balance their collective interest in the security of Europe with individual and more
diverse interests outside Europe. It surveys the historical experience on out-of-area
issues, looks at the global dimension of Western security in terms of both interests and
vulnerabilities, and assesses the efforts by the allies to manage out-of-area challenges.
The problems of consultation and policy coordination are examined. The paper also
considers the idea of European cooperation on out-of-area issues although it is rather
sceptical about this.

699 The Alliance: A Gulf post mortem.

Michael Brenner.   *International Affairs*, vol. 67, no. 4 (October 1991),
p. 665-678.

A perceptive and highly critical appraisal of the performance of the European allies
during the Gulf War. The author concludes that the United States is the only country
with the capacity to use significant military force, that the Europeans could not form a
unified position, and that Allied behaviour was either deferential or independent
towards American leadership. In addition, the analysis covers US public opinion, the
ambivalence toward the war, and the American belief that the allies should share
responsibility in such situations. Bonn's and Tokyo's roles as virtual non-players, the
West European efforts to open discussions with Saddam Hussein, and the French role
as negotiator are all considered. The article concludes that the allies must accept more
responsibility while the US must be prepared to give up some of the traditional
prerogatives of leadership.

700   **The Atlantic Alliance and the Middle East.**
Edited by Joseph I. Coffey, Gianni Bonvicini.   Pittsburgh,
Pennsylvania: University of Pittsburgh Press, 1989. 316p.

Places the NATO out-of-area issue in historical perspective, while also highlighting the particular problems in the Middle East. There are good chapters on the level of conflict and the use of force in the Middle East, while Maurizio Cremasco provides an interesting analysis of what he terms 'Do it yourself: The national approach to the out-of-area question'. In addition, Reinhardt Rummel examines political perceptions and military responses to out-of-area challenges, while Geoffrey Edwards has an incisive analysis of multilateral coordination. The editors provide an excellent set of conclusions and recommendations.

701   **The United States, Western Europe and Military Intervention Overseas.**
Edited by Christopher Coker.   London: Macmillan, 1987. 190p.

This book, in the RUSI Defence Studies Series, is not about NATO as such. Its focus, however, is the extent to which Western Europe is able, either independently or in association with the United States, to intervene militarily outside the NATO area. Consequently, it is highly relevant to the NATO debate about out-of-area challenges and responses. A chapter by the editor on European responses to security challenges in the Third World is followed by an examination of how the Anglo-American special relationship has worked in relation to extra-European contingencies. The third chapter examines patterns of convergence and divergences in the approach of NATO members to the Persian Gulf, a chapter that was subsequently given added interest by the war with Iraq over Kuwait. The chapter outlines different national perspectives on the possibility of military action in the Gulf. Other chapters deal with NATO's interests in the South Atlantic, and with African out-of-area problems for the Alliance. Douglas Stuart's chapter on Africa is particularly valuable for its four-fold typology of out-of-area situations: those involving burden-sharing and requests for assistance; those involving concerns about guilt by association with colonial actions; those involving competition for influence between NATO allies; and those in which there are fundamental differences about the out-of-area threat posed by the Soviet Union. An example of each kind is discussed. There is also a useful chapter by John Chipman which examines French attitudes and policies towards NATO and regional conflict in Africa.

702   **NATO, the Warsaw Pact and Africa.**
Christopher Coker.   London: Macmillan, 1985. 302p.

This study details the relationship between the Western Alliance and Africa and looks at interventions by members of NATO in Africa. As such, it fills an important gap. In his conclusion, the author cautions against any attempt to redefine NATO's area of responsibility, but suggests that some of the members, on occasion, will want to use force, either individually or acting collectively. As he notes, the allies and the alliance are not always the same thing. This is a helpful and interesting study.

703   **The Allies as Petro-Partners.**
Melvin A. Conant.   *Washington Quarterly*, vol. 4, no. 4
(Autumn 1981), p. 101-106.

Starting from the premise that throughout the 1980s Europe's need to import oil and gas will be a cause of tension and division in the Atlantic Alliance, the author highlights the differences in perspective between Washington and the allies on both the

Persian Gulf and the Soviet Union. He looks at European energy dependence and emphasizes the imbalance between interests and roles in the Middle East and the Gulf – with the Europeans having the most at stake but a secondary role and the United States the converse. In relation to the Soviet Union he notes the European emphasis on creating interdependencies as part of the détente process. Conant has written a succinct and informative article.

704 **Improving Capabilities for Extra-European Contingencies: The British Contribution.**
Peter Foot.   Aberdeen, Scotland: Centre for Defence Studies, Aberdeen University, Spring 1981. 48p. (Aberdeen Studies in Defence Economics, No. 18).

Looks at the out-of-area issue in NATO and the contribution that Britain might make to out-of-area contingencies. The author recognizes the British impulse to take a broad view of the challenges to security but makes clear that British capabilities to respond to these challenges are strictly limited. The author dissects the comments in the 1980 Defence White Paper on this issue and makes clear that all that is proposed is a series of low-cost improvements which do not give Britain much of a capability to act without its allies. The paper looks at non-military instruments of policy as well as military. What was not foreseen in the paper – or indeed in government policy – was the kind of operation which Britain would mount the following year in response to the Argentine invasion of the Falklands.

705 **NATO and the Gulf Crisis.**
Jonathan Howe.   *Survival*, vol. 33, no. 3 (May-June 1991), p. 246-259.

Written by the Commander in Chief of Allied Forces in NATO's Southern Region, this article examines NATO's response to a new locus of security threats. The author highlights both the direct Iraqi threat to Turkey and the indirect threat posed by Iraq's potential to command the 'petro-weapon'. In addition, he looks at the general characteristics of NATO's response and some of the specific responses, including defence and warning activities in Turkey. Howe also focuses on the lessons learned and on implications for the future. The most interesting elements of the article are those detailing what were termed Southern Guard military measures in Turkey and the Mediterranean.

706 **The Atlantic Community and the World.**
Hans Kohn.   *Orbis*, vol. 1, no. 4 (Winter 1958), p. 418-427.

Kohn looks at anti-Western movements in the Third World and the challenge of building new relationships with the peoples of Asia and Africa. He emphasizes the importance of the fact that the North Atlantic Community is the first open society in history.

707 **Europe: The Partial Partner.**
Edward A. Kolodziej.   *International Security*, vol. 5, no. 3 (Winter 1980-81), p. 104-131.

Argues that European–American relations are best described as a partial or incomplete partnership – with the degree of partnership varying from issue to issue. Kolodziej sees Western Europe and the United States are drifting apart for a variety of reasons. He believes that European perceptions of US global policies combine concerns over

American decline with anxieties over the wisdom of Washington's strategy in much of the Third World. Differences over détente and its meaning are also important. Although Kolodziej acknowledges that misunderstandings, impaired communications and flawed consultation contribute to the problems, he concludes that the fundamental causes lie in divergent interests and perspectives on both geographical areas and functional issues.

708   **NATO and the Persian Gulf: Examining Intra-Alliance Behaviour.**
    Charles A. Kupchan.   *International Organization*, vol. 42, no. 2
    (Spring 1988), p. 317-346.
Looks at the evolution of NATO policy towards the Gulf and explains both cooperative and non-cooperative behaviour among the allies. The author examines several determinants of cooperation, including external threats, the coercive potential of the alliance leader, the notion of collective action as a public good, and the impact of domestic politics. American coercion is seen as crucial in terms of political cooperation but as something which has less impact on the economic components of alliance behaviour.

709   **The Persian Gulf and the West: The Dilemmas of Security.**
    Charles A. Kupchan.   Boston, Massachusetts: Allen and Unwin, 1987.
    254p.
The focus of this study is the perennial debate in the West about the threats to security that arise outside the NATO area, taking the Persian Gulf as a case-study of regional security problems. The book provides a historical perspective, before focusing attention upon the situation after the revolution in Iran and the Soviet invasion of Afghanistan. After a chapter dealing with the development of Central Command the author turns his attention to the Alliance dimension and explains why European and American perspectives on the Middle East and the Persian Gulf have frequently diverged. Following this is a chapter which deals with the debate within NATO over the out-of-area issue. This deals not only with American demands for compensation, facilitation and where possible participation by its allies in out-of-area contingencies, but also examines European attitudes and concerns. The analysis is very revealing on the debates of the 1980s and provides helpful background to any discussion of the war against Saddam Hussein in 1991.

710   **Economics, Energy, and Security in Alliance Perspective.**
    Robert J. Lieber.   *International Security*, vol. 4, no. 4 (Spring 1980),
    p. 139-163.
Focuses on the security implications of the energy problem, with particular attention to French and American policy responses. The author analyses these issues in the context of the Western alliance and considers the impact of these issues on alliance unity. Although both unexpected events and slow moving crises can cause problems, Lieber argues that crisis strains can be alleviated to some degree by prior planning. To achieve this, however, US leadership and cooperation with France will be essential.

711   **Out-of-Area Crises and the Atlantic Alliance.**
Edited by General Robert Reed, Roger Weissinger-Baylon.   Menlo
Park, California: Strategic Decisions Press, 1989 137p.

This publication consists of a series of papers presented at a NATO Workshop on
Political–Military Decision Making held in Heemskerk, Holland, in May 1988. The
Conference brought together academics and practitioners, both military and civilian
and this is reflected in a wide-ranging group of papers which deal with various aspects
of NATO decision-making and out-of-area contingencies. As well as dealing with crisis
management both in the Southern Region and out of area, the papers also deal with
the future of the Soviet Union. A helpful summary chapter attempts to distil the main
lessons identified in the papers and offers certain recommendations. Designed to be of
practical help rather than academic, these papers are particularly useful as a guide to
the approach of key decision-makers in NATO and in various national governments.

712   **Israel in NATO: Basis for a Middle East Settlement?**
Alvin Z. Rubinstein.   *Orbis*, vol. 22, no. 1 (Spring 1978), p. 89-100.

Starting from the premise that another Arab–Israeli war would be a disaster for the
West and that Western involvement in a settlement is vital the author looks at the
arguments for and against a Western-sponsored settlement based on the admission of
Israel to NATO. The arguments both in favour of and against this option are explored
and Rubinstein suggests that a NATO-engineered settlement would advance its
position in the Middle East, counter Soviet ambitions in the region and provide
considerable benefits to Europe. Having looked at the arguments to the contrary, he
suggests that Israel should become a member of NATO. An interesting and unusual
analysis which, if not entirely persuasive, is different from most analyses of NATO and
out-of-area issues.

713   **Defending the NATO Alliance: Global Implications.**
Peter N. Schmitz.   Washington, DC: National Defense University
Press, 1987. 178p.

Starting from the premise that NATO is an alliance caught in a struggle with its own
identity, the author – the first German officer in the United States National Defense
University International Fellows Program – looks at the reasons for NATO's disarray.
He argues that one of the most crucial problems is the inability of the members to
cooperate politically and economically beyond the military dimension of the Atlantic
relationship. Consequently, he emphasizes the need for a global defence strategy. The
author also considers some of the prerequisites for this. These include: the
development of a common foreign policy, the need to strengthen both the principles
and the procedures of consultation, and the need to agree upon equal rights and equal
obligations in relation to global issues.

714   **The Out-Of-Area Debate: The Atlantic Alliance and Challenges beyond
Europe.**
Elizabeth D. Sherwood.   Santa Monica, California: Rand
Corporation, May 1985. 24p. (Rand Note N-2268-USDP).

Sherwood starts from the presumption that effective management of out-of-area issues
is crucial to the maintenance of cohesion between Western Europe and the United
States. She looks at the reasons why out-of-area issues took on greater importance in
the 1970s and 1980s and identifies informal bilateral and multilateral forms of

consultation between the United States and key European allies. The focus is on attitudes towards out-of-area issues in the United States, the United Kingdom, France, Germany and Italy. The author concludes that while the United States should continue to emphasize the importance of out-of-area issues for allied security, the informal approach is better than efforts formally to extend the domain of allied responsibility. She notes that there will be no permanent solutions to out-of-area problems for NATO but that these problems will be a permanent feature of alliance politics.

715 **Allies in Crisis: Meeting the Global Challenges to Western Security.**
Elizabeth D. Sherwood.   New Haven, New Jersey: Yale University Press, 1990. 245p.
A perceptive and timely addition to the literature on NATO's out-of-area debate. Sherwood examines in detail the history of NATO's out-of-area experiences and non-experiences from the Korean war to the first Persian Gulf war. Her conclusions run contrary to much of the conventional wisdom on NATO's out-of-area performance. Sherwood believes the NATO experience has been a success, in that such potentially divisive issues have not been allowed to shatter alliance consensus concerning NATO's core mission in Europe. She argues that an informal 'shadow' alliance has developed within NATO which allows for consultation and cooperation among those members of a like mind on a given issue. It is the habit of consultation, rather than a sense of obligation that has strengthened the alliance and its ability to respond to crises. Writing before the Kuwait crisis she concluded rightly that the shadow alliance would probably be of even greater importance in the post-Cold War era.

716 **The Future of NATO.**
Jasjit Singh.   *Strategic Analysis*, vol. 13, no. 9 (December 1990), p. 979-990.
The justification for continuation of NATO with contemplated new roles is examined, in the context of the end of the Cold War in Europe. The author focuses on what he portrays as US plans to increase NATO involvement outside its formal area of responsibility. He is also highly critical of an extra-regional military role of this kind, portraying it as a spread of Western military hegemony on the developing world and as a threat to the role of the United Nations. In the author's view, the UN should be restructured, reinforced and redefined in order to save it from being usurped by NATO. An interesting and unusual perspective.

717 **The Limits of Alliance: NATO Out-of-Area Problems since 1949.**
Douglas Stuart, William Tow.   Baltimore, Maryland: Johns Hopkins University Press, 1990. 383p.
This comprehensive and detailed study of security challenges outside NATO's formal area of responsibility places the issue in historical perspective and provides the most definitive account yet to appear. The authors set out to compare and contrast out-of-area crises in terms of their origins, their management and their impact. Their basic theme is how difficult it is to maintain a regionally demarcated multilateral alliance when the member-nations have important security interests beyond the formal scope of the alliance. To highlight this theme the book examines the out-of-area issue on a country-by-country basis. There are individual sections on the United States, Britain, and France, while a fourth section deals with the other NATO members. The book has some incisive observations on broader issues such as the nature of alliances and

burden-sharing, and is very good on national preferences and policies. This is the most important treatment of this subject.

718 Nato's Out-of-Region Challenges and Extended Containment.
William T. Tow. *Orbis*, vol. 28, no. 4 (Winter 1985), p. 829-856.

Tow looks at out-of-area issues as a source of dispute in the mid-1980s, and argues that some of the peripheral areas to NATO are, in fact, important to its security. Consequently, the author applies the notion of extended containment to the Arctic/ Northern Atlantic region, the Greenland–Iceland–UK gap, Southwest Asia, the Aegean/Mediterranean Crescent, and the South Atlantic Cape route. He argues that NATO has not been successful in coordinating policies to deal with such areas, but suggests some ways in which out-of-area burden-sharing and coordination for responding to out-of-area crises might be enhanced.

719 Global Threats and Trans-Atlantic Allies.
Gregory F. Treverton. *International Security*, vol. 5, no. 2 (Fall 1980), p. 142-158.

Starts from the premise that events in Afghanistan and Iran in 1979 and 1980 revealed that the most probable threats to Western security stemmed from outside Europe. Treverton also looks at the nuclear issue and at the possible impact on alliance solidarity of domestic politics or external shocks. Much of the article, however, focuses on the out-of-area issue and the author emphasizes the divergence of interests and analyses between Western Europe and the United States. He also considers whether this particular crisis in NATO represents a more serious rupture than past crises.

720 Europe, American and South Africa.
Gregory Treverton, Claude Cheysson, Donald F. McHenry, Herman W. Nickel, Francis Pym, Max van der Stoel. New York: Council on Foreign Relations, 1988. 138p.

Part of the Council on Foreign Relations Series on European–American relations, this volume addresses the issue of South Africa as a possible source of strain in Atlantic relations. Treverton provides a very useful framework and the other contributors – some of whom are distinguished practitioners – offer interesting reflections on specific aspects of the problem. They all agree that the allies need to coordinate their policies more closely. Although overtaken by developments in South Africa itself, this small volume does look at an issue that is rarely looked at with reference to the members of NATO.

721   **The US Raid on Libya – and NATO.**
Frederick Zillian.   *Orbis*, vol. 30, no. 3 (Fall 1986), p. 499-524.

The United States raid on Libya in 1986 was very controversial in Europe. The author explores the purposes of this raid and considers the European attitudes on the issue. After exploring the political context and highlighting the divergences between the United States and the European allies over policies to counter terrorism, the author looks at the raid itself and the reactions, especially in Britain which allowed US air bases to be used, and France which denied overflight rights to United States aircraft. He concludes that the raid galvanized the allies to adopt positions closer to that of the United States, but that European policies reflected a mixture of interests – economic, humanitarian, domestic, as well as their bilateral relationships with both the United States and Libya. It is also suggested that out-of-area issues will continue to pose problems for the Atlantic Alliance.

Domestic Pressures, Public Opinion and NATO

722 **Crisis of Will in the NATO Alliance. Hearing before the Subcommittee on European Affairs of the Committee on Foreign Relations, United States Senate.**

Washington, DC: Government Printing Office, 19 September 1985. 81p.

An interesting hearing, with testimony on European and American public and élite opinion given by John Reilly and Catherine Kelleher. In addition, Earl Ravenal presents a very critical analysis of the Alliance and the United States nuclear commitment.

723 **NATO at the Moral Crossroads.**

David Abshire. *Washington Quarterly*, vol. 7, no. 3 (Summer 1984), p. 3-12.

Abshire argues that the public consensus supporting the Alliance must be broadened and that this can be achieved in part through addressing the moral issues and choices related to NATO policies. He looks at the Bishops' Letter on nuclear weapons and at the arguments of the peace movement. The author also suggests that Flexible Response needs to be made more flexible, but emphasizes the dangers of an aversion to nuclear weapons that is not shared by the Soviet Union. The article ends by reiterating the values for which NATO stands and which it is intended to uphold. Although this could be dismissed as an exercise in moral cheer-leading for the Alliance, it does convey a real sense of the debate in the first half of the 1980s.

724 **French Public Opinion and the Atlantic Treaty.**

Raymond Aron. *International Affairs*, vol. 28, no. 1 (January 1952), p. 1-8.

Written by an eminent French sociologist and strategic analyst, this article examines French attitudes towards the North Atlantic Treaty. While French opinion saw the Treaty as a necessary corollary to the Marshall Plan there was uncertainty about whether it should be an implicit or explicit agreement. The article also dissects three arguments against the Treaty: that it is likely to provoke Russia; that it offers no real security guarantee to France; and that German rearmament is dangerous. Aron argues that without NATO there would be a military vacuum in Europe and also notes that although a segment of French opinion favours neutrality, this is not a practical alternative. French misgivings about the Treaty are attributed partly to French ambivalence about capitalism, partly to the existence in France of the largest communist party in Western Europe, and partly to the fact that French fears about Germany outweigh fear of Russia.

725   A Change of Course: The West German Social Democrats and NATO, 1957-1961.
Stephen J. Artner.   Westport, Connecticut: Greenwood Press, 1985. 242p.

Traces the shift in the policy of the Social Democratic Party in Germany from opposition to German rearmament and Western military integration to becoming the champion of Alliance military strategy. While the author suggests that the transformation was not as abrupt or strange as sometimes suggested, he concludes that it stemmed largely from a recognition that the initial SPD preferences had proved unacceptable both domestically and internationally. The study is very useful both in its own right and as background for an understanding of the SPD position in the debate over theatre nuclear force modernization in the 1980s.

726   Politics and the Peace Movement in West Germany.
Jeffrey Boutwell.   *International Security*, vol. 7, no. 4 (Spring 1983), p. 72-92.

Boutwell examines both the political forces involved in the German anti-nuclear movement, and the changed domestic context within which these forces operated. He looks at the anti-nuclear protest of the 1950s and highlights the reasons for its limited impact. The nature of the movement in the 1980s is also discussed and Boutwell argues that in the early 1980s the Federal Republic of Germany was heading towards an increasingly polarized debate about security.

727   American Domestic Priorities and the Demands of Alliance.
David P. Calleo.   *Political Science Quarterly*, vol. 98, no. 1 (Spring 1983), p. 1-15.

Focuses upon the tensions between America's domestic policies and priorities on the one side and its international role on the other. Calleo examines American public opinion towards the Alliance, and the changes in that opinion stemming partly from the criticisms of the allies made by members of the United States élite during the early 1980s. Consideration is also given to the anti-nuclear movement, and to ethnic lobbies. The major thrust of the argument, however, is that US economic constraints have resulted in the growth of protectionist sentiment and that to prevent this increasing and damaging Atlantic relations, there has to be a greater sharing of costs and responsibilities within the Alliance.

728 **Defense and Public Opinion.**
David Capitanchik, Richard C. Eichenberg. London: Royal Institute
of International Affairs, 1983. 96p.

An informed and well-constructed survey and assessment of public opinion on security
issues in a period of great controversy and debate in Western Europe. The study
examines public opinion on a variety of issues including burden-sharing, nuclear
deterrence and the deployment of long-range theatre nuclear forces. The authors are
balanced in their conclusions. The authors provide a number of useful tables which are
helpful in understanding the evolution of opinion.

729 **A Widening Atlantic? Domestic Change and Foreign Policy.**
Ralf Dahrendorf, Theodore C. Sorensen. New York: Council on
Foreign Relations, 1986. 107p.

This book deals with the paradox that although the countries of Western Europe share
with the United States a common heritage and a set of traditional values and beliefs,
during the 1980s they increasingly appeared to have divergent perspectives and
interests. It looks at the roots of this in the domestic politics of the United States and
its major allies in Europe. Dahrendorf identifies a series of trends which he interprets
in terms of what he calls the Europeanization of Europe – arguing in passing that there
is also an Americanization of America taking place. He concludes, however, that such
developments are quite normal and need not be seen as a threat to the Atlantic
Alliance. Sorensen addresses five European fears – of militant right-wing unilateralism;
of timid left-wing isolationism; of the Pacific Basin focus; of American perceptions of
Western Europe as an economic loser; and of US troop withdrawal – before suggesting
reasons why they are unfounded. He also considers the idea of generational change.
His conclusion is that there has to be a re-examination of NATO and some adjustment
but that the Alliance should be able to survive this through careful management on
both sides of the Atlantic.

730 **The INF Controversy: Lessons for NATO Modernization and
Transatlantic Relations.**
Jacquelyn K. Davis, Charles M. Perry, Robert L. Pfaltzgraff.
Washington, DC: Pergamon-Brassey's, 1989. 125p.

A comparative assessment of the INF controversy as it evolved in Britain, The
Netherlands and Germany. The focus is on public opinion and the political parties.
The authors conclude that the INF agreement was seen by the peace movements as
vindication of their activities.

731 **Arms Control and the Atlantic Alliance: Europe Faces Coming Policy
Decisions.**
Karl Deutsch. New York: John Wiley, 1967. 167p.

Starting from the premise that France and West Germany were the crucial nations in
terms of the success or failure of arms control, the author provides a comprehensive
survey of attitudes based on élite interviews, mass opinion data, content analysis of
newspapers and the like. The author highlights disconnections between French
attitudes towards a national nuclear deterrent and government policy. He also looks at
changing images of the threat. This work was a forerunner for many of the studies of
domestic opinion and the peace movements in the 1980s.

732   Consensus Lost: Domestic Politics and the "Crisis" in NATO.
      William K. Domke, Richard C. Eichenberg, Catherine M. Kelleher.
      World Politics, vol. 39, no. 3 (April 1987), p. 382-407.
Based on opinion poll data dealing with security issues, this article challenges some of
the conventional wisdom of the first half of the 1980s about the erosion of the domestic
consensus and the loss of support for NATO. The authors found that governments
were in close accord with public opinion apart from the nuclear issue and that the main
divisions in European publics were based on partisanship rather than the generational
shift identified by many observers.

733   Shattering Europe's Defense Consensus: The Antinuclear Protest
      Movement and the Future of NATO.
      Edited by James E. Dougherty, Robert L. Pfaltzgraff, Jr.
      Washington, DC: Pergamon-Brassey's, 1985. 226p.
A useful collection of essays which examines the anti-nuclear protest movements in
Europe. The volume contains specific chapters on the protest movements in Italy,
Britain, The Netherlands and France. One of the strengths of the book is its explicit
acknowledgement that there is no monolithic peace movement in Europe; another is
that there is a systematic effort to explore the intellectual roots of the protest
movements. Although the final chapter by Robert Pfaltzgraff is critical of anti-
nuclearism, this book certainly helps to explain and understand the phenomenon in its
various national manifestations.

734   Public Opinion and National Security in Western Europe.
      Richard C. Eichenberg.   Ithaca, New York: Cornell University Press,
      1989. 293p.
In the 1980s nuclear strategy became a focus of public attention, especially in Western
Europe where large and active peace movements opposed the deployment of cruise
and Pershing missiles. Accordingly, this book combines a study of national security
issues with the methodology of opinion analysis. It examines public perceptions of the
military balance and the confidence of the Europeans in NATO's deterrence and
defence capabilities; public attitudes towards the use of force, deterrence and arms
control; public support for NATO; and popular support for increased defence
spending. The final chapter focuses upon the degree of continuity and change in
European attitudes, as well as the extent to which these attitudes differ from those of
European leaders and from American public opinion. This is a well-documented study
which yields several interesting conclusions. Eichenberg argues that European opinion
has the complexity of a glacier with the new politics of generational change providing
an additional layer on the continuing polarization resulting from the old politics of
ideology and partisanship. He also concludes that European public opinion has
developed largely in reaction to leadership opinion and that by the mid-1980s it was
very similar to American public opinion. The book contains a great deal of supporting
data and a valuable section on sources.

735   The Myth of Hollanditis.
      Richard C. Eichenberg.   *International Security*, vol. 8, no. 2
      (Fall 1983), p. 143-159.
Looks at public opinion in Holland and challenges much of the conventional wisdom
about the dominance of pacifist and neutralist views on security policy – a phenomenon

often described as 'Hollanditis'. Eichenberg notes that although Dutch public opinion is sceptical of higher defence spending there is still strong support for NATO membership. He contends that Dutch public opinion has had a unique impact because Dutch parliamentary politics is fragmented into numerous parties. The visibility and intensity of opposition to the INF deployment has prevented the Dutch government from accepting the deployment – but this does not mean that there is a rejection of NATO, partly because the pacifist tradition in Holland is balanced by a pragmatic tradition.

736   Energy and Security Concerns in the Atlantic Community.
Edited by Werner J. Feld.   Boulder, Colorado: Westview Press, 1985. 107p.

A small collection which focuses on both the civilian and military dimensions of nuclear power. Francis Beer looks at nuclear weapons and the anti-nuclear movement, and Heinrich Schneider focuses on peace movements, with particular reference to the two German states and Austria.

737   NATO and the Atlantic Defense: Perceptions and Illusions.
Werner Feld, John K. Wildgen.   New York: Praeger, 1982. 171p.

An attempt to examine the disarray in NATO which developed in the late 1970s through an analysis of public perceptions and attitudes on both sides of the Atlantic. The book explores US attitudes towards European security issues using both public opinion data and a content analysis of United States newspaper articles dealing with NATO. It looks at NATO's public information efforts in the United States and concludes that most Americans were fairly sentimentally committed to NATO. When it looks at European opinion, it concludes that dovish views were becoming stronger and that there was a growing conceptual gap between European and American opinion. Among the findings was that the age of European respondents did not seem to be an important variable. The final chapter examines some of the ways in which NATO could attempt to reduce the impact of these disparities of attitudes and opinions.

738   The Internal Fabric of Western Security.
Edited by Gregory Flynn.   London: Croom Helm, 1981. 250p.

An examination of how domestic considerations have increasingly influenced the security policy priorities of the Atlantic Alliance. The result of a major project undertaken by the Atlantic Institute, this volume examines the internal as well as the external security agenda which faced the major European states in the 1980s. It recognized that the internal agenda was inextricably bound up with the new social rights embodied in the welfare state. This raised questions about the general perceptions of the need for defence, the balance between internal and external security needs, and the intra-Alliance dimensions of this balancing act. Having been set up by Flynn, these issues are explored in a series of country studies on Germany, France, Britain and Italy. Contributors include Josef Joffe, Laurence Martin and Stefano Silvestri. Finally, Flynn considers the implications of these national studies for consensus on security priorities in the Alliance. His conclusions are sombre and he rightly noted that during the 1980s burden-sharing was likely to be an acrimonious issue in the Alliance.

739 **Public Images of Western Security.**
Gregory Flynn, Edwina Moreton, Gregory Treverton. Paris: Atlantic Institute, June 1985. 92p. (The Atlantic Papers, No. 54-55).
Looks at public attitudes on security and attempts to explain why these have changed. The basic thesis is that controversy is normal and that it was the first two decades after the Second World War which were really unusual. Edwina Moreton explains this in terms of the evolution of public assessments of the Soviet threat which no longer emphasize ideology but simply focus on the fact that the Soviet Union is a strong military power. Gregory Treverton traces a similar shift in Atlantic relations as the Europeans have gone from complete dependence on the United States to an uneven partnership. Gregory Flynn looks at the implications of this new ambivalence for the relationship between NATO governments and publics.

740 **Limited War, Unlimited Protest.**
Lawrence Freedman. *Orbis*, vol. 26, no. 1 (Spring 1982), p. 89-103.
Explains the rise of the peace movement in Europe largely in terms of European fears about American plans to fight a limited war in Europe, combined with fears that such a war might start as a result of a superpower clash outside Europe. The policies of the Reagan Administration, which were seen by large segments of European opinion as dangerously irresponsible, exacerbated this concern. This is a succinct and helpful analysis.

741 **Mood Contrast and NATO.**
Michael R. Gordon. *Washington Quarterly*, vol. 8, no. 1 (Winter 1985), p. 107-130.
Argues that what makes the NATO crisis of the mid-1980s so serious are two divisive and unprecedented trends: a psychological gulf across the Atlantic caused by divergent mood-shifts and the increasing intrusion of mass publics into foreign policy. The author shows how different attitudes at both the public and élite levels have caused tensions in Atlantic relations. Although he is overly pessimistic about the ability to salvage the alliance in spite of these strains, this is a distinctive, informative and careful analysis which offers considerable insight not only into domestic attitudes in Europe and the United States but also into the impact of these attitudes on Atlantic relations.

742 **American Public Opinion on NATO, Extended Deterrence, and Use of Nuclear Weapons: Future Fission.**
Thomas W. Graham. Lanham, Maryland: University Press of America, 1989. 148p. (Harvard University, CSIA Occasional Paper, No. 4).
Based on a comprehensive examination of over ninety public opinion surveys, this study argues that in the 1980s there was no legitimacy for the first use of nuclear weapons by the United States on behalf of its NATO allies. The author also makes clear that this was less a departure from previous attitudes than is often suggested. Yet the American public has strongly and consistently supported the use of US troops to defend Western Europe. From the 1950s to the 1980s there has never been majority support for reducing the number of troops in Europe, although there has been a stable attitude that the European allies have not been doing enough and that the United States has been spending too much on their defence. These conclusions are supported by four detailed appendices.

743 **Peace and Survival: West Germany, the Peace Movement and European Security.**
David Gress.   Stanford, California: Hoover Institution Press, 1985.
266p.

This volume deals with the rise of what the author calls 'nationalist neutralism', the ideology of the West German peace movement, the change in the SPD from an Ostpolitik aimed at liberalizing Eastern Europe to what is portrayed as a policy of appeasement of the Soviet Union, and the revival of interest in the national question. He is very critical of the neutralist worldview but makes great efforts to locate it within a broader cultural and philosophical context. A highly opinionated and excessively critical study which nevertheless offers some very perceptive insights into the West German debate over NATO and its military strategy.

744 **Peace and Populism: Why the European Anti-Nuclear Movement Failed.**
Josef Joffe.   *International Security*, vol. 11, no. 4 (Spring 1987),
p. 3-40.

The author explains why the peace movement failed to block the deployment of INF missiles. He suggests that the rise of the peace movement was a cyclical trend rather than a fundamental break with the past and considers the implications for the Atlantic Alliance. Looking at both public opinion data in European countries and theories of revolt, Joffe concludes that the key factor in the protest movement seems to have been party affiliation and especially the radicalization of large parties in key countries such as Germany. He also contends that the crucial thing in taking the sting out of anti-nuclear sentiment is a greater sense of safety.

745 **America Looks at Europe: Change and Continuity in the 1980s.**
Catherine M. Kelleher.   *Washington Quarterly*, vol. 17, no. 1
(Winter 1984), p. 33-49.

The article focuses on American images of Europe and the way these images are changing, and argues that during the post-war period the United States defined Europe as like the United States and planned to defend it in virtually the same way as it planned to defend the United States itself. The author argues that this image of incorporation is undergoing important changes, but that there is continued acceptance of the need for a framework of cooperation in Atlantic relations. Kelleher also notes that US images of Western Europe are inextricably bound up with the images of the United States' role in the world.

746 **The New Nationalism.**
Edited by Werner Link, Werner J. Feld.   New York: Pergamon, 1979.
165p.

Although six chapters focus on sub-national regionalism, the overall concern of this volume is the impact on Atlantic relations of the New Nationalism, which is described as defensive and inward-looking in character. New interdependencies and new demands on government lead to foreign policies increasingly concerned with economic security. The implications of this for coordination of policies in the Atlantic area and, therefore, for the solidarity and cohesion of the Atlantic relationship are also examined. The work includes chapters by Fred Northedge, Wolfram Hanreider and Edward Morse.

747   Origins of Estrangement: The Peace Movement and the Changed Image
of America in West Germany.
Harald Mueller, Thomas Risse-Kappen.   *International Security*,
vol. 12, no. 1 (Summer 1987), p. 52-88.
Draws on extensive opinion poll data to explain the changing image of the United
States in Germany. The authors trace the changing images of the United States to the
war in Indochina, but conclude that what transformed a less favourable image into
anti-nuclear protest was the Reagan Administration's foreign and strategic policies.
The concomitant, they argue, is that a new détente would do much to dissipate the
negative feelings about the United States.

748   Alliance Politics.
Richard E. Neustadt.   New York: Columbia University Press, 1970.
167p.
Examines the Suez and Skybolt crises between Britain and the United States and
shows how in both cases each government's preoccupations with domestic issues
reduced its sensitivity to the needs and particular problems of the other. This study
provides considerable insight into the more subtle ways in which domestic politics can
influence Alliance relations.

749   Campaigns against Western Defense: NATO's Adversaries and Critics.
Clive Rose.   London: Macmillan, 1985. 318p.
Written by a former British Permanent Representative on the North Atlantic Council,
this book focuses on the pressures and influences which are designed to erode the
political support for the strategy on which the defence of the West is based. Part Two
of the volume focuses on adversaries and looks at Soviet exploitation of West
European fears and the manipulation of International Front Organizations. The third
section examines the critics in the indigenous peace movements in Western Europe and
Rose makes clear that there is no central direction of these movements and that the
basis of shared policies is pragmatic. Part Four includes a chapter on unofficial peace
activities in Eastern Europe and there are also several appendices focusing mainly on
Soviet front organizations.

750   Theater Nuclear Forces: Public Opinion in Western Europe.
Bruce Russett, Donald R. Deluca.   *Political Science Quarterly*,
vol. 98, no. 3 (Summer 1983), p. 179-196.
Some observers have charged Europeans with becoming pacifist, neutralist, or anti-
American. A careful analysis of public opinion in the major countries over the past two
decades supports none of those accusations, but the results suggest that Europeans
have developed serious doubts about the prudence of American leaders, and about
reliance on the threat of first use of nuclear weapons to defend Europe against
conventional attack.

751   The Third World War Scare in Britain: A Critical Analysis.
Philip A. G. Sabin.   London: Macmillan, 1986. 191p.
The NATO decision of December 1979 to modernize its long-range theatre nuclear
forces sparked off a major protest movement. One of the bases for this was fear. This
study sets out to provide a comprehensive overview of this upsurge of anxiety from the

perspective of an analyst who is sceptical about the risk of war. It looks at images of World War Three, the nature of the scare, the reasons for the scare, and its impact. The author makes good use of opinion poll data and includes discussion of British attitudes to NATO.

752   Challenges to NATO'S Consensus: West European Attitudes and U.S. Policy.
Stanley Sloan.   Washington, DC: US Government Printing Office, May 1987. 82p.

This report, which was prepared for the Subcommittee on Europe and the Middle East of the Committee on Foreign Affairs, US House of Representatives by Stanley Sloan of the Congressional Research Service, analyses the level of consensus within and among the member-nations of NATO. It looks at the debate over the Soviet threat, over NATO's strategy and especially the reliance on nuclear weapons to meet that threat, and over ballistic missile defence. The report surveys attitudes of governments, opposition parties and European publics; Norway, Denmark, West Germany and the United Kingdom are all explored in some detail. Particular attention is given to the strategic preferences of the Labour Party in Britain. A final section spells out what needs to be done to restore consensus. A good analysis of some of the political problems faced by NATO in the mid- and late 1980s.

753   US–West European Relations during the Reagan Years: The Perspective of West European Publics.
Steven K. Smith, Douglas A. Wertman.   New York: St Martin's Press, 1992. 318p.

Based on extensive public opinion survey data, this study focuses on the major issues and controversies in transatlantic relations during the Reagan years, including the INF deployment, economic relations, counter-terrorist activities and out-of-area threats. It looks at both United States and Soviet efforts to influence opinion in Western Europe and, based on almost a hundred multinational opinion surveys, assesses the impact of these efforts. There is a very good chapter on European images of the United States. The volume also contains a large number of very useful tables and figures.

754   The Atlantic Alliance, Nuclear Weapons, and European Attitudes: Reexamining the Conventional Wisdom.
Wallace J. Thies.   Berkeley, California: Institute of International Studies, University of California, Berkeley, 1983. 59p. (Policy Papers in International Affairs, No. 19).

Attempts to place the crisis in NATO over the deployment of Long-range Theatre Nuclear Forces in historical perspective and asks whether it really is more serious than earlier crises over nuclear weapons. The second purpose of this succinct analysis is to consider the lessons of previous crises for resolving the problems of the 1980s. After analysing public opinion data, the author concludes that the conventional wisdom is wrong and that the crisis of the early 1980s is not significantly worse than earlier periods of crisis. A useful and sensible study which makes some pertinent observations.

755   **Attitudes of NATO Countries toward the United States.**
C. M. Woodhouse.   *World Politics*, vol. 10, no. 2 (January 1958),
p. 202-218.

Explores the changing attitudes of West Europeans to the United States through the
1950s, highlighting the divergences within nations and the fluctuations over time. The
argument is that there has been no real shift of attitude, only a series of temporary
variations in the proportion of fear and admiration. United States action in Korea was
widely approved in Europe, but the subsequent thaw in superpower relations led to
criticisms from France and Germany that the United States was gullible, and criticisms
from Scandinavian countries that Washington had not been responsive enough to
Soviet overtures. The crises of 1956 over Suez and Hungary led to a greater awareness
of European dependence, together with increased questioning of American depen-
dability. Although a majority of Europeans were not particularly sympathetic to the
United States, this had little impact on governments who were committed to
maintaining the Atlantic Alliance.

NATO and East—West Trade

756 Western Security and Economic Strategy towards the East.
David Buchan.   London: International Institute for Strategic Studies, 1984. 54p. (Adelphi Paper 192).
Looks at the impact of Western technology on the Soviet economy and its contribution to Soviet weapons development. The author also explores the debate in the West about tighter controls on trade in strategic items. He concludes that there are several principles which should guide a more comprehensive Western policy: avoid enhancing Soviet military power and eroding the West's technological lead; recognize the limits of economic leverage in terms of influencing either Soviet military capabilities or political decisions; and avoid trade or commodity dependence on the Soviet Union while trying to differentiate Western economic policies in favour of reformist Eastern European regimes.

757 Technology Transfer to the Soviet Bloc.
David Buchan.   *Washington Quarterly*, vol. 7, no. 4 (Fall 1984), p. 130-135.
Looks at the tensions between the Reagan Administration and the European allies over the issue of technology transfer to the Soviet Union. A short, succinct analysis which focuses on the underlying reasons for the dispute and considers how it might be resolved.

758 Technology Transfer and East–West Trade: A Reappraisal.
J. Fred Bucy.   *International Security*, vol. 5, no. 3 (Winter 1980-81), p. 132-151.
Argues that the demise of superpower détente in the late 1970s provided a new opportunity for the United States to develop and implement a more coherent policy on technology transfer to the Soviet Union. Although most of the article looks at the problem from a United States perspective, there is a section dealing with relations with the European allies on this issue. The author succinctly notes why the approach of the

Europeans on the issue is different from that of Washington but then argues that a greater effort must be made to develop a concerted set of policies.

759 NATO's Troubles with East–West Trade.
Ellen Will Frost, Angela E. Stent. *International Security*, vol. 8, no. 1 (Summer 1983), p. 179-200.

Looks at the divisions in the Atlantic Alliance over trade and technology transfer to the Soviet Union and suggests ways in which these divisions might be healed. Many of the problems stem from conflicting interpretations of security and the fact that the United States sees it almost exclusively in military terms whereas the Europeans see it as much in economic terms as in military. Noting the debilitating impact of public quarrelling on the issue, the authors prescribe a two-track policy for the Western Alliance. The first track would be based on a common allied definition of security and agreed criteria for evaluating all major projects. The second would be a recognition that it is legitimate to use East–West trade for more short-term purposes. The difficulties of moving in this direction are also discussed and the trade-offs and compromises that would be necessary are identified. A valuable contribution to the debate on this issue.

760 Pipeline Politics: The Complex Political Economy of East–West Energy Trade.
Bruce W. Jentleson.   Ithaca, New York: Cornell University Press, 1986. 263p.

A crucial element in the Cold War was a restrictive trade policy towards the Soviet Union. This became a particularly controversial issue in Atlantic relations in the early 1980s, however, as the Europeans and the United States clashed over the Siberian gas pipeline. Members of the Reagan Administration argued that European dependence on the Soviet Union for energy supplies would be a source of leverage for Moscow while also providing it with hard currency which would finance the modernization of its military and industrial establishment. Jentleson puts this controversy in proper perspective, arguing that the trade issue had simmered in the 1950s, surfaced in the 1960s and worsened in the 1970s. He also explores why the United States was unable to change the policies of the European allies. For all those interested in East–West trade as well as the role of the Coordinating Committee on Export Controls (COCOM), this is essential reading.

761 Technology Management as an Alliance Issue: A Review of the Literature.
Sherry Rice.   *Washington Quarterly*, vol. 13, no. 1 (Winter 1990), p. 219-235.

A useful survey of the literature which looks at the debates in the United States and in NATO over the transfer of technology to the East. The author assesses the impact of the Soviet reform process, the effect of changes in the United States' economic position, and the growing importance of commercial and trade considerations. Although the subsequent demise of the Soviet Union has changed some aspects of the issue, this article nevertheless provides good background to the changing nature of an issue which has traditionally aroused considerable controversy in Atlantic relations.

762   **From Embargo to Ostpolitik: The Political Economy of West German–Soviet Relations, 1955-1980.**
Angela Stent.   Cambridge, England: Cambridge University Press, 1981. 328p.

A comprehensive analysis of East–West trade and the German problem. The author traces the gradual divergence in United States and German approaches to economic sanctions as an instrument of pressure against the Soviet Union. It not only shows how Soviet–West German trade was affected by the broader political relationship but also examines the economic content of Bonn's Ostpolitik. The last chapter deals with the impact of Afghanistan on NATO and the issue of linkage between economic and security matters. An important analysis which provides the basis for a fuller understanding of the tensions in Atlantic relations during the early 1980s over East–West trade.

763   **Western Security and that Eastern Bloc Economy.**
Heinrich Vogel.   *Washington Quarterly*, vol. 7, no. 2 (Spring 1984), p. 42-49.

Shows how the transatlantic arguments over technology transfer to the Soviet Union reflected two distinct strategies for bring about change in the Soviet Union – change through rapprochement versus change through denial. Vogel looks at the underlying assumptions of both these approaches and explores the grounds for a possible consensus while arguing that positive strategies for influencing Soviet foreign policy and encouraging change deserve more attention.

764   **Western Policies on East–West Trade.**
Stephen Woolcock.   London: Routledge and Kegan Paul for the Royal Institute of International Affairs, 1982. 87p. (Chatham House Papers, No. 15).

The Soviet invasion of Afghanistan in 1989, followed by the crisis over the imposition of martial law in Poland, precipitated major divisions between the United States and its European allies about the use of trade sanctions as an instrument of foreign policy towards the Soviet Union. Woolcock provides an incisive analysis of the central issues in this debate. He focuses on three issues: the relevance and utility of economic sanctions against Moscow; the issue of what export controls are necessary to ensure that the United States and Western Europe do not export products to Moscow which enhance its military effort; and the long-term security implications of increased economic linkages between Western Europe and the Soviet Union. Woolcock examines divergent transatlantic conceptions of the role of trade, identifies the major patterns of East–West trade, and explores the basis for both American and European approaches. Overall, he provides an intelligent and helpful summary of the economic issues which became a key element in the internal NATO debate of the first half of the 1980s.

NATO Collaboration

765 **The Two Way Street: Cooperation or Counterattack?**
Armed Forces Journal International (December 1988).
Considers the notion of a 'two-way street' across the Atlantic in defence trade and assesses the effectiveness of efforts to establish more transatlantic exchanges. There are several good articles, including one by Thomas Callaghan whose ideas on both the two-way street and the structural disarmament caused by the increasing expense of weapons systems were very influential. There is also much detail about the two-way trade in defence products. Several authors express concerns about the need for the United States to protect its own defence industrial base.

766 **Weapons Procurement Collaboration: A New Era for NATO?**
F. M. Anderson. *Orbis*, vol. 20, no. 4 (Winter 1977), p. 965-990.
This article outlines the advantages of greater collaboration in weapons equipment. It also identifies some of the constraints which inhibit a process that would make better use of resources, enhance military effectiveness and contribute to Western Europe integration. The author argues that the Allies should make a long-term commitment to improved collaboration, should try to get full French participation and encourage the United States to pursue a policy which promotes European as well as transatlantic collaboration.

767 **NATO Countries: Arms Industry as "Victim of Peace"?**
Ian Anthony. New York: Oxford University Press, 1990, p. 331-338.
(*SIPRI Yearbook 1990*).
Deals with the controversy over the future of the military–industrial base in NATO countries. The article considers the debate between those who argue that the loss of the arms industry would undermine industrial capacity which is a pillar of deterrence, and those who contend that NATO members should not fight change and should recognize that the status quo cannot be maintained. The chapter also deals with the changes in the West European arms market. A useful contribution to the discussion on the impact of the end of the Cold War for the defence industries.

768 **Cooperation or Competition: Defense Procurement Options for the 1990s.**
Martyn Bittleston.   London: International Institute for Strategic Studies, Spring 1990. 82p.

An interesting analysis of defence procurement practices which starts with an explanation of past efforts at rationalization, harmonization and the integration of national and alliance requirements. It focuses on the contribution to future progress of the Action Plan devised by the Independent European Programme Group and contends that more radical change is necessary. The likely impact of the creation of the European single market is assessed and the author concludes with the argument that Western Europe and North America should allow market forces to bring about a radical restructuring of defence procurement.

769 **International Collaboration in Weapons and Equipment Development and Production by the NATO Allies: Ten Years Later – and Beyond.**
Alexander H. Cornell.   The Hague: Martinus Nijhoff, 1981. 233p.

Having analysed this issue in 1969 the author explored it again ten years later to see what had changed. There were successful endeavours in collaboration – and details of these are provided – but the whole process still consisted of little more than a series of ad hoc efforts. This is a very detailed and comprehensive analysis which contains a judicious and thorough assessment of arguments for and against collaboration and also looks at some of the new initiatives and possibilities which were opening up in the late 1970s and early 1980s.

770 **European Defense Equipment Collaboration: Britain's Involvement, 1957-87.**
Alan G. Draper.   London: Macmillan, 1990. 132p.

In 1957 NATO began to use the term 'interdependence' to describe the relationship amongst its members. This study looks at the concept and implementation of interdependence in relation to weapons acquisition. The focus is very much on the British experience and the author argues that early collaborative projects had little success in the period from 1957 to 1976 but that between 1976 and 1987 much greater progress was made. Looks at the NATO emphasis on equipment standardization and at the activities of the Conference of National Armaments Directors set up by NATO. The author argues, though, that it was with the Independent European Programme Group (IEPG) that the European allies, with the encouragement of the Carter Administration, really began to collaborate more successfully. Specific examples of collaboration are examined and the author concludes on a positive note about the future of collaborative equipment ventures in NATO.

771 **France and Arms for the Atlantic Alliance: the Standardization–Interoperability Problem.**
Eliot R. Goodman.   *Orbis*, vol. 24, no. 3 (Fall 1980), p. 541-571.

Argues that the French rejection of standardization of equipment for NATO forces has a very damaging effect in spite of French acceptance of the less stringent notion of interoperability. It is suggested that French policy on this issue wastes resources, undermines NATO's capabilities, and undercuts efforts to establish a European arms industry which would be more competitive with that of the United States. The conclusion is that French policy helps to perpetuate the United States domination that France so dislikes.

772 NATO Arms Co-operation: A Study in Economics and Politics.
Keith Hartley.   London: Allen and Unwin, 1983. 228p.

A study which examines weapons standardization in NATO and sets out to answer a series of questions about standardization and why it has not occurred. Hartley suggests that the reason standardization of weapons systems has been lacking in NATO is that decisions about defence procurement are political and are influenced by voters, politicians, bureaucracies, and interest groups of both producers and consumers. If the author is aware of the political realities, however, he also provides a systematic economic analysis which assesses the possible magnitude of savings from weapons standardization. The second part of the volume tests several hypotheses about the effects of alternative procurement policies with a detailed study of the aerospace industry where there has been a series of joint European projects. Hartley examines the benefits of these projects and compares them with alternatives such as buying off the shelf. One of the best studies of procurement in NATO, this volume ends with a set of recommendations which centre around the advantages of introducing greater competition into the NATO arms market.

773 The Alliance and Europe: Part VI The European Programme Group.
D. C. R. Heyhoe.   London: IISS, Winter 1976-77. 27p.
(Adelphi Paper 129).

Looks at how the prospects for European collaboration in armaments cooperation have been enhanced by the inclusion of France in the Independent European Programme Group. The author, a civil servant in the British Ministry of Defence, traces the background of the IEPG and considers its relationship with NATO and the United States. A detailed and useful analysis.

774 The Independent European Programme Group: The Failure of Low-Profile High-Politics.
Stephen Kirby.   *Journal of Common Market Studies*, vol. 18, no. 2 (December 1979), p. 175-196.

Looks at the issue of weapons standardization as discussed in NATO in the latter half of the 1970s. The author argues that this debate has highlighted differences in the political, strategic, and economic interests of the United States on the one side and Western Europe on the other. The European allies promoted European-wide arms collaboration not only to reduce the costs of defence, but also to promote high technology and the economic competitiveness of European industry. For its part, the United States has promoted alliance standardization to protect its technological leadership and its arms sales in Europe. The tension between the European and Atlanticist options has helped to render the Independent European Programme Group relatively ineffective.

775 **The Dreadful Fury: Advanced Military Technology and the Atlantic Alliance.**
Michael Moodie. New York: Praeger, 1989. 140p. (Washington Papers, No. 136).

The main concern of this study is with how NATO can best exploit advanced technology to strengthen its conventional forces on the battlefield of the future. The focus, however, is on the broad context within which this occurs and the author examines not only the shifting industrial landscape within which technological change occurs but also some of the issues NATO confronts in responding to this change. These include technology and the battlefield, technology transfer and control, and cooperation in procurement. The author examines a case-study in each of these areas – Follow-on Forces Attack, the Toshiba–Kongsberg Affair, and the European Fighter Aircraft. A valuable study which draws on the author's knowledge and his experience as Special Assistant to the United States Ambassador to NATO.

776 **A High Technology Gap? Europe, America and Japan.**
Frank Press, Hubert Curien, Carlo De Benedetti, Keichi Oshima.
New York: Council on Foreign Relations, 1987. 114p.

Part of the Council on Foreign Relations Series on European–American relations, this volume addresses the issue of the technology gap between Western Europe on the one side and Japan and the United States on the other, looks at the reasons for this gap, its implications and how it can be narrowed. The study offers a series of essays and does not have a conclusion. Nevertheless, it identifies the key problems in Europe as stemming from the inability to exploit advances in science and technology and capitalize on investments in research and development.

777 **Weapons Standardization in NATO: Collaborative Security or Economic Competition?**
Phillip Taylor. *International Organization*, vol. 36, no. 1 (Winter 1982), p. 95-112.

An interesting article which examines the NATO commitment to rationalization, standardization and interoperability and suggests that in spite of the rhetoric and the desire for greater efficiency, progress has been very limited. The author looks at several case-studies and concludes that one of the most important factors explaining the modest progress is the rise of European defence industries and the increased national competition.

778 **Towards Rationalizing Allied Weapons Production.**
Gerdiner Tucker. Paris: Atlantic Institute, 1976. 54p. (The Atlantic Papers, No. 1, 1976).

Identifies a trend towards 'destandardization' in NATO weapons systems and shows how this reduces the compatibility amongst the armed forces of NATO members. The author explores ways in which this trend can be reversed and NATO get greater value for money.

779   **Lessons from Aerospace: The Prospects for Rationalization in NATO.**
Bernard Udis.   *Orbis*, vol. 25, no. 1 (Spring 1981), p. 165-196.
Identifies and assesses the innovations in the NATO weapons planning process. These innovations, which include the establishment of a NATO Armaments Planning Review, are intended to produce greater rationalization in the weapons acquisition process.

780   **NATO and 1992: Defense Acquisition and Free Markets.**
Simon Webb.   Santa Monica, California: Rand Corporation, July 1989. 127p. (Rand Paper R-3758-FF).
Starting from the premise that defence acquisition by NATO members has been dominated by domestic economic and political factors, the author looks at both the effort to create a single market in Europe and the US–Canada free trade agreement and considers whether these free markets should be extended to defence industries. He also considers whether 1992 will establish new barriers to transatlantic defence trade. His conclusion is that a free-bidding system should operate NATO-wide, although he recognizes that the Independent European Programme Group is a useful forum for European cooperation.

781   **Trade Liberalization as a Path to Weapons Standardization in NATO.**
Charles Wolf, Jr., Derek Leebaert.   *International Security*, vol. 2, no. 3 (Winter 1978), p. 136-159.
Starting from the assumption that standardization and rationalization will increase economic efficiency and military effectiveness but may conflict with other political or economic goals within member countries, the authors nevertheless argue that the increasing technical complexity and cost of modern weapons systems encourage the sharing of development and production costs. They make a case for trade liberalization along the lines of comparative advantage and are critical of offset deals which they see as distorting the normal market incentives. Wolf and Leebaert argue that there are opportunities for increased civil sector exports by European NATO members to the United States and that these include high-technology product categories. They also contend that liberalization which allowed more competitive bidding would take advantage of economies of scale, whether in the United States or in Europe. The difficulty is that efforts to promote economic integration in the European Community involve preferential treatment on tariffs and the like, and discriminatory trade practices against non-Europeans. A more integrated Atlantic Alliance requires more co-ordinated, reciprocal, and collaborative arrangements across the Atlantic. The authors argue that this should take precedence over the European Community.

NATO and Arms Control

782 **Mutual Force Reductions in Europe: The Political Aspects.**
Christoph Bertram. London: The International Institute for Strategic Studies, 1972. 34p. (Adelphi Paper 84).
A study which looks at the background to and the incentives for NATO to initiate conventional arms control negotiations with the Soviet Union and its allies. This study helps to explain why MBFR negotiations took place and by focusing on the political context also offers some insight into why they yielded no result. It discusses differences in the Alliance over the negotiations and suggests that MBFR has considerable divisive potential in NATO.

783 **After INF: Toward Conventional Arms Control in Europe? Conceptual Problems of Conventional Arms Control.**
Robert D. Blackwill. *International Security*, vol. 12, no. 4 (Spring 1988), p. 28-47.
A leading arms control specialist and former ambassador to the MBFR negotiations identifies five sets of problems involved in efforts to achieve conventional arms control in Europe: integrating arms control proposals into a cohesive political vision; determining appropriate US force size and structure in Europe; analysing the conventional balance; assessing the reliability of conventional deterrence as part of NATO strategy; and verifying compliance of an agreement in view of Soviet resistance to intrusive measures. Blackwill acknowledges that there is increasing public pressure for arms control, but cautions that a rigorous standard of verification and compliance must be met for agreements to be meaningful.

784 **Specific Approaches to Conventional Arms Control in Europe.**
Robert D. Blackwill. *Survival* vol. 30, no. 5 (September-October 1988), p. 429-447
Written by a former US Ambassador to the MBFR negotiations, this article looks at the conventional stability talks. It outlines NATO's objectives, and considers the

virtues of a step-by-step approach of the kind advocated by Senator Nunn as opposed to a more far-reaching approach for equipment ceilings advocated by the author and Jim Thomson of the Rand Corporation. Many of the limitations proposed are very close to those which were finally agreed upon in the CFE agreement. For anyone interested in the moves towards this agreement, this article is a must.

785 **Constraining Ground Force Exercises of NATO and the Warsaw Pact.**
Robert D. Blackwill, Jeffrey W. Legro. *International Security*, vol. 14, no. 3 (Winter 1989-90), p. 68-98.

This article sets out to assess the utility of confidence- and security-building measures as part of the European conventional arms control process. The authors examine the goals and the nature of NATO and Warsaw Pact exercises, the purposes and substance of constraint proposals, and the trade-offs inherent in accepting training limitations. They consider the extent to which constraints on exercises would enhance the prospects for an early detection of a Warsaw Pact attack, strengthen effective decision-making within the Alliance, help defend West Germany, diminish the Soviet ability to attack Western Europe, or reduce the Soviet capacity to intimidate Eastern Europe. Constraints on the size, number, frequency, duration, geographical location, and activities of ground forces are all discussed. Blackwill and Legro conclude that most of these CSBM proposals would not offset Warsaw Pact quantitative advantages or reduce its offensive potential. Select CSBMs, however, such as a lower notification floors and increasing inspections would decrease the immediate threat of a surprise attack even though they would still leave open the possibility of a large offensive after Soviet mobilization.

786 **Regaining the High Ground: NATO's Stake in the New Talks on Conventional Armed Forces in Europe.**
Barry M. Blechman, William J. Durch, Kevin P. O'Prey. New York: St Martin's Press, 1990. 217p.

Looks at the changing political context of European arms control, the background to the CFE negotiations, the objectives of the major participants, alternative types of agreements that might be possible and the likely military impact of these agreements. This is a useful study containing much detail.

787 **Mutual Force Reductions in Europe from a Soviet Perspective.**
John Borawski. *Orbis*, vol. 22, no. 4 (Winter 1979), p. 845-873.

Argues that the lack of progress in MBFR reflects a fundamental divergence of approach in which NATO sees Soviet superiority as destabilizing while the Soviet Union sees it as stabilizing. Borawski notes that although this would make for a continued impasse, Moscow could try to use the talks to achieve other objectives such as alleviating the threat posed by NATO's forward-based nuclear systems. A good alternative perspective which adds to our understanding of why conventional arms control in Europe took so long to achieve.

788   **Toward Conventional Stability in Europe?**
      John Borawski.   *Washington Quarterly*, vol. 10, no. 4 (Autumn 1987),
      p. 13-30.
Looks at NATO's approach to the conventional stability talks in Europe and highlights
the divergences between NATO and Warsaw Pact conceptions of stability. Also looks
at the role that CSBMs can play in enhancing stability in Europe.

789   **The Stockholm Agreement of September 1986.**
      John Borawski, Stan Weeks, Charlotte E. Thompson.   *Orbis*, vol. 30,
      no. 4 (Winter 1987), p. 643-662.
This article elucidates and assesses the confidence-building measures agreed upon in
the 1986 Stockholm Agreement. This accord placed restrictions on the size of troop
movements which could be made without advance notification. The authors spell out
the nature of these restrictions and assess their contribution to European security.

790   **Limiting Conventional Forces in Europe.**
      William R. Bowman.   Washington, DC: National Defense University
      Press, 1985. 84p.
Subtitled 'An Alternative to the Mutual and Balanced Force Reduction Negotiations',
this short monograph looks briefly at the history of the MBFR negotiations which
formally opened in 1973. The analysis focuses partly upon the problems which
prevented an agreement. The second chapter examines the conventional balance in
Europe. The third chapter discusses the relationship between the negotiations and
conventional stability. The author's central thesis is that an MBFR agreement could
accentuate rather than ameliorate some of NATO's problems which stemmed more
from Soviet armaments than troop levels. Accordingly, the final chapter suggests that
more emphasis should be placed on confidence-building measures which should be
negotiated through the Conference on Disarmament in Europe. Although this
alternative is not fully developed, the author expresses the growing sense of frustration
which led in 1989 to the replacement of the MBFR negotiations by the Conventional
Armed Forces in Europe (CFE) talks which covered the area from the Atlantic to the
Urals and yielded an agreement in November 1990.

791   **Mutual Force Reductions: A Military Perspective.**
      Steven Canby.   *International Security*, vol. 2, no. 3 (Winter 1978),
      p. 122-135.
Canby's main argument is that NATO can benefit from mutual force reductions only if
the Warsaw Pact agrees to large asymmetrical cuts. He views mutual force reductions
(MFR) as militarily dangerous to NATO and argues that the common ceiling concept
is particularly ill-advised. Canby discusses geographical and offensive asymmetries and
concludes that these problems cannot really be dealt with through arms control. More
generally, he contends that NATO's real problems include its tactical doctrine,
organization for combat, and pattern of deployment. Although the conclusion is that
NATO must solve its internal problems before it can come to the negotiating table
from a position of comparability, the author claims that dealing with these problems
would actually enhance the prospects for the negotiations.

792 **Rethinking European Security.**
Edited by Furio Cerutti, Rodolfo Ragionieri.   New York: Crane
Russak, 1990. 182p.

An interesting collection of papers based on a conference held in September 1988
which stemmed from the Forum on the Problems of Peace and War founded at the
University of Florence in 1984. After an introductory section which contains chapters
by Michael Howard and Johan Galtung, the focus shifts to security in Europe. This
section includes chapters by Soviet, German, American and Italian authors and
highlights some of the more innovative approaches to European security such as
common security and third-generation confidence-building measures. The third and
final section of the book contains a series of chapters dealing with defensive defence
from both supporting and critical perspectives. An interesting and unusual collection.

793 **Arms Control and European Security: A Guide to East–West**
   Negotiations.
Joseph I. Coffey.   New York: Praeger, 1977. 271p.

Written largely while the author was a Research Associate at the International
Institute for Strategic Studies, this book offers a snapshot of arms control in the mid-
1970s and assesses its impact on European security. As a prelude to a detailed
assessment of arms control, the author discusses the military balance between NATO
and the Warsaw Pact moving from strategic nuclear forces through theatre nuclear
systems to the conventional balance. Although the author acknowledges the limits of
arms control he also presents its rationale and identifies the various ways in which it
can enhance European security. As well as looking at arms control restrictions on
forces deployed in Europe and on those that would be used in any war beginning in
Europe, Coffey also considers other possibilities such as restrictions on particular
classes of weapons, constraints on military budgets, deployment restrictions, and the
establishment of restricted areas. Throughout the analysis the focus is on the impact of
particular proposals or measures on perceptions of security. The final chapter,
however, is not optimistic and emphasizes the difficulty of enhancing security through
arms control when security is defined in so many different ways by different states. It
also suggests that the answer could be to move forward with unilateral initiatives which
might induce a response by the adversary. Although time bound in terms of many of
the details, this is a useful guide to the way arms control was approached in the 1970s.

794 **Detente, Arms Control and European Security.**
J. I. Coffey.   *International Affairs*, vol. 52, no. 1 (January 1976),
p. 39-52.

Focuses on how divergent views on détente influence the willingness of NATO
members to accept arms limitations. The author also considers how perceptions of the
effects of détente influence alliance cohesion. In addition, the implications of arms
control for security and détente are assessed. The author suggests that détente should
be approached in ways that enhance rather than undermine security and recommends
that both alliances re-examine their military programmes.

795 **The CFE Treaty: An Overview and an Assessment.**
Ivo H. Daalder.   Washington, DC: Johns Hopkins Foreign Policy
Institute, 1991. 45p.

A very useful assessment of the CFE Treaty which also contains a copy of the Treaty itself as an appendix. The author looks at the background to the Treaty, describes the transition from MBFR to CFE, provides a brief overview of the CFE negotiations themselves, and highlights the major provisions of the Treaty. Daalder also offers a useful assessment of the agreement, highlighting its utility in defusing the Cold War confrontation in Europe while also pointing up its limitations in relation to post-Cold War Europe. He notes that CFE deals with past problems rather than future security challenges, especially those facing the countries of East and Central Europe.

796 **Watershed in Europe: Dismantling the East–West Military Confrontation.**
Jonathan Dean.   Lexington, Massachusetts: Lexington Books, 1987.
286p.

A comprehensive analysis of the military confrontation in Europe and how it can be dismantled through arms control. The author looks at the breakdown of the Western defence consensus, the efforts by NATO to move to conventional deterrence, the opportunities for conventional and nuclear arms control and the political aspects of East–West relations in Europe. Although the author – like most other commentators – underestimated the speed with which the military confrontation in Europe would be dismantled, this is an important study which provided a judicious yet imaginative approach to military change in Europe. The work is supplemented by tables and figures.

797 **MBFR: From Apathy to Accord.**
Jonathan Dean.   *International Security*, vol. 7, no. 4 (Spring 1983),
p. 116-139.

Argues that the opportunity for costs savings and the need for escalation management both require that conventional arms control receive more attention. The author explains the slow progress of the MBFR negotiations in terms of a lack of compelling incentives to force the pace, disagreement over data, and different Western and Eastern negotiating styles. He also suggests that high-level political leadership in the West has been lacking. Dean traces the changing course of the negotiations, identifies the continuing obstacles to an agreement, highlights and counters the criticisms that are made of the talks, and suggests ways in which they might be brought to completion.

798 **Zonal Arms Limitations in Europe.**
James E. Dougherty.   *Orbis*, vol. 7, no. 3 (Fall 1963), p. 478-517.

Suggests that the disengagement debate of the 1950s highlights the need to find a solution to arms problems in Europe. Looks at the various schemes for disengagement and in particular at the proposals for zonal arms limitations which, their proponents argue, would lessen tensions in Central Europe and create conditions for political–military détente. The author identifies what he sees as the drawbacks with such proposals, especially the likelihood that disengagement would facilitate the Soviet goal of separating West Germany from NATO.

799 **NATO after Global Double Zero.**
Lewis Dunn. *Survival*, vol. 30, no. 3 (May-June 1988), p. 195-209.
After briefly surveying the content of the Intermediate Nuclear Forces Treaty and describing the highlights of the negotiations which led to it, the author looks at the benefits for NATO stemming from the elimination of Soviet INF missiles. He then explores the lack of consensus in the alliance on what it should do in response to the elimination of its own INF. He also identifies guidelines for NATO nuclear policy and considers the various options for ensuring that NATO retains an effective strategy of nuclear deterrence. A sensible contribution to an often heated debate.

800 **Conventional Force Reductions: A Dynamic Assessment.**
Joshua Epstein. Washington, DC: Brookings Institution, 1990. 275p.
An analysis of the conventional balance in Europe that was done on the eve of the momentous political changes, but that was relevant to the CFE negotiations and continues to have some relevance to post-Cold War Europe. One of Joshua Epstein's main questions concerned the impact of implementing the CFE agreement that was being negotiated through 1989 and much of 1990. He also tried to think through the kind of arrangements and issues which would be relevant to the period after CFE was reached. Although this analysis was in many respects very forward-looking – and was designed to go beyond a CFE agreement to follow-on negotiations – the political changes have cast question marks over its relevance. Yet if it appears to be more of a snapshot of the military balance in Europe when the Cold War ended rather than an analysis of post-Cold War scenarios, there is still much of value. Epstein is so systematic and rigorous in his methodology, that he provides a model for analyses of conventional balances in post-Cold War Europe.

801 **What War in Europe? The Implications of Legitimate Stability.**
Lawrence S. Finkelstein. *Political Science Quarterly*, vol. 104, no. 3 (Fall 1989), p. 433-446.
The author argues that the Berlin crisis of 1958-62 confirmed that neither NATO nor the Warsaw Pact would risk nuclear war in Europe. The East–West European equilibrium subsequently attained diplomatic legitimacy and was maintained whatever the perceived force ratios or political circumstances. In these circumstances, political cohesion was more important than military requirements. Moreover, it was possible to use arms control negotiations to dispense with some costly forces and move towards non-threatening deterrence and a period of relaxation.

802 **Arms Control and Stability in Europe: Reductions are Not Enough.**
Stephen J. Flanagan, Andrew Hamilton. *Survival*, vol. 30, no. 5 (September-October 1988), p. 448-465.
After looking at the military requirements of NATO's forward defence and Soviet force generation potential the authors argue that if instability in Europe is to be reduced it is necessary to go beyond arms reductions and develop an approach which combines increased transparency of military activity with zonal force ceilings and operational constraints. It is argued that such measures would form the durable foundation of a more stable military situation in Europe.

803 **Defining Stability: Conventional Arms Control in a Changing Europe.**
Schuyler Foerster, William A. Barry III, William R. Clontz, Harold F. Lynch, Jr. Boulder, Colorado: Westview Press, 1989. 112p.

A succinct and well-done analysis which defines conventional stability, identifies the criteria for a stable security relationship in Europe and assesses the role of conventional arms control in bringing about that relationship. A chapter on the political environment looks at the impact of resource constraints while another chapter provides a good overview of the debate on the military balance, looking at both the optimistic and the pessimistic assessments. The authors show how arms control can contribute to both military and political stability and apply their framework to the CFE negotiations. A useful and constructive book, although somewhat overtaken by the CFE agreement and other developments in Europe.

804 **Security in Europe: A Crisis of Confidence.**
Bernd A. Goetze. New York: Praeger, 1984. 225p.

Writing in a period of increased tension between East and West in Europe, the author proposes ways in which the deep suspicions about the purposes of military activities by either side could be eased. The book sets out a concrete proposal for the development, negotiation and implementation of a mandatory regime of confidence- and security-building measures to be achieved through the Conference on Security and Cooperation in Europe. Various sets of measures are discussed under four categories: information, notification, stabilization and verification. The book also contains a number of appendices related to efforts to build greater confidence.

805 **Disengagement.**
Eugene Hinterhoff. London: Stevens, 1959. 454p.

This book exhaustively reviews the various proposals for disengagement – or a mutual pull-back of military forces in Central Europe – between the two blocs in Europe that were made in the mid- to late 1950s. As a basic resource on early ideas for arms control in Europe it is essential reading. One of its values is that it reproduces details of many of the proposals in a series of appendices. The author also presents his own proposal for a gradual withdrawal of forces from Germany, Poland, Czechoslovakia and Hungary.

806 **Disengagement and Western Security.**
Michael Howard. *International Affairs*, vol. 34, no. 4 (October 1958), p. 469-476.

Written by an eminent British military historian this article questions the value of military disengagement – that is a Soviet military withdrawal from Eastern Europe and a similar withdrawal of Western forces. The focus is on two proposals: the Gaitskell Plan to create a disengaged area in Central Europe; and the more far-reaching suggestions of George Kennan for the complete withdrawal of US forces in Europe. The article discusses the reasons why NATO governments were opposed to such proposals.

807   **Overcoming Threats to Europe: A New Deal for Confidence and Security.**
Edited by Sverre Lodgaard, Karl Birnbaum.   New York: Oxford University Press, 1987. 235p.

Looks at the main threats to European security, national threat perceptions, and policies to alleviate threats. The opening chapter by Lodgaard looks at the threats to European security and distinguishes between First World War and Second World War types of threat. Subsequent chapters look at how these can be alleviated. This is an interesting and helpful analysis.

808   **Conventional Arms Control and the Security of Europe.**
Edited by Uwe Nerlich, James A. Thomson.   Boulder, Colorado: Westview Press, 1988. 251p. 3 maps.

Edited by a prominent American and a prominent German analyst, this volume contains the collected papers from a conference on Conventional Arms Control and the Security of Europe which was held in September 1987 in West Berlin under the auspices of Richard Burt, the United States Ambassador to the Federal Republic. The conference was called in anticipation of the INF agreement which was widely viewed in the strategic analysis community as a measure which would accentuate the asymmetry of conventional power in Europe. Accordingly, the papers look not only at the political–military setting, but also at the needs of conventional defence. Contributors include Zbigniew Brzezinski, Lothar Ruhl, Phillip Karber and Karl Kaiser. In addition, there are some very interesting pieces on conventional arms control by Robert Blackwill and Richard Haas. The final section of the book provides a synthesis of the view presented at the conference. This volume is useful as an indicator of how the United States and some of the European allies were thinking about the changed context for conventional arms control in the late 1980s before the massive changes which led to a revision in many of the prevailing assessments of what was required. Some tables are included.

809   **Mutual and Balanced Force Reduction: Issues and Prospects.**
William B. Prendergast.   Washington, DC: American Enterprise Institute, 1978. 75p.

A good overview of the background to and the early stages of the negotiations between NATO and the Warsaw Pact on mutual force reductions. The author looks at some of the proposals of the 1940s and 1950s and then traces the steps which led to the opening of the negotiations in Vienna in October 1973. He deals succinctly with the substance of the negotiations and looks at some of the problems which made it so difficult to achieve real progress. His conclusion was that the talks continue because each side believes it may derive some advantage from them; yet neither side has real incentives to reach an accord. This was an apt description of talks which were designed in large part to forestall a Congressionally mandated unilateral reduction in American forces in Europe. As a straightforward introduction to the negotiations which preceded the Conventional Forces in Europe talks which resulted in an agreement in November 1990, this little book is hard to beat.

810   **Force Reductions in Europe: Starting Over.**
Jeffrey Record.   Cambridge, Massachusetts: Institute for Foreign
Policy Analysis, 1980. 92p.

Looks at the eroding conventional balance in Europe and the efforts by NATO to deal with it through negotiations on conventional arms control. Argues that the emphasis in MBFR on reducing manpower is ill-advised and that NATO should focus instead on establishing a regime of on-site inspections that would minimize the prospects of a surprise attack – which is the biggest danger to NATO given the capacity of Soviet forces to launch an unreinforced attack.

811   **The Zero Option: INF, West Germany and Arms Control.**
Thomas Risse-Kappen.   Boulder, Colorado: Westview Press, 1988.
202p.

This is one of the most comprehensive studies available on the deployment and subsequent elimination of Intermediate Nuclear Forces in NATO. The author skilfully traces the origins of NATO's dual-track decision of December 1979, suggesting that the availability of technological options, the threat perceptions, domestic require-ments, arms control considerations, Alliance policy, and military strategy resulted in a decision based upon rather contradictory grounds. He then examines the negotiations and deployment which took place from 1980 to 1983, before describing the breaking of the stalemate and the gradual move towards the INF Treaty which removed all missiles with a range between 500 and 5,500 kilometres from Europe. The study is particularly good on the debate in West Germany and on the relationship between Bonn and Washington.

812   **MBFR: Lessons and Problems.**
Lothar Ruehl.   London: International Institute for Strategic Studies,
Summer 1982. 37p. (Adelphi Paper 176).

Highlights the problems which have hindered progress in MBFR but suggests that financial and demographic pressures compel NATO to seek an agreement.

813   **American Arms and a Changing Europe: Dilemmas of Deterrence and Disarmament.**
Warner R. Schilling, William T. R. Fox, Catherine Kelleher, Donald J.
Puchala.   New York: Columbia University Press, 1973. 218p.

This book essentially does three things. In the first place it highlights many of the strategic dilemmas facing NATO, especially the tension between extended deterrence and strategic stability. Second, it looks at the change in strategic, political, and economic environments and examines possible European futures against the back-ground of these changes. Eight models of possible security arrangements for Europe are delineated. Third, the book examines the choices facing the United States in relation to arms and arms control in Europe. It suggests that there is more to be obtained from moving down the arms control path than trying to maintain extended deterrence based on strategic superiority.

814 **Arms Control and Alliance Commitments.**
Jane M. O. Sharp.   *Political Science Quarterly*, vol. 100, no. 4
(Winter 1985-86), p. 649-667.

West European dependence on the American nuclear security guarantee exacerbates the security dilemma common to all military alliances. The allies oscillate between the fear of abandonment in a crisis and the fear of entrapment in a superpower conflict. Attempts to alleviate this cycle of anxiety by reducing the allies' dependence on nuclear weapons have foundered because NATO critics and reformers alike overestimate the requirements of extended deterrence. Reducing the nuclear deterrent does not require a compensatory increase in conventional forces because nuclear weapons are useful only to deter. They do not compensate for conventional inadequacy and do not therefore require conventional compensation when reduced. Nuclear deterrence forces need only be invulnerable, they need not balance the nuclear forces of the potential adversary.

815 **Conventional Arms Control in Europe.**
Jane M. O. Sharp.   New York: Oxford University Press, 1989,
p. 370-426. (*SIPRI Yearbook 1989*).

Analyses European arms control diplomacy in 1988, focusing primarily on the developments at the third follow-up meeting of the CSCE and the prospects for two new sets of negotiations on military security: CFE and CDE-II. A good snapshot of an area in which very rapid progress was soon to take place.

816 **Conventional Arms Control in Europe.**
Jane M. O. Sharp.   New York: Oxford University Press, 1991,
p. 442-451. (*SIPRI Yearbook 1991*).

Focuses on NATO reductions in the Atlantic to the Urals (ATTU) zone in 1990. These reductions – which took place prior to the CFE Agreement of November 1990 – reflected the movement of forces to the Persian Gulf as well as a mix of domestic fiscal constraints and a reduced threat assessment. The article deals specifically with budget cuts and base closures in the United States, Britain, France and Germany.

817 **Conventional Arms Control and Europe's Future.**
Stanley R. Sloan.   New York: Foreign Policy Association, 1989. 72p.

A very accessible analysis which looks at prospects for the CFE negotiations against a background of the previous talks on Mutual and Balanced Force Reductions and the Conference on Security and Cooperation in Europe.

818 **After INF: Toward Conventional Arms Control in Europe? Limiting Conventional Forces: Soviet Proposals and Western Options.**
Jack Snyder.   *International Security*, vol. 12, no. 4 (Spring 1988),
p. 48-77.

An analysis which manages to be both sensitive to change in the Soviet Union and cautious about the impact on European security. The author examines the impact of *perestroika* on Soviet military doctrine, addresses civil–military relations in the Soviet Union and looks at spiralling Soviet military expenditures. Snyder argues that the change in the Soviet approach to conventional arms control is not propaganda but that Moscow wants reciprocity from NATO for arms reductions. He looks at considerations

NATO should take into account in its response and some of the possible trade-offs (e.g. airpower for armour) which might facilitate agreement. An interesting and serious article which appeared when Soviet intentions were still uncertain.

819 **Nuclear and Conventional Forces in Europe: Implications for Arms Control and Security.**
Edited by Thomas W. Wander. Washington, DC: American Association for the Advancement of Science, 1987. 205p.

A collection of essays which looks at various aspects of the defence of Europe and at the dimensions of theatre arms control in Europe. There are good essays by Jane Sharp, Fen Hampson, Stanley Sloan, and Jonathan Dean amongst others. Topics include the military balance, emerging technology, the validity of the United States nuclear and conventional guarantees to European security, arguments for and against missile defence in Europe, as well as chapters on various aspects of European arms control.

820 **Arms Control and the Politics of European Security.**
Theodore H. Winkler. London: International Institute for Strategic Studies, 1982. 43p. (Adelphi Paper 177).

Deals with the crisis in European arms control in the early 1980s. The author suggests that arms control has become politically more vulnerable than in the past, that its contribution to European security is uncertain, and that Soviet military superiority in some areas has made it even more problematic. He argues that negotiations will be increasingly protracted and will pose a profound challenge to the cohesion of the Western Alliance. In fact, the success or failure of arms control will be evaluated largely with respect to intra-Alliance relations, and if neglected will inevitably cause cracks in NATO. The author recommends improved consultative mechanisms to ensure better policy coordination within the Western Alliance.

821 **Beyond SALT II: European Security and the Prospects for SALT III.**
David Yost. *Orbis*, vol. 24, no. 3 (Fall 1980), p. 625-655.

Highlights the complexity of West European reactions to SALT II and outlines the main arguments used by European supporters and opponents of the Treaty. The article also identifies several factors which the author believes condition perceptions in Britain, West Germany and France. There is also a section which considers the prospects for SALT III. Although these negotiations never took place, being replaced by START, this article identifies what some of the expectations were during and just after the debate over ratification of SALT II.

NATO after the Cold War

822 The Atlantic Alliance Transformed.
David M. Abshire, Richard Burt, R. James Woolsey. Washington, DC: Center for Strategic and International Studies, August 1992. 128p.

Argues that in the post-Cold War period NATO is an agent for stability in Europe and has important political and military functions including crisis management. The role of the US presence in Europe is also considered. There are three useful appendices, one by Don Snider which looks at alternative US force levels in Europe, a study of NATO armaments cooperation by Robin Niblett, and a selection of key NATO documents from 1991-92. This is a very useful study.

823 Science and International Security: Responding to a Changing World.
Edited by Eric H. Arnett. Washington, DC: The American Association for the Advancement of Science, 1990. 523p. (Fifth Annual AAAS Colloquium on Science and Security, Critical Choices: Setting Priorities in the Changing Security Environment).

Contains twenty-eight contemporary essays on the changing nature of the security environment. Topics include new challenges for the 1990s, technological advances, Third World armament, Soviet defence policy, the new face of European security, nuclear strategy, and arms control, verification, and confidence-building measures. Contributors are both distinguished academics and high-level government practitioners from both sides of the Atlantic. Of particular note are Ian Gambles' 'NATO without the Warsaw Pact', Catherine Guicherd's 'Nuclear weapons in Europe', and Jed C. Snyder's contribution on arms control in Europe.

824 A United Germany.
Ronald Asmus. *Foreign Affairs*, vol. 69, no. 2 (Spring 1990), p. 63-76.

Writing in a period of transition, Asmus identifies the major reasons why a unified Germany would still want membership in NATO. He notes that the USSR remains the dominant land power in Europe, and that it is nuclear-armed whereas a united Germany is non-nuclear. He also suggests that close security ties with the West would help ensure German democracy. Perhaps most important of all, the author identifies the alternatives to German membership in NATO and shows how unattractive these are. Asmus endorses the 'two plus four' concept for negotiating Germany's future while noting that democracy and ties to the West are the best prescription for German stability. A useful analysis which reveals some of the concerns during the transition from a divided to a united Germany.

825　**A New Flag.**
Brian Beedham.　*The Economist*, vol. 316, no. 7670
(1 September 1990), p. 1-18.

A detailed examination of the emerging European security order after the Cold War and the opportunities it presents. The author favours the preservation of NATO, arguing that it is an alliance of like-minded states and not simply a pact between geographical neighbours. Beedham is critical of German Chancellor Helmut Kohl's bilateral negotiations with Soviet President Mikhail Gorbachev which led to the agreement on withdrawal of Soviet troops from Eastern Germany. Also covered in the study are the competing institutional frameworks for European security and some possible alternative postures for NATO itself. Gives a good sense of some of the concerns in the period immediately after the end of the Cold War.

826　**Why Russia should Join NATO.**
Coral Bell.　*The National Interest*, no. 22 (Winter 1990-91), p. 27-47.

Argues that the best way for NATO to become obsolete is to extend eastward and offer membership to Russia and other major members of the defunct Warsaw Pact. Part of the argument is that if a traditional enmity such as that between Greece and Turkey can be accommodated and restrained by membership of the Atlantic Alliance, then it should be possible to do the same between Germany and Russia. The author argues that the potential gains for stability in what has been historically a very unstable zone of *Mitteleuropa* would compensate for whatever is lost by enlargement of membership. The argument is provocative but not wholly convincing.

827　**Systems for Peace or Causes of War? Collective Security, Arms Control, and the New Europe.**
Richard K. Betts.　*International Security*, vol. 17, no. 1
(Summer 1992), p. 5-43.

An original and incisive critique of collective security and arms control, which argues that in post-Cold War Europe both approaches to international security may worsen rather than reduce instability. Betts notes, for example, that if legal constraints are in place they may make military build-ups seem more ominous – even though these build-ups might be initiated for defensive rather than aggressive purposes. The major thrust of Betts's argument on arms control, however, is that efforts to freeze military parity between particular states may do nothing to achieve overall parity because of the uncertainty about patterns of alignment in the post-Cold War era. In terms of collective security, his argument is that such a system is too rigid and could transform relatively minor issues into major conflicts. He also suggests that a post-Hobbesian pacific anarchy in Europe is certainly conceivable and that this should be based on strategic *laissez faire*.

828 **Steps toward Stable Peace in Europe: A Theory and Practice of Coexistence.**
Ken Booth. *International Affairs*, vol. 66, no. 1 (January 1990), p. 17-46.

Noting the rapid changes in East–West relations, Ken Booth proposes a three-stage course over the next twenty-five years to create a stable peace. After discussing 'regressive mindsets' – including ethnocentrism, doctrinal realism, ideological fundamentalism, and strategic reductionism – the author lays out a plan for peace. He begins with the short-term goal of constructive engagement (1995-2000) which would focus on the prospects of reform, reaction, or revolution in the communist world, the emergence of a new economic and political superpower (the EC), and the requirements for enhanced security. The article also discusses the medium-term goal – a legitimate international order (2000-2015) and the long-term goal of a stable peace. An agenda offering specific proposals to promote alternative security ideas is also included. Although overtaken by events which moved faster than his timetable, Booth's analysis contains some interesting ideas about stability and how to achieve it.

829 **Beyond NATO: Complementary Militaries.**
Paul Bracken, Stuart E. Johnson. *Orbis*, vol. 37, no. 2 (Spring 1993), p. 205-222.

The authors argue that the best approach to US–European military ties in the post-Cold War period is to develop a framework for a new division of labour based on comparative military advantages. For the United States these are command, control, communications and intelligence capabilities, global mobility and a capacity for sustained maritime operations. For the Europeans they are proximate ready forces, local knowledge and specialized expertise. Against this background, the authors argue that the United States should get away from the sterile debate about how many troops should be maintained in Europe and consider ways in which it can complement European capabilities rather than substituting for them. A bottom-up approach based upon an assessment of core capacities that are needed to fulfil various roles and missions is advocated. An interesting and thoughtful analysis.

830 **The European Security Order Recast: Scenarios for the Post Cold War Era.**
Barry Buzan, Morten Kelstrup, Pierre LeMaître, Elzbieta Tromer, Ole Waever. London: Pinter, 1990. 282p.

This is one of the first book-length studies to deal with the overall impact of the revolutions of 1989 on the Cold War security order in Europe. After examining the concept of security and exploring the place of the European security system in the global pattern of security, the authors consider the break-up of the Cold War order. They examine the German problem and trace the transition from division to reassociation to unification. The most interesting part of the book, however, deals with various scenarios for the future of European security. The first scenario considered is a possibility of a third Cold War. The second is what is described as the triumph of integration in which the European community provides the core of a Europe of concentric circles. The key element in this notion is that the integration process in Western Europe would be accompanied by increased interdependence between Western Europe and the states of Eastern Europe as well as the Soviet Union. This is clearly the most optimistic scenario although one which is analysed rigorously and critically by the authors. The third scenario is the triumph of anarchy. The idea is that there would be a re-nationalization of defence policies and that Europe would be fragmented once again. Two forms of fragmentation are identified: malign fragmentation in which there is a return to balance-of-power politics and benign fragmentation in which a European regime is established. For those who want to think seriously about the future shape of Europe and the continued role of NATO, this book is a good place to start. It is far from providing the last word, but is nevertheless extremely useful.

831 **NATO at 40: Confronting a Changing World.**
Edited by Ted Galen Carpenter. Lexington, Massachusetts: D. C. Heath, 1990. 275p.

Edited by the Director of Foreign Policy Studies at the Cato Institute, this volume contains a wide range of opinions regarding the future of NATO. In his introductory chapter the editor identifies three points of view on NATO – all included in his volume. The first – represented most vigorously by Joseph Joffe – is that NATO has been crucial to the security of the West including the United States and, with minor adjustments, will continue to be of importance. The second group of contributors, while agreeing on the importance of NATO argues that fundamental reform is essential if the Alliance is to remain relevant. A third group – represented among others by Ronald Steel and Melvyn Krauss – contends that the Atlantic Alliance has already outlived its usefulness and that the United States should disengage from Western Europe. The book itself is divided into four parts: the Alliance under stress; the costs and benefits of NATO; the implications of a changing strategic environment; and alternatives to the status quo. It contains some good chapters and is representative of the gamut of opinion about the future of NATO.

832 **Beyond the Alliance System: The Case for a European Security Organization.**
Malcolm Chalmers. *World Policy Journal*, vol. 7, no. 2 (Spring 1990), p. 215-250.

Chalmers argues that with the disintegration of the Warsaw Pact, it is inappropriate for Western Europe and the United States to cling on to NATO as the major security institution in Europe. The moves towards German unification are seen as a catalyst for the creation of a wider European peace order, which would replace the military alliances and function within the framework established by the Conference on Security and Cooperation in Europe. Although the analysis greatly exaggerates the problems for a united Germany of continued membership in NATO, it develops the idea of a European Security Organization in an interesting if rather idealistic and far from persuasive manner. This work is important mainly as an example of the kinds of alternative to NATO which have been discussed in the aftermath of the changes in Eastern Europe.

833 **Collective Security in Europe and Asia.**
Inis Claude, Sheldon Simon, Douglas Stuart. Carlisle, Pennyslyvania: US Army War College, March 1992. 78p.

A useful publication by the Strategic Studies Institute of the US Army War College, this study contains three essays dealing with collective security. Although all three are useful in thinking about European security after the Cold War, the most relevant is that by Douglas Stuart which deals with 'The Future of the European Alliance: Problems and Opportunities for Coalition Strategies'. This article briefly surveys the transatlantic debate of the last years of the Cold War, looks at the problems of instability facing Europe and considers the capacity of other institutions to respond to these problems. Stuart then argues that NATO should be redefined as a pan-European institution which would stand between the United Nations and the European Community/Western European Union as the paramount organization for pan-European security cooperation and peacekeeping. A constructive and forward-looking analysis. No index is included.

834 **Beyond East–West Confrontation: Searching for a New Security Structure in Europe.**
Edited by Armand Clesse, Lothar Ruhl. Luxembourg: Nomos Verlagsgesellschaft, 1990. 640p.

This massive volume, the result of a conference held in Luxembourg in July 1990, contains fifty-seven chapters by a wide variety of experts on European and Atlantic security. It has sections on Alliance security and Collective Security, on views from Western Europe, on Central and East European perspectives and on the transatlantic dimension, as well as an annex providing a series of shorter and more specific comments. Although the volume is somewhat unwieldy, it nevertheless provides a good starting point for thinking about European security after the Cold War and about the continued role of NATO as opposed to other institutions.

835 **Transforming the Atlantic Alliance.**
Peter Corterier. *Washington Quarterly*, vol. 14, no. 1 (Winter 1991), p. 27-37.

Starting from the premise that NATO retains an important role in European security in the future the Secretary-General of the North Atlantic Assembly looks at the outcome of the London Summit of July 1990 and offers some further reflections on the role of NATO in the new security architecture in Europe. He places the Summit and the London Declaration in a wider perspective while also highlighting their significance for post-Cold War Europe.

836 **European Security without the Soviet Union.**
Edited by Stuart Croft, Phil Williams. London: Cass, 1992. 165p.

Based on a conference held at the University of Pittsburgh in 1991, this volume has contributions by a number of eminent commentators on European and Atlantic security issues including Jack Snyder, Admiral Sir James Eberle, James Goodby, Joseph Pilat, Robbin Laird, Stephen Szabo, Lawrence Kaplan and Dr. Willem van Eekelen. Topics discussed include nationalism and instability in the former Soviet Empire; peacekeeping; British, German and French policies; the future role of the United States in Europe; and the role of the Western European Union.

837 **Cooperative Arms Control: A New Agenda for the Post-Cold War Era.**
Ivo Daalder. College Park, Maryland: Center for International Security Studies, Maryland School of Public Affairs, October 1992. 73p.

A gem of a study which begins the process of reconceptualizing arms control for the post-Cold War era. The author surveys the whole arms control arena including the need for further restructuring of conventional forces in Europe. Although not writing directly on NATO, Daalder provides a good sense of the new environment in which NATO has to operate.

838 **Emerging Dimensions of European Security Policy.**
Edited by Wolfgang F. Danspeckgruber.   Boulder, Colorado:
Westview Press, 1991. 337p.

One of the problems with many books written in the late 1980s about NATO and European security was that they were rapidly overtaken by events. While this book suffers to some extent from this problem, it also represents one of the early efforts to come to grips with the changes set in motion by the end of the Cold War in Europe. Although it was written before the Soviet Union disintegrated and when Moscow was still deemed to pose a security problem for the West, the book provides a good overview of European security issues in 1989-90. The first section deals with theoretical, strategic and political considerations and includes interesting chapters on the future role of nuclear weapons in Europe by Thomas Risse-Kappen and Stuart Croft. The second section looks at the place of conventional arms control in European security, while the third part contains three contributions on economic dimensions. Part Four is entitled 'A European Architecture' and as well as exploring the future of the security system in Europe has useful contributions on European and American public opinion on European security. Although the book contains some good analysis it is perhaps best seen as representing some of the early efforts to think through the consequences of the end of the Cold War rather than as a real analysis of the post-Cold War security system.

839 **Planning for Long-Term Security in Central Europe: Implications of the New Strategic Environment.**
Paul K. Davis, Robert D. Howe.   Santa Monica, California: Rand
Corporation, August 1990. 50p. (Rand Report R-3977-USDP).

This report from the Rand Strategy Assessment Center prepared for the Under-Secretary of Defense for Policy, identified five objectives that the authors regarded as essential to the attainment of stability in Europe when the Soviet Union was still intact. These objectives were: deter without provocation a Soviet invasion of Western Europe; deter without provocation a Soviet re-entry into Eastern Europe; maintain strategic equivalence in the East–West competition; deter rearmament; and reduce the sources of conflict and tension. The major actions required to attain each of these objectives are spelled out in some detail in what is a thoughtful and systematic treatment of the requirements of stability in a Europe in which the spectre of Soviet power had not fully disappeared. Although an interim assessment, some of the ideas continue to have relevance in a Europe without the Soviet Union but in which Russia remains a major military power.

840 **The Future of NATO: Facing an Unreliable Enemy in an Uncertain Environment.**
S. Nelson Drew, Keith W. Dayton, William J. Ervin, M. Barry Keck,
Philip C. Marcum.   New York: Praeger, 1991. 206p.

Written by officers in the US armed forces who participated as National Security Fellows at Harvard's Kennedy School, this study sets out to look at the military implications of the changes in Europe in 1989 and 1990. The authors emphasize the need for a new vision especially in relation to NATO strategy. They offer a blueprint for what they describe as resilient defence in a period of lower force levels. They are cautious about the new environment and consider the implications of losing a reliable enemy for NATO's political consensus. The book has considerable detail on military strategy and tactics but even though it is forward-looking has been overtaken by events. The new security problems for NATO are no longer deterrence and defence but crisis management and peacekeeping.

841 **Military Planning after the Cold War: Escalators and Quagmires: Expectations and the Use of Force.**
Lawrence Freedman. *International Affairs*, vol. 67, no. 1 (January 1991), p. 15-32.

Using the analogies of escalation and quagmires, Freedman warns that the real danger of military action is not so much uncontrolled development, but distorted political decision-making. As such, military policy must be informed by political and national goals to a greater extent than in the past. Freedman argues that with the end of the Cold War holding alliances together will be even harder. He also suggests that the United Nations may prove to be the best framework for coordinating and enforcing military action in the future.

842 **Europe Transformed: Documents on the End of the Cold War.**
Lawrence Freedman. London: Tri-Service Press, 1990. 516p.

A very useful compendium of documents which covers the security framework established in the aftermath of the Second World War; détente in the 1970s; arms control in the 1980s; and speeches, statements, and declarations in the period preceding and following the breach in the Berlin Wall. The documents include the Brussels and Atlantic Treaties, the Paris Agreements of 1954, NATO and Warsaw Pact communiqués and speeches by individual leaders such as Gorbachev. Overall, a very good reference source.

843 **Europe in Turmoil: The Struggle for Pluralism.**
Edited by Gerald Frost. New York: Praeger, 1991. 377p. (*European Defense and Strategic Studies Annual 1990-91*).

Consisting largely of papers published by the conservative European Institute for Defense and Strategic Studies, this volume has four sections: the Gorbachev phenomenon; information openness and freedom of movement; British and French perspectives on a changing world; and the impact of tyranny and the seeds of revolt, with particular reference to Romania and the crisis in Yugoslavia. The contribution on the British Conservatives and Defence by Christopher Coker stands out for both its wit and its acidity.

844 **Eastern Europe's Search for Security.**
Howard E. Frost. *Orbis*, vol. 37, no. 1 (Winter 1993), p. 37–53.

Starting from the perception that the governing élites of Eastern Europe see a security vacuum, the author looks at the steps they have taken to improve their security situation and then considers the implications for the role of the West, especially NATO, in further efforts to enhance security in the region. The author argues that these élites see NATO as crucial and considers ways in which the Alliance can respond to this positively while avoiding over-extensions. He considers the various forms this might take and the pace at which this process of establishing security for Eastern Europe might move.

845 **NATO: A Changing Alliance Faces New Challenges.**
General Accounting Office.   Washington, DC: GAO, July 1992. 40p.
(Report to the Chairman, Subcommittee on Conventional Forces and
Alliance Defense, Committee on Armed Services, US Senate).
Provides the results of a review undertaken by the General Accounting Office (GAO)
which looked at NATO's new strategic concept, the national defence plans of NATO
members and the extent to which they reflect the new strategy, and obstacles to the
implementation of the strategy. US plans for contributing to the new force structure
are considered, while the level of the US contribution to the overall effort in the future
is assessed. The report suggests that even though the total US contribution to NATO is
declining, the US portion of troops in Germany will increase as other nations bring
home a higher percentage of their troops than does Washington.

846 **Why NATO is Still Best: Future Security Arrangements in Europe.**
Charles Glaser.   *International Security*, vol. 18, no. 1 (Summer 1993),
p. 5-50.
An attempt to offer a systematic analysis of various possible security arrangements in
Europe and their strengths and weaknesses for dealing with the main kinds of threat.
The author argues that there are three kinds of threat that might occur – a resurgent
Russia, war in Eastern Europe that could draw in the West, and war within Western
Europe. He contends that in designing policies to meet these threats the United States
and its allies need to decide what interests are at stake. Against this background the
author examines five security structures to deal with the three types of possible war: a
refashioned NATO; an integrated Western Europe; a continent-wide collective
security system; a concert of major powers; and the development of defensive
unilateral security in which countries focus on defence capabilities and reduce their
ability to attack others. The author concludes that NATO provides a better hedge than
any of the alternatives.

847 **Reforging European Security: From Confrontation to Cooperation.**
Edited by Kurt Gottfried, Paul Bracken.   Boulder, Colorado:
Westview Press, 1990. 226p.
This volume looks at the new security environment as it was emerging by the end of
the 1980s. The editors argue that in light of the changes the United States should move
to a relationship with Western Europe very similar to that with Japan – in which
reliance is placed on air and sea forces rather than the commitment of ground forces.
Part two of the book by Jonathan Dean and Stanley Resor – two experienced
commentators and practitioners – looks at the emerging framework of European
security with particular reference to the CFE negotiations. Part three looks at ways in
which NATO and United States forces might be restructured for a new situation, while
a fourth section consists of relevant documents including an address by Gorbachev and
the Declaration by NATO Heads of State at the London Summit.

848   **Homeward Bound? Allied Forces in the New Germany.**
Edited by David G. Haglund, Olaf Mager.   Boulder, Colorado:
Westview Press, 1992. 299p.

This useful volume explores the implications of the end of the Cold War for the future of NATO forces deployed in Germany. Unlike many collections of essays this is both well conceived and carefully structured. After a very useful introduction by the editors which provides a helpful introduction to the issues, Helga Haftendorn explores what the editors call the 'structural context' within which the role of allied forces on German territory evolved. She not only explores the legal, military and political dimensions of this presence but also offers a succinct overview of German unification and the questions which arise now that the Federal Republic has ceased to be a front-line state. Some of the initial moves by NATO to adapt to this are explored in a chapter on defence planning and one on the role of multinational formations. Since the future presence of troops will be determined in part by their domestic legitimacy the chapter on German domestic opinion is particularly important. Part two of the volume moves from the context to the stationing policies of those states with troops in Germany. There are chapters on the United States, Britain, France, Belgium, Canada and The Netherlands. United States stationing policy, of course, is particularly important given the United States role in European security since the late 1940s. In his chapter on this, David Haglund argues very convincingly that the United States has been freed from the dictates of security which made a large presence of American troops in Europe inevitable. The element of what he terms 'voluntarism' in the American position raises a real question mark about the medium- and long-term future of American military involvement in Europe. The editors conclude that the case for maintaining the stationing regime is strong since the need for reassurance does not depend upon the existence of a single clearly identifiable enemy.

849   **Nuclear Weapons in a Changing Europe.**
Edited by Vilho Harle, Pekka Sivonen.   London: Pinter, 1991. 210p.

Based on a series of workshops held between November 1988 and April 1990 the papers in this volume explore the role of nuclear weapons in Europe after the Cold War. The individual chapters by such analysts as Simon Duke, Caroline Kennedy, Matthias Dembinski, and Hans Gunter Brauch explore the military and political functions of nuclear weapons during the Cold War and the prospects for the future given the kinds of political changes taking place. Dembinski is particularly good on this, developing what he terms the 'concept of minimized extended deterrence'. The most interesting essay, however, is that by Brauch who looks both at the prospects for moving from collective defence to collective security in Europe and at the role of military force within a collective security system. Brauch relates his discussion to the analyses by John Mearsheimer and others concerning the likely impact of the end of the Cold War on European security. Although the individual contributions are worthwhile, however, the editors have not provided any kind of useful framework and offer neither an introduction nor a conclusion. While this weakens the book, this is still a useful starting point for those interested in the future role – or lack of one – for nuclear weapons in the European security system after the Cold War.

850 **Europe Beyond Partition and Unity: Disintegration or Reconstruction?**
Pierre Hassner. *International Affairs*, vol. 66, no. 3 (July 1990),
p. 461-475.

An incisive analysis which emphasizes the urgent need to integrate Western and Eastern Europe. Hassner suggests that the end of the Cold War has been followed first by pan-European rapprochement, and then by fractional splintering between East and West. Consequently, integration in the West, disintegration in the East, and East–West unity are simultaneously vying for dominance. This is useful as a point of departure for thinking about NATO's role in the new system – which the author himself suggests is very limited now that the threat has disappeared.

851 **Europe and America beyond 2000.**
Pierre Hassner, David Calleo, Robert Hormats, Johan Jorgen Holst,
David Owen, Richard Perle. New York: Council on Foreign
Relations, 1990. 157p. (Europe/America, No. 8).

Unlike the other studies in this series, which tended to look at current problems, this volume looks ahead to the changing shape of European security arrangements. Unfortunately it was written just prior to the events which overcame the division of Germany and of Europe. Nevertheless, there are some illuminating essays. Pierre Hassner emphasizes the priority of constructing Western Europe, while there is a helpful piece on military stability and political order by Johan Holst. For the most part, however, the contributors do not really look beyond 2000 in the way that was intended. They also have a starting point that is already outmoded.

852 **NATO: An Institution under Threat.**
Jan Willem Honig. New York: Institute for East–West Security
Studies, 1991. 69p. (Occasional Paper Series, No. 22).

This succinct and useful study addresses the crucial question as to whether NATO has any useful role in Europe now that the Cold War is over. After examining proposals for reform of the Alliance from the United States, Britain, France, Germany and the smaller allies, the author turns his attention to the way NATO has functioned in the past. He takes issue with the conventional wisdom that the military forces of the member-states have been integrated into a common military organization, arguing instead that NATO has provided an invaluable framework for military planning, coordination and cooperation in the Atlantic region. Attempts to broaden the Alliance geographically and to deepen military integration have not been successful. Nevertheless, the author argues, NATO has a future, based on its military role. Central and Eastern Europe, Northern Africa, and the Middle East are all characterized by political and economic instability and a high probability of armed conflict. In these circumstances, a NATO which continues to provide the framework for military cooperation between the United States and Western Europe remains of continued relevance and importance.

853 **The Future of European Security.**
Robert Hunter. *Washington Quarterly*, vol. 13, no. 4 (Autumn 1990),
p. 55-68.

Looks at the implications of the Soviet retreat from Eastern Europe and suggests the future security in Europe must in large part be about political and economic systems, performance and relationships. Hunter examines the capabilities a new European security system must have if it is to remain viable. He also looks at problems in Eastern Europe, the role of Germany and the future of the European Community. An interesting essay which offers some valuable observations.

854 European Security beyond the Cold War: Four Scenarios for the Year 2010.
Adrian Hyde-Price. London: Sage for the Royal Institute of International Affairs, 1991. 272p.

A systematic analysis of the prospects for the European security system now that the Cold War is over. The book highlights the main features of the Cold War security system in Europe, identifies and assesses the determinants of change, and explores four scenarios for the year 2010. While acknowledging the difficulties of modelling alternative security futures, the author does an excellent job of elucidating the range of possibilities. His scenarios are: NATO and an Atlanticist Europe; a West European Defence Community; a pan-European collective security system; and Europe of states. In his conclusions Hyde-Price notes that the actual outcome will be determined in large part by the performance of the existing institutions in dealing with specific crises and security challenges. In addition, he suggests ten principles which should be incorporated into whatever system finally emerges. Overall, this is an excellent analysis which offers an incisive treatment of the possibilities for the post-Cold War security system.

855 Collective Security and the Future of Europe: Failed Dreams and Dead Ends.
Josef Joffe. *Survival*, vol. 34, no. 1 (Spring 1992), p. 36-50.

A strong critique of collective security based on both theoretical and empirical considerations. After disposing of arguments in favour of a new collective security system in Europe, the author develops a strong case for maintaining NATO as the central institution for the promotion of European security. He argues that NATO's past successes, its reservoir of experience and training and the fact that it is the only institution which links the United States and Western Europe are crucial. The author suggests that the new dilemma of European security is that NATO has the means but not the mission and that the European Community/Western European Union and the Conference on Security and Cooperation in Europe have the mission but not the means.

856 A NATO Vehicle for the Road Ahead.
Sir Brian Kenny. *Parameters*, vol. 21, no. 3 (Autumn 1991), p. 19-27.

Written by the Deputy Supreme Allied Commander Europe, this article looks at the modifications in NATO which followed the end of the Cold War. After noting the change in Soviet attitudes towards NATO, Kenny argues that in spite of the end of the Cold War there are still security challenges which have to be met – resulting from religious and ethnic tensions and the resurfacing of old rivalries. He then outlines the kinds of changes NATO has made in response to this changed environment. Particular emphasis is placed on multinational forces and the need for rapid responses to crisis situations. Although the article touches on the idea of the Western European Union playing a larger role in European security matters, the author is unequivocal that NATO is the only organization with a proven military command structure capable of acting effectively in crises.

857   **Perceptions of Germany and the United States on NATO.**
Emil Kirchner, James Sperling.   University of Essex, Dept of Politics
and Government, July 1991. 26p. (Essex Papers in Politics and
Government, No. 80).

The central purpose of this paper is to answer the question whether the collapse of the
Warsaw Pact and reunification of Germany make NATO redundant. The focus,
however, is primarily historical and looks at the role of NATO as a framework for
dealing with Germany. The authors argue in conclusion that increasing emphasis will
be placed by Germany on the European Community and that this will allow Germany
to act as broker when conflicts of interest develop between the United States and the
European allies over trade and monetary issues. At the same time they acknowledge
that German security will continue to depend upon the goodwill of its neighbours and a
nuclear guarantee extended by either France, Britain or the United States.

858   **The Evolving New European Architecture – Concepts, Problems and
Pitfalls.**
Joachim Krause, Peter Schmidt.   *Washington Quarterly*, vol. 13, no. 4
(Autumn 1990), p. 79-92.

A helpful analysis which acknowledges the uncertainty over the future European
security architecture and focuses on what the authors believe will be a lengthy
transition period. During this period, concrete political and economic problems will
have to be addressed and this will do much to determine the final architecture.
Accordingly, the authors address the problems of the transitional phase such as forging
new relationships with the formerly socialist states. The article provides a necessary
caveat to great architectural designs for European security and the future of NATO.

859   **Concerts, Collective Security and the Future of Europe.**
Charles A. Kupchan, Clifford A. Kupchan.   *International Security*,
vol. 16, no. 1 (Summer 1991), p. 114-161.

Can collective security work effectively in the radically changed landscape of post-Cold
War Europe? The authors make a case that it can and that, in particular, a concert-
based collective security arrangement may be most effective for several reasons. First,
collective security arrangements strengthen cooperative peaceful relationships more
than balance-of-power relationships do. Second, a concert-based arrangement in which
only the major powers participate allows for more flexible, timely, and coordinated
decision-making in a still-evolving European security situation. Moreover, present
European conditions are ripe for a concert-based system: there is general satisfaction
with the status quo, general agreement about the uselessness of a major war,
reciprocity, and high transparency. Thus, Kupchan and Kupchan argue that CSCE
should be reformulated to serve as a concert-based collective security organization –
but that NATO should be retained until the European security situation is stabilized
and CSCE can take the leading role in ensuring peace and security in Europe.

860 **Long Memories and Short Fuses: Change and Instability in the Balkans.**

F. Stephen Larrabee. *International Security*, vol. 15, no. 3 (Winter 1990-91), p. 58-91.

Starting from the assumption that in the 1990s the main threat to European security is likely to come not from Soviet military power but from ethnic conflict and political fragmentation in the Balkans, Larrabee analyses the problems of democracy and political chaos in post-communist Balkan states. He looks at the Yugoslav crisis as well as other festering and potential ethnic conflicts such as the Kosovo, Macedonian, Bessarabian questions, the Hungarian minority in Romania and the Turkish minority in Bulgaria. Western policy towards the region is also discussed and some policy guidelines proposed. Specifically, Larrabee argues, the United States should support the process of democratization in post-communist Southeastern Europe and should make political and economic reforms a precondition for economic aid. Additionally, the United States should defer to third-party mediation from the UN or CSCE to deal with deep-seated ethnic disputes; should encourage regional cooperation among the Balkan states and the 'Europeanization' of Southeastern Europe, and should coordinate its policies with those of Western Europe.

861 **Halt! Who Goes Where: The Future of NATO in the New Europe.**

John Leech. London: Brassey's (UK), 1991. 156p.

Based on ideas expressed at a meeting of forty diplomats, defence specialists and politicians organized by the West–West Agenda, this slim volume looks at the changes in Europe in 1989 and 1990 and considers how NATO should respond. It argues that the Alliance has unfinished business in the short and medium terms but that it has to be converted from an instrument appropriate to the Cold War to an organization which can enhance confidence-building in Europe. Attention is given to the need to move from confrontation with the East to peacekeeping, to provide aid, and to adapt NATO strategy to the new circumstances. Since the book was written, NATO has in fact gone much further in some of the directions specified. Nevertheless, this is useful as a snapshot taken in mid-1990 of thinking about future security requirements.

862 **The United States and Europe: Redefining the Relationship.**

Joseph Lepgold. *Current History*, vol. 90, no. 559 (November 1991), p. 353-357.

Argues that NATO is of uncertain relevance to the kind of security problems that Europe faces in the aftermath of the Cold War. Also discusses the frictions between the United States and Western Europe on a variety of issues including trade. Lepgold gives succinct and useful analysis.

863 **Transition and Turmoil in the Atlantic Alliance.**

Edited by Robert Levine. New York: Crane Russak, 1992. 285p.

Resulting from a Rand Corporation project which began in 1988 this volume consists primarily of a series of chapters on NATO member-nations. The editor has a chapter on the United States, Ronald Asmus on a unified Germany, Gregory Flynn on France, Phil Williams on the United Kingdom, Ian Lesser on Italy, Richard Bitzinger on the Low Countries, and John Lund on Scandinavia. Perhaps the most interesting aspect of the book, however, is the introduction in which Levine looks at the way issues flow through NATO and the timetables on which decisions must be made. His conclusion is also valuable as it explores the interactions between these two dimensions and makes some recommendations for United States policy.

864   **Security and Strategy in the New Europe.**
Edited by Colin McInnes.   London: Routledge, 1992. 250p.
A useful collection of essays divided into three parts and containing contributions by, amongst others Ken Booth and Nicholas Wheeler, Adrian Hyde-Price, Peter Foot, John Baylis, Stuart Croft, and Michael Brenner and Phil Williams. The first section of the book is perhaps the most interesting as it focuses upon future possibilities for the European security system. Part Two deals with strategy after the Cold War, while the third section has five chapters which focus on national concerns and perspectives.

865   **Back to the Future: Instability in Europe after the Cold War.**
John Mearsheimer.   *International Security*, vol. 15, no. 1
(Summer 1990), p. 5-56.
An important and highly controversial article which argued that the breakdown of bipolarity and its replacement by multipolarity together with the move from nuclear to conventional deterrence in Europe would mean an end to stability. The conditions in the security system would be more permissive and would allow ethnic animosities to fuel instability. The author argues that the best way to prevent this is to maintain as much of the Cold War system as possible, including NATO and its nuclear deterrence capability. As part of the effort to maintain stability he argues that Germany should be encouraged to become a nuclear power. Mearsheimer's diagnosis of the problem was much better than the proposed solution, but for anyone interested in the role of NATO in European security after the Cold War this is a must.

866   **Challenges to NATO in the 1990s.**
Sam Nunn.   *Survival*, vol. 32, no. 1 (January-February 1990), p. 3-14.
The text of the 1989 Alastair Buchan lecture given by the Chairman of the Armed Services Committee in the United States Senate. Nunn looks at the changes taking place in Europe and highlights ways in which the positive developments in the European security environment can be consolidated. Looks at Western assistance to Hungary and Poland and NATO policy towards the Soviet Union.

867   **Reshaping Western Security: The United States faces a United Europe.**
Edited by Richard N. Perle.   Washington, DC: AEI Press, 1991. 162p.
Starting with an introduction by the editor which castigates the European allies for their performance in the Gulf, this volume contains several articles which consider ways in which the post-Cold War system in Europe can be made more stable. Henry Nau looks at US objectives for change against a background of complex interactions among political, economic and security factors; Josef Joffe examines the stability of the Cold War order and looks at the principles that should guide the post-Cold War system; Joseph Fitchett looks at defence industries in the 1990s; Brian Beedham looks at the demise of the Warsaw Pact; and the Undersecretary of Defense in the Bush Administration, Paul Wolfowitz, elucidates US goals for a future Europe. There are also commentaries on the substantive chapters by other analysts. A somewhat eclectic but interesting collection.

868 **NATO's Future Role: An American View.**
Robert L. Pfaltzgraff, Jr. *Proceedings of the Academy of Political Sciences*, vol. 38, no. 1 (1991), p. 176-186.
An interesting analysis which argues that the major issue for NATO in the 1990s is not about the appropriate strategy but about the principal security issues confronting the US and the West European allies and the appropriate frameworks for their resolution. Although decisions about security needs will be dictated more by budgetary considerations than strategic logic, without NATO the task of formulating a security concept for the West as a basis for equilibrium, however defined, would be virtually impossible. And if there is a broader concept of security which encompasses economics as well as defence and arms control, the roles of NATO and the European Community will increasingly intersect and overlap. NATO, however, will have a continued role in ensuring European political–military equilibrium and providing a security framework within which the unfolding links to the East can be most fully developed. An interesting analysis which goes some way to developing a post-Cold War rationale for NATO.

869 **Keeping Deterrence: Nuclear Weapons and the Abolition of War.**
Michael Quinlan. *International Affairs*, vol. 67, no. 2 (April 1991), p. 293-302.
An interesting if rather conservative analysis by a former Permanent Under-Secretary in the British Ministry of Defence. Sir Michael Quinlan argues that even in a dramatically new security environment, nuclear weapons still have an important role to play in deterring war. Although their numbers could probably be reduced, nuclear weapons should still remain a key element in NATO's security posture in an uncertain and unstable environment.

870 **Did 'Peace through Strength' End the Cold War? Lessons from INF.**
Thomas Risse-Kappen. *International Security*, vol. 16, no. 1 (Summer 1991), p. 162-188.
An interesting analysis which sets out to explain the end of the Cold War and examines the INF negotiations as a source of insights into this process. The author highlights the way in which Gorbachev transformed Soviet INF policy in a way which made possible the 'double zero' option. He suggests that the INF negotiations revealed that the political environment is more important than a specific bargaining strategy and that the significance of domestic politics is difficult to overstate. Finally, Risse-Kappen attributes the end of the Cold War primarily to Soviet domestic developments, rather than Western pressure.

871 **NATO's Future Role: A European View.**
David Robertson. *Proceedings of the Academy of Political Science*, vol. 38, no. 1 (1991), p. 164-175.
For Europeans, NATO is viewed as only one among a plethora of multinational agreements and organizations in Europe, and its popularity stems more from it latent functions than its overt purposes. Although recent developments have undermined NATO's main purpose, Robertson argues that it can still serve an important role as an international security organization in Europe in the absence of better alternatives. Ethnic tensions and the old issue of the German question provide the main rationale

for NATO, but it must also make crucial decisions regarding its future membership, political justification and operational doctrine and force structure.

872   **European Security beyond the Year 2000.**
Edited by Robert Rudney, Luc Reychler.   New York: Praeger, 1988.
317p.

An interesting collection of essays in which eighteen authors from non-Communist European countries were asked to look ahead and see where Europe and its security were headed in the long term through a focus on national perspectives. The book is divided into four sections – NATO Center, NATO North, NATO South and the Neutrals – and each section consists of a series of country studies. For Britain, France and Germany there are two chapters each, while other European countries are dealt with in single chapters. The authors were asked to define their country's long-term threat perceptions, to evaluate official security policies and their domestic legitimacy, and to make prescriptions for improving security policies over the next thirty years. Although the book was rapidly overtaken by events, with contributors including Ken Booth, Jan Siccama, Hans Gunter Brauch, Baard Knudsen and Bo Huldt, it is still worth looking at, especially as it provides a useful survey of national perspectives relatively shortly before the massive changes in Europe.

873   **European Security Policy after the Revolutions of 1989.**
Edited by Jeffrey Simon.   Washington, DC: National Defense
University Press, 1991. 640p.

This volume, which evolved from a conference held at the National Defense University (NDU) in June 1990, offers one of the first relatively comprehensive assessments of the consequences of the political changes in Europe for the force structures of NATO and the Soviet Union, for the Southern and Northern Flanks, and for the states of Central Europe. Particular attention is given to the impact of the changes on mobilization and deployment patterns. The book is far more than simply a reporting of development, however, and several chapters, including one on US reinforcement options, prescribe changes that the authors feel need to be made as military structures adapt to changed political conditions. As well as looking at the core states, Germany, France and Britain, the contributions also focus on the countries on the periphery – Czecho-slovakia, Poland, Hungary, Belgium, Holland and Denmark. Another section deals with three flank countries, Norway, Romania and Bulgaria, while yet another has chapters on NATO's Southern Flank – Greece, Turkey, Italy, Spain and Portugal. One for the main conclusions of the volume is that if NATO is to remain relevant it must evolve into, or at least facilitate, a pan-European security structure that includes Germany, the United States and the USSR. One of the first books to offer an assessment of security problems in post-Cold War Europe, this volume is particularly good on the military consequences of poltical change.

874   **Does Eastern Europe belong in NATO?**
Jeffrey Simon.   *Orbis*, vol. 37, no. 1 (Winter 1993), p. 21–35.

Starting from the premise that NATO is in danger of becoming irrelevant and that a security vacuum has developed in Central and Eastern Europe, the author argues that NATO should enlarge its mission to include this region. He suggests that it should hold out the prospect of membership to the states of the region. The article contains a very useful summary of the steps already taken by NATO in relation to Eastern Europe through the North Atlantic Cooperation Council (NACC), and argues that although great progress has been made more needs to be done. He suggests associate membership – and ultimately full membership – status for all NACC members who observe certain norms of behaviour and argues that this will give the states of Central and Eastern Europe an incentive for observing these standards of behaviour.

875 **NATO's Future in a New Europe: An American Perspective.**
Stanley R. Sloan. *International Affairs*, vol. 66, no. 3 (July 1990), p. 495-512.

Provides a useful perspective on the implications of Soviet and East European change for NATO. After discussing the revolutionary changes and the victory of democratic principles Stanley Sloan highlights several short-term policy imperatives: the need to balance Soviet power while respective legitimate Soviet security interests; to acknowledge the right of a unified Germany to full sovereignty; and to avoid actions which might force the Warsaw Pact countries back to the USSR. He also outlines various national perspectives, considers institutional frameworks for the future, and assesses the implications for the role of the US in Europe. He suggests that NATO should be preserved as an essential safety net.

876 **The New Germany and the New Europe.**
Edited by Paul Stares. Washington, DC: Brookings Institution, 1992. 406p.

This excellent collections of essays attempts to assess the implications of German unification on political, economic and security relations and patterns in post-Cold War Europe. Part I deals with the new Germany and includes chapters on security and on foreign policy. Part II looks at designs for a new Europe and includes a valuable analysis by Paul Stares and John Steinbruner of cooperative security in the new Europe. For anyone interested in the implications of a unified Germany for the future of European security and NATO this volume is a must.

877 **The Year of European (Dis)Unification.**
Gregory F. Treverton. *Current History*, vol. 91, no. 568 (November 1992), p. 353-358.

Deals with the continued implementation of the European goal of a single market, noting the various difficulties. On the military side, Treverton believes NATO is not suitable for future possible security problems in Europe which are likely to resemble the situation in Yugoslavia. He contends that the United States should not object to the Europeans promoting greater defence cooperation among themselves which would complement, not compete with, NATO. NATO would act as a deterrent against a renewed threat from the East and provide reassurance to all Europe. NATO should also adapt to the new security problems and develop greater capabilities for peacekeeping operations.

878 **Securing Europe.**
Richard H. Ullman. Princeton, New Jersey: Princeton University Press, 1991. 183p.

A stimulating and incisive if somewhat optimistic study of Europe after the Cold War. The author argues that there is no longer a serious likelihood of war among Europe's major states and that there is a new impetus to seek security through cooperation. He believes that the key to institutionalizing European security is to build on CSCE and the Western European Union and establish a new European Security Organization that would, in effect, be NATO transformed. The integrated military organization would disappear and the European Security Organization would become the key structure for maintaining security in Europe. Ullman also acknowledges that American administrations may well react to the changes in Europe by clinging to NATO as the favoured institution for linking the two shores of the Atlantic, but contends that this would be a mistake as NATO is essentially a Cold War institution. An index is included.

879 **Military Cooperation: What Structure for the Future?**
René Van Beveren. Paris: Institute for Security Studies, Western European Union, January 1993. 50p.
Looks at traditional patterns of military cooperation within NATO – including staff agreements and integrated command structures – and considers the extent to which these are still appropriate and probable given the changes in the strategic environment and the responses of both NATO and the Western European Union.

880 **Primed for Peace: Europe after the Cold War.**
Stephen Van Evera. *International Security*, vol. 15, no. 3 (Winter 1990–91), p. 7–57.
A useful contribution to the debate on European security after the Cold War which considers the likelihood of war in Europe in view of the Soviet withdrawal from Eastern Europe and the further fragmentation of the Soviet Union. The author criticizes the more pessimistic views of Europe's future and argues that the European wars of the twentieth century grew from military factors and domestic conditions that will not return. The nuclear revolution has dampened security motives for expansion, and the domestic orders of most European states have changed in ways that make renewed aggression unlikely. The most significant domestic changes include the spread of democracy, the levelling of highly stratified European societies, the resulting evaporation of 'social imperial' motives for war, and the disappearance of states governed by revolutionary élites. Accordingly, Van Evera discounts three common strands of pessimism about the increasing risk of European war: that a multipolar world is less stable than the old bipolar arrangement; that Germany may rearm and become a security threat; and that the democratic revolutions in Eastern Europe may not be completed. He cautions, though, that ethnic tensions increase the risk of war. Consequently, the last part of the article consists of four policy prescriptions for helping to maintain peace in Europe: pursue a comprehensive European settlement; promote democracy and dampen nationalism and militarism in Eastern Europe; manage nuclear proliferation; and maintain a US military presence in Europe as a stabilizer.

881 **Why Europe Matters, Why the Third World Doesn't: American Grand Strategy after the Cold War.**
Stephen Van Evera. *Journal of Strategic Studies*, vol. 13, no. 2 (June 1990), p. 1–51.
This analysis makes a strong case for continuing to give Europe the top priority in American foreign and security policies even though the Cold War is over. Although the latter part of the article is focused on the lack of US interests in the Third World, the first part focuses on US interests in Europe. The author argues that although geopolitical considerations no longer carry the same weight as in the past, the United States still has a significant interest in maintaining peace and prosperity in Europe. Part

of the argument is based on the notion that if Europe becomes unstable then the United States could be dragged into another major war there. At the same time the author acknowledges that the United States can maintain its security commitment with a much lower level of forces than that projected by the Bush Administration. Whereas Bush and the Pentagon had argued that 150,000 was an irreducible minimum Van Evera sees little problem with reducing forces to somewhere between 50,000 and 100,000.

882   **Three Competing Europes: German, French, Russian.**
Ole Waever.   *International Affairs*, vol. 66, no. 3 (July 1990),
p. 447-494.

Looks at the divergent conceptions of Europe in the post-Cold War era and suggests that there is a bargaining process between Germany and the two losers of the postwar peace – France and Russia. After describing German Europe (based on *Mitteleuropa* and East–West détente), French Europe (respecting the full sovereignty of the nation-state and centred on Western Europe) and Russian Europe (which emphasizes the Common European Home), the author argues that although Germany is in a very strong position, France and Russia must be accommodated. The views of the United States, Britain, Poland are also considered. Although the focus is not on NATO, this article does deal with changes in the political context which will do much to determine NATO's future.

883   **The New Europe: Revolution in East–West Relations.**
Edited by Nils H. Wessell.   New York: The Academy of Political
Science, 1991. 214p. (*Proceedings of the Academy of Political Science*,
vol. 38, no. 1).

This volume focuses on Europe's dichotomous evolution. In Eastern Europe and the Soviet Union the dominant theme is disintegration while in contrast Western Europe is going through a period of accelerated integration. The volume is divided into four sections. Section One, 'Security in a new light', and Section Four, 'Alternative Futures', merit special attention. Contributions to Section One include F. Stephen Larrabee on 'The new Soviet approach to Europe', Stephen F. Szabo's 'The New Europeans: Beyond the balance of power', and Robbin Laird's 'France, Germany, and the future of the Atlantic alliance'. Section Four includes Wessell's 'Alternative Soviet futures and the new Europe' and articles by Robertson and Pfaltzgraff which are dealt with as separate items (*see* items 871 and 868).

884   **The New European Security Calculus: Implications for the US Army.**
Thomas-Durell Young.   Carlisle, Pennsylvania: Strategic Studies
Institute, US Army War College, January 1991. 65p.

Looks at the implications of the changes in Europe for the United States Army. The author contends that in the medium term, as Europe evolves towards a post-Cold War security structure, the stabilizing effects of NATO are indispensable. He also acknowledges, however, that at some point this need for stabilization will end and a more fluid regional political structure will emerge. It is crucial to keep Germany within the Western Alliance and West European economic and political institutions – an objective which will require efforts to avoid any singularization of Germany. As part of this it might be necessary for the United States to conduct its large-scale military exercises in North America – and to invite European participation. Although Young argues that US forces in Europe provide stability, he emphasizes that they have to be in radically different formations configured for new missions.

885 Reforming NATO's Command and Operational Control Structures: Progress and Problems.

Thomas-Durell Young, William T. Johnsen.   Geneva, Switzerland: Graduate Institute of International Studies, 1992. 46p.

Examines and assesses NATO's efforts to reorganize its command and control requirements to accord with the Alliance's new strategic concept. Shows how the distribution of command positions involves influence and status of member-nations. The implication is that the reform process is likely to be a political process rather traditional reorganization. Nevertheless, the authors offer some astute comments on how this process might be carried out more effectively. In doing so they look at Allied Forces Central Europe and the other commands as well as issues related to the Rapid Reaction Force. The paper also contains a number of very useful organizational charts.

886 Europe's Security: A Great Confusion.

Jan Zielonka.   *International Affairs*, vol. 67, no. 1 (January 1991), p. 127-137.

This article identifies the major questions in the post-Cold War debate about the future of European security. It contends that the West must move from old conduct to new thinking on three levels: spending for traditional defence purposes vis-à-vis assistance for democratic and economic reforms in Eastern Europe; export control policy towards Eastern Europe; and the issue of whether or not NATO is the most appropriate institution to handle Europe's security situation. The article identifies possible threats to European security and discusses the future role of a united Germany, the role of the United States in Europe, and the future of the Atlantic Alliance. The article concludes with three models for future European security: preserving the stable and predictable bipolar system; creating a new security regime in Europe; and providing security though comprehensively integrating Europe.

Alliance Theory and NATO

887 **Alliances; Latent War Communities in the Contemporary World.**
Edited by Francis A. Beer.   New York: Holt, Rinehart and Winston,
1970. 348p.

Starting from Robert Osgood's definition of alliances, the editor has compiled an excellent collection of essays. Particularly noteworthy is Elliott Vandevanter's chapter which compares NATO and the OAS alliance systems as well as the Olson and Zeckhauser chapter outlining their economic theory of alliances.

888 **Security makes Strange Bedfellows: NATO's Problems from a
Minimalist Perspective.**
Ken Booth.   *Journal for Defense Studies*, vol. 120, no. 4
(December 1975), p. 3-14.

A very incisive analysis which suggests that when analysing and evaluating NATO it is important not to expect too much from what is an alliance of sovereign states, each of which has its own distinct interests and perspectives and a particular set of domestic pressures and problems to contend with. This is a good antidote to those who expected NATO to be more harmonious than it was. Booth offers some useful insights into the limits of alliances and provides some excellent observations about the level of cohesion that can reasonably be expected in an alliance like NATO. He also suggests that NATO has suffered primarily from problems of success.

889 **The Future of European Alliance Systems: NATO and the Warsaw Pact.**
Arlene Idol Broadhurst.   Boulder, Colorado: Westview Press, 1982.
316p.

Based on a symposium held in May 1981, this volume is divided into four sections. The first offers some conceptual perspectives, including one by the editor which provides a very good analysis of the conditions which facilitate the maintenance of alliance cohesion and those which lead to disintegration. There is also an iconoclastic analysis by Hedley Bull, which looks briefly and rather dismissively at alliance theory and then assesses NATO and the Warsaw Pact in terms of their durability. Part Two contains four essays on NATO. One of these, by Pierre Lellouche, deals with the role of West European cooperation within the Atlantic framework. The third section has four essays on the Warsaw Pact, while the final section has just one chapter dealing with patterns of resource allocation within the two alliances. A useful collection with a rather different kind of focus to most.

890 **NATO: The Dynamics of Alliance in the Postwar World.**
H. Fedder Edwin.   New York: Dodd, Mead and Co., 1973. 155p.

This interesting book contains a good overview of NATO. It explores international coalitions and identifies ways in which NATO is unique. It also looks at the reasons the Alliance came into being and identifies three reasons why there has been conflict amongst members of the Alliance: some have nuclear roles and others are confined to non-nuclear roles; there is a diversity of goals among the member-states, stemming largely from differences of power; and member-states perceive and assess the threat in very different ways. Having outlined the conditions for conflict in the Alliance, Fedder looks at the policy-making process and identifies some of the characteristics of collective action. In the final chapter, he considers the possible reform of NATO, with particular emphasis on the idea of the Europeans taking on a greater role. He claims that NATO should be re-invigorated or replaced by a more dynamic and more relevant organization in which there is an integrated army under direction of a supranational Western European Union. The book contains some useful diagrams on NATO's structure and organization and is generally helpful although rarely definitive.

891 **Alliance in International Politics.**
Edited by Julian R. Friedman, Christopher Bladen, Steven Rosen.
Boston, Massachusetts: Allyn and Bacon, 1970. 383p.

A comprehensive collection of essays which looks at the functions fulfilled by alliances in international politics, has some general theories about alliances offered by a variety of authors including Olson and Zeckhauser who present their economic theory, and considers various facets of alliance including limits and size.

892 **Security in Europe.**
Robert Hunter.   London: Elek, 1969. 188p.

A very incisive study which locates the formation of NATO within a process of hostility and mistrust which developed between the Soviet Union and the West in the late 1940s and which fed off the uncertainty over the balance of power. The author also looks at how differences over the assessment of the Soviet threat caused problems for Alliance cohesion. There are also interesting chapters on institutions, strategy, and non-military roles of the Alliance. This is certainly a book which repays another look, both for the incisive nature of much of its analysis and the fact that it offers what can be seen as a mildly revisionist account of the formation and functioning of NATO.

893 **When Trust Breaks Down: Alliance Norms and World Politics.**
Charles W. Kegley, Jr., Gregory A. Raymond.   Columbia, South Carolina: University of South Carolina Press, 1990. 331p.

A broad-ranging analysis of how alliance norms change and how alliances come to an end. The volume is wide-ranging but includes some interesting observations on commitment which is at the core of alliances.

894   **How the West was One: Representational Politics in NATO.**
Bradley S. Klein.   *International Studies Quarterly*, vol. 34, no. 3
(September 1990), p. 311-325.
Klein argues that NATO's success and longevity was due more to the alliance's ability
to manage the periodic crises occurring amongst the allies than to its deterrence of
Soviet aggression. Deterrence, Klein concludes, would not have succeeded without the
underlying bonds of alliance. The author sees these bonds as existing beyond the
narrow arena of military cooperation and suggests that the West ultimately prevailed in
the Cold War because it had established its political and cultural identity. The
dissolution of the Eastern bloc provides an opportunity to extend the boundaries of
this Western identity.

895   **Nations in Alliance.**
George Liska.   Baltimore, Maryland: Johns Hopkins University Press,
1962. 301p.
An important contribution to the understanding of what alliances are, why states align,
and those factors which make alliances cohesive and effective as well as those which
can lead to their dissolution. The author also looks at parallels and differences between
Soviet and Western alliances. Although it does not focus exclusively on NATO, this
work does contribute to an understanding of the Western Alliance.

896   **Semialignment and Western Security.**
Edited by Nils Orvik.   London: Croom Helm, 1986. 286p.
An unusual and incisive collection of essays which looks at the phenomenon of NATO
members who in certain respects qualify their membership, or practise what some
critics see as partial participation in the Alliance. The notion of semi-alignment is
somewhere between full alignment and non-alignment. The editor sets up the
conceptual framework at the outset and this is followed by chapters which deal
respectively with Denmark, Greece, The Netherlands, Canada and Norway. The final
section contains two views assessing the impact of semi-alignment on the Alliance. An
unusual and valuable collection which has been very effectively integrated into an
overall assessment by the editor.

897   **The Security Dilemma in Alliance Politics.**
Glenn Snyder.   *World Politics*, vol. 36, no. 4 (July 1984), p. 461-495.
A systematic, stimulating and original analysis which looks at the security dilemma in
alliances in terms of the twin fears of abandonment (defection) and entrapment.
Snyder argues that in a bipolar world the alliance security dilemma is less severe
because the risks of abandonment are very low. Not only does the adversary dilemma
dominate, but the fact that there are few risks of defection mean that the allies can
adopt independent policies towards the adversary. This leads the author to some
counter-intuitive conclusions. Among them is the contention that the crisis in NATO in
the early 1980s is not a prelude to the collapse of NATO but a function of the fact that
in a bipolar world the Alliance cannot collapse. 'This structural guarantee against
disintegration encourages unilateralism and inhibits compromise. Policy conflicts may
not be resolved because the cost of not resolving them does not include a risk to the
alliance itself' (p. 495). An important, albeit somewhat theoretical analysis.

898 **NATO: Issues and Prospects.**
Harold von Riekhoff.   Toronto, Canada: Canadian Institute of
International Affairs, 1967. 170p.

The main focus of this study is whether there is a role for an institution like NATO
which relies on common planning and coordination of policies rather than more
ambitious forms of supra-nationalism. The book contains an incisive analysis of many
of NATO's problems, especially those stemming from what the author terms the
imbalanced vulnerability of its members. There is a good chapter on the nuclear
control problems and also a chapter which deals with the smaller members and their
particular problems and dilemmas. The author's suggestion that NATO could well
become increasingly important as a stabilizing mechanism under conditions of rapid
political change looks remarkably prescient from the perspective of the 1990s.

899 **The Origins of Alliances.**
Stephen M. Walt.   Ithaca, New York: Cornell University Press, 1987.
321p.

Although the case-studies Walt examines are taken from the Middle East, his
theoretical analysis of why alliances are formed, his discussion of the literature on
alliances and his consideration of whether states engage in bandwagonning behaviour
or balancing behaviour have great relevance for NATO.

Indexes

There follow three separate indexes: authors (including editors, compilers, contributors, translators and illustrators); titles of publications; and subjects. Title entries are italicized and refer either to the main titles or to other works cited in the annotations. The introductory definite or indefinite article is omitted. The numbers refer to bibliographical entries, rather than page numbers. Individual index entries are arranged in alphabetical sequence.

Index of Authors

A

Abshire, David M. 114, 323, 376-377, 723, 822
Acheson, Dean 1-2, 162
Achilles, Theodore C. 3, 29
Adomeit, Hannes 545, 558, 561
Alford, Jonathan 124, 304, 372, 679
Aliboni, Robert 529
Allin, Dana 504
Allison, Graham 380
Alstyne, Richard Van 78
Amme Jr., Carl H. 221-222
Anderson, F. M. 766
Andren, Nils 511
Andrianopoulos, Argyris G. 94
Anthony, Ian 767
Archer, Clive 512, 548
Arlinghaus, Bruce E. 337
Arnason, Robert T. 513
Arnett, Eric H. 823
Aron, Raymond 108, 223, 684, 724
Artner, Stephen J. 725
Ashcroft, Geoffrey 178-179
Asmus, Ronald 824, 863

Aspin, Les 546
Ausland, John C. 514

B

Bahr, Egon 509
Ball, George 84
Ball, Mary Margaret 643
Bare, C. Gordon 603
Barnet, Richard J. 48
Barry III, William A. 803
Bartlett, Dewey 564
Baumann, Carol Edler 115
Baylis, John 4, 5, 224, 275, 864
Beach, Hugh 124
Beaton, Leonard 225
Beaufre, André 84, 234, 644
Beedham, Brian 825, 867
Beer, Francis A. 180, 604, 736, 887
Bell, Coral 65, 484, 826
Bellany, Ian 378
Bentinck, Marc 698
Bertram, Christoph 494, 523, 679, 782
Betts, Richard K. 116, 194-195, 253, 358-359, 827

Biddle, Stephen D. 571
Binnendijk, Hans 274
Birnbaum, Karl 807
Birrenbach, Kurt 145, 235, 572
Bittleston, Martyn 768
Bitzinger, Richard 528, 573, 863
Bjarnason, Bjorn 515
Bjol, Erling 516
Blackwell, Jr., James A. 66
Blackwill, Robert D. 783-785, 808
Bladen, Christopher 891
Blair, Bruce 198
Bland, Douglas L. 181
Blechman, Barry M. 137, 495, 786
Bluth, Christoph 385, 679
Boll, Michael M. 530
Bonomo, James 399
Bonvicini, Gianni 700
Booth, Ken 275, 828, 864, 872, 888
Borawski, John 787-789
Boutwell, Jeffrey 276, 726
Bowie, Robert R. 92, 236-237, 260
Bowman, William R. 790

255

Boyer, Yves 121, 413, 474
Boyle, Peter G. 6
Bracken, Paul 196,
   574-575, 829, 847
Brady, Linda P. 414
Brandt, Willy 81, 496
Brauch, Hans Gunter 576,
   849, 872
Brenner, Michael 146, 277,
   606, 645, 699, 864
Briefs, Henry W. 84
British Atlantic Committee
   381
Broadhurst, Arlene Idol
   889
Brodie, Bernard 7, 226,
   260
Brody, Richard I. 386
Brooks, Linton F. 406
Brosio, Manlio 182
Brown, James 531
Brown, Seyom 148
Brzezinski, Zbigniew 148,
   808
Buchan, Alastair 80, 82-83,
   197, 238, 260, 646
Buchan, David 756-757
Bucy, J. Fred 758
Bull, Hedley 119, 647, 889
Bundy, McGeorge 207,
   360
Burrows, Bernard 648-649
Burt, Richard 127, 220,
   273, 380, 822
Buteux, Paul 278-279
Buzan, Barry 830
Buzzard, A. W. 280
Byers, R. B. 517

C

Cahen, Alfred 650-651,
   654
Callaghan, Thomas 765
Calleo, David P. 159, 415-
   416, 652, 727, 851
Campen, S. I. P. 45, 95
Camps, Miriam 147
Canby, Steven L. 324-327,
   375, 877, 791
Capitanchik, David 728
Carnovale, Marco 239, 653
Carpenter, Ted Galen 831

Carter, Ashton B. 198
Cartwright, John 117, 281
Carver, Field Marshal
   Lord, 361
Cerny, Karl H. 84
Cerutti, Furio 792
Chalmers, Malcolm 578,
   832
Chance, James 148
Charles, Daniel 199
Cheysson, Claude 720
Childs, Marquis W. 8
Chipman, John 532, 701
Church, Frank C. 417
Cimbala, Stephen J. 208,
   254, 282-283
Clark, Asa A. 337
Clark, Susan 558, 605
Clarke, Michael 654
Claude, Inis 833
Clawson, Robert W. 107,
   538
Clesse, Armand 9, 834
Cleveland, Harlan 85, 149
Cleveland, Harold Van B.
   655
Clontz, William R. 803
Close, Robert 328, 579
Coffey, Joseph I. 93, 150,
   700, 793-794
Cohen, Benjamin 159
Cohen, Eliot A. 118, 580
Cohen, Samuel T. 284, 314
Coker, Christopher 119,
   126, 485, 606-607,
   701-702, 843
Cole Paul M. 518
Combs, Jerald A. 10
Conant, Melvin A. 703
Connally, Tom 11
Connell, Jon 581
Connery, Robert H. 86
Cook, Don 12
Cooper, Charles 637
Cordesman, Anthony 304
Cordier, Sherwood S. 519
Cornell, Alexander H. 769
Corterier, Peter 835
Cotter, Donald 119, 198,
   332, 375
Cottrell, Alvin 49, 78
Covington, Stephen R. 547
Craig, Gordon A. 70, 497

Cremasco, Maurizio 700
Critchley, Julian 281, 549
Croan, Melvin 448
Croft, Stuart 387, 836, 838,
   864
Cromwell, William C.
   151-152, 418, 656
Cross, John 121
CSIA European Security
   Working Group 533
CSIC Study Group on
   International Crisis
   Communications 200
Curien, Hubert 776
Cyr, Arthur 419ˉ

D

Daalder, Ivo H. 227,
   388-389, 795, 837
Dahrendorf, Ralf 729
Danchev, Alex 13
Daniel, Donald 124
Dankert, Pieter 657
Danspeckgruber,
   Wolfgang F. 838
Davis, Jacquelyn K. 730
Davis, Paul K. 93, 582, 839
Dawisha, Karen 561
Dawson, Raymond H. 183
Dayton, Keith W. 840
De Benedetti, Carlo 776
De Santis, Hugh 120
De Rose, François 255,
   304, 362
Dean, Jonathan 256, 329,
   796-797, 819, 847
Dean, Vera Micheles 14
Debouzy, Olivier 420
Deger, Saadet 608-609
Deibel, Terry 421
Delmas, Claude 15
Delors, Jacques 658
Deluca, Donald R. 750
Dembinski, Matthias 849
Denoon, David B. H. 610
DePorte, Anton W. 50, 97,
   130
Deschamps, Louis 390
Dettke, Dieter 150
Deutsch, Karl 153, 498,
   659
Di Nolfo, Ennio 16

Newhouse, John 448, 476
Niblett, Robin 822
Nicholson, George E. Jr.
183
Nickel, Herman W. 720
Nitze, Paul 460
Nogueira, Albano 33
Nolting, Frederick 51
Norstad, Lauris 79, 84, 162
North Atlantic Assembly,
NAA 629
North Atlantic Treaty
Organization, Defence
Planning Committee
630
Northedge, Fred 746
Nunn, Sam 137, 449, 564,
866
Nurick, Robert 304
Nye, Joseph S. 600

O

O'Leary, James 454
O'Neill, Robert 67, 220
O'Prey, Kevin P. 786
Odom, William 396
Olson Jr., Mancur 631, 891
Oneal, John R. 632-633
Ortona, Egidio 34
Orvik, Nils 112, 896
Osgood, Robert E. 60, 89,
138, 171, 523
Oshima, Keichi 776
Owen, David 851
Oye, Kenneth A. 440

P

Palmer, Glenn 634
Palmer, John 687
Papacosma, S. Victor 130
Park, William 60
Pearson, Lester B. 263
Perle, Richard 624, 851,
867
Perry, Charles M. 730
Perry, William 382
Petersen, Nikolaj 35
Petersen, Phillip 558
Pfaltzgraff Jr., Robert L.
56, 80, 170, 730, 733,
868

Pierre, Andrew J. 86, 90,
148, 212, 349, 688
Pilat, Joseph 836
Platt, Alan 171
Posen, Barry R. 264-265,
412, 598-599
Powell, Colin L. 450
Prendergast, William B.
809
Press, Frank 776
Puchala, Donald J. 813
Pym, Francis 720

Q

Quinlan, Michael 869

R

Radway, Laurence 451
Ragionieri, Rodolfo 792
Raj, Christopher S. 452
Rallo, Joseph C. 689
Randle, Michael 370
Rathjens, George W. 70,
266
Ravenal, Earl C. 148,
213-214, 454, 722
Raymond, Gregory A. 893
Record, Jeffrey 305-306,
344, 453, 810
Reed Jr., John A. 505
Reed, Robert 711
Reid, Escott 36-37
Reilly, John 722
Rendel, Alexander 38-39
Resor, Stanley 847
Reychler, Luc 872
Rice, Condelezza 276
Rice, Sherry 761
Richardson, James L. 506
Richey, George 492
Ridgley, Stanley K. 635
Risse-Kappen, Thomas
747, 811, 838, 870
Riste, Olav 40-41
Robertson, David 871
Rogers, Bernard W. 119,
139, 189, 218, 350
Rogers, Paul 370
Roman, Peter 74

Roper, John 374, 392, 661,
679
Rose, Clive 201, 794
Rosen, Steven 891
Ross, Dennis 219
Rothchild, Donald 440
Rothschild, Baron Robert
42
Royal Institute of
International Affairs
75
Rubenson, David 399
Rubin, Mark R. 130
Rubinstein, Alvin Z. 712
Rudney, Robert S. 477-
478, 872
Ruehl, (Ruhl) Lothar 563,
808, 812, 834
Ruiz Palmer, Diego A. 479
Rummel, Reinhardt 678,
690, 700
Russett, Bruce 750

S

Sabin, Philip A. G. 751
Sabrosky, Alan Ned 351,
404, 686
Sandler, Todd 628
Schear, James A. 600
Schelling, Thomas C. 9,
162, 260, 307
Schilling, Warner R. 813
Schlesinger, James 53, 129
Schlor, Wolfgang 507
Schmidt, Helmut 129,
267-268, 508
Schmidt, Peter 678, 858
Schmitz, Peter N. 713
Schmuckle, Gerd 202
Schneider, Heinrich 736
Schulze, Franz-Joseph 352,
367, 382
Schuman, Robert 691
Schwartz, David N.
308-309, 372
Schwarz, Hans-Peter 106
Schweitzer, Carl-Christoph
565
Scott, John F. 269
Scrivener, David 512
Serfaty, Simon 93, 110, 137

260

262

Index of Titles

264

266

267

268

269

273

275

277

Index of Subjects

281